Ethics and Auditing

Ethics and Auditing

Tom Campbell and Keith Houghton
(Editors)

ANU

THE AUSTRALIAN NATIONAL UNIVERSITY

E PRESS

Acknowledgements

The editors gratefully acknowledge the support of the Academy of The Social Sciences in Australia (ASSA), the Centre for Applied Philosophy and Public Ethics (CAPPE) and the Australian National Centre for Audit Assurance and Research (ANCAAR).

ANU

E PRESS

Published by ANU E Press
The Australian National University
Canberra ACT 0200, Australia
Email: anuepress@anu.edu.au
Web: http://epress.anu.edu.au

National Library of Australia
Cataloguing-in-Publication entry

Ethics and auditing.

Bibliography
Index

ISBN 1 920942 25 4
ISBN 1 920942 26 2 (online)

1. Auditing. 2. Auditing - Moral and ethical aspects.
3. Auditors - Professional ethics. I. Campbell, Tom,
1938- . II. Houghton, Keith A.

657.45

Edited by Ewen Miller
Cover design and photograph by Brendon McKinley

Contents

List of figures

List of tables

List of contributors

Stephen Bottomley is Professor of Commercial Law and Director of the Centre for Commercial Law at the Australian National University, Canberra. He is co-author (with Roman Tomasic) of *Directing the Top 500: Corporate Governance and Accountability in Australian Companies* (1993) and (with Tomasic and R. McQueen) *Corporations Law in Australia* (Federation Press, 2002).

Tom Campbell is Professorial Fellow at the Centre for Applied Philosophy and Public Ethics (CAPPE), Charles Sturt University, Canberra, and Visiting Professor at the School of Law, King's College, London. He was formerly Professor and Dean of Law at the Australian National University and Professor of Jurisprudence at the University of Glasgow. His books include *Justice* (Macmillan, 2001) and *The Legal Theory of Ethical Positivism* (Dartmouth, 1996).

Barry J. Cooper is Professor of Accounting Education at the Royal Melbourne Institute of Technology (RMIT). After gaining experience as an auditor, Professor Cooper joined RMIT University in 1972, where he taught auditing and financial accounting. He was Head of Accountancy at Hong Kong Polytechnic from 1987 to 1991, and at RMIT University from 1993 until 1997, when he took leave to join CPA Australia as National Director, Member Services. He returned to RMIT University in December 2000. Professor Cooper has undertaken a number of research projects and published in the areas of auditing, ethics and accounting education.

Nicholas P. Courtney is an honour's graduate of the University of Melbourne. His research focuses on audit and governance. After graduation, Nick became a member of the specialist accounting firm Korda Mentha and worked on one of Australia's most high-profile administration and liquidation projects – that of Ansett Airlines. He now works in the accounting profession in the United Kingdom.

Jane Hamilton is a Senior Lecturer at the University of Technology (UTS), a position she has held since 2000. Prior to joining UTS, Jane held appointments at La Trobe University and Bendigo College of Advanced Education. Before joining the tertiary education sector in 1989, Jane worked for the National Australia Bank. Her research background is in financial accounting and auditing, and she has recently submitted a Ph.D. thesis for examination at Monash University. She is a member of CPA Australia. Ongoing research projects are partially funded by the Co-operative Research Centre for Technology Enabled Capital Marks and the School of Accounting at UTS.

Keith A. Houghton is the Professor of Business Administration and Dean of the Faculty of Economics and Commerce at the Australian National University. Keith is a member of the Australian Audit and Assurance Standards Board, and is one of the two independent reviewers of the Australian practice of the accounting firm Peat Marwick Mitchell & Co (KPMG). He regularly provides expert evidence on audit quality and financial reporting in litigation and commercial arbitration matters. He was twice called to give evidence to the recent Australian parliamentary inquiry into auditor independence.

Bryan Howieson is a Senior Research Fellow at the University of South Australia in Adelaide. His interests are in financial reporting, accounting standard-setting, and professional ethics and corporate governance. Bryan has published extensively, including a monograph for the Australian Accounting Research Foundation. He has undertaken a number of consultancies in the private and public sectors in the areas of financial reporting and codes of conduct. He has also served in various ethical policy and educational roles for the Institute of Chartered Accountants in Australia. Bryan is on the board of the Accounting and Finance Association of Australia and New Zealand, and is Vice-President-at-Large of the International Association for Accounting Education and Research.

Christopher Ikin is Associate Director of the Australian National Centre for Audit and Assurance Research at the Australian National University, having spent many years as an auditing practitioner, including a period as a partner of an antecedent firm to one of the present Big Four auditing firms. He was also engagement partner for one of Australia's largest manufacturing companies.

Shireenjit Kaur Johl is a Ph.D. graduate of the University of Melbourne and is currently a senior member of the Faculty of Management at the Multimedia University of Malaysia.

Christine A. Jubb is Professor of Accounting at Deakin University. She has previously lectured at Monash University and the University of Melbourne, and was seconded to the Australian Accounting Research Foundation during 2001 and 2002 as Second-in-Charge of the Foundation.

Doreen McBarnet is an Economic and Social Research Council Professorial Fellow and a fellow of Wolfson College. She is based at the Centre for Socio-Legal Studies, where she runs the centre's research programme on business and the law. She is also a fellow of Oxford University's Said Business School, where she runs the core course on corporate responsibility for the MBA. Major publications include *Conviction* and (with Chris Whelan) *Creative Accounting and the Cross-eyed Javelin Thrower* (Wiley, 1999).

Kay Plummer is a Senior Lecturer in Accounting at the Charles Sturt University (CSU) and a Senior Research Fellow of the Australian Centre for Co-operative Research and Development. Prior to joining CSU she lectured at UTS, has held senior positions in Technical and Further Education (TAFE) NSW, and has undertaken two volunteer projects for the Australian Executive Service Overseas Program. She has worked in auditing for KPMG.

Roger Simnett is Professor at the University of New South Wales. Roger's research interests cover a range of financial accounting and auditing topics, including auditor decision processes, development of specialist skills, corporate governance and financial disclosure issues. He was a member of the Auditing and Assurance Standards Board from 1995 to 1999, and currently serves as Associate Editor for *Accounting & Finance*. He is on the editorial boards of a number of accounting journals. In 2002, Roger was elected as the first academic onto the International Auditing and Assurance Standards Board.

Alana Smith is a first class honours graduate from the University of New South Wales. Her current position is Accountant, Group Finance, QBE Insurance Group.

Edward Spence lectures in moral philosophy and applied and professional ethics in the School of Communication, Charles Sturt University, Bathurst. He holds an honours degree and a Ph.D. degree in philosophy from the University of Sydney. Edward is a Research Fellow at the Centre for Applied Philosophy and Public Ethics (CAPPE) in Canberra. Prior to taking up philosophy, Edward was a practicing accountant. He is the architect, founder and producer of the 'Philosophy Plays' project, whose aim is the introduction of philosophy to the general public.

Donald Stokes is Professor of Accounting at UTS, a leading party in the Cooperative Research Centre for Technology Enabled Capital Markets. Donald is one of the leading international researchers in the economics of auditing markets. He has been involved in delivering research for industry partners including PricewaterhouseCoopers, Altium Ltd, the Securities Industry Research Centre for Asia-Pacific, the Australian Centre for Global Finance, Computershare, Credit Suisse First Boston, the Australian Stock Exchange, ABN Ambro, the Australian Securities Investment Commission, the Australian Auditing and Assurance Standards Board, the Australian Accounting Research Foundation and the NSW Department of Information and Technology Management. Donald has served as President of the Accounting Association of Australia and New Zealand (1997-98) and on editorial boards of international research journals.

Carolyn A. Windsor has been Senior Lecturer in the Faculty of Commerce and Management at Griffith University, Queensland, since receiving her Ph.D. Prior to Carolyn's academic career, she worked for 15 years in administrative and management positions. She is a member of the Australian Society of CPAs, as well as of international accounting bodies such as the American Accounting Association and the European Accounting Association. Carolyn has published papers on accounting and auditing in top international journals. She was recently awarded the competitive Velux Visiting Professorship Program to research auditor independence at the University of Southern Denmark in 2004.

Foreword: Restoring public trust

Bill Edge, *PricewaterhouseCoopers*
Australian Auditing and Assurance Standards Board (2002-04) Chairman

Enron, Parmalat, WorldCom, HIH – these corporate failures and accounting scandals have shaken the foundations of investor confidence in the transparency, integrity and accountability of corporations and capital markets. There has also been public disquiet about the role professional auditors and audit firms have played in these corporate scandals.

The consequences for many of the players in the market for financial information have been enormous; reputations both of key individuals and organisations are in ruins, jobs have been lost, and pension funds have been wiped out. The damage, both economic and social, has been incalculable, and the implications are far-reaching for corporate management, company directors, audit firms and the investing public.

An array of factors contributed to these events, but one thing is for certain – the billions of dollars in corporate value lost was due in significant part to unscrupulous management and boards of directors that failed to meet their responsibilities. The accounting profession, including auditors, also played a major role in these events. While the story behind these corporate failures is always complex, a lack of ethical behaviour by many individuals is a big part of it.

For the audit profession, these developments have again highlighted the gap between public expectations and the reality of the role of the auditor. With Enron in particular, the public perception was that the auditor should have acted as a control on unscrupulous management practices. The conclusion reached by many members of the public (and parliamentarians) was that the auditors failed in this responsibility because their independence from the management of Enron was compromised. While it is by no means as simple as that, the audit profession must acknowledge and address these types of perceptions, or indeed facts, if it is to restore trust in both the capital markets and itself.

The biggest challenge ahead for auditors is to identify *how* ethical behaviour can be – and be seen to be – restored, as it is this that will be the basis for the reconstruction of public trust in the profession and in the practice of auditing. This book does not purport to provide all the answers, but it highlights the importance of ethics and provides some thought-provoking commentary on the means in which ethical behaviour can be embedded in our personal and professional culture – one of the essential components to restoring public trust.

The response: regulation, regulation, regulation ...

The response of governments worldwide to corporate scandals has been greater regulation. This response is often taken in the name of supporting the need for protecting the public's interest. Attention has been focused on flaws in the capital market and reforms to corporate reporting and accounting/auditing that may rectify them.

Stock exchanges, global and local accounting and auditing standard-setters, institutional investors and other stakeholders have called for transparency and accountability in corporate governance, business ethics and corporate reporting. New laws and best practice guidance require strict monitoring of auditor independence, codes of ethical conduct, more disclosures, and CEO/CFO certification of various key statements in corporate reports. The aim of these requirements is to ensure effective checks and balances are in place so that good corporate governance and business ethics are observed.

Regaining trust

Why regulation isn't the only answer

Regulation alone will not regain public trust. Confidence in the capital markets depends on confidence that the reporting and regulatory process will deliver accountability and transparency. This in turn depends on integrity – and integrity depends on one's core ethical beliefs and behaviours.

A state of mind: ethical behaviour

Ethical behaviour is not simply conforming to legal and professional rules; it is a state of mind, the following of unwritten principles, a culture of 'doing the right thing'.

An individual's interpretation of ethical behaviour is influenced by a variety of factors including industry and company guidelines, social and economic pressures, laws and regulations, and the surrounding values and beliefs. These influences develop a set of written and unwritten principles which are drawn on when faced with an ethical dilemma.

Auditors face ethical questions on a daily basis, and in a way that is unique to our profession. Arguably the underlying principle of the auditing profession's ethics is independence. Auditors must balance their duty to their clients, their profession, society and numerous other stakeholders. An actual or perceived conflict of interest may arise as a result of these competing interests and lead to public distrust – a familiar sight in recent years. Confidence is quickly lost and slowly regained in these instances.

By the time people enter their professional careers, their personal ethics have been largely shaped. However, these ethics can be reinforced or, conversely, strained or even shattered by the corporate culture in which they work. It is essential that audit firms – and, for that matter, all organisations – entrench a culture that fosters ethical behaviour.

The framework for rebuilding public trust: an ethical code of conduct

It is inevitable that an auditor will be faced with ethical decisions during the course of their career. It is therefore fundamental that appropriate and professional decision-making protocols and behaviours are ingrained in the culture in which they work.

A strong code of professional and personal ethical guidelines is a critical starting point to embedding ethical behaviour. The accounting bodies in Australia each have a code of conduct to provide authoritative guidance on professional conduct. The codes set out general guidelines on concepts such as independence, competence and honesty, as well as statements addressing specific issues of professional behaviour. These guidelines are backed with the power to monitor and penalise non-conforming members.

Similarly, staff and partners of the Big Four auditing firms operate within global codes of conduct, which articulate the principles of integrity and accountability by which generations of audit professionals have been guided.

Written codes of conduct that are comprehensive and clear are now seen as an essential element of good governance and ethics for all organisations.

Codes of conduct are pro-active statements about an organisation's position on ethical and compliance matters. They are not usually legally binding and they are not a complete or exhaustive list. The essential elements of a code should include:

- an emphasis on communication and training around core values
- building a culture that motivates responsible business conduct
- encouraging employees to ask questions about ethics and report potential violations, without fear of reprisal
- values that are clear and meaningfully reinforced
- the establishment of confidential reporting frameworks to encourage communication and protect whistleblowers
- incident management processes that support due process and consistent enforcement
- processes in place to monitor the program as well as emerging standards and risks to ensure ongoing improvement.

Leading ethical and compliance programs enable forward-thinking, continuous improvements and effective change management. Common attributes of successful programs include:

- 'tone at the top' board management styles
- a values-driven code of conduct
- whistleblower protection
- integration of business processes.

'Tone at the top' board management styles

'Tone at the top' is characterised by the board and senior management (or, in an audit firm, its leadership team and the partnership) having a strong, unified vision of ethics and the purpose of the ethics program. Management are delegated responsibility for the planning and implementation of effective ethics and compliance policies, with board-leadership team oversight ensuring the implementation occurs and ongoing corporate responsibilities are met.

The board-leadership team must live by the code of conduct, just as they expect all others in the organisation to live by it. People in an organisation pick up quickly on how the 'the top' deal with outliers of the ethical code. The board-leadership team must infuse an organisational culture of ethics, and effective communication is essential to achieve this culture.

A values-driven code of conduct

The code of conduct must be clearly written and outline both management and key stakeholders' values. The code must be meaningfully communicated to employees and associated parties. A sample of topics covered by the accounting bodies' codes of conduct includes:

- fundamental principles
  - public interest
  - integrity
  - objectivity
  - independence and conflicts of interest
  - confidentiality
  - competence and due care
- other matters
  - resolution of ethical conflicts
  - advertising, publicity and solicitation
  - changes in professional appointments
  - incompatible business
  - opinion requests.

A further sample of the key topics that individual organisations, including auditing firms, might cover in their codes of conduct are listed in Table 1:

Table 1. Sample topics to be covered in a code of conduct

Affirmative action/equal opportunity/non-discrimination	Financial reporting/record-keeping	Product safety and suitability
Antitrust/fair trading/competition	Gifts and entertainment	Professional development
Bribery and kickbacks	Insider information and trading	Protection of proprietary and confidential information
Community service and philanthropy	Intellectual property/copyrights	Responsible supply chain
Compensation and benefits	Joint ventures and strategic alliances	Sexual and other harassment
Conflicts of interest	Media relations and public image	Substance abuse
Corporate giving	Money-laundering and fraud	Travel and expense reporting
Corporate governance and structure	Personal use of company assets	Union relations
Criminal convictions and civil actions	Political activities/lobbying/contributions	Use of communications tools
Employee health, safety and welfare	Privacy	Wage laws and fair labour practices
Environmental compliance	Private investments and outside business activities	Work/life balance

The code of conduct can be contained in a variety of materials, to ensure it is embedded into the organisational culture. Some suggested elements of a comprehensive code of conduct framework are listed in Table 2.

Table 2. Elements of a code of conduct framework

Introductory materials	Ethical conduct policies	Compliance administration
Organisational mission statement	Statement of relevant values and the policy's positive intent	Ethics and compliance certification form
Letter from the CEO	Clear and succinct statement of the policy	Directory of key contact persons
Statement of values/organisational principles	Brief examples of acceptable and unacceptable conduct	Links/references to related information
General statement of compliance with laws and regulations	Consequences of misconduct to the organisation and employees	Compliance and ethics reporting procedures (e.g., hotline / whistleblower protection)
	Reference to specific policies	Due process regarding ethics and compliance
		Decision-making assistance

Whistleblower protection

Whistleblower protection is one of the hot topics of corporate ethics. While it is a vital element of any corporate governance strategy, a whistleblower protection policy will not of itself work to ensure corporate ethics are observed. Employees will not utilise help lines or report misconduct if they are not satisfied that their actions will be supported, as the ramifications can be significant to an individual's personal and professional life.

For auditors, the focus must be on supporting audit teams in any dispute with a client. Audit partners must know that they will be protected – even rewarded – if they take a firm stance against an accounting practice they feel is potentially misleading.

Integration of business processes

Finally, integration of business processes ensures that the ethics and compliance program becomes operational and effective. This includes:

- developing clear policies and procedures
- communicating to, and training, employees about the code of conduct and related practices
- monitoring progress
- reporting to management/partners and the board-leadership team
- fine-tuning strategies
- communicating the company's successful performance to key stakeholders.

Measuring the effectiveness of ethics programs is difficult, but it is essential to ensuring ethical behaviour is integrated into the organisational processes. There are a number of ways to monitor and assess the successful embedding of ethical behaviours. Some of the more common performance indicators include:

- code of conduct awareness signatures
- helpline awareness, call resolution and trends
- adequacy of program documentation
- risk management and early detection
- consistency of enforcement
- ethical culture surveys and employee opinions
- management's response to issues raised.

Conclusion

Corporate governance, business ethics and effective compliance management are increasingly critical to an organisation's reputation and success. To regain public trust, safeguard reputation and grow market share, all organisations need to embed ethics and compliance into their culture and core business processes. They also need a mechanism so that they can be seen by the public at large to have these processes working effectively.

A framework and process for corporate governance, business ethics and compliance management that weaves together a 'top-down' approach to managing accountability with 'bottom-up' compliance processes is a large step in the right direction.

The ultimate success or failure of an organisation's code of conduct and business ethics program will rest upon the values and culture created by the board of directors or leadership team, and ultimately embraced by all its people.

References

DiPiazza, S. A., Jr. & Eccles, R. G. 2002, *Building Public Trust – The Future of Corporate Reporting*, John Wiley & Sons, New York.

PricewaterhouseCoopers (US) 2003, *Governance, Business Ethics and Compliance – What Works Best* (unpublished article).

Introduction: The ethics of auditing

Tom Campbell

Accountancy and auditing are complex and technical processes. Ethics, in contrast, might be considered relatively simple. The difficult part of ethics, it may be argued, is not knowing what we ought to do, but getting ourselves, and others, to do the right thing. Truthfulness, honesty, care, loyalty, integrity: we know what they require, but we do not know if and how these requirements can be met. If this is indeed the case, and we want to promote ethical auditing, then we need to attract decent people into the profession, train them well, and not subject them to more temptation than they can cope with. Beyond that, all that is required is a code of ethics laying down minimum standards of professional conduct, with a complaints and disciplinary process to deal with any errant behaviour that comes to the attention of professional bodies, such as CPA Australia and the Institute of Chartered Accountants, who jointly issue a Code of Professional Conduct for the guidance of their members.

There is sufficient truth in this scenario to explain, but not to justify, the minimal attention that is given to ethics in the training of accountants and auditors, despite the growing international literature on the subject (Albrecht 1992; Maurice 1996; Morse & Blake 1998), and the absence of ethical debate and concern within the profession. Provided the expertise is there, it is assumed that ordinary moral sensibility, together with the good example of senior colleagues, can take care of the ethical side of the business. Attention to the ethics of auditing engages the professional firms only with respect to risk minimisation in relation to the serious illegal activities of the occasional 'bad apple' and the likelihood of legal liabilities and a general concern for their reputation. In these circumstances, it is understandable that research into the ethics of accountants and auditors is focussed on discovering how to maximise compliance with generally accepted principles of professional conduct.

If this analysis of professional attitudes is now somewhat out of date (see, for instance, Howieson, Chapter 13; Duska & Duska 2003), this is because of the exceptional publicity given to auditing failures revealed in the disastrous collapses of major corporations, whose accounting practices are revealed to have been seriously deficient and downright dishonest, not to say often unlawful and even criminal in more than a merely technical sense (Clarke, Dean & Oliver 1997; HIH Royal Commission 2003). The crisis of public confidence in the accounting profession arising from these events is perceived as a threat not only to the business of auditors but to business itself. If there have to be unexpected major corporate insolvencies before serious auditing irregularities come to light, what trust can we have in the reliability of the accounting and auditing standards and procedures generally? And, more specifically, if we cannot trust an audit, has it any value?

Gross auditing failures can always be dismissed as atypical lapses deriving from the wickedness of key players involved. This feeds off the assumption that ethical problems relate to occasional non-compliance with agreed standards of professional conduct. Yet focussing on ethics in the context of auditing catastrophes reveals that determining what is ethical or legal in auditing is not such a simple matter after all (see McBarnet, Chapter 2). We may easily elicit a large measure of agreement as to the relevant moral values and their accompanying virtues, such as truthfulness, honesty and law-abidingness, but what these should be taken to mean with respect to conduct in the context of assessing the financial reports of business organisations turns out to be far from clear when we get down to the – not very fine – detail. Determining what is and is not ethical in auditing turns out not to be simply a matter of detecting fraud, corruption and other criminal conduct.

Ethical disagreement about auditing arises, in part, because there is no agreement as to what the central purpose of an audit is. And since the ethical significance of the conduct of individual players in the audit depends on the moral justification of the system in place, disagreement about the purpose of the audit generates disagreement about how audits ought to be conducted. This means that, although ethics in auditing does involve the conduct of auditors, any serious attempt to assess that conduct must take account of the nature and purpose of auditing and the economic and social functions it is intended to serve. Evaluating auditor performance requires, for instance, raising questions as to what constitutes conformity with official guidelines and the standard of professional practice, and about the attitude of those involved to auditing and accounting rules, legal and otherwise, and the ways in which they are interpreted and applied. It requires reference to the systems for decision-making and control within auditing firms, and the openness and honesty of the corporations under audit. All this goes far beyond seeking conformity with obvious and agreed standards and conduct. Beyond these matters, the ethics of auditing involves a critique of the content of legal and professional norms and the regulatory system within which they feature, including the adequacy of the legal frameworks in which accounting and auditing takes place. Do the existing professional cultures and accounting norms adequately serve the ends that justify the existence of the economic system they purport to serve?

In raising the complex interrelationship of issues concerning how auditors ought to behave, what rules and principles they ought to adopt and follow, and how to promote a culture in which we can expect compliance with these norms, it is helpful to classify the ethical issues that arise in relation to auditing by distinguishing three spheres of activity; (1) the practice of auditor(s), (2) the management and culture of auditing firms, and (3) the setting of auditing standards and laws.

Ethically, things may seem relatively straightforward at the level of the individual auditors engaged in the practice of auditing. Auditors ought to carry out their standard procedures carefully, diligently and punctually in accordance with their instructions and the appropriate auditing standards and procedures. The virtues of integrity, objectivity, independence, confidentiality, upholding technical and professional standards, competence and due care, which are all highlighted in the Australian Code of Professional Conduct, seem particularly appropriate in this first sphere.

Even supposing the adequacy of such categorisations of virtues (Libby & Thorne 2004), putting these virtues into practice is not a simple matter. There may be morally relevant problems for practicing auditors when tasks are set that go beyond what the time and expertise available render feasible. In these circumstances, should those involved seek to disguise the limitations of their work, thereby risking the displeasure of their superiors and hazarding their career prospects, or should they just do what they can, perhaps in the dim awareness that their superiors might prefer not to be informed of weaknesses in the process that they are not themselves in a position to remedy?

The options available to the hard-pressed auditor may be analysed purely in terms of self-interest. How hard to work, how often to seek assistance, how open to be about difficulties – these may be regarded as tactical questions within a career strategy that is aimed at personal advancement and material gain, questions best approached through a calculation of the short- and long-term benefits of alternative courses of action for the individuals concerned. These calculations may turn out to be in conflict with more evidently moral or ethical questions: considerations of fairness to other members of the team, obligations to employers, duties to clients, and perhaps a concern for other groups who may rely on the audit for one reason or another.

Only a little reflection is required to demonstrate the difficulty of balancing such a variety of considerations. What weight, if any, should be given to self-interest in such circumstances? Some would say none at all. Morality is all about considering other people, not calculating one's own gains and losses. Yet there is also a powerful moral tradition that endorses the idea of people having duties to themselves which may be balanced against duties to others. And every system of morality has a place for legitimate self-interest. Even if we put self-interest to one side, similar problems arise when we consider the interests of other people and try to think through how to approach employees' duties to their colleagues, their employers and the public. Are all these interests morally relevant? If so, how can these be compared? And when making such comparisons, should we consider short- or long-term consequences, and what sort of consequences are morally salient anyway?

At this point it is easy to fall back on a few simple maxims. Individual auditors should work as hard as they can, in accordance with their instructions, and they should always make a full report to their superiors of any problems they encounter. Slacking, fudging and dissemblance are simply wrong. If there are complex moral balances to be taken into account, this is not something that should affect practicing auditors at work. Their duties are clear and they should do their best to fulfil them. It is also almost certainly in their long-term self-interest so to do. But that is not a calculation for them to make.

A similarly firm line may be taken to another ethical dilemma that is said to be endemic in auditing. This arises when pressure is brought to bear on the auditor not to draw attention to irregularities or problems that have emerged in the course of the audit, pressure that is often related to a real or perceived threat to the future commercial relationship between the auditee and the auditor. This is a manifestation of what is a straight conflict of interest at the core of the standard auditee/auditor relationship – that the auditor is financially dependent on the auditee (see Spence, Chapter 6). The integrity of a professional auditor might suggest that such pressure is always to be totally resisted, but the legitimate need to earn a living, and retain clients in a way that the auditor's employers have a right to expect, mean that there will always be some moral reason to compromise on such matters from time to time.

The more robust approach to such moral dilemmas is characteristic of 'deontology', the view that morality is all about duty and duty is all about not wronging other people (Fried 1978; Nagel 1986, Chapter 10). Ethics, according to the deontologist, is a matter of understanding and following certain general imperatives or rules, such as the Ten Commandments: 'work hard', 'tell the truth' and 'be kind' are examples of such moral imperatives. Moral rules are held to be binding independently of the consequences of putting them into practice. Murder is wrong, full stop. It is not for us to calculate the consequences of truthfulness, just to be truthful. A moral person knows what is right and must be what is right simply because it is right (Kant 1953).

The standard view is that deontology (or 'rule-morality') comes into direct conflict with 'consequentialism', the theory that an act is right or wrong depending on its consequences for all those affected by the action, including the agent in question (Mill 1910 (1861)). The most famous brand of consequentialism – 'utilitarianism' – holds that the consequences that matter morally are pleasures and pains, the morally right act being that which maximises the balance of pleasure over pain, with each person's hedonic experiences being given equal weight in the calculation. This is summed up in Jeremy Bentham's famous commitment to 'the greatest happiness of the greatest number' (Bentham 1948 (1823)). Other consequentialists argue that other types of consequence may feature in moral calculations, including, most typically, well-being in the sense of 'interests', and within economics, 'wealth' – either in monetary terms ('welfare economics') or with respect to consumer goods.

In all moral choices there is a tension between doing what is right according to the rules and working out what is right according to the consequences. It is dogmatic to say that one is characteristically more moral than the other, yet trite to hold that an adequate moral approach requires a measure of both ingredients. The trouble is that appeals to consequences do undermine a commitment to rules, and an absolute commitment to rules drives out what may be seen as a proper sensitivity to the social consequences of conduct. Moreover, allowing people to pick and choose between rules and consequences opens the way for self-serving choices that are determined by the self-interest of the particular agent. This is central to auditing ethics and regulation, as it is to ethics in general (see Campbell, Chapter 5; Tweedie 1988).

However, the sharp contrast between rules and consequences can be misleading, especially in a technical field such as auditing. One attempted compromise between deontology and consequentialism, a compromise that seeks to avoid the twin problems of partiality and insensitivity, is 'rule-consequentialism'. According to rule-consequentialism, individuals ought to follow pre-established moral rules when making particular decisions, but the rules themselves should be determined by consequentialist moral reasoning (Hare 1981; Smart & Williams 1973). This analysis is certainly an improvement on the sort of pure deontology in which the moral rightness of rules is simply 'intuited'. Many rules are quite evidently justified in terms of the good consequences that flow from their general application. However, problems remain to the extent that at least some rules (such as not killing one innocent person to save the lives of many innocent persons) appear to have a powerful non-consequentialist basis. And, even for rule-consequentialists, questions still arise as to whether it is ever right to depart from a rule in a specific case because of its exceptionally bad consequences. There is also controversy over the question of who has the authority to decide which rules should be adopted – albeit on the grounds of their perceived beneficial consequences – and at what point in time they may engage in such rule-making and rule-reform.

In matters of private morality, both making exceptions to rules in particular cases and changing the rules themselves is something for each individual to consider and determine, although they must be prepared to take the consequences in terms of other people's responses to their behaviour. But when it comes to working within an organisation or carrying out a public function, there are moral and practical constraints that go along with such involvement. Organisations must have their internal rules, and those offering a service to the public have to take notice of what are regarded as the legitimate expectations of society. In such circumstances, individuals have less room for manoeuvre with respect to the moral stances that they take. In these contexts, authorities normally set the rules and, as a matter of individual morality in collective circumstances, it is up to those involved to follow them in all but exceptional circumstances.

Thus, in the case of the hard-pressed auditors, it would appear that they ought to take a deontological or rule-morality approach to their work-related moral choices, whereas those who set the rules within or for the organisation might be expected to take a more consequentialist view, at least when making the rules. It may be, therefore, that as we ascend the ladder of authority within an organisation, the moral choices become more consequentialist, and therefore more open and more complex. And beyond the organisation, there are further hierarchies of standard-setters, professional bodies and regulators, culminating in the State, which has the political and perhaps the moral right to establish the legal rights and duties of all individuals and groups within a society.

This hierarchy of authority with the associated differences in moral reasoning seems to apply in most institutional settings. The ethics of organisational life must assume that, on the whole, members of organisations have a moral obligation to conform to the organisational or community rules that they had no part in creating. And it is certainly true that moral choices have to be made by those in authority that are much more complex than those that arise for others lower down in an organisation. Further, there is no doubt that joining an organisation – rather like being a member of a society and a citizen of a country – does involve a certain commitment to abiding by the rules of such entities.

However, it is a defining feature of morality – at least within the Western tradition, with its stress on individual autonomy (Kant 1953) – that all moral persons have, ultimately, to make up their own minds as to what is morally right and wrong, and this includes deciding whether or not to conform to socially and institutionally authoritative moral norms. Notwithstanding that there are moral reasons to abide by the rules of the group, there is always an overriding moral responsibility for the individual to accept or reject those reasons in particular circumstances. Where they judge the rules to be grossly immoral, or the consequences of following generally beneficial rules in certain circumstances are on balance morally unacceptable, then every moral agent has a duty to make up their own mind as to how they ought to act.

It is therefore a general feature of ethics that no one can entirely excuse themselves by saying that they were just following the rules or obeying a higher authority or doing what everyone else is doing. Ethics begins and (some would hold) ends with individual responsibility. This is particularly the case with members of a group or profession which is publicly committed to following certain values that transcend their own self-interest and the normal obligations that apply to all competent human beings. In such circumstances, there is something like a collective obligation to uphold these professional values that includes both a commitment to follow the rules of the profession in a way that serves the values of the profession, and a duty to resist and if necessary disobey rules that the individual member believes to be morally wrong in the context of those values, even when they carry the imprimatur of higher authority.

It follows that, while all accountants and auditors have moral reasons to conform to the norms of conduct accepted as authoritative in their profession, nevertheless all accountants and auditors, even those with limited experience and seniority, have an obligation to take a critical attitude to their own and their colleagues' conduct and to the rules and procedures that define and govern their professional practice. The appropriate ethical attitude for rank and file members of a profession towards rules of practice may appear quite straightforward, but this is not the case. The straightforward aspect is rule compliance: that the rules are there to be followed conscientiously and meticulously without the intrusion of the practitioners' personal opinions as to what these rules should be or departures prompted by inattention or lack of effort. The complicating factor is that this attitude of deference to rules should not be a matter of blind obedience to their authority, but should be based on an awareness of the rationales behind having such rules and the purposes that the activity in question is designed to serve.

Awareness of rule rationales is possible only after a professional education that enables the qualified professional to understand what accounting and auditing systems are designed to do, and the role that their constitutive and regulative rules play in enabling them to fulfil these purposes. The importance of such awareness is not primarily a matter of motivating compliance, although knowledge of the function of rules does promote rule-following (see Plummer, Chapter 12). Its significance lies more in its contribution to the understanding of rules and how they are best interpreted and implemented in particular circumstances. Some accounting procedures are purely computational and can be understood and applied without an appreciation of the larger purpose of the exercise in which they feature. However, these rules are all normally related to other rules in which the categorisation of what is being subjected to arithmetical analysis involves judgments that are far from mechanical. The 'creative' or flexible accounting practices that typify the seedy side of much contemporary business practice involve stretching the conceptual boundaries of what counts as 'interest' as distinct from 'capital expenditure', or whether this or that business entity is a 'subsidiary' from a legal point of view (see McBarnet, Chapter 2).

The categorisation of financial transactions requires transparency and consistency so that the processes involved can be duplicated, and can thus be used to make meaningful historical and cross-organisational comparisons between the financial standing of companies. An appreciation of the importance of consistency in rule-interpretation involves an appreciation of the purpose of accounting practices, whether this be internal control, provision of data relevant to rational business decision-making, or external assessments of profitability.

For these reasons, it is as much the consistency of the rule-application as the content of the rules themselves which ensures the validity of the process and the comparisons that are derived from it. The ethics of rule-interpretation and rule-following here are a function of the value of the particular accounting or auditing system and the purposes it serves – thus the importance in an audit of checking that accounting systems are consistently following pre-established categories in the representation of their financial position. It is this that enables those using the accounts to make meaningful and reliable comparisons between the performance of different companies. It follows that conformity to the rules that determine how business phenomena are to be financially represented is a crucial accounting and auditing virtue. It is not only a technical accounting failure not to follow such rules, but a moral failure in that it undermines the purposes that justify external accounting, and hence also the worth of auditors' reviews of such accounts. This point is often lost in emotive critiques of moral 'legalism' (Maurice 1996, p. 18), which might be better directed at those who try to twist the rules to suit their own illicit ends (see McBarnet, Chapter 2) than those who seek to promote the benefits of consistency through competent rule-interpretation and a commitment to rule-conformity.

Not all departures from ordinary accounting standards are due to incompetence or lack of awareness of the nature of the process. Sometimes accounting deviations and failure to pick them up and respond to them on the part of auditors is brought about by the self-interest of the auditee (and maybe also auditor) in giving a false and misleading view of their financial situation (and on the auditor's part, in putting the commercial relationship with the auditee in jeopardy). Indeed, the core ethical issue of external accounting is that there is a vested interest on the part of companies to misrepresent their financial position in order to maintain or attract investment and enhance the (short-term) profitability of the company. The fundamental ethical issue in auditing is that there is a business interest on the part of auditors to collude with the auditee who is the source of the fees from which they derive their income.

Here we come to the need for rules of a different kind; not rules that govern the presentation and inspection of accounts so that they can be reliably used for comparative purposes, but rules that are designed to counter the tendency of companies and their auditors to depart from or manipulate accounting and auditing standards in their own illicit financial interests. With respect to auditing, these rules are designed to promote what is called 'auditor independence' – that is, to promote both the reality and the appearance of an objective assessment of the truth or accuracy of the auditee's accounts. Such rules may prohibit auditors having a financial interest in the company being audited, or providing non-audit services to that company. These rules are designed to ensure the trustworthiness of the process in itself, so that it is not contaminated by extraneous factors. Thus, in accordance with professional norms and legal requirements, no one may audit the financial reports of an organisation in which they have a financial interest. To break this rule is immediately to bring the independence of the audit into question. These are rules that have a significance that derives from their application in each and every case because the consequences of ignoring the rules are directly harmful to the exercise in question. This is independent of any contribution this may make to the consistency, and hence the validity, of a system.

Clearly audit firms are subject to the same ethical duties as practising auditors with respect to the observance of the accounting rules and standards that serve to make audits useful to their end-users. However, firms have additional collective responsibility to provide support and guidance for individual auditors in carrying out their tasks and working with auditees. The provision of adequate resources and training, the creation of a culture that supports auditor integrity, and the subordination of maximising profit to the maintenance of auditing standards are amongst the particular responsibilities of auditing firms. Lacking that leadership, employee auditors and junior partners cannot be expected to sustain ethical conduct in the field.

Traditionally, rules of both kinds, those establishing accounting and auditing procedures and those establishing auditing independence, have their origins within the domain of the accounting and auditing profession. In theory this has meant that auditing firms as well as individual auditors have been subject to the governance of the profession as a whole, or a plurality of professional bodies, although the recent dominance of the profession by a few exceptionally large accounting firms has blurred the practical distinction between accounting firms and accounting bodies. The ethical issues that arise in the setting of standards, and how they are to be enforced, have all the complexity of consequentialist reasoning in institutional settings, with the additional problems of identifying which consequences matter, and for whom. At this point, the interests of the auditor's clients have to be juxtaposed with the public interest in having a reliable auditing system. Working that out is a highly technical matter, but these technicalities do not exclude – indeed, they ought properly to be at the service of – the moral justifications that underpin the economic and social system of which the audited companies are part.

This need for taking a broader view has bearing on a particular ethical issue that arises where the professional bodies may be tempted to adopt or recommend rules and standards that benefit the auditing profession at the expense of the public interest (see Simnett & Smith, Chapter 3). Perhaps on account of this 'moral hazard', accounting and auditing standards and the regulation of the auditing process have increasingly been shared between professional bodies and governments intent on shoring up the public's trust in the professional conduct of auditors. This co-regulation (rather than 'self-regulation') model is explored in Part II of this book. It is a topic that adds another layer of moral complexity, for governmental views of ethical auditing may differ from those of some of the more professional groups, thus creating not only moral disagreement, but also a moral dilemma on the part of auditors as to whether or not they ought to conform to legal requirements where these conflict with what they see as their duty to their profession.

This brief overview of the complexities that arise in considering what constitutes an ethical audit does something to explain the scope and methodology of this book. The subject matter of the chapters that follow includes (but transcends) the moral dilemmas facing the practicing auditor, and takes in not only the moral duties of audit firms in relation to supporting and managing auditing practice, but the normative issues that confront both professional and governmental regulators in deciding what the auditing standards should be and how these standards are to be monitored and enforced.

These substantive issues are approached via a number of different disciplines and theoretical perspectives. Most contributions come from academic auditors with considerable professional experience who have conducted empirical and theoretical research on auditing practice and its regulation. They deploy a variety of techniques, including behavioural and economic empirical methodologies, drawing on a diversity of experience in the practice and governance of auditing. These are supplemented by legal, philosophical and sociological contributions that place professional auditing expertise in the wider context that is, I argue, required for addressing the ethics of auditing.

The book is divided into four parts. Part I, 'Approaches to the critique of auditing', introduces the themes of the book from the point of view of a practitioner, a sociologist, a lawyer, an economist, an international regulator and a philosopher. Part II, 'Auditor independence', addresses the current crisis in auditing via the core concepts – independence and conflicts of interest – deployed in this area, and presents empirical evidence relevant to this debate. Part III, 'Beyond the auditor: the search for solutions', brings together chapters that focus on audit regulation and ethical education for accountants. 'The Conclusion, Restorative strategies', summaries the very disparate themes arising out of the book and cautions against both complacency and the hasty application of symbolic regulatory changes.

The objective of the book is not to provide an ethical primer for auditors or a systematic account of auditing ethics, but to stimulate critical thought and openness to empirical evidence by bringing out the moral and institutional complexities of the auditing function. No ethical quick fixes are offered and no one line of reform is suggested, but all the chapters raise important arguments that bear on the ethical problems that confront professional auditors, their clients, regulators and the public, whose interests ought to be paramount in the crafting and implementation of acceptable auditing standards and practices.

References

Albrecht, W. S. 1992, *Ethical Issues in the Practice of Accounting*, South-Western Publishing, Cincinnati, OH.

Bentham, J. 1948 (1823), *Introduction to the Principles of Morals and Legislation*, Basil Blackwell, Oxford.

Clarke, F. L., Dean, G. W. & Oliver, K. G. 1997, *Corporate Collapse – Regulatory, Accounting and Ethical Failure*, Cambridge University Press, Melbourne.

CPA Australia & ICAA (Institute of Chartered Accountants in Australia) n.d., *Code of Professional Conduct*, www.cpaustralia.com.au. http://www.cpaustralia.com.au

Duska, R. F. & Duska, B. S. 2003, *Accounting Ethics*, Basil Blackwell, Oxford.

Fried, C. 1978, *Right and Wrong*, Harvard University Press, Cambridge, MA.

Gowthorpe, C. & Blake, J. (eds) 1998, *Ethical Issues in Accounting*, Routledge, London.

Guy, D. M., Carmichael, D. R. & Lach, L. A. 2001, *The CPA Guide to Professional Ethics*, John Wiley & Sons, New York.

Hare, R. M. 1981, *Moral Reasoning*, Clarendon, Oxford.

HIH Royal Commission 2003, *The Failure of HIH Insurance*, Commonwealth of Australia, Canberra.

Kant, I. 1953, 'The Moral Law', in H. J. Paton (trans.), *Groundwork of the Metaphysic of Morals*, Hutchinson, London.

Libby, T. & Thorne, L. 2004, 'The Identification and Categorization of Auditors' Virtues', *Business Ethics Quarterly*, vol. 14, no. 3, pp. 479-98.

McBarnet, D. & Whelan, C. 1999, *Creative Accounting and the Cross-Eyed Javelin Thrower*, John Wiley & Sons, Chichester.

Maurice, J. 1996, *Accounting Ethics*, Pitman Publishing, London.

Mill, J. S. 1910 (1861), 'On Liberty', in A. D. Lindsay (ed.), *Utilitarianism, Liberty, Representative Government*, Dent, London, pp. 65-170.

Nagel, T. 1986, *The View from Nowhere*, Oxford University Press, New York.

Smart, J. C. C. & Williams, B. 1973, *Utilitarianism: For and Against*, Cambridge University Press.

Tweedie, D. 1988, 'True and Fair vs The Rule Book: which is the answer to creative accounting?', *Pacific Accounting Review*, vol. 1, no. 1, pp. 1-21.

Part I. Approaches to the critique of auditing

Chapter 1. Governance and accountability: a legal approach to auditing

Stephen Bottomley

Abstract

This chapter examines the legal context of company auditing from the perspective of the Australian legal setting for public company audits.[1] It outlines the recent history of legislative review and reform, describes the current legal setting — as set out in legislation and court decisions — for company audits and auditor liability, and investigates the debates concerning auditor independence and the limitation of auditor liability.

Introduction

The legal regulation of company audits in Australia has come under significant scrutiny in the past three years, prompted by some significant corporate collapses in 2001, most notably HIH Insurance (which led to an inquiry by a Royal Commission) and One.Tel. In the wake of these events, there were four major and separately conducted reviews of the legislative framework governing auditors and audit work. These reviews culminated in the *Corporate Law Economic Reform Program (Audit Reform and Corporate Disclosure) Act 2003* (Cwlth).

The first of these reviews commenced in August 2001, when the Federal Minister for Financial Services commissioned Professor Ian Ramsay to review the requirements for the independence of auditors and audits, the findings of which were published in October that year (Ramsay 2001). In addition to the impetus supplied by the recent company failures, the review was also prompted by a perception that overseas developments on auditor independence had moved ahead of the Australian requirements (Ramsay 2001, p. 6). Six months later, in April 2002, the Federal Parliament's Joint Standing Committee on Public Accounts and Audit commenced its own review of independent auditing, reporting in August of that year (JSCPAA 2002). This was the first time that the Committee had undertaken an inquiry into private-sector audit issues (JSCPAA 2002, p. *vi*). Then, in June 2002, the Federal Treasurer announced a review of audit regulation as part of the government's Corporate Law Economic Reform Program. The outcome of

---

[1]This chapter is based on, but develops material in, Tomasic, Bottomley and McQueen (2002), Chapter 7.

that review (known colloquially as 'CLERP 9')[2] was published in September 2002 (CLERP 2002). Finally, the three-volume report of the HIH Royal Commission was published in September 2003, containing, as part of its broad inquiry into the HIH collapse, a review of and reform proposals for auditor independence, audit reports and audit committees (HIH Royal Commission 2003). Each of these reports was factored into the drafting of the Corporate Law Economic Reform Program (Audit Reform and Corporate Disclosure) Bill 2003 (Cwlth), which was introduced into Parliament in December 2003. The Bill was debated and amended in Parliament, and was assented to on 30 June 2004. The resulting Act made significant changes to many aspects of the Corporations Act. Most notably these include to the law relating to the conduct of audits, to the appointment and independence of auditors, and to company financial reporting requirements.

The audit requirement

It has long been a basic statutory requirement that a company must have its annual financial report audited and must obtain an auditor's report about the conduct of the audit. Currently, this requirement is found in s. 301 of the *Corporations Act 2001* (Cwlth).[3] This requirement has been imposed since the earliest Australian company law statutes. The first Australian companies legislation to include mandatory financial reporting requirements, the *Companies Act 1896* (Vic), was enacted 'in the wake of large-scale company losses, land fraud, and bank and building society failures' (Peirson & Ramsay 1983, p. 288). Section 28(1) of that Act stated that:

> No balance-sheet of any company shall deemed to be filed ... unless the same shall have subscribed thereto or indorsed thereon a certificate signed by the duly appointed auditors that such auditors have audited the same and have certified to the correctness or otherwise of the said balance-sheet.

Before outlining the current legal requirements for company audits, it is useful to examine some of the rationales that have been provided for these mandatory audit rules over the past 100 years.

Rationales for the audit requirement

The mandatory audit requirement must be understood against the underlying requirements about the public disclosure by companies of their financial affairs. Mandatory public financial reporting was introduced in the United Kingdom by the Joint Stock Companies Act in 1844. Whilst these requirements were de-

---

[2]This was the ninth report published by the Program.
[3]Similar requirements apply elsewhere; for example, see the Companies Act, s. 9, in the United Kingdom, and the Canada Business Corporations Act, ss. 155 and 169. In Australia, the audit requirement also applies to other corporate entities such as managed investment schemes. It does not apply to small proprietary companies unless this is required by at least 5% of the voting shareholders (Corporations Act, s. 293).

emphasised in the subsequent Companies Act 1862, they have since formed a major part of modern corporate legislation and corporate regulation. At the time, these requirements were prompted by concerns over the incidence of corporate fraud. The rationale for these requirements was summed up (some 70 years later) in Mr Justice Brandeis' famous aphorism that 'sunlight is the best disinfectant, electric light the best policeman' (Brandeis 1913, cited in Weiss 1979, p. 575). This concern about the importance of protecting investors from financial fraud has persisted as one of two interwoven rationales for mandatory financial audits. It is premised on ideas of investor susceptibility and lack of expertise. The assumption is that potential victims of corporate misconduct will be able to take note of this publicly available and professionally verified information, and take appropriate steps to protect themselves, or to seek their own remedies.

The second rationale is that audits promote confidence and empower investors to make rational and informed financial decisions. This policy was described by Street CJ in Eq in *re Castlereagh Securities Ltd* ([1973] 1 NSWLR 624, p. 638) in the following way:

> A sound share market and the ability of shareholders to reach reliable conclusions are dependent upon shareholders, brokers and financial experts having access to full and reliable information concerning the affairs of companies. The courts do not, and directors should not, yield to the laconism that the only financial information most shareholders want is the figure on their dividend cheques. It is the clearly discernible intention of the companies legislation that companies should make adequate disclosures to enable shareholders individually, and the market collectively, to reach informed judgments. Over value and under value are both obnoxious. Where authentic details are not forthcoming, inference and even speculation inevitably take over. Decisions based on gossip or on inside information are concomitants of an unhealthy market.

Economic theory has also emphasised this argument. For example, audits are said to 'improve the reliability of financial statements, make them more credible and increase shareholders' confidence in them' (Panel on Audit Effectiveness 2000, cited in Ramsay 2001, para. 4.01). In this way audits are said to 'add value' to the financial statements and to the capital markets in general (Ramsay 2001, para. 4.02). The statutory requirement for an audit is then said to reinforce these credibility-enhancing and value-adding functions, providing an independent third party who can verify the financial information produced by a company. In theory, this reduces the costs that users of that information would otherwise incur if they had to verify it themselves. Auditors thus serve as 'reputational intermediaries', assisting the efficient operation of the market for corporate information (Corbett 1994, p. 850, referring to Gilson & Kraakman 1984).

A different justification for the mandatory imposition of audit requirements can be found in the 'concession' theory of company incorporation. According to this theory, the grant by the State of independent legal status to a company creates a private actor with special powers and capacities (for example, the company's capacity to issue shares and to enter into contracts). This special status is therefore said to carry certain obligations.[4] On this view, the requirement that a company should publicly disclose its financial affairs on a regular basis and be subject to an audit is the quid pro quo for the grant of incorporation by the State. On this view, when an auditor is engaged to meet the company's statutory audit requirement, they can thus be said to be performing a dual function. The first function may be described as 'private'. It arises from the contractual relationship between the auditor and the company. This contract imposes various duties on the auditor, which are discussed later in this chapter. Breach of these duties may result in an action for damages brought by the company against the auditor. Secondly, there is a more public function. The companies legislation not only requires that an auditor should report to the company about its financial statements, but also that this report should become part of the public record about the company. Moreover, while they are conducting the audit and reporting to the company, the auditor is under a number of *statutory* obligations which cannot be contractually modified. The auditor is prohibited by the statute from contracting out of any liability for breach of their duties to the company (Corporations Act, s. 199A). Furthermore (as noted below), an auditor is required to inform the Australian Securities and Investments Commission (ASIC, the regulator responsible for enforcing the Corporations Act) if the auditor suspects a contravention of the Act has occurred. In this sense, the audit is part of the wider public system of corporate regulation. There is, clearly, a tension between these private and public roles which is most evident when considering the question of an auditor's liability to persons outside the contractual relationship (a topic dealt with later in this chapter).

The auditor's appointment and removal

The following discussion focuses on the audit obligations of public companies. A public company is required to appoint an auditor (ss. 327A & B). Following the CLERP 9 reforms, the auditor may be either an individual, a firm or a company (s. 324AA).[5] This requirement first applies within one month after a company has been registered, and this initial appointment must be made by the directors. The auditor who is appointed at this time holds office until the first annual general meeting of the company (s. 327A(2)). At that meeting the company,

---

[4]There is disagreement about the contemporary relevance of concession theory, given the relative ease with which companies can now be registered. For a discussion, see Bottomley (1999).
[5]As discussed later, CLERP 9 introduced the possibility that an audit firm may incorporate as a company (Corporations Act, Pt 9.2A).

acting through its voting members, is required to appoint an auditor who will hold office until either death, removal from office, resignation, incapacity by reason of lacking the relevant qualifications, or because of a 'conflict of interest situation' (ss. 327B(2)-(2C)).[6]

Two features of these requirements are worth emphasising. First, in the absence of any disqualifying factor, the auditor holds office indefinitely, not for a fixed term. One qualification to this is found in the new provisions (introduced by CLERP 9) concerning audit rotation for companies listed on a stock exchange. If an individual plays a significant role[7] in the audits of a listed company for five successive years, then they cannot play a significant role in the audit of that company for another two years (s. 324DA). Thus, if the company has appointed an *individual* as its auditor, a new auditor must be found at the end of the five-year period. But, on the other hand, if the auditor is a firm or company, and the lead or review auditor[8] has played a significant role in audits for the past five successive years, then the firm or company may continue to act as auditor, provided that it uses another person in the lead or review capacity (ss. 324DC & DD).

Secondly, in formal terms, the appointment of the auditor is a decision that is made by the members of the company, rather than its directors. Indeed, the Act requires that before the annual general meeting, the auditor must be nominated by a member (s. 328B). This underlines the theory that the auditor is part of a process whereby members are able to monitor the performance of the directors and managers of the company. Of course, in practice the board has a significant degree of influence on the selection and appointment of the auditor. The members will usually make their decision by following the recommendation put to them by the board.

The auditor's formal accountability to the members is also emphasised by the fact that an auditor may only be removed from office by a resolution passed at a general meeting, initiated by the directors or members of a company (s. 329). ASIC has indicated its view that this section 'is designed to protect the auditor from manipulation by directors and to protect members of the company from an auditor who wishes to resign rather than conclude an audit which is proving difficult or controversial' (ASIC 1992, para. 2). Notwithstanding the obvious purpose of this section, it is rarely used. For example, a study of the annual general meetings of 271 Australian listed companies found that the removal of the auditor had not been an agenda item in any of the meetings held between 2001 and 2003 (Bottomley 2003, p. 36).

---

[6] 'Conflict of interest situations' are discussed later in this chapter.
[7] A person 'plays a significant role' if they are appointed and act as the auditor or prepare the audit report for the company, or if they are the lead or review auditor for a firm or company that is appointed as auditor (s. 9).
[8] The lead auditor is the person in the firm or company who is primarily responsible for the conduct of the audit. The review auditor is the person who is primarily responsible for reviewing the conduct of the audit (s. 324AF).

Statutory functions of the auditor

The statutory function of an auditor is to provide an independent and expert assessment of the annual and half-yearly financial reports prepared by a company, and to prepare a report to the company's members.[9] The statutory framework for company audits is narrowly defined. First, it does not extend to audits outside the annual and half-yearly timetable. A company may choose to undergo an audit outside of this framework (for example, in preparation for a potential takeover defence).[10] Second, within the framework of annual or half-yearly audits, as Fogarty and Lansley point out, the auditor's role 'is restricted to commenting on historic financial statements produced by the company twice-yearly: … it does not extend into arguably the most important area of disclosure – continuous disclosure' (Fogarty & Lansley 2002, p. 412). Nor does the audit involve any assessment of 'the prudence of business decisions made by management' (Ford, Austin & Ramsay 2003, p. 521). And third, the statutory framework does not regulate non-audit work performed by auditors. The CLERP 9 reforms did not impose any prohibition or restriction on the supply of non-audit services by auditors to audit clients. Instead, amendments to s. 300 simply require the directors of a listed company to include in the company's annual report a statement that describes the dollar amount paid to the auditor for non-audit services during the year, to state whether the directors are satisfied that the provision of those services is compatible with the general standard of independence for auditors, and to explain the reasons why the directors are satisfied about this (s. 300(11B)). This contrasts with the position in the United States, where the Sarbanes-Oxley Act of 2002 prohibits auditors from providing certain non-audit services contemporaneously with the audit (see s. 201).

Looking at the statutory functions in more detail, when conducting the audit of a company's annual or half-yearly financial report, the auditor is required to:

- form an opinion about whether the financial report complies with the Corporations Act and with the applicable accounting standards, and gives a true and fair view of the company's financial position. The auditor must then report to the members about the opinion they have formed.[11] If the auditor forms the opinion that the financial report does not satisfy any of these requirements, then the auditor's report must state why (ss. 307(a), 308(1) & (2))
- form an opinion about whether:
  - the auditor has been given all information, explanations and assistance that is necessary for the conduct of the audit

---

[9]Half-yearly reports may be reviewed by the auditor, rather than being fully audited (ss. 302(b) & 309(3)).
[10]As occurred in the case of *AWA v. Daniels* (1993) 9 ACSR 383, discussed elsewhere in this chapter.
[11]The requirement to report to the members is a strict liability offence (s. 308(5)).

- sufficient financial records and registers have been kept by the company to enable a financial report to be prepared and audited
- other records and registers required by the Corporations Act have been kept (ss. 307(b)-(d)).

These requirements that the auditor must 'form an opinion' reflect the common law requirement which, as we will see, says that auditors should conduct their audits actively, rather than relying passively on information supplied by company officers and employees. In addition to these 'opinion forming' requirements, the auditor must also:

- conduct the audit in accordance with the auditing standards that are made by the Auditing and Assurance Standards Board (s. 307A). This requirement was introduced by the CLERP 9 reforms; its intention is to give legislative backing to the auditing standards (CLERP 2002, p. 27)
- give the directors of the company a declaration that the auditor has not contravened the auditor independence requirements in relation to the audit (s. 307C, introduced by CLERP 9: the auditor independence requirements are discussed later)
- report on and describe any defect or irregularity in the company's financial report, including any 'deficiency, failure or shortcoming' relating to the corporation's financial records, other records and registers, and information given to the auditor (s. 308(3)). The company has a right to sue for damages as a result of a breach by the auditors of this duty (*AWA Ltd v. Daniels* (1993) 9 ACSR 383, p. 386)
- notify ASIC if the auditor has reasonable grounds to suspect that there has been a contravention of the Act that is either significant or is one that cannot be adequately dealt with in the auditor's report or by bringing it to the attention of the directors. As a consequence of the CLERP 9 amendments, the auditor must also notify ASIC of any attempt to unduly influence, coerce, manipulate, mislead or otherwise interfere with the conduct of the audit (s. 311).[12]

Statutory powers

To discharge their statutory audit and reporting requirements, the auditor has certain powers and entitlements under the Corporations Act.

The auditor has a right of access to the books of the company, and may require any company officer to provide such information, explanations or assistance as the auditor needs for the purposes of the audit (s. 310). For their part, company officers are under a positive obligation to allow the auditor access to the books

---

[12]This CLERP 9 proposal was criticised by peak accounting bodies because of its possible impact on relations between auditors and their audit clients; see *Butterworths Corporation Law Bulletin* (2004), 7 [202].

(including registers and general documents) and to give the auditor any information, explanation or assistance which is required (s. 312).

In an unlisted company the auditor is *entitled* to attend the general meeting and to be heard on matters concerning the audit (s. 249V). If the auditor does attend the AGM then the members must be given a reasonable opportunity to question the auditor about the conduct of the audit, the preparation of the audit report, the accounting policies used by the company in preparing its financial statements, and the independence of the auditor (s. 250T). As a result of the CLERP 9 reforms, the situation for listed companies is different. In this type of company members have the right to submit written questions to the auditor prior to the AGM (s. 250PA). Moreover, the auditor of a listed company is *required* to attend or be represented at the company's AGM (s. 250RA). The impact of this mandatory attendance requirement will be slight. The study of 271 AGMs referred to earlier found that auditors already attended the AGM in 94% of cases. Having said that, the study also suggests that this attendance has frequently been symbolic rather than functional: the study suggests that most questions directed to the audit report will be answered by the chair of the meeting instead of the auditor, and that auditors rarely speak at meetings (Bottomley 2003, pp. 31-2).

Contract and tort duties and liabilities

In addition to statutory requirements, auditors must also comply with duties imposed by the common law concerning the conduct of the audit and the detection of malpractice. These duties are based in the tort of professional negligence, arising from the relationship between the auditor and anyone to whom the auditor owes a duty of care, and also in contract, arising from the engagement contract with the company.

Duties to the company

The basic duty of an auditor when conducting an audit is to use a reasonable degree of skill and care. The parameters of this duty were first set out in the late 19th century in a series of cases culminating in *re Kingston Cotton Mill Co (No 2)* ([1896] 2 Ch 279). In that case, Lopes LJ used what became a frequently invoked metaphor, stating that the auditor's role was to act as 'a watch-dog, but not a blood-hound'. This meant that:

> ... [the auditor] is justified in believing tried servants of the company in whom confidence is placed by the company. He is entitled to assume that they are honest, and to rely upon their representations, provided he takes reasonable care. If there is anything calculated to excite suspicion he should probe it to the bottom; but in the absence of anything of that kind he is only bound to be reasonably cautious and careful ([1896] 2 Ch 279, pp. 288-9).

During the 20th century, however, the courts gradually moved away from this image of the auditor as an alert but passive watch-dog. As Moffitt J put it in 1970 in the landmark case of *Pacific Acceptance Corporation Ltd v. Forsyth*:

> Since the classic statements concerning the auditors were made last century there have been considerable changes in the organisation of the affairs of companies either operating singly or as groups, in their merger or takeover and in their accounting systems, and there have been continuing and increasing experience of and notoriety of danger signs in respect of mismanagement, fraudulent or otherwise, of companies often brought to light by "economic squeezes" as they are termed ((1970) 92 WN (NSW) 29, p. 73).

Justice Moffitt's judgment contains a lengthy and sustained analysis of the auditor's duty of skill and care in the conduct of a company audit. The case involved an action by a company against its auditors, alleging negligence arising from a breach of contractual duty. In finding for the company, Justice Moffitt acknowledged that 'auditors are not insurers' — that is, they are not expected to detect any and all errors and fraud that may occur in company financial statements.[13] Nevertheless, he held that in planning and carrying out a company audit, the auditor 'must pay due regard to the possibility of error or fraud' ((1970) 92 WN (NSW) 29, p. 63). The auditor's duty is to go behind the company's books and determine the true financial position of the company ((1970) 92 WN (NSW) 29, p. 63). This means that the auditor must design and carry out procedures which have a reasonable expectation of detecting 'a substantial or material error or fraud' in the company's affairs ((1970) 92 WN (NSW) 29, p. 65). The auditor will design those procedures by drawing on his or her previous experience of how fraud and error are likely to be hidden in corporate financial statements. The implementation of the audit program requires that the auditor must personally check and examine these matters. In particular:

> ... if the existence of a document which is under the control of the company is material to the audit, it is the duty of the auditor acting reasonably to examine the document for himself unless there are some specific circumstances which make it reasonable to accept something less than proof by inspection ((1970) 92 WN (NSW) 29, p. 70).

In contrast to the approach taken in the *Kingston Cotton Mills Case*, Moffitt J held that an auditor does not comply with the standard of reasonable skill and care by simply relying on the assumption that company directors and officers have fulfilled their respective duties to the company. Thus, the auditor is required to make inquiries at the appropriate level. The auditor may rely on the corpora-

---

[13] (1970) 92 WN (NSW) 29, p. 60, citing Lindley LJ in *re Kingston Cotton Mill Co (No 2)* [1896] 2 Ch 279, p. 284.

tion's system of internal control, but only after it has been appraised, its strengths and weaknesses have been ascertained, and it has been tested.

The next major Australian case concerning an auditor's duties to the company did not introduce any new dimensions to the duties already discussed, but the magnitude of the claim did attract considerable attention to the issue of auditors' liability. The case involved an action for breach of contract brought by Cambridge Credit Corporation Ltd against its auditors.[14] Cambridge Credit was a finance corporation involved in real estate development. It had issued debentures under the terms of a trust deed. The money raised from the debentures was invested in real estate. The trust deed imposed a limitation on the ability of Cambridge Credit to issue further debentures. This limitation required the company to maintain a certain ratio of debentures to shareholders' funds; if that ratio was breached, the trustees were empowered to appoint a receiver. The company's 1971 annual accounts wrongly overstated the value of the shareholders' funds. Nevertheless, the auditors certified that the accounts gave a true and fair view of the company's financial position, and also certified that the issue of further debentures would not breach the ratio defined in the trust deed. Cambridge Credit continued to conduct business and to invest in real estate. During the crash of the property market in 1974, Cambridge Credit, along with a number of other property companies, collapsed. When it failed to make an interest payment to the debenture holders, the trustee appointed a receiver to the company. Cambridge Credit sued the auditors, alleging a breach of contract in relation to the certification of the 1971 accounts. At first instance, Rogers J held that the auditors had been negligent in failing to require that adjustments be made to the 1971 accounts. If those adjustments had been made, the trustee would then have been alerted and appointed a receiver. At that time the company's deficit would have been significantly less than that which existed in 1974. That breach of duty in 1971, said Rogers J, was the substantial cause of the collapse of the corporation in 1974, since the corporation had continued trading on an inadequate financial basis. His Honour ordered that $145 million damages be paid by the auditors. On appeal, the decision was overturned by a majority on the grounds that, while the 1971 audit involved a breach of contractual duty, this was not the cause of the loss suffered by the corporation in 1974. The Court of Appeal found that the collapse of the property market, due to government intervention, broke the chain of causation. It was also held that the loss was too remote from the negligent act.

As Chief Judge of the Commercial Division of the NSW Supreme Court, Rogers J had a further opportunity to rule on the duties of auditors, five years later, in

---

[14]The case was ultimately decided by the Court of Appeal in New South Wales: *Alexander v. Cambridge Credit Corporation Ltd* (1987) 12 ACLR 202. However, the decision of the trial judge is also relevant; see *Cambridge Credit Corporation Ltd v. Hutcheson* (1985) 9 ACLR 545.

the landmark *AWA Ltd v. Daniels* decision ((1992) 10 ACLC 933). AWA Ltd had entered into what was then the relatively new world of foreign exchange dealings. The lone employee appointed to manage AWA's foreign exchange operations was initially very successful: AWA's foreign exchange operation looked as though it would become 'the largest dollar generating department' in the company ((1992) 10 ACLC 933, p. 985). Over time, however, the situation became quite different. Ultimately the employee's foreign exchange activities caused a loss to AWA of almost $50 million. This loss was concealed by various methods, including the making of unauthorised borrowings from a number of banks on behalf of AWA.

During this period the defendant audit firm, Deloitte Haskins & Sells, was engaged by AWA to conduct two audits. The firm had a long association with AWA. The partner in charge of audits (Daniels) was a long-standing friend of both the general manager and the internal auditor of AWA. The first audit was a statutory audit of the company's 1985/86 financial statements; the second was a non-statutory audit conducted between late 1986 and early 1987 in response to AWA's fears of a possible takeover. In neither of the audits was the full extent of the company's foreign exchange problems disclosed, although the Court found that the audit partner had recognised and noted the defects in AWA's system of internal control as early as June 1986.

AWA admitted that, in relation to foreign exchange dealings, its systems of internal control and record- and account-keeping were deficient. Nevertheless, the company sued the auditors for damages from breach of contract, claiming that the loss was caused by the auditor's failure to draw attention to these deficiencies and to note the problems in its reports. The company's claim was that the auditors were responsible for detecting and reporting deficiencies or inadequacies in the company's systems. For their part, the auditors denied any breach of duty to AWA, and claimed for contributory negligence on the part of the company.

Justice Rogers found that the auditors had been negligent. He also upheld the auditor's claim of contributory negligence. His Honour found that AWA's responsibility for negligence was 20%, while the auditor was 80% responsible. The AWA chief executive officer was ordered to contribute 10% of the auditor's 80% liability.[15] In dealing with the liability of the auditors, Justice Rogers emphasised the point made by Moffitt J in the *Pacific Acceptance Case*, namely that an 'auditor's duty has to be evaluated in the light of the standards of today' ((1992) 10 ACLC 933, p. 990). Justice Rogers' decision highlighted a number of specific aspects of the auditor's basic duty to exercise care and skill:

---

[15]The apportionment of liability is reported in *AWA Ltd v. Daniels (No 2)* (1992) ACLC 1643.

- *A duty in relation to the examination of the company's financial records*: Rogers J emphasised that, consistently with the obligation that is now found in the Corporations Act, s. 307(c),[16] the auditors should form an opinion that proper financial records have been kept by the company. In the *AWA Case*, His Honour found that the auditors had failed in this regard.

- *A duty in relation to the process of gathering information*: when doubts were raised about the scope of authority of the employee in charge of the foreign exchange operations, the auditors were then under a duty to make inquiries from senior management to ascertain the true position about the nature and extent of that authority. As Rogers J put it, 'in case of doubt, an auditor is required to inquire' ((1992) 10 ACLC 933, p. 954).

- *A duty to bring matters to the attention of management during the conduct of the audit*: according to Rogers J, the auditors were under an obligation to bring deficiencies in the company's internal controls to the attention of management in the first instance. This duty persisted for the duration of the audit process. His Honour observed that it was 'negligence of the first order' for Daniels to have waited until the conclusion of the audit to bring these matters to the attention of the managers ((1992) 10 ACLC 933, p. 990).

- *A duty to follow up*: when it became apparent that management had failed to respond adequately, Rogers J held that the auditors had a further obligation to report the matter to the board: '[T]he absence of internal controls in AWA ... were of such importance that the defendants came under a duty to report them initially to management. Failing action to rectify the position, they had to be reported to the Board' ((1992) 10 ACLC 933, p. 964).

On appeal by the auditors, Justice Rogers' findings on the negligence of the auditor were upheld (*Daniels v. Anderson* (1995) 13 ACLC 614). The Court of Appeal disagreed, however, with the apportionment of liability made by Rogers J, and reduced the damages by one-third. Nevertheless, the Court stressed the responsibilities of an auditor when problems are discovered:

> If the auditor in the course of evaluating internal control and other auditing procedures becomes aware of material weaknesses in or an absence of internal controls the auditor must ensure, usually by a communication in writing, that management becomes aware of these weaknesses on a timely basis. If management does not react appropriately the auditor must report the weaknesses to the board ((1995) 13 ACLC 614, pp. 645-6 per Clarke and Sheller JJ).

---

[16]The section requires an auditor to form an opinion about whether the company has kept financial records sufficient to enable a financial report to be prepared and audited.

Duties to persons outside the company

The private/public role of the auditor in conducting a statutory audit raises the question whether the auditor owes duties of care to individuals outside the company. Given that the audit report becomes a matter of public record, is a duty owed to anyone who has access to the audited accounts? In other words, do auditors play a role in the policy of investor protection for which a wider liability is justified?

In Australia, the answer to this question was finally settled in 1997 by the High Court's decision in *Esanda Finance Corporation Ltd v. Peat Marwick Hungerfords* ((1997) 23 ACSR 71).[17] This decision resolved a difference between two lines of cases. One line of cases suggested a broad approach, under which auditors would owe a duty of care to a wide class of persons. One of the most influential decisions in this group of cases was *Scott Group Ltd v. McFarlane* ([1978] 1 NZLR 553), where a majority of the Court of Appeal in New Zealand held that auditors owe a duty of care to any person whom the auditors could reasonably foresee would need to use and rely upon the audit report when dealing with the company. This conclusion was applied subsequently in a number of cases.[18]

The second line of cases – upheld by the High Court – supports a narrow interpretation of auditors' liability to third parties. These decisions have often taken their lead from the words of Cardozo CJ in the US case *Ultramares Corporation v. Touche*. His Honour remarked that the liability of accountants (and auditors) for negligent misstatement ought to be restricted, otherwise they would be exposed 'to a liability in an indeterminate amount for an indeterminate time to an indeterminate class' (255 NY 170, p. 179 (1931)).

Prior to the *Esanda Case*, the standard-bearer for this narrow view of auditors' liability to third parties was the House of Lords decision in *Caparo Industries plc v. Dickman* ([1990] 2 AC 605). That case dealt with two questions: is any duty owed by an auditor to potential investors in a company who do not already own shares in the company, and is any duty owed by an auditor to existing shareholders in the company? On the first question, the House of Lords held that the auditors of a public company owe no duty of care to investors who rely on the audited accounts in deciding to buy shares in the company. The Court acknowledged that it might be foreseeable that potential investors would use the audited accounts, but foreseeability by itself is insufficient to establish a duty. The Court stressed that proximity was also required as a separate element, and that there was no sufficiently proximate relationship between the auditor and a potential investor to give rise to any duty.

---

[17]This confirmed a trend which had been developing in earlier cases; see Baxt (1990, 1993).
[18]For example, *JEB Fasteners Ltd v. Marks, Bloom & Co (a firm)* [1981] 3 All ER 289, and *Twomax Ltd v. Dickson, McFarlane & Robinson* 1982 SC 113. See also *Columbia Coffee & Tea Pty Ltd v. Churchill* (1993) 9 ACSR 415.

On the second question, the House of Lords held that the auditor's duty in performing his or her statutory function is owed to the shareholders as a body, not to individual shareholders. The Court accepted that facts might arise which established a sufficiently proximate relationship between the auditor and an individual shareholder. This would require the auditor to know that the statement would be communicated to the shareholder for the purpose of a particular transaction or type of transaction, and that the shareholder would rely on the statement in connection with that transaction ([1990] 2 AC 605, p. 641 per Lord Oliver). In such a case, however, the resulting duty of care would only protect the shareholder from losses in the value of shares which he or she already held. It would not protect the shareholder for losses resulting from the purchase of additional shares in reliance on the auditor's report. This is because, as a share purchaser, the shareholder would be in the same position as any other potential investor, to whom the auditor owes no duty ([1990] 2 AC 605, p. 627 per Lord Bridge). Some Australian courts had already accepted and applied the *Caparo* decision prior to the *Esanda Case*.[19]

In *Esanda Finance Corporation Ltd v. Peat Marwick Hungerfords* ((1997) 23 ACSR 71), the High Court was able to lay down decisive guidelines for Australian law about the liability of auditors to third parties. The Esanda finance company had lent money to a number of companies associated with a company called Excel. The loans were guaranteed by Excel. In deciding to make the loans, Esanda had relied on the accounts of Excel, which had been audited by Peat Marwick Hungerfords. The audited accounts did not disclose Excel's true financial position. Excel subsequently went into liquidation and Esanda claimed to have suffered financial loss as a result of the loan transactions. Esanda brought an action against the auditors, claiming that they were negligent in the audit of Excel's accounts.

The High Court held that the auditors did not owe a duty of care to Esanda. The Court confirmed that in an action for economic loss arising out of negligence, mere foreseeability of the possibility of harm arising from giving information or advice is not sufficient to impose a duty of care on the person giving the information or advice. Esanda needed to prove that the auditor knew, or ought reasonably to have known of, three things ((1997) 23 ACSR 71, p. 78 per Brennan CJ). First, 'that the information or advice would be communicated to the plaintiff, either individually or as a member of an identified class'; second, that the information or advice would be communicated for a purpose that would be very likely to lead the plaintiff to enter into a transaction of the kind that the plaintiff did enter; and third, 'that it would be very likely that the plaintiff would enter into such a transaction in reliance on the information or advice'.

---

[19] E.g., *R Lowe Lippmann Figdor & Franck v. AGC (Advances) Ltd* (1992) 10 ACLC 1168.

Justice McHugh identified several factors in support of this confined scope of liability ((1997) 23 ACSR 71, pp. 102-8), including a mixture of policy-based and empirical claims that:

- imposing a duty of care on auditors in favour of third parties would lead to an increase in the cost of auditing services, a decrease in competition for such services as smaller firms are forced out of business, and a reduction in the standard of those services as auditors reduce overheads in order to absorb the higher cost of insurance
- the intended beneficiaries of such a duty are 'a sophisticated group who have the means in most cases to take steps to avoid the risk of loss'
- the plaintiff's loss is caused primarily by the conduct of the company which is audited, while the role of the auditor in causing the loss is secondary
- sophisticated investors will face problems in proving reliance on the audit report, given that they are likely to regard the report as only one of many factors to take into account
- 'the factual issues that arise in auditor's liability cases ... make it almost impossible for an auditor to avoid a trial or settlement even when the auditor is not liable to the plaintiff'
- such a duty would carry a prospect of 'vexatious or near vexatious litigation'
- such a duty would require an auditor to compensate investors for loss arising from their self-induced reliance where they were not prepared to pay for the auditor's work.

The *Esanda* decision indicates a significant shift away from the broad investor protection rationale discussed earlier in this chapter. It also favours a private conception of the audit function, as opposed to the public role identified earlier.

Current legal issues

Auditor independence

The corporate collapses of the 1980s were seen primarily as the result of neglect and mismanagement by company directors and officers. This led to major reforms to the law, both statutory and judicial, on directors' duties. By comparison, critical scrutiny of the collapses of 2001 has concentrated more on the role of the auditors.[20] In particular, there has been considerable speculation about the extent to which a lack of auditor independence contributed to the high-profile corporate collapses in Australia during 2001.[21] Both the Ramsay Report and the report of the Joint Standing Committee on Public Accounts and Audit had as

[20] The role of directors has not been ignored. There have been some significant cases brought against directors, for example *ASIC v. Adler (No. 3)* (2002) 20 ACLC 576 (relating to the collapse of HIH Insurance), and *ASIC v. Rich* (2003) 21 ACLC 450 (relating to the collapse of One.Tel).
[21] A similar concern with auditor independence is apparent in the United States (see the Sarbanes-Oxley Act of 2002, ss. 201-206) and the United Kingdom (see Companies (Audit, Investigations and Community Enterprise) Act 2004).

their main focus the problem of maintaining auditor independence (Ramsay 2001; JSCPAA 2002), and over half of the reforms in the CLERP 9 legislation were directed at audit reform. Whether this unfairly perpetuates the scapegoating of auditors for company failure is a matter of debate (Fogarty & Lansley 2002, pp. 418-19). Nevertheless, as the Ramsay Report noted, 'the importance of independence in the auditing context has become such that the terms "independent" and "auditor" can no longer be separated' (Ramsay 2001, para. 8.15).

Concerns about auditor independence are not new. There have long been provisions in the Corporations Act and in professional codes of conduct dealing with aspects of auditor independence (Ramsay 2001, para. 4.14). The courts have also commented on the importance of the auditor's independence, and the difficulties in maintaining it. In *Pacific Acceptance Corporation Ltd v. Forsyth*, for example, Moffitt J noted that while the shareholders appoint the auditor, most often it is the directors or senior managers who determine this appointment. Therefore the auditor may be under some pressure to produce a report which pleases those managers. The auditor 'is put in a position where there must often be a real and practical conflict ... between his duty to the shareholders and his interest not to take action which may prejudice his reappointment or his relations with those with whom he works' ((1970) 92 WN (NSW) 29, p. 131).

Prior to the CLERP 9 reforms, the statutory independence requirements for auditors were relatively straightforward. A person could not be appointed as an auditor if they were an officer of the company, or if they, or any corporation in which they were a substantial shareholder, owed more than $5000 to the company or its related entities. As the Ramsay Report noted, these provisions fell short of a general requirement of auditor independence (Ramsay 2001, para. 5.03). The CLERP 9 reforms, based upon the recommendations of the Ramsay Report but also taking into account findings of the HIH Royal Commission, cast the net of auditor independence much more widely and are expressed in much more detail. These reforms include the auditor rotation requirements discussed earlier in this chapter.[22]

Following the CLERP 9 reforms, the Corporations Act specifies both general and specific independence requirements for auditors. The general requirement focuses on the need to avoid 'conflict of interest situations'. It is set out in ss. 324CA-CC (applying, respectively, to individual auditors, members of audit firms and directors of audit companies). A 'conflict of interest situation' exists whenever the auditor is not capable of exercising objective and impartial judgment in conducting the audit, or at least a reasonable person would conclude that this is the case. This involves looking at the relationship between the auditor and the company,

---

[22] In addition, the Act now imposes a two-year post-audit 'cooling off' period for auditor partners who wish to join a company client as a director or officer (ss. 324CI & CJ).

and its current or former directors and managers (s. 324CD). The effect of this general requirement is that if an auditor engages in audit activity and they are aware of the existence of a conflict of interest situation, they commit an offence unless they take all reasonable steps to end that situation. They must also inform ASIC within seven days of becoming aware that the conflict of interest situation exists. If the auditor is not aware of the situation, they commit an offence if they do not have in place a quality-control system that would have been reasonably capable of making them aware that the conflict of interest situation exists.

The specific independence requirement creates further offences, focusing on particular 'relevant relationships' that constitute a breach of the auditor's independence when they are engaged in audit activity. The Act defines 19 such relationships (s. 324CH). Some are role relationships (e.g., where the auditor is an officer or employee of the audited company), others are property relationships (e.g., where the auditor has an asset that is an investment in the audited company), and the remainder are financial relationships (e.g., where the auditor owes money to, or is owed money by, the audited company). The Act then lists the persons associated with the audit to whom these different types of relationships apply (ss. 324CE-CG). The listed persons include immediate family members of the audit team, and suppliers of non-audit services from the audit firm.

These independence requirements are reinforced by the further requirement that the auditor must declare to the directors of the audited company whether there have been any contraventions of the auditor independence requirements (including the auditor rotation requirements) (s. 307C).

Notwithstanding their detail, the regulation of auditor independence goes beyond these new statutory requirements. The independence requirements introduced by the CLERP 9 reforms are primarily concerned with what Michael Power calls 'organizational independence' (Power 1999, p. 132). That is, the reforms define the independence problem in terms of the relationship between the company and the auditor. Power argues, however, that there is a second dimension to audit independence – he calls it 'operational independence' – which focuses on the *audit process* rather than the auditor (Power 1999, p. 132). Here there are two questions. First, regardless of their degree of organisational independence, how much does/should the auditor rely on company managers for information? This is a question that has tended to occupy the courts, typified by the *Pacific Acceptance* decision described earlier. For example, in defining the common law duties of auditors, the courts have concentrated on the obligation to 'go behind the company's books' and determine the company's true financial position. Of course, auditors must be dependent, at least to some extent, on information supplied by the company. This was recognised in the *AWA Case*, where the court emphasised the auditor's duty to inquire. So the second question is whether the auditor is able to draw independent conclusions from this information. Power suggests that for this to be possible, auditors must have an independent knowledge base on which to assess the information: there must be 'clear rules of auditee conduct and robust techniques for determining compliance with these rules' (Power 1999, p. 133). This aspect of operational independence is the domain of the auditing (and accounting) standards referred to earlier in this chapter. When it is seen with these added dimensions, auditor independence becomes a much more complex regulatory goal.

Limiting auditors' liability

Since the 1970s the quantum of civil claims against auditors has produced continuous debate about the extent to which auditors should be liable for economic loss incurred when a company fails financially. The auditing profession has expressed its concern that there is an 'expectation gap' between the auditors' legally defined role and what the investing public expects:

> The general public believes that the auditor has a responsibility for detecting *all* fraud, while the auditing profession believes its responsibilities are limited to *planning* the audit so that there is a reasonable expectation of detecting *material* fraud (Gay & Pound 1989, p. 118, emphasis in original).

The question has been whether the narrowing of this expectation gap is best left to the episodic application by judges of concepts such as foreseeability, proximity and reliance, or whether statutory intervention is required. On one view, legislative reforms are unnecessary, given the tight limitations imposed on auditors' liability to third parties in the *Esanda Case*, and the use of contributory negligence principles in *Daniels v. Anderson* (Fogarty & Lansley 2002, p. 425). The other view looks for legislative certainty. In Australia, the CLERP 9 reforms have taken the latter approach.

CLERP 9 introduced two methods by which the liability of auditors for loss might be restricted.[23] First, the reforms introduced a system of proportionate liability for economic loss or property damage arising from misleading or deceptive conduct in relation to a financial product or financial services. The idea of proportionate liability is that the defendant's liability is directly proportionate to the degree of their responsibility for the loss or damage that has been incurred. This scheme replaces the system of joint and several liability under which a plaintiff can recover the whole amount of the loss from any one or more of the

---

[23]In addition to these methods of reducing liability, it should be noted that under legislation in New South Wales and Western Australia (the *Professional Standards Act 1994* (NSW) and the *Professional Standards Act 1997* (WA)), professional associations (including accountants) can limit (or 'cap') the liability of their members for financial loss in certain situations. Under the *Treasury Legislation Amendment (Professional Standards) Act 2004* (Cwlth), this state legislation is applied to certain types of liability under the Corporations Act and the Trade Practices Act.

defendants, regardless of the relative degree of fault of the defendants.[24] Secondly, the reforms permit an audit firm to incorporate as a limited liability company on certain conditions (for example, each director of the company must be a registered company auditor). The immediate consequence of incorporation is that the company, unlike a partnership, is a separate legal actor. Prima facie, it is the company, rather than its members or directors, that incurs legal liability for its actions. This separation of the company's liability from that of the auditor members of the company[25] does not, however, insulate the auditor members from liability. An audit member who is negligent in the conduct of an audit may be liable along with the audit company. The advantage of incorporation, though, is that other non-negligent auditor members will be shielded from liability.

Conclusion

It is too early to say what effect the flurry of legislative reforms that were introduced in the wake of the corporate failures of the early 21st century might have. Indeed, the broader literature on law reform and legislation suggests that, notwithstanding the number of reports, reviews and inquiries that preceded these changes, it may be difficult to produce conclusive assessments of their impact and effect. There are likely to be different views about what is to count as an effect of this legislation, and how this is to be measured. This is not a new problem; some years ago John Griffiths drew attention to the distinction between the direct and indirect effects of legislation (Griffiths 1979, pp. 351-6).[26] Direct effects occur when the people to whom the legislation is directed comply with the letter of the rules. Indirect effects are the consequences of that compliance. In the case of the CLERP 9 reforms, the intended direct effects presumably include the delivery of audit services by auditors who are not disqualified by 'relevant relationships' with the audited company. This should be relatively easy to measure. The indirect effects that are hoped for (presumably) are audit processes and reports that are trusted by shareholders and that 'add value' to the company's financial statements. This will be less easy to gauge. One thing is clear, however: the prevention and regulation of corporate wrongdoing and failure cannot be made the responsibility of any one group. Since the 1980s, the roles of directors, senior managers, institutional shareholders and auditors have each come under regulatory scrutiny in Australia. In the United States, lawyers have been added

---

[24]Two things should be noted about the proportionate liability scheme introduced by CLERP 9. First, it is not restricted to auditors. It applies to any person who causes loss or damage as a result of misleading or deceptive conduct in relation to financial services (see Corporations Act, s. 1041H). Secondly, at the time of writing it is not clear whether the reforms actually apply to audit reports. This is because r. 7.1.29(3)(a) currently excludes the auditing of financial reports from the definition of 'financial service'. It is possible that new regulations will be introduced to correct this.
[25]This is not the same thing as 'limited liability'. In a company context, limited liability refers to the fact that a member's liability *to the company* is limited.
[26]Griffiths also notes the occurrence of independent effects and unintended effects.

to this list.[27] Problems of corporate governance and accountability are complex; regulatory responses need to avoid attempts at simple fixes.

---

[27]See the Sarbanes-Oxley Act of 2002, s. 307 (requiring lawyers to report evidence of material violation of securities law or breach of fiduciary duty to the chief legal counsel or chief executive officer of the company, at first instance, and to the audit committee thereafter).

References

ASIC (Australian Securities and Investments Commission) 1992, Policy Statement 26: Resignation of Auditors, viewed 5 April 2004, http://www.asic.gov.au/asic/pdflib.nsf/LookupByFileName/ps26.pdf/%24file/ps26.pdf.

Baxt, R. 1990, 'The Liability of Auditors – The Pendulum Swings Back', *Company and Securities Law Journal*, vol. 8, no. 4, pp. 249-57.

Baxt, R. 1993, 'A Swing of the Pendulum (Value of Auditors Reports)', *Charter*, vol. 64, no. 1, p. 20.

Bottomley, S. 1999, 'The Birds, the Beasts, and the Bat: Developing a Constitutionalist Theory of Corporate Regulation', *Federal Law Review*, vol. 27, no. 2, pp. 243-64.

Bottomley, S. 2003, 'The Role of Shareholders' Meetings in Improving Corporate Governance', Centre for Commercial Law Research Report, Australian National University, Canberra.

Butterworths Corporation Law Bulletin 2004, 7 [202].

CLERP (Corporate Law Economic Reform Program) 2002, 'Corporate Disclosure: Strengthening the Financial Reporting Framework', Commonwealth of Australia, Canberra.

Corbett, A. 1994, 'The Rationale for the Recovery of Economic Loss in Negligence and the Problem of Auditors Liability', *Melbourne University Law Review*, vol. 19, no. 4, pp. 814-67.

Fogarty, M. & Lansley, A. 2002, 'Sleepers Awake! Future Directions for Auditing in Australia', *University of New South Wales Law Journal*, vol. 25, no. 2, pp. 408-33.

Ford, H. A. J., Austin, R. P. & Ramsay, I. M. 2003, *Ford's Principles of Corporations Law*, 11th edn, Butterworths, Sydney.

Gay, G. & Pound, G. 1989, 'The Role of the Auditor in Fraud Detection and Reporting', *Company and Securities Law Journal*, vol. 7, no. 2, pp. 116-29.

Gilson, R. & Kraakman, R. 1984, 'The Mechanisms of Market Efficiency', *Virginia Law Review*, vol. 70, no. 4, pp. 549-644.

Griffiths, J. 1979, 'Is Law Important?', *New York University Law Review*, vol. 54, no. n/k, pp. 339-74.

HIH Royal Commission 2003, *The Failure of HIH Insurance*, Commonwealth of Australia, Canberra.

JSCPAA (Joint Standing Committee on Public Accounts and Audit) 2002, Review of Independent Auditing by Registered Company Auditors, Report 391, Commonwealth of Australia, Canberra.

Peirson, G. & Ramsay, A. 1983, 'A Review of the Regulation of Financial Reporting in Australia', *Company and Securities Law Journal*, vol. 1, no. 6, pp. 286-300.

Power, M. 1997, *The Audit Society: Rituals of Verification*, Oxford University Press.

Ramsay, I. 2001, *Independence of Australian Company Auditors: review of current Australian requirements and proposals for reform*, Report to the Minister for Financial Services and Regulation, Department of Treasury, Canberra.

Tomasic, R., Bottomley, S. & McQueen, R. 2002, *Corporations Law in Australia*, 2nd edn, Federation Press, Sydney.

Weiss, J. 1979, 'Disclosure and Corporate Accountability', *The Business Lawyer*, vol. 34, no. 2, pp. 575-603.

Chapter 2. 'Perfectly legal': a sociological approach to auditing

Doreen McBarnet

Abstract

This chapter offers a sociological perspective on ethics and auditing, drawing on empirical research to put current auditing issues in context and to demonstrate the need for a new ethical approach to law. Taking Enron as its starting point, it widens the focus from outright accounting fraud to techniques of 'creative accounting', which are carefully constructed to undermine accountability and transparency while still claiming to be 'perfectly legal'. The use of such techniques is a matter of routine business practice, and their acceptance a matter of routine audit practice. The chapter suggests that this practice is fostered by a culture which sees it as legitimate to manipulate the letter of the law in ways which defeat its spirit. Changes in the law itself, or in the structuring of auditor independence, will not lead to a change in practice unless this culture is itself addressed, and a new ethical attitude to law adopted by business and auditors alike.

Introduction

The perspective taken in this chapter is that of neither an accountant nor an ethicist but of a sociologist of law. It takes Enron as the starting point for an analysis of accounting practice and accounting law, and ends by raising questions for accounting ethics. In particular, it raises questions about the ethics of both auditors and management in their approach to and application of law, as evidenced not only in fraudulent accounting but in 'creative accounting'. The great attraction of creative accounting over fraud is that it allows companies to circumvent legal control in ways which can nonetheless claim to be 'perfectly legal', complying literally with the letter of the law while nonetheless defeating its spirit. Enron has laid bare not only extensive examples of fraud but extensive examples of creative accounting. But Enron is only the tip of the iceberg. This chapter draws on empirical research to demonstrate the routine nature of creative accounting practice, the challenges it poses for law and the questions it raises for ethics in the preparation and audit of financial reports.[1]

Beyond fraud

Enron in the late summer of 2001 was the world's largest energy trader, the seventh largest corporation in the United States and darling of market analysts, who were urging investors to buy its shares. By 2 December 2001 Enron had filed for bankruptcy, till then the largest bankruptcy in US history. In between, on 16 October, it had announced its third-quarter results for 2001 would include, completely out of the blue, a charge against earnings of US$585 million and previously unreported debts of US$1.2 billion (Powers 2002). The regulators, the Securities and Exchange Commission (SEC), began to investigate, and by November Enron had restated its accounts of the previous five years. As the story unfolded over succeeding months, it emerged that Enron had 'not only wiped out $70 billion of shareholder value but also defaulted on tens of billions of dollars of debts' (Partnoy 2002, p. 1).

The public has been left reeling over how such a huge collapse could occur without warning, and how such enormous debts and losses could have been hidden from the market. Enron has become an icon for corporate wrongdoing on a massive scale, not just for the accounting issues but for all that followed: employees losing their retirement benefits, locked into Enron shares as the value of those shares vanished, while senior executives had been selling at still high rates and taking multimillion-dollar bonuses; accountancy firm Arthur Andersen shredding masses of Enron-related documents; auditors and analysts in general coming under scrutiny and criticism for lack of independence and new structures being introduced to counter this[2] ; allegations of political and regulatory corruption. Civil and criminal lawsuits are in process, there has been a series of investigations by Congress, as well as the SEC and Justice Department, and there has been a rush to new legislation and regulation. Enron's audit firm, Arthur Andersen, has paid the price with its own demise.

Enron is being treated as a watershed. 'After Enron', or the 'post-Enron world', are phrases used repeatedly in the press and in academic analysis to suggest an event of enormous significance, and there may be some temptation to demonise Enron, and Arthur Andersen, in order to shore up the notion that they are rotten apples in an otherwise basically sound and honest corporate world. 'Enron's

---

[1]This chapter draws on research on 'Regulation, responsibility and the rule of law' funded by the ESRC under its Professorial Fellowship Scheme, as well as earlier work on 'creative compliance'. Papers drawing on the same material on Enron and creative compliance as in this chapter, but focussing on the role of corporate social responsibility rather than on 'ethical compliance', were presented at the colloquium of the International Society of Business, Economics and Ethics, Melbourne, July 2004, and at the colloquium on *Governing the Corporation*, Belfast, September 2004. The Belfast presentation, 'After Enron: Corporate governance, creative compliance and the uses of Corporate Social Responsibility', will be published by John Wiley in O'Brien (ed.) (2005).
[2]This reaction has not, of course, been confined to the United States. Australia, for example, beset by its own examples of audit and accounting failure, instigated the Ramsay review of independence of Australian company auditors (Ramsay 2001).

demise is not business as usual in America', said one investigating Congressman (Tauzin, Subcommittee on oversight and investigations 2002b, p. 32). This chapter focuses on the issues at the heart of the Enron case – its corporate structuring and financial reporting practices – and there the question has to be raised of what 'business as usual in America' – and the United Kingdom and elsewhere – actually is, in order to put Enron in context and draw out its wider implications for business and professional ethics.

There have to date been 30 indictments for fraud in relation to Enron's practices, going to the very top of the executive chain, and it would be easy to focus attention only on the clear breaches of law at the heart of those indictments – outright fraud or law-breaking in the form of lies about products being marketed, structures improperly accounted for in that they failed to comply with the rules on the treatment adopted, insider dealing, frauds against Enron and obstruction of justice. Yet to do so would be to create a disjunction between the legal charges brought by regulators in court and many of the charges made by Congress, the media and the general public. For them part of the outrage of Enron lies simply in the fact that the market was fundamentally misled on Enron's financial status by its use of off balance sheet accounting devices, and the issues this raises for the reliability of financial reporting in general. As two congressional investigators put it, 'Off the books transactions were purposefully designed to mislead shareholders about Enron's precarious financial profits' (Greenwood, Subcommittee on oversight and investigations 2002b, p. 2), and the 'broader issues are capital systems and transparency in accounting' (Deutsch, Subcommittee on oversight and investigations 2002a, p. 4).

These concerns take us deeper than fraudulent accounting. They necessarily raise issues about the widespread and endemic practice of creative accounting.

Enron used a multitude of fraudulent and creative practices to keep profits high, liabilities low, stock prices rising and credit ratings good, but the core technique was the use of what are variously known as Special Purpose Entities (SPEs), Special Purpose Vehicles (SPVs) or 'non-subsidiary subsidiaries'. These were partnerships constructed to fall outside the rules requiring their finances to be consolidated in Enron's group accounts, thus keeping them 'off balance sheet' (OBS). It could be argued from SEC guidelines that if just 3% of the capital investment in the SPV came from an independent outside body and remained at risk throughout the transaction, and the independent owner exercised control of the SPV, then the vehicle could be treated as 'off balance sheet' (Partnoy 2003, p. 210); that is, Enron did not have to include its losses or liabilities (or, in theory, profits or assets, but unsurprisingly OBS vehicles rarely have those) in its group accounts. Complex deals largely using derivatives were then done between the SPVs and Enron itself both to formally manage risk and to further enhance reportable financial performance. Some 4300 SPVs were in play by the time of Enron's demise.

These transactions were astonishingly complex and the indictments involve clear allegations of fraud in the construction of the deals. My concern, however, is broader, and it is this: much has been made of Enron's breach of accounting and other rules, and in relation to the core SPVs, the fact that they did not always comply with the rules which allow such entities to remain off the balance sheet. There were instances, for example, where 'the 3% rule' was invoked to justify an accounting treatment, but not, as later investigation demonstrated, actually adhered to (Powers 2002). Yet even if it had not broken the rules, it seems clear that Enron would have been misleading the market just as much. If it had only engaged in OBS structuring within the rules, it could still have kept significant debts and losses out of its own accounts. Indeed, it is arguable that much of Enron's OBS activity did not breach the rules. Rather, it creatively exploited the rules or utilised regulatory gaps, including the 'regulatory black hole' of derivatives (Partnoy 2002, p. 2).[3] Certainly, Enron's OBS vehicles were not, as has sometimes been said, 'secret' partnerships. Their existence was disclosed in the notes to the accounts as is required by the rules. They may have been disclosed in ways which were economic with the truth, or via other forms of 'non-disclosing disclosure' (McBarnet 1991), but they were disclosed.

This is not to defend Enron. On the contrary, it is merely to refine the charges. It is to suggest that Enron engaged in creative accounting as well as fraudulent accounting, and to underline the fact that the creative accounting, just as much as the fraudulent accounting, was, to cite our first congressman again, 'purposefully designed to mislead shareholders about Enron's precarious financial profits' (Greenwood, Subcommittee on oversight and investigations 2002b, p. 2). What is more, Enron has been far from alone in engaging in such creative accounting, raising with a vengeance the 'broader issues' which so concerned our second congressman, the issues of 'capital systems and transparency in accounting' in general (Deutsch, Subcommittee on oversight and investigations 2002a, p. 4).

Public reaction has been raised not only by the outright fraud involved, but by the capacity of both business and auditors to mislead the market and violate trust through OBS structuring – whether fraudulent or not – and indeed through creative accounting more generally. And that to me is the more fundamental issue. Indeed, the second biggest collapse in history – Enron has been upstaged in size if not complexity by WorldCom – could still have happened, completely out of the blue, even if it had *not* been breaking specific rules. It has certainly happened before.

---

[3]Partnoy (2002) has also observed in testimony to an investigating Senate Committee: 'Even if Enron had not tripped up and violated the letter of these rules, it would still have been able to borrow 97% of the capital of its special purpose entities without recognising these debts on its balance sheet'.

There are parallels, for example, with Polly Peck in the United Kingdom (*re Polly Peck International plc* 1996). Polly Peck went bust in August 1991, just weeks after the analysts had been describing it as 'undervalued' and a 'must-buy'. When it collapsed, what had been reported in the books as £2 billion in assets was suddenly redefined as £1.5 billion in liabilities. As with Enron, there were allegations of fraud on related issues, but the accounting figures themselves were largely down to creative use of the rules – or, in this case, of gaps in the rules. One commentator noted: 'This is the other side of the Polly Peck miracle. Stated profit margins ... are perfectly correct within generally accepted accounting standards, but they tell a misleading story' (David Brewerton, *The Times*, 2 October 1990).

That is why we need to contextualise Enron in the wider world of corporate legal practice and to see that if Enron is unusual, it may be unusual not because it misled the market – not because it used SPVs and other OBS techniques to do so – but because it sometimes used them improperly, because it got caught out and had to expose the reality behind the façade, and perhaps because it was an extreme case, not so much using creative accounting to enhance a business as to create one. There is a lot of technically proper but still thoroughly misleading creative accounting going on out there. There may also be a lot of technically *improper* accounting that never gets exposed. Certainly, large numbers of US corporations seemed to suddenly find it necessary to restate accounts after Enron and before the new Sarbanes-Oxley legislation took effect. But the important point is this: even where accounting is technically proper and can claim to be, in the oft-repeated phrase 'perfectly legal'[4] , – creatively exploiting rules and regulatory gaps rather than engaging in outright fraud – it can still be highly misleading.

Outright fraud is not, then, the only practice to raise ethical questions in accounting and audit. Significant questions are also raised by the construction of 'perfectly legal' techniques of creative accounting. In the following sections this chapter will, first, set the practices of Enron and Arthur Andersen in context by looking briefly at the kind of 'perfectly legal' OBS structures which have constituted widespread, routine corporate practice, regularly receiving auditor approval. Second, it will ask what can be done through accounting law to constrain creative accounting, and will assess some such attempts. Third, it will explore the culture underlying creative accounting and the ethical questions it raises for business and the accounting profession.

---

[4] This is not only used frequently in research interviews, but is something of a cliché in newspaper stories on creative accounting, tax avoidance or similar practices.

Enron in context: perfectly legal creative accounting

Enron is far from alone in setting up OBS SPVs to hide liabilities and create paper profits, and Arthur Andersen far from alone in endorsing this in audit. Nor is the practice new. My own research in the United Kingdom in the late 1980s and 1990s demonstrated the widespread use of SPVs and other OBS techniques to manipulate accounts. [5] Creative accounting more generally was, indeed, shown to be rife in the United Kingdom in this period (Griffiths 1986, 1995; Smith 1992). Similar practices are in use in the United States.[6] Nor is creative accounting an Anglo-Saxon phenomenon. One Enron indictment concerns abuse of reserves but again our past research, this time in Germany, demonstrated use of reserves to be common practice there as a way of manipulating accounts.

OBS SPVs were commonly used in the United Kingdom in the 1980s to manipulate accounts. 'Non-subsidiary subsidiaries' were set up, companies which were in economic substance subsidiaries, but which were carefully structured in their legal form to fall outside the rules defining a subsidiary (subsidiaries' finances having to be included in group accounts). Debts or losses could then be tidied away in them, off the balance sheet, and therefore out of the accounts of the company setting them up. Such techniques were used routinely by household-name companies such as Cadbury Schweppes, Habitat, Burtons, Storehouse, Dixons and many more.

As company law rules defining subsidiaries stood, it was far from difficult to keep bad financial news hidden in a way which could claim to be not breaking the rules but complying with them and therefore 'perfectly legal'. True, company law also contained the overriding principle that accounts should give a true and fair view, and the accounts produced after the set-up of such SPVs, it could be (and was) argued, did not do that, but accountants and lawyers looked to the detail of the law, to specific definitions and precedents, queried the meaning of 'true and fair' and its capacity to override specific rules, and endorsed the practice. Companies could properly claim they had the approval of their advisers. Auditors endorsed their accounts. Just like Enron.

Also like Enron, they sometimes had to shop around to get accountants and lawyers who would say that some of their more exotic structures and accounting

---

[5] I will draw on this research, much of which was carried out with Chris Whelan, in this section of the chapter and the next (see, for example, McBarnet 1991, 2003; McBarnet & Whelan 1991, 1997, 1999). Key parts of this body of work are also brought together in a recent volume of collected essays (McBarnet 2004b). The final section of the chapter relies on new research being conducted under the ESRC Professorial Fellowship Scheme.

[6] In hard-hitting testimony to the investigating Senate Committee, Partnoy (2002, p. 4) noted:

> Transactions designed to exploit these accounting rules have polluted the financial statements of many US companies. Enron is not alone. For example, Kmart Corporation — which was on the verge of bankruptcy as of January 21, 2002, and clearly was affected by Enron's collapse — held 49% interests in several unconsolidated equity affiliates. I believe this committee should take a hard look at these widespread practices. Partnoy notes too that 'accounting subterfuge using derivatives is widespread' (Partnoy 2002, p. 5).

innovations were indeed perfectly legal. But then there was and is no requirement to disclose just how much 'opinion shopping' had gone on until an endorsement was achieved. So long as one barrister was prepared to take a 'bullish' interpretation of the law in providing a legal opinion, and one accountancy firm to accept that, or posit its own bullish approach in audit, this was all that was needed in practice to claim reporting treatments were perfectly legal.

OBS SPVs were used for all sorts of things, including manufacturing paper profits. A property development company, for example, would set up an SPV to do its development for it. It then lent it money for the purpose and charged interest. The SPV did not pay the interest but since the interest was *payable*, the company could add it to its books to enhance its profits (by many millions of pounds at a time). Meantime, the SPV used another creative accounting technique, defining the interest as capital expenditure so the cost did not appear on its own profit and loss account (as a loss). The result is like magic: profits from nowhere and vanishing losses. Just like Enron. Property development company Rosehaugh, for example, had 16 SPVs. Just like Enron, their existence was disclosed in the notes to the accounts (at length, indeed, with seven pages of detail) but, also just like Enron's 'impenetrable footnote disclosure' (Partnoy 2002), or 'obtuse' provision of information (Powers 2002, p. 17), disclosure was so opaque that it was later said by one analyst that one would need to be a professor of accounting to have any hope of deciphering their significance (Christopher Hird, *House of Cards*, Radio 4 (UK), 1991). Such 'non-disclosing disclosure' is a recurrent theme in both creative accounting and tax avoidance (McBarnet 1991; McBarnet & Whelan 1999).

Unlike Enron, most companies did not collapse, but they were still misleading the market. And keeping debts off the balance sheet and profits up had a number of valuable consequences, indeed purposes. Performance-related pay and bonuses for senior executives could boom. Just like Enron. Huge debts could be taken out that would not have been possible if they had to go on the balance sheet – or at least would not have been possible without upsetting the debt/equity ratio. This ratio is key in corporate finance and corporate governance. It is used most obviously for assessing good/bad buys in the stock market. But it is also used as a trigger in loan covenants for calling in loans if banks think the company's debt is getting out of hand, and is also frequently used in a company's 'constitution', its memorandum and articles of association, as a trigger requiring shareholder consultation before, for example, directors may make a highly leveraged acquisition. Artificially protecting the debt/equity ratio, then, meant basic corporate governance controls could be bypassed.

This was exemplified in the case of Beazer, a UK housebuilding company. It acquired, through an SPV, the US corporation Koppers, worth twice Beazer's own value, in a deal described by Angus Phaure, an analyst at County NatWest, as 'impossible' and 'sheer magic' (*Accountancy*, April 1988, p. 9). Just as in Enron, derivatives formally shifted the risk, which, however, ultimately fell on Beazer not the SPV, and indeed came back to haunt it within a few years (McBarnet & Whelan 1997; *The Times*, 26 June 1991).

And some companies did collapse. When property development company Rush and Tomkins went bust in 1991, an estimated £700 million-worth of hitherto unreported debts suddenly emerged from associated but OBS joint ventures (*The Times*, 30 April 1990). Sometimes the scope to take on more debt than could really be sustained itself led to collapse – or fraud to try to hide it. Again, just like Enron. Maxwell Corporation is best remembered for raiding pensions, but one of the reasons it did so was because it had overextended itself by buying MacMillan via huge debts (Bower 1992). The purchase was made via an OBS SPV. It could not have been done without it, there being too much debt already. But in practice, as is often ultimately the case, the risk came back to Maxwell.

There are many other direct parallels with Enron. One Enron SPV was set up to take advantage of the beneficial regulatory treatment available for wind farms it owned (*SEC v. Fastow* 2002). If the wind farms were more than 50%-owned by an electric utility or electric utility holding company, they would not be eligible for the benefits, and since Enron was about to acquire Portland General Electric it would lose out. It therefore used an SPV to buy the wind farms. There is a close parallel to this in the United Kingdom in the context of broadcasting. A broadcasting company, EMAP, wanted to take over another broadcasting company, but if it did so it would hold eight licences. Since the statutory limit for one company's holding was six, the takeover would be disallowed. It therefore set up an OBS SPV to formally make the takeover. This was contested as mere form but upheld in court (*R v. Radio Authority* 1995).

In short, Enron's manipulation of its accounts, and Arthur Andersen's auditing, need to be understood in this wider context of normal business practice – normal and arguably 'perfectly legal' practice, 'creative' rather than fraudulent accounting, yet nonetheless routinely frustrating the whole idea of true and fair accounts, and routinely distorting market information.

What is to be done? Strategies for legal control and their limits

The immediate reaction to a scandal such as Enron is a demand for legal change. The United States has already produced the Sarbanes-Oxley Act. Auditor independence has become a key issue, with new rules aimed at securing this proposed or established in and beyond the United States.[7] But new structures for auditor independence are not themselves likely to be enough, as we shall see, and new

---

[7] For discussion of this in the context of Australia, see Ramsay (2001).

law in general is not always the panacea hoped for. Such problems as compromises built into new law, inadequate sanctions and inadequate resources for policing can all be listed as potential factors in the law's failure to offer effective control. It is also increasingly recognised that new rules, even if they are fully resourced and uncompromised, can themselves prove inadequate simply because of the ability of the regulated to adapt to them. A new rule may stop today's objectionable creative accounting device, but leave the way open for the new device ingeniously constructed tomorrow to thwart the new rule. The more specific and prescriptive the rule is, the clearer the criteria the new structure has to meet or circumvent.

In the post-Enron United States, proposals have therefore been put forward not just for a tightening of regulations and strengthening of sanctions, but for a change of regulatory style. The suggestion is that there should be less emphasis on specific rules and more on principles.[8] Harvey Pitt, for example, former SEC chairman, noted to the House of Representatives: 'We seek to move toward a principles-based set of accounting standards, where mere compliance with technical prescriptions is neither sufficient nor the objective' (Pitt 2002; and see Bratton 2004). This is exactly the strategy adopted by the United Kingdom in the 1990s in a bid to constrain creative accounting and specifically OBS financing.

Enron's SPVs were built on rules and guidelines which determined whether or not an entity should be consolidated into a group's accounts partly on the basis of specific thresholds of equity ownership. This was also the case in 1980s' company law in the United Kingdom. The rules on consolidation (the requirement for a holding company to include all its subsidiaries in its group accounts) at that time involved two questions for determining whether Company B was a subsidiary of Company A, and therefore had to have its financial accounts included in A's. First, does A own more than 50% in nominal value of B's equity share capital? Second, is A a member of B and does it control the composition of B's board of directors?

There were simple and complicated ways to ensure B fell outside these criteria and therefore could stay off A's balance sheet. It would be one of the aforementioned 'non-subsidiary subsidiaries'[9], a subsidiary in substance but not in form. One way was to set up a 'diamond structure', in which A set up two subsidiaries, B and C, owning 100% of B and 50% of C. B and C then owned 50% each of D. A in effect owned 75% of D, but D fell outside the definitions of a subsidiary. Another route was for A to get a friendly bank, B, to hold 50% of the SPV, C, in the form of preference shares. C had a board of four directors, two from A and two from the bank, but A's directors had more voting rights and A therefore

---

[8]Many have advocated this approach; see, for example, Partnoy (2002), p. 5. The Sarbanes-Oxley Act has charged the SEC with producing a more principle-based regime (Sarbanes-Oxley Act 2002, s. 108(d)).
[9]There were various other terms for this kind of structure, e.g. a 'controlled non-subsidiary' or an 'orphan subsidiary'.

controlled the vote of the board without controlling, as the statute phrased it, its 'composition'. Though such practices might have been constrained by concerns over a challenge under the purportedly 'overriding' principle that accounts give 'a true and fair view', the *Argyll Case* (Ashton 1986; McBarnet & Whelan 1999, p. 90), and wider legal discussions of the exact nature and status of the 'override', provided ammunition to counter any such challenge, and indeed encouraged the spread of the practice.

Creative accounting using OBS techniques was rife, but there also followed scandals, collapses, review committees, a campaign to clean up accounting (spearheaded by David Tweedie, then chair of the UK's Accounting Standards Board, now chair of the International Accounting Standards Committee, the IASC) and significant changes in law and in accounting regulation. The story, and the changes made, are complex and are detailed elsewhere (McBarnet & Whelan 1999), but for the purposes of this chapter the point is that radical changes in the law were made with the express purpose of controlling creative accounting, and specifically the abuse of OBS financing and SPVs. What were these changes, and how has the new regime fared?

At the core of the new regime was the view that law was failing to control creative accounting because of weak enforcement, inadequate regulation and too much emphasis on rules. Precise rules and thresholds were too easy to circumvent; creative accounting thrived on repackaging transactions and structures to fall just outside them. They provided too clear a recipe for avoidance. Changing from one precise rule to another to catch the latest device simply stimulated the creation of yet another new device designed to escape the latest legal criteria. A new approach had to be adopted. Lord Strathclyde, for example, in the House of Lords, stated: 'Our intention is to curb the use of off balance sheet financing schemes through controlled non-subsidiary undertakings. Any definition of the term will encourage attempts to avoid the provision by artificial constructions with the intention of escaping from the letter of the definition' (Strathclyde, Hansard, HL Deb, vol. 03, col. 1018).

In essence, therefore, the new regime adopted a philosophy of shifting regulatory style from detailed prescriptive rules to broader purposive principles, from narrow criteria to broader catch-all ones in the drafting of definitions, and from an emphasis on legal form as the criterion for deciding on appropriate accounting treatments to an emphasis on economic substance. There was also a revision of the law on the 'true and fair override' to make it more accessible. The stated mission was that there be a shift of focus in financial reporting, and by implication in auditing, from the letter of the law to its spirit (e.g., Sir Ron Dearing, *The Times*, 24 January 1991). A new standard-setting body was set up under creative accounting's arch-enemy, David Tweedie, and a new agency, the Financial Reporting Review Panel, was set up to investigate accounts, policing no longer being left entirely to auditors. New sanctions were introduced for directors found in breach of regulations.

The OBS SPVs of the 1980s, and the rules which were interpreted as permitting them, were clearly targeted. So in the 1989 Companies Act (itself implementing European company law's Seventh Directive), the definitions of a subsidiary included a 'catch-all' definition which avoided mention of 50% thresholds or precise forms of control and instead required consolidation in broader terms. B would have to be included in A's group accounts, in the event of A having 'a participating interest' in B (which might take forms other than equity ownership) and 'exercising an actual dominant influence' ('actual' rather than in any particular legal form). A linchpin of the new regime was Financial Reporting Standard 5 (ASB 1994). This stated categorically that transactions should be reported according to their economic substance, putting economic reality before formal legal structuring. It also specifically tackled 'quasi-subsidiaries', entities which fulfilled the functions of a subsidiary despite falling outside the statutory definitions of one, and required their inclusion in the accounts of the 'quasi-holding company'.

Great hope has been attached by opponents of creative accounting to the potential of a principle-based regime for avoiding the limitations of rule-based regulation and providing a more effective means of controlling creative accounting. Tweedie noted, for example: 'We believe this is the surest means of forming standards that will remain relevant to innovations in business and finance and which are most likely to discourage ingenious standards avoidance practices' (FRC 1991, para. 5.5). Close analysis of the new regime, however, and of other jurisdictions following similar strategies[10] , suggests even a shift to principles poses problems for effective legal control. Again, this is detailed elsewhere (McBarnet & Whelan 1991, 1999; McBarnet 2003) and I will simply note some of the main problem areas.

First, there is a problem with sustaining principles as principles. There are too many factors which can produce a drift from principles to rules, clarifying and narrowing the ambit of their control, and providing more recipes for creative accountants to work on. Lobbying, demand for guidelines, court cases and just the build-up of informal precedents on what is allowed in practice and what is not are examples of the factors that eat away at principles and can convert them in effect back to rules.

Second, our empirical research suggests enforcers face problems in putting principles, and indeed stronger powers in general, into practice. There is too much room for contestability over what is true and fair − what is substance. There is concern about losing in court. Indeed, there is concern about winning

---

[10]For example in relation to tax avoidance in the United Kingdom, Germany and Australia.

in court if the win would nonetheless lead to tighter definitions of what is not allowable, and by implication what is. There is concern about losing control to the judges.

The strength of a principle-based regime as a means of control also lies in the uncertainty it generates. Hence David Tweedie's response, when asked early in the new regime how it would fare: 'We're like the cross-eyed javelin thrower at the Olympic Games. We may not win but we'll keep the crowd on the edge of its seats...'[11] Not knowing where the regulatory javelin will fall may make for greater caution among would-be creative accountants and their auditors. It also encourages settling with enforcers rather than contesting them; there is reluctance to be the company that puts its head on the block to test the legal interpretation of the new regime. On the other hand, if uncertainty is strength, the last thing the regime wants is to have its limits clarified, and regulators too may be too wary of a court case to flex their muscles too much. Yet there is a paradox here, because if the javelin is never wielded it will cease to deter.

What is more, the strength provided by uncertainty is also a potential weakness in terms of issues of legitimacy. Principle-based regimes can be readily open to criticism as too uncertain, as open to retrospectivity, as giving regulators too much power, as opening the way to arbitrary decision-making. The strategic response to creative accounting is itself susceptible to critique as 'creative control', and as an unacceptable violation of the rule of law. One empirical consequence of this is a tendency on the part of enforcers to limit themselves in how they use their powers. In turn, the consequence of that is to limit in practice the theoretical scope of the principle-based regime for control.

Whether rule-based or principle-based, there are then problems in controlling creative accounting through law. Yet one could argue that ultimately creative accounting is only a problem because of another issue, and that is not just the law itself but the attitude taken toward law by those allegedly subject to it, and those policing it. Turning to that takes us from accounting law to accounting ethics.

Towards ethical compliance?

Even principle-based systems can fall prey to creative accounting. Regulations, even regulations based on principles, have to be based on words, and even abstract words can be scrutinised for creative interpretations or uses. Alternatively, co-existing rules or even other principles can be brought in to limit the reach of the principles in question.

The 1989 Companies Act, we saw, introduced the 'catch-all' phrase 'actual dominant influence' in an effort to stop novel methods of control slipping through

---

[11]Providing Chris Whelan and myself with the title of our book (McBarnet & Whelan 1999).

the net of more specific definitions. Yet that phrase then spawned 'deadlocked joint ventures', where A and B set up a partnership, C, in which the equity was held 50-50 and the power of each was 'deadlocked': neither A nor B exercised 'actual control' and C remained off the balance sheets of both. Rush and Tomkins' partnerships, unheard of until its bankruptcy as noted above, were deadlocked joint ventures of this kind. Though further regulations, especially FRS5, might be thought to catch this now, accountancy firms have suggested there could still be ways of constructing entities to keep them, arguably, OBS; for example by making C a corporate joint venture, and using an exemption in the Companies Act to avoid consolidation. Another suggested route was to use 'revolving chairs', with A and B appointing a chairman for C with a casting vote each alternate year. Other sections of company law, and GAAP[12] principles on consistency, could then be invoked to keep C out of the accounts of both (Ernst & Young 1997). Even the idea of 'substance over form' itself has been used creatively and counter-purposively.[13]

In fact, whatever law, and whatever kind of law, is put in place as a mechanism for controlling business, it is mined for opportunities for circumvention. That is the reality of business regulation in action, whether in the arena of accounting or elsewhere.[14] Routine techniques are to search out gaps in the law ('Where does it say I can't?'); to scrutinise the 'ex-files' of law – exemptions, exclusions, exceptions – to see whether transactions or structures can be repackaged to fit within them, whether they naturally do so or not; to find or press for specific definitions and thresholds as guidance then 'work to rule'; and to construct completely innovative techniques which the law has not yet regulated and avoid control that way. Examples of all of these techniques can be found in creative accounting.[15] The OBS SPV, whether Enron's variation or the UK examples demonstrated here, are examples of 'working to rule'. They depended on close scrutiny of the rules and guidelines defining what *forms* of business entity or relationship require inclusion in group accounts, in order to construct or recon-struct forms which fall outside those definitions – even if they are equivalent in *substance*.

What this underlines is not just the nature and inherent limitations of law, but the fact that limitations of law are also a product of the way law is received and acted upon. Creative accounting is in fact the product of two factors. Limitations inherent in the nature, substance and enforcement of law provide the opportun-

---

[12]Generally Accepted Accounting Principles.
[13]For example via 'in-substance defeasance'. See McBarnet and Whelan (1999), Chapter 11; Rosenblatt (1984); FASB (1996).
[14]Tax avoidance, a close cousin of creative accounting, is another obvious example, but legal creativity is to be found in any legal area where there are attempts to control corporate activity through law, be it in the context of employee protection, environmental issues, health and safety, food and drugs or tenancy controls (McBarnet 1988). The concept 'creative accounting' captures the practice in financial reporting, but we need a broader concept to capture the pervasiveness of the practice. I've dubbed it 'creative compliance' (in McBarnet & Whelan 1997, for example).
[15]For examples of all of these techniques in action, see McBarnet and Whelan (1999).

ity, but that opportunity also has to be actively taken up by those subject to the law and by those charged with guiding and policing them – in this case, corporate management, their professional advisers and their auditors. It is not just how law is constructed and enforced that determines its impact but how it is received. If change is to come, therefore, it is not just the law we need to address but the attitude towards law assumed by those subject to it. The same is true of those charged with enforcing the law. Focussing on structures or rules to secure the independence of auditors will not resolve the situation so long as auditors, whether structurally independent or not, share the same attitude to law. The issue is not just legal or structural, but cultural and ethical.

What is the culture underlying, and facilitating, creative accounting? Ongoing research[16] suggests the following characteristic attitudes to law:

- The attitude to law is essentially one of 'Why not?' If a practice is not expressly and specifically defined as illegal, why should it not be used and claimed as legal? If a particular type of transaction is expressly outlawed, why should it not be refashioned in form if not in substance and claimed to be different?

- It is an attitude which defines compliance in a minimalist way, focussing on compliance with the letter of the law rather than its spirit, and which sees it as the responsibility of legislators and regulators to get the letter of the law right. If the way the law is drafted allows loopholes to be teased out, then it is deemed perfectly legitimate to utilise them, regardless of the intentions of the lawmakers.

- It is an attitude which treats law not as an authoritative and legitimate policy to be complied with, but as an obstacle to be circumvented, indeed as a 'material to be worked on' (McBarnet 1984) and, regardless of the policy behind it, tailored to one's own interests.

- It is an attitude which is highly attentive to law, but which looks to law not to ask, 'Is what I want to do allowed by law?', but, 'How can I find a way to justify it regardless?'

- It is an attitude in which law is a game, a game in which it is legitimate to come up with any interpretation one can, any argument one can dream up, however, *in one's one view*, 'spurious', 'bullish' or 'sailing close to the wind' that argument may be.[17]

This approach to law raises issues that can be addressed in a number of ways.[18] In the context of this book, the key question must be, 'Is this ethical?' *Should* this approach to law be seen as acceptable in either business ethics or professional

---

[16]Research in progress under the ESRC Professorial Fellowship Scheme.
[17]To cite from interviews with senior lawyers, accountants and business executives.
[18]These traits could be seen, for example, as reflecting a formalistic or positivistic approach to law.

ethics? It can be seen as ethical if business and professional ethics are equated with compliance with law, *and* if compliance with law is defined at a minimalist level as literal, 'bullishly' interpreted compliance. But the debates sparked by Enron and other accounting scandals may provide an ideal moment for those premises to be questioned, and for an expectation to be fostered that *ethical* compliance means compliance with the spirit and not just the letter of the law.

There may be ways in which law itself can be further enhanced to ensure compliance with the spirit and not just the letter, and we have yet to see what signals the Enron cases finally give out. But it may be time to also tackle the other side of the coin, not only the way law is made and enforced but the way it is received. It may be time to put the spotlight on the corporate and professional culture which sees as acceptable, indeed applauds as smart, the manipulation of law and defeat of legal control. It may be time to question the ethics of this attitude to law, and to ask *why* creative compliance is deemed legitimate when fraud is not. The intention, to defeat legal control, and the consequences, in terms of the frustration of legal policy and the impact on victims, are after all the same. What is clear is that changes in the law alone will not lead to a change in practice unless this culture is addressed, and a new, more ethical attitude to law and compliance is adopted by business and auditors alike.

This issue is not purely speculative. Many companies in their codes of conduct have made a point of declaring their commitment to compliance with the law. Indeed, Enron did just that, stating in its last social and environmental report that: 'We are dedicated to conducting business according to all applicable local and international laws and regulations' (Enron 2000). Given the fraud that was going on as this code was published, this does not do much to foster confidence in codes of conduct. More to the point of this chapter, however, even if Enron had complied totally with its code, it would have done nothing to constrain creative as opposed to fraudulent accounting. Although Enron's code committed it to compliance with the law, it did not spell out *how* the company would comply. A commitment only to minimalist, literal and creative compliance would foster, not prevent, creative accounting.

That point is, however, beginning – implicitly – to be acknowledged. We are already seeing a handful of companies expressly committing themselves in their codes of business ethics not just to compliance with the law, but to compliance with the *spirit* of the law.[19] Not all commitments in corporate codes of conduct can be taken at face value, as Enron amply demonstrates (though even commitments undertaken lightly may rebound when they are used to hold their instig-

[19]The current trend in big business of adopting policies of 'corporate social responsibility', though also complex and in need of critical assessment (McBarnet 2004a), might also prove a facilitative factor here.

ators to account).[20] And commitment to the spirit of the law could yet raise all kinds of legal controversies. However, the move suggests some acknowledgement, at least at the level of rhetoric, that it is not just breaking the letter of the law but breaking the spirit of the law that raises ethical questions. Helping place this issue on the agenda for corporate and professional ethics could prove one of Enron's more constructive consequences.

---

[20]See McBarnet (2004a) for an analysis of how rhetoric can rebound. Even if a code is seen mainly as PR, companies can still find themselves held to account on their commitments, with negative reputational and market consequences.

Bibliography

References

ASB (Accounting Standards Board) 1994, *FRS5 Reporting the substance of transactions*, London.

Ashton, R. K. 1986, 'The Argyll Foods case: a legal analysis', *Accounting and Business Research*, vol. 17, no. 65, pp. 3-12.

Bower, T. 1992, *Maxwell: The Outsider*, BCA, London.

Bratton, W.W. 2004, 'Rules, principles and the accounting crisis in the United States', *European Business Organization Law Review*, vol. 5, no. 1, pp. 7-36.

Enron 2000, Corporate Responsibility Annual Report.

Ernst & Young 1997, UK GAAP, Macmillan, Basingstoke.

FASB (Financial Accounting Standards Board in the United States) 1996, Statement of Financial Accounting Standards (SFAS) 125, 'Accounting for transfers and servicing of financial assets and extinguishment of liabilities', Norwalk, CT.

FRC (Financial Reporting Council) 1991, *The State of Financial Reporting: A Review*, London.

Griffiths, I. 1986, *Creative Accounting: How to Make your Profits What you Want Them to be*, Sidgwick & Jackson, London.

Griffiths, I. 1995, *New Creative Accounting*, Macmillan, London.

McBarnet, D. 1988, 'Law, policy and legal avoidance', *Journal of Law and Society*, vol. 15, no. 1, pp. 113-21.

McBarnet, D. 1991, 'Whiter than white collar crime: tax, fraud insurance and the management of stigma', *British Journal of Sociology*, 42, pp. 323-44.

McBarnet, D. 2003, 'When compliance is not the solution but the problem: from changes in law to changes in attitude', in V. Braithwaite (ed.), *Taxing Democracy*, Ashgate, Aldershot.

McBarnet, D. 2004a, *'Human rights and the new accountability'*, in T. Campbell & S. Miller (eds), Human Rights and Moral Responsibilities of Corporate and Public Sector Organisations, Kluwer, Dordrecht.

McBarnet, D. 2004b, *Crime, Compliance and Control*, Ashgate Dartmouth, Aldershot.

McBarnet, D. & Whelan, C. 1991, 'The elusive spirit of the law: formalism and the struggle for legal control', *Modern Law Review*, vol. 54, no. 6, pp. 848-73.

McBarnet, D. & Whelan, C. 1997, 'Creative compliance and the defeat of legal control: the magic of the orphan subsidiary', in K. Hawkins (ed.), *The Human Face of Law*, Oxford University Press.

McBarnet, D. & Whelan, C. 1999, *Creative Accounting and the Cross-eyed Javelin Thrower*, John Wiley & Sons, Chichester.

O'Brien, J. (ed.) 2005, *Governing the Corporation: Regulation and Corporate Governance in the Age of Scandal and Global Markets*, John Wiley & Sons, Chichester.

Partnoy, F. 2002, 'The Unregulated Status of Derivatives and Enron', Testimony at Hearings before the US Senate Committee on Governmental Affairs, 24 January.

Partnoy, F. 2003, *Infectious Greed*, Profile Books, London.

Pitt, H. L. 2002, Testimony Concerning the Corporate and Auditing Accountability, Responsibility, and Transparence Act before the Committee of Financial Services, US House of Representatives, Washington, DC, 20 March.

Powers, W. C., Jr. 2002, 'Report of Investigation,' Special Investigative Committee of the Board of Directors of Enron Corp, W. C. Powers, Jr. (Chair), R. S. Troubh, H. S. Winokur, Jr., 1 February.

Ramsay, I. 2001, *Independence of Australian Company Auditors: review of current Australian requirements and proposals for reform*, Report to the Minister for Financial Services and Regulation, Department of Treasury, Canberra, http://www.treasury.gov.au.

Rosenblatt, M. 1984, 'In-substance defeasance removes long-term debt from balance sheet', *Corporate Finance* (Euromoney).

Smith, T. 1992, *Accounting for growth*, Century Business, London.

Subcommittee on Oversight and Investigations Hearing 2002a, 'The Financial Collapse of Enron – Part 3', Committee on Energy and Commerce, US House of Representatives (107th Congress: 14 February 2002), Serial No. 107-89.

Subcommittee on Oversight and Investigations Hearing 2002b, 'The Financial Collapse of Enron – Part 4', Committee on Energy and Commerce, US House of Representatives (107th Congress: 14 March 2002), Serial No. 107-90.

Cases

re Polly Peck International plc (in administration) (No 3) [1996] 2 All ER 433.

R v. Radio Authority ex parte Guardian Media Group [1995] 2 All ER 865.

SEC v. Andrew Fastow, US District Court Southern District of Texas, Houston Division 2, October 2002.

Chapter 3. Public oversight: an international approach to auditing

Roger Simnett
Alana Smith

Abstract

The predominant structure initiated or proposed by various jurisdictions for reforming all of the recent ills attributed to the auditing standard-setting processes has been a public oversight board (POB). This includes mainly people independent of the audit profession, who oversee the activities of the standard-setting board (which includes mainly auditing practitioners). The rationale behind this structure is that there is a public-interest dimension to auditing. The aim of this chapter is to compare and contrast the various structures that have been instigated or proposed by the leading national and international bodies with regards public oversight of the auditing standard-setting process. This chapter compares and contrasts the oversight structure that is to be set up in Australia under the CLERP 9 reforms against similar recent initiatives in Canada, the United Kingdom and the United States, as well as the International Auditing and Assurance Standards Board (IAASB) of the International Federation of Accountants (IFAC). This comparison and contrast is undertaken on the following dimensions: membership, the procedures relating to appointment on the POB, the relationship between the POB and the standard-setting board, the powers of the POB, and whether the POB assumes responsibility for both accounting and auditing oversight.

Introduction

One of the key initiatives that has become a popular mechanism for reforming all of the recent ills attributed to the auditing standard-setting processes has been to instigate public oversight over these processes. The predominant structure initiated or proposed by various jurisdictions has been a public oversight (or equivalent) board (POB) (which includes mainly people independent of the audit profession), the purpose of which is to oversee the activities of the standard-setting board (which includes mainly auditing practitioners). The rationale behind this structure is that there is a public-interest dimension to auditing. It is generally, although not universally, believed that the setting of standards requires significant practical and technical expertise, and that this resides largely with practicing auditors. However, if auditors are given free rein to produce the standards that are required to be followed by members of the auditing profession, the concern is that they will produce standards that reflect the interests of the profession, rather than the public's interest.

The aim of this chapter is to compare and contrast the various structures that have been instigated or proposed by the leading national and international bodies with regards public oversight of the auditing standard-setting process. Such an oversight structure is to be set up in Australia under the CLERP 9 reforms, and follows similar recent initiatives at the national level in Canada, the United Kingdom and the United States, as well as at the international level with regards the International Auditing and Assurance Standards Board (IAASB) of the International Federation of Accountants (IFAC). The second section of this chapter examines what public oversight entails and what it is expected to achieve. The third section compares and contrasts the POBs in these jurisdictions on the following dimensions: membership, the procedures relating to appointment on the POB, the relationship between the POB and the standard-setting board, the powers of the POB and whether the POB assumes responsibility for both accounting and auditing oversight.

The fourth section of the chapter evaluates specific implications for Australia of moving to the proposed POB structure. (The issues considered may also have implications to varying degrees for other national bodies.) It firstly examines the tension that is created between oversight of a national standard-setting process and convergence with international auditing standards. The advantages of having public oversight at the national level, given that there is public oversight at the international level, and the proposed convergence of national with international auditing standards are also examined. A related consideration of the tensions produced by having national POBs set objectives that compete with a policy of converging with international auditing standards is also discussed. Finally, the extent of the POB's responsibilities in Australia with regards the development of auditing and assurance standards for assurance services other than financial report audits are considered.

The final section of the chapter contains a summary of the major findings and implications for Australia. In the Appendix, a comparison and summary of the key characteristics of POBs in the major national and international jurisdictions is provided. This includes all of the dimensions discussed in the chapter, as well as a comparison of some of the more structural aspects of POBs — oversight structure and funding mechanisms.

What is public oversight and what will it achieve?

Public oversight has been defined by the European Commission as comprising 'the responsibility for the education, the licensing and registration of statutory auditors as well as for standard setting on ethics and auditing, quality assurance and disciplinary systems' (European Commission 2003a). It has been operation-alised by way of independent national bodies charged with the responsibility to carry out one or more of the above functions. In Australia, it has been proposed that public oversight will become the responsibility of an expanded Financial Reporting Council (FRC)[1] , whilst the Companies Auditors and Liquidators Disciplinary Board (CALDB) will maintain its responsibility for taking disciplinary action in the case of auditor misconduct. The FRC's duties will include monitoring, advising, reporting and assessing the audit standard-setting process, independence issues and systems to deal with them, compliance with audit-related disclosure requirements, teaching of professional and business ethics, and the disciplinary procedures of the accounting bodies (CLERP 2002).

It has been widely claimed (both nationally and internationally) that the 'present audit standards and practices are severely deficient' (Sharav 2003). This apparent deficiency has been associated with a loss of credibility of the audit profession as investors become aware of the largely self-regulatory nature of this profession, and the conflicts of interest evident within such a structure (European Commission 2003a). It has also been widely accepted that the solution for restoring investor confidence in the audit profession is to improve its independence and transparency.[2] Public oversight of the profession has been the often suggested[3] and accepted solution[4] ; it is posited to be a 'major element in the maintenance of confidence in the audit function' (European Commission 2003b).

Theoretically, public oversight by an independent body will restore confidence in the audit profession through the introduction of neutrality and transparency. However, the manner in which this theoretical solution is operationalised will severely impact the degree to which it achieves its goals of protecting 'the interests of investors and further[ing] the public interest in the preparation of informative, fair and independent audit reports' (PCAOB n. d.).

---

[1]Internationally, similar bodies include the Public Companies Accounting Oversight Board (PCAOB) in the United States, a restructured FRC taking on the roles of the Accounting Foundation in the United Kingdom, and in Canada the Auditing and Assurance Standards Oversight Council (AASOC), which will oversee standard-setting, whilst the Canadian Public Account-ability Board (CPAB) will oversee the conduct of audits.
[2]Auditor independence and transparency are the 'two main thrusts' (PNG Institute of Directors n. d.) of CLERP 9.
[3]The Ramsey Report was one of many documents to make this suggestion. More recently, the Task Force on Rebuilding Public Confidence in Financial Reporting, an independent group commissioned by IFAC, released its report entitled 'Rebuilding Public Confidence in Financial Reporting', which also outlines the merits of public oversight. The European Commission has further put forward a set of principles for public oversight on the EU audit profession (see European Commission 2003a).
[4]As seen in the establishment of public oversight bodies in Australia, the United Kingdom, Canada and the United States, the principles of the European Commission and IFAC's current process of creating an oversight function (IAASB n. d.).

A comparison and evaluation of the dimensions of public oversight

This section compares and contrasts the approaches that have been adopted by the various jurisdictions with respect to POBs, and the implications of this for the proposed oversight structure in Australia. This comparison and contrast concentrates on the following dimensions: membership, the manner of appointment to the POB, whether clear separation of the POB and the audit standard-setting body is achieved, the powers of the POB, and whether the POB assumes responsibility for both accounting and auditing oversight.

Membership

There has been much international debate as to who should form the membership of a POB. The European Commission identified significant participation by non-practitioners as an essential characteristic of an oversight body, with independence being critical to maintaining public confidence (see European Commission 2003 a). However, of equal importance in an oversight regime is the capability of board members to understand the practical implications of the audit framework, and for them to have appropriate knowledge, experience and capability (McNamee 2002).

In addressing the appropriate balance between experience and independence, Australia has taken a passive, neutral approach. As in the United Kingdom and Canada, Australia's oversight board, the FRC, is comprised of 'senior-level stakeholders from the business community, professional accounting bodies, governments and regulatory agencies' (CLERP 2002, p. 24). There are no rules regarding members' responsibilities, rather they are simply 'required to act independently and not as representatives of any stakeholder group' (Priest 2003). This can be contrasted to the stringent attitude employed in Canada, whereby the chairman and a majority of the Auditing and Assurance Standards Oversight Council (AASOC) members must be drawn from outside the accounting profession (CICA n. d.). Similarly, three of the five members of the US Public Company Accounting Oversight Board (PCAOB) must not be certified accountants, whilst currently four of the five, including the chairman, have no public experience in accounting (McNamee 2002).

The absence of a specific policy regarding the proposed Australian POB's composition induces uncertainty regarding the intended level of neutrality and experience of this body. Whilst recent appointments have been made independently from the nominations of key stakeholder groups (Priest 2003), one may question the ability of such members to always act truly independently of their originating body, as well as the level of experience such members possess. In comparison to the structures in other jurisdictions, what Australia is lacking is not a balance between experience and independence, but some guidance on how this balance should be struck.

Appointment to the board

The manner in which members are appointed to POBs is an important factor in ensuring the independence and transparency of the oversight process.[5] Theoretically, for an oversight body that aims to 'increase public confidence in … standard setting activities' (IAASB n. d.), members should be appointed by the public. Practically, however, the costs of such a process would likely outweigh the benefits.

In Australia, the Treasurer will continue to appoint members to the FRC, either on the basis of nominations from key stakeholder groups[6] or independently.[7] This method of appointment is similar to the United States where the SEC appoints members of the PCAOB, and can be contrasted to that of both the United Kingdom and Canada, where the FRC and AASOC, or subcommittees thereof, appoint members to their own boards.[8]

There are clear advantages and disadvantages to both methods of appointment. A system of self-appointment may decrease the transparency of the process and independence of members. In such a structure, the council could develop its own agenda and appoint members in this pursuit. Conversely, appointment by a government agency has been described as a 'contentious and politicized process' creating 'doubts about the group's credibility and capability' (McNamee 2002). It is not possible to determine which method would induce a greater bias; a government may have larger incentives to manipulate the council[9] , but also faces larger political costs (disincentives) for doing so (Watts & Zimmerman 1986).

One area of general agreement is that the procedure for appointment 'should be subject to a high level of scrutiny that is expressed in an independent and transparent nomination procedure' (European Commission 2003a). Such a procedure exists in Australia, providing support for the current process. Thus, whilst Australia's current appointment system is not perfect, it is no less perfect than the alternative and must simply be monitored for undue political influence.

---

[5]Principle 2 of the European Commission's Principles for Public Oversight states that 'persons involved in public oversight should be selected under an independent and transparent nomination procedure' (European Commission 2003a).
[6]Nominations are currently made by the Business Council of Australia, the Australian Institute of Company Directors, the Securities Institute of Australia, the Australian Institute of Financial Services Association, ICAA, CPAA, the Australian Shareholders' Association, the Australian Stock Exchange, ASIC and the Commonwealth, state and territory governments.
[7]See http://www.frc.gov.au/content/about.asp
[8]In the United Kingdom, an appointment committee comprised of FRC members and its chairman have the responsibility of appointing members to their FRC.
[9]In the United States, it has been alleged that the 'PCAOB was designed to be [a] weak underling for SEC Chairman' (McNamee 2002, p. 37).

Separation of standard-setting and oversight

'Clear separation between standard setting and regulatory oversight' (ACCA n. d.) is essential in ensuring the credibility of a 'transparent independent oversight' (CPA Australia & ICAA n. d.) regime. If there was not clear separation, the new regime would be no more independent than the old, in which auditors oversaw their own standard-setting. The approach taken by Australia conforms to this generally accepted best practice, whereby the FRC will 'oversee auditing standard setting arrangements' (CLERP 2002, p. 1) and monitor the profession, whilst the AuASB will continue to independently set the auditing standards. This is consistent with the United Kingdom, Canada and IFAC, where standard-setting responsibilities have remained with existing bodies, which have come under the supervision of an independent oversight council.[10]

The United States has taken a different, and arguably less independent, approach. The PCAOB has 'put an abrupt end to the era of self regulation' (Carlino 2003) by announcing that it will take on the role of setting auditing standards to apply to all SEC-listed entities (*Accounting Office Management and Administration Report* 2003). An advisory committee containing 15 to 30 'experts' (*Business Times* 2003) from the business community, with less than one third of this membership comprising accountants, will be established to aid in this pursuit.[11] Whilst standards are subject to SEC approval, the fact that this so-called 'oversight' body sets rather than oversees an independent standard-setting process suggests that public oversight was not the primary objective. On the basis of the above discussion, the Australian system, which 'set[s] standards by calling on the experience of those who are on the front lines, doing audits every day, and learning from every audit they conduct' (Rankin 2003), is arguably superior to the US system. It allows independent oversight whilst ensuring the most efficient and effective body remains responsible for the setting of standards.

Powers

According to the European Commission, 'public oversight must include the exercise of investigative and disciplinary powers' because 'without such powers public oversight would lack public credibility' (European Commission 2003a). However, there also exists the view that 'in principle … standard setting should be separated from enforcement' (ACCA n. d.). It is argued that this separation of activities is essential to ensure the transparency, independence − and thus credibility − of the oversight council.

---

[10]Namely, the FRC in the United Kingdom, AASOC in Canada and the PIOB for IFAC respectively.
[11]This indicates the independence is highly valued in the United States, even at the expense of experience. The minimal experience, however, raises doubts as to how effective the standard-setting process will be.

The United Kingdom has successfully applied both principles through the establishment of the Investigation and Discipline Board (IDB). The IDB operates under the FRC and has the ability to 'impose appropriate sanctions, including removing the eligibility to perform an audit' (Williams 2003). The establishment of this body as separate from the standard-setters, but working under the umbrella of the same oversight council, has been commended as 'a balanced and robust approach' (Hewitt 2003).

In contrast, the PCAOB in the United States has been granted 'sweeping powers' (Hudson 2003). The PCAOB will not only set audit standards and monitor compliance with them, but will also 'enforce compliance with the act, the rules of the Board, professional standards, and the securities laws relating to the preparation and issuance of audit reports' (KPMG LLP 2003). In fulfilling this role, the PCAOB will conduct trial-like hearings where board staff act as both prosecutor and hearing officer, the latter having the authority to 'render a written decision, including findings of fact and conclusion of law' (PCAOB 2003). The PCAOB explains that this hearing officer will be 'insulated from the enforcement staff by a "Chinese Wall"' (PCAOB 2003), suggesting acknowledgement by the PCAOB that the transparency and independence of their system is flawed – and that their sweeping powers oppose the foundations upon which public oversight was established.

Not only will the PCAOB act as prosecutor and judge, it will also act as the only appeals commission; 'in the event of an appeal, the Board will render the final decision' (PCAOB 2003). Such sweeping powers in an area of public interest give cause for concern. The concentration of power within this board eliminates any credibility being placed upon its judgment – and can evoke feelings that such judgments are simply the outcome of political witch-hunts. It has been argued that 'the board's broad powers … might do more harm than good' (Hudson 2003). Given the dictator-like powers that it has over the accounting profession, such a claim indeed seems warranted.

The FRC in Australia, however, may equally be criticised for sitting at the other end of the continuum; it possess no disciplinary powers. Instead, disciplinary procedures have been left in the hands of the professional bodies, with the FRC fulfilling passive responsibilities to monitor, advise, report, promote and assess. The highest power the FRC possesses is to advise government if improvements are required, and to refer matters to the CALDB or to ASIC. Whilst many have commended this approach as 'achieving an appropriate balance between self-regulation and co-regulation' (McGregor 2002), a more cynical critic might express concern regarding the FRC's lack of authority, particularly in comparison to the approach being employed in the United Kingdom. Given that the PCAOB has been described as 'a weak underling for SEC Chairman' (McNamee 2002), one questions how Australia's FRC could be viewed as anything other than a mere veil of oversight established to induce perceptions of an efficient oversight regime.

Separate oversight bodies for auditing and accounting?

It is generally believed that a separation between responsibility for accounting and auditing standard-setting oversight is beneficial to enhancing the perceived quality of the auditing function. Where auditing and accounting standard-setting oversight is undertaken by the same body, some concerns have been expressed that the auditing function is perceived as the 'poorer cousin' by being prioritised below the accounting oversight responsibility.

As outlined in the Appendix, the United States, Canadian and other international auditing and accounting standard-setting processes are all overseen by separate independent bodies. In the United Kingdom, the FRC oversees both the Accounting Standards Board (responsible for setting accounting standards) and the Auditing Practices Board (responsible for setting auditing and assurance services standards). In addition, the Professional Oversight Board for Accountancy of the Accountancy Profession (POAB) oversees the application of accounting standards and also supervises the Audit Inspection Unit, which monitors the public company audits.

The structure proposed in Australia is closest to that used in the United Kingdom, where the FRC will undertake responsibility for oversight of both the auditing and accounting standard-setting function. It is hard to compare the relative merits of the different approaches. It is anticipated that having one oversight body will achieve a reduction in oversight costs. However, this must be offset by the fact that effective oversight of both bodies may be hard to achieve unless considerable new resources are added to the current ones. Another consideration is that oversight of accounting and auditing may require separate oversight expertise, a reason for separating such supervision. However, if you consider the constituencies of the various oversight bodies of accounting and auditing standard-setting in order to see whether these constituencies are separate and distinct, it is not clear that this is so.

Specific implications of public oversight for Australia

There are a number of issues arising as a result of recent developments in the area of public oversight of the auditing standard-setting process. One of these is that, with the recent IFAC proposal to have public oversight of the international auditing standard-setting process, if countries are planning to converge with international auditing standards, the benefits of an additional level of oversight are less clear. It may even be that the oversight at the national level may create additional tensions with the objective of converging with international auditing standards. Finally, auditing standards boards have traditionally undertaken broader agendas than only setting financial statement auditing standards for public-interest entities, including setting assurance standards for other services and setting auditing standards for private entities. Tensions arising from these issues are examined in the following sections.

Do we require public oversight at both the national and international level?

The advantages arising from public oversight of the auditing standard-setting process for Australia and other countries planning to converge[12] with international auditing standards become less clear given that the IAASB is also working towards establishing a public-interest oversight board (PIOB) for the setting of International Standards on Auditing (ISAs) (IFAC 2003). Australia, like Europe, has adopted a policy of converging with ISAs as from January 2005 (AuASB 2003). It must be questioned whether there is a need for public oversight at a national level if a country is proposing to converge with ISAs that are developed under a public oversight structure. On the whole, the agenda for standard-setting will be set at the international level, and it is at this level that the content of the actual standards will also be determined.

One possible advantage of this dual level of public oversight may be an increase in the perceived independence of the standard-setting process of the individual country. There is also the potential advantage that if a country works towards what is commonly being termed an 'ISA+ model' (which involves including additional material in the ISAs as a result of the specific national requirements), the national POB may have a role in overseeing the process by which the ISAs are added to in the creation of the national auditing standards. These benefits must, however, be balanced against the significant increased costs associated with national public oversight.

Will tension develop between public oversight at a national level and achieving other objectives?

Where a country has an objective of converging with ISAs, and the national POB sets any other objective for the national standard-setting body, it is possible that these objectives may conflict. For example, in Australia it has been flagged that attempting to get a category one rating from the PCAOB for the Australian audit standard-setting process is an objective that may be considered desirable and be pursued by the FRC.[13] Although it is not yet clear as to what would be

---

[12]In this situation, convergence is defined as adoption of international auditing standards with minimal change.
[13]Mr Charles Macek, Chairman of the FRC, at the advisory meeting of the AuASB, October 2003.

required in order to gain such a rating, it is possible that such an objective may conflict with the policy of convergence with ISAs.

It is also possible that other objectives, such as legislative backing for auditing standards, as is proposed for Australia, may conflict with the policy of convergence with ISAs. To the extent that legislative backing will involve the rewriting of any auditing standards (there have been a number of comments claiming that the current standards are too detailed and unclear for such backing), such an objective has the potential to conflict with a convergence policy.

Thus, it can be argued that greater clarity is needed as to the functions that are expected of the POB in Australia or any other country that is contemplating convergence with ISAs. The role of any national POB in these circumstances will be limited. In fact, any POB will be very limited in its ability to do anything other than oversee convergence with ISAs. A desire to set any other objective or agenda for the auditing standards board which will impact the content of standards or the process of standard-setting will have the potential to conflict with the international convergence objective.

Will the public oversight body assume responsibility for audit and assurance services other than those under the Corporations Act?

Auditing standard-setting bodies have traditionally undertaken more activities than just setting standards for the financial statement auditing of public-interest entities. For example, they have also taken responsibility for setting assurance standards for other services such as performance auditing or reporting on internal controls, as well as setting auditing standards for private entities. In Australia, it is unclear as to whether the FRC will assume an oversight responsibility for the setting of auditing standards for other than Corporations Act audits. If the FRC is not to assume this responsibility, then the accounting bodies would have to run an equivalent standard-setting process for non-Corporations Act audits. This will be similar to the system which is proposed in the United States, with the PCAOB taking responsibility for SEC registrant audits and AICPA taking responsibility for providing standards and guidance for non-SEC registrant audits. Such an approach has the advantage of focussing resources on the audits of greater public interest, but this needs to be compared with the costs associated with the inefficiencies of running two parallel standard-setting processes within a particular country.

It is also unclear to what extent national POBs will assume responsibility for the setting of assurance standards, which may or may not be under their mandate, and, if they do assume responsibility, what attention they will pay to these services. The advantages and disadvantages of the national POB taking responsibility for oversight of such services is similar to the arguments for and against when considering providing oversight for the setting of auditing standards for other than public-interest audits; the advantage of focussing resources on the services of greater public interest compared with the costs associated with the inefficiencies of running parallel standard-setting processes.

Conclusion

There is much empirical evidence to suggest that high-quality audits are demanded (and thus supplied) by the market to protect firm reputation (Carcello et al. 2002), decrease the cost of capital (Blackwell, Noland & Winters 1998), avoid legal liability (Carcello et al. 2002) and avoid agency cost (Abdel-khalik 1993; Carcello et al. 2002; Carey, Simnett & Tanewski 2000). The demise of Arthur Andersen, as a result of its loss of credibility and associated exodus of clientele, has also been cited as proof that market mechanisms ensure audit quality (Gunther & Moore 2002). Commentators have thus criticised governments and policymakers for their failure to consider the successful track record of the market in 'disciplining ineffective auditors and promoting an effective audit function' (Gunther & Moore 2002). Such critics argue that governments 'should avoid restrictive measures that unnecessarily increase audit costs' (Gunther & Moore 2002) and rely instead upon the proven disciplinary procedures evident in the market. In support of such views, it is often argued that 'structures, standards and regulations can never be a complete defence against individuals bent on wrongdoing' (Hewitt 2003).

Whilst the oversight structure proposed in Australia is less authoritative than some of its overseas counterparts, those who believe in the efficiency of the market may argue that the Australian model appears superior. Unlike the US response, it can be argued that the proposals under CLERP 9 are not guilty of ignoring the effect of market forces in disciplining auditors. This can be seen in the fact that the professional bodies are still largely responsible for disciplining members. Rather than developing black-letter laws to ensure audit credibility, the Australian Government is 'supporting a system of "competitive capitalism" … strong enough to create confidence among investors while not so over-regulated that "those who are doing nothing wrong are treated as if they are"' (Abernethy 2002b).

It has been claimed that 'what is developing in this country [Australia] is the world's best system of co-regulated corporate governance'[14] , based in part on CLERP 9's proposal to establish public oversight of the audit profession. In addressing the issue of public oversight, the Commonwealth Government's actions mirror those of governing bodies worldwide, although the manner in which

---

[14]Steven Harrison, CEO of ICAA, cited in Abernethy (2002a), p. 38.

Australia has responded differs in some respects from that of other nations. Whilst Australia's response can be criticised for lacking black-letter laws and an oversight body containing enforcement power, perhaps it is the more mature one. It establishes oversight to increase investor confidence, without imposing regulations that will hinder market efficiency or create the authority for further misuse of powers.

However, the functioning of any POB must be considered alongside competing aims such as the policy of harmonisation and convergence with international standards. As the ISAs board moves to establish a public oversight body of its standard-setting process, and the policy of convergence with ISAs means that the setting and contents of standards will be carried out at an international rather than national level, the roles, duties and expectations of any national public board overseeing the development of auditing standards must be clearly established.

References

Abdel-khalik, A. R. 1993, 'Why Do Private Companies Demand Auditing? A Case for Organisational Loss of Control', *Journal of Accounting, Auditing and Finance*, vol. 8, no. 1, pp. 31-52.

Abernethy, M. 2002a, 'Heads of agreement', *CA Charter*, vol. 73, no. 10, pp. 37-9.

Abernethy, M. 2002b, 'Accountants and accountability', *CA Charter*, vol. 73, no. 8, pp. 57-9.

ACCA (Association of Chartered Certified Accountants) n. d., 'Shake up of UK accountancy regulation is welcome by ACCA', viewed 30 April 2004, http://www.accaglobal.com/news/release/827689.

Accounting Office Management and Administration Report 2003, 'New public standards will be set by the PCAOB', vol. 3, no. 6, p. 2.

AuASB (Auditing and Assurance Standards Board) of Australia 2003, 'Policy on harmonisation and convergence with International Standards on Auditing (ISAs)' (policy statement), Melbourne.

Blackwell, D. W., Noland, T. R. & Winters, D. B. 1998, 'The Value of Auditor Assurance: Evidence from Loan Pricing', *Journal of Accounting Research*, vol. 36, no. 1, pp. 57-70.

Business Times 2003, 'US accounting oversight board decides to set new auditing standards', (online edition).

Carcello, J. V., Hermanson, D. R., Neal, T. L. & Riley, R. A. 2002, 'Board Characteristics and Audit Fees', *Contemporary Accounting Research*, vol. 19, no. 3, pp. 365-84.

Carey, P., Simnett, R. & Tanewski, G. 2000, 'Voluntary Demand for Internal and External Auditing by Family Businesses', *Auditing: A Journal of Practice and Theory*, vol. 19 (Supplement), pp. 37-51.

Carlino, B. 2003, 'PCAOB finally gets new chairman', *Accounting Today*, vol. 17, no. 8, p. 1.

CICA (Canadian Institute of Chartered Accountants) n. d., 'Auditing and Assurance Oversight; About AASOC', viewed 30 April 2004, http://www.cica.ca/index.cfm/ci_id/205/la_id/1.htm. http://www.cica.ca/index.cfm/-ci_id/205/la_id/1.htm

CLERP (Corporate Law Economic Reform Program) 2002, 'Corporate Disclosure: Strengthening the Financial Reporting Framework', Commonwealth of Australia, Canberra.

Corcoran, T. 2003, 'Bolkenstein unveils radical audit plans and renews attack on US registration', *The Accountant*, no. 5995, viewed 30 April 2004, http://www.lafferty.com/newsletter/newsletter_04_article_display.asp.

CPA Australia & ICCA (Institute of Chartered Accountants in Australia) n. d., 'Communiqué – Corporate Reporting and Public Accountability Forum', viewed 30 April 2004, http://www.cpaaustralia.com.u/01_information_centre/13_ext_report/1_13_4_0_communique.

European Commission (Commission of the European Communities) 2003a, Note to members of the EU Committee on Auditing Subject: Principles for public oversight on the EU audit profession, viewed 30 April 2004, *International Market DG, Financial Markets, Accounting and Auditing* (Brussels), DG Markt G4/2003/04, http://europa.eu.int/comm/internal_market/.

European Commission (Commission of the European Communities) 2003b, 'Communication from the Commission to the Council and the European Parliament: Reinforcing the statutory audit in the EU', viewed 30 April 2004, http://www.cnmv.es/publicaciones/StatutoryAudit.pdf.

Gunther, J. W. & Moore, R. R. 2002, 'Auditing the auditors: Oversight or overkill?', *Federal Reserve Bank of Dallas Economic and Financial Policy Review*, vol. 1, no. 5, viewed 30 April 2004, http://dallasfedreview.org/-pdfs/v01_n05_a01.pd.

Hewitt, P. 2003, 'A balanced and robust approach', *AccountancyAge.com*, viewed 30 April 2004, http://www.managementconsultancy.co.uk/Print/1132438. http://-www.managementconsultancy.co.uk/Print/1132438

Hudson, K. 2003, 'Auditing watchdog aims for speedy thorough reforms', *Denver Post*, 23 June.

IAASB (International Auditing and Assurance Standards Board) n. d., Action Plan 2003-04, viewed 30 April 2004, http://www.ifac.org.

IFAC (International Federation of Accountants) 2003, *Reform proposals*, viewed 30 April 2004, http://www.ifac.org.

KPMG LLP 2003, *Comparison of Canadian and U.S. regulatory changes*. (KPMG LLP is the Canadian member firm of KPMG International.)

McGregor, G. 2002, 'Back to the future', *Australian CPA*, viewed 30 April 2004, http://www.cpaaustralia.com.au/03_publications/02_aust_cpa_magazine/-2002/46_dec/3_2_46_8.

McNamee, M. 2002, 'Accounting watchdog – or lapdog? Here's how you'll know', *Business Week*, no. 3801, 11 November, p. 37.

PCAOB (Public Company Accounting Oversight Board) 2003, 'Working Paper regarding Board Investigations and Disciplinary Proceedings', 21 April, viewed 30 April 2004, http://pcaobus.org.

PCAOB (Public Company Accounting Oversight Board) n. d., Mission statement, viewed February 2005, http://pcaobus.org.

PNG Institute of Directors n. d., 'Australia's Response to Corporate Governance Issues', viewed 30 April 2004, http://www.pngid.or.pg/austres.html.

Priest, A. 2003, 'Appointment to the Financial Reporting Council', *Treasury* (Australia), viewed 30 April 2004, http://www.treasurer.gov.au/.

Rankin, K. 2003, 'PCAOB could strip CPAs of standard-setting duties', *Accounting Today*, vol. 17, no. 1, p. 3.

Sharav, I. 2003, 'If Sarbanes-Oxley is to work, be wary of certain offers', *Accounting Today*, vol. 17, no. 10, p. 6.

Watts, R. L. & Zimmerman, J. L. 1986, *Positive accounting theory*, Prentice Hall, Englewood Cliffs, NJ.

Williams, P. 2003, 'Official Green Light To Review of Accountancy Regulations', *Financial Director*, April, p. 45, viewed 30 April 2004, http://www.financialdirector.co.uk/briefing.

http://www.accountingfoundation.com, viewed 30 April 2004.

www.pcaobus.org http://www.pcaobus.org , viewed 30 April 2004.

http://www.fe.be/issues/auditing.htm, viewed 30 April 2004.

http://www.cica.ca, viewed 30 April 2004.

http://www.ifac.org/IAASB, viewed 30 April 2004.

http://www.iosco.org, viewed 30 April 2004.

http://www.frc.gov.au/content/about.asp, viewed 30 April 2004.

Appendix
Summary of key characteristics of public oversight boards in major jurisdictions *

	Australia (proposed)	US	UK	Canada	International (proposed)
Oversight structure	Proposed that FRC be expanded to oversee audit setting process, advise on issues of independence and monitor aspects of the profession. Original role of	Public Company Accounting Oversight Board (PCAOB) established by Sarbanes-Oxley Act. Broad powers to oversee and discipline audit profession.	Financial Reporting Council (FRC) taking on roles of Accountancy Foundation to form new regulator which will have three responsibilities: to	Auditing and Assurance Standards Oversight Council (AASOC) established October 2002 by Canadian Institute of Chartered	Proposed that IFAC create a public interest oversight board (PIOB) for its activities which would include the IAASB. The PIOB shall be

	overseeing work of AASB remains.		oversee setting of accounting and auditing standards, enforcement or monitoring of standards and oversight of regulatory activities of professional accounting bodies.	Accountants (CICA) to oversee activities of ASB. Canadian Public Accountability Board (CPAB) is an independent body which oversees the conduct of audits of public companies.	responsible for overseeing the public interest activities of IFAC related to auditing, giving priority, at least initially, to those standard-setting activities related to audits and other financial statement assurance activities.
Membership	Comprised of senior level stakeholders from the business community, professional accounting bodies, governments and regulatory agencies.	Five members, four of whom have no public track record in accounting. Must have three members that are not CPAs.	Include wide and balanced representation at the most senior levels of preparers, auditors, users of accounts and others interested in them.	AASOC: 9-12 members. The chair and majority of members must be drawn from outside the audit profession; that is, not be CAs. Consists of prominent leaders from business, finance, government, accounting, legal professions and regulators. CPAB: 11 members including seven non-CAs.	The precise size of the PIOB, yet to be determined, shall not be more than 10 members. Members shall not be currently in public practice as auditors or working for a firm that performs audits, but might be persons practicing in another area of auditing (e.g., an auditor-general) or accounting.
Member selection	Members appointed by the Treasurer on nomination by the Business Council of Australia, Australian Institute of Company Directors, Securities Institute of Australia, Investment and Financial Services Association, ICAA, CPAA, Australian Shareholders Association, ASX, ASIC, and Commonwealth, state and territory governments.	SEC appoints members.	An appointment committee is responsible for the appointment of members to both the FRC and its subsidiary units. This committee comprises the chairman, deputy chairman and three other members of the FRC.	AASOC appoints own members. CPAB members will be appointed by a group, the chair of which is Ontario Securities Commission Chair.	PIOB members shall be selected by the current members of the monitoring group – currently, the International Organization of Securities Commissions (IOSCO), the Basel Committee on Banking Supervision (Basel Committee), the International Association of Insurance Supervisors (IAIS), the World Bank and the European Commission.
Funding of body	AuASB will be established under ASIC Act, and funded by government, accounting profession and business.	Annual levy on all listed companies with market capitalization greater than US$25 million. This level is higher for managed funds.	Costs of FRC will be shared by government, business and the professional bodies. Costs of cases coming before IDB borne by professional bodies. Costs of audit inspection unit borne by audit firms.	Individual firms will have to meet the additional costs of this new regime.	It is expected that initially the annual budget will not exceed US$1.5 million. As a general principle, both IFAC and the monitoring group consider it to be in the public interest that parties other than IFAC shall fund at least 50% of the cost of the PIOB.

Powers/roles of body	Responsibilities to oversee audit standard-setting, advise professional bodies on independence issues, monitor and report on systems of firms to deal with independence issues, monitor and report on companies compliance with audit-related disclosure requirements, advise on adequacy of teaching of professional and business ethics, and monitor and assess adequacy of the disciplinary procedures of the accounting bodies. FRC cannot involve self in setting of standards. FRC will not have direct role in disciplining members, but rather refer attention to CALDB or government.	Primary functions include registration of public accounting firms, to establish or adopt the auditing, quality control, ethics, independence and other standards relating to the preparation of audit reports, conducting inspections of public accounting firms, conducting investigations and disciplinary proceedings and imposing appropriate sanctions upon registered public accounting firms, enforcing compliance with Sarbanes-Oxley Act, rules of board, professional standards and securities laws relating to audit reports, and performing other duties or functions as the board or SEC determines appropriate. Advisory group will help board set new auditing standards and will include experts from the accounting profession, corporate finance and investments.	Will form the umbrella under which separate bodies will set audit standards, review alleged departures from standards, hear disciplinary cases, and review regulatory activities of professional bodies. APB will set audit standards as well as independence, objectivity and integrity standards. Professional oversight board will have audit inspection unit which will monitor the audit of listed companies and major charities/pension funds. Investigation and Discipline Board (IDB) will be forum for hearing significant public-interest disciplinary cases, and will have power to impose sanctions and remove eligibility to perform audits.	AASOC to oversee Assurance Standards Board (ASB), providing input, strategic direction and the perspective of users into the setting of auditing and assurance standards in Canada. Will be responsible for appointing its own members, and those of ASB, provide input into activities of ASB, inform ASB of diversity of views represented on AASOC, be satisfied that standard-setting process is appropriate, and monitor and evaluate ASB. It reports publicly at least annually. Meetings are open to public observation at the discretion of the chair. CPAB will conduct rigorous inspection of auditors of public companies. There are tougher auditor independence rules and quality control requirements for firms auditing public companies.	The PIOB shall approve the terms of reference (i.e., duties and scope of work, charter, operating procedures, etc.) of relevant IFAC boards and committees, such as the Ethics Committee, Education Committee and the IAASB, as well as their consultative advisory group(s) (CAGs). The PIOB shall have the authority to finally approve or reject the choice of the chair of the IAASB. The PIOB shall have the right to meet with all or some of the members of the IFAC boards or committees, to discuss matters of interest to the PIOB. The PIOB chair may attend, or may designate a PIOB member to attend as an observer, any IFAC meeting (other than those held in executive session) which it considers might have an impact on the public interest.
Separate oversight bodies for auditing v. accounting	The Financial Reporting Council will be responsible for overseeing both accounting and auditing functions as outlined in the recent CLERP 9 regulations.	The Public Company Accounting Oversight Board (PCAOB), established by the Sarbanes-Oxley Act 2002, oversees auditors of public companies. Auditing rules made by the PCAOB do not take effect unless approved by the SEC. The Financial Accounting Standards Board (FASB) is the private-sector body responsible for establishing	The Financial Reporting Council (FRC) oversees both the Accounting Standards Board (responsible for setting accounting standards) and the Auditing Practices Board (responsible for setting auditing and assurance services standards). An additional subsidiary of the FRC, the Professional Oversight Board for Accountancy of the Accountancy	The Accounting Standards Oversight Council oversees the accounting function. It does so through supervision of the Accounting Standards Boards (AcSB), responsible for establishing accounting and reporting standards applicable to the private sector, and the Public Sector Accounting Board, responsible for the accounting and reporting	The International Auditing and Assurance Standard Board (IAASB) will be overseen by its own PIOB. This will be separate from the oversight of accounting, undertaken by the International Accounting Standards Committee Foundation.

| | | financial accounting and reporting standards. The SEC has statutory authority to establish financial accounting and reporting standards for publicly held companies (Securities Exchange Act 1934), however the SEC's policy is to rely on the private sector for this function. | Profession (POAB), will oversee the accounting standards. The POAB will also supervise the Audit Inspection Unit which will monitor the public company audits. | standards applying to the public sector. The Auditing and Assurance Standards Oversight Council (AASOC) oversees the auditing function through supervision of the Auditing and Assurance Standards Board (AASB). The AASB has the authority to establish audit and assurance standards for both the public and private sectors. | |

* These jurisdictions were chosen due to the similarity of the environment in which the audit takes place. They were chosen based on comparisons most frequently made within the literature and are not an exhaustive list of possible comparable oversight frameworks.

Chapter 4. The role of markets: an economic approach to auditing

Jane Hamilton
Donald Stokes

Abstract

The current institutional regulatory framework for auditing is a product of the philosophy that individual property rights exist and are to be protected. These notions of property rights create the tension to which auditing is a partial solution.

In this chapter, we describe the institutional regulatory framework for auditing and its relationship to markets, corporations and professional associations. Our thesis is that all the institutional arrangements are incentivised as contracting cost-reducing mechanisms to deliver 'audit reform' but residual losses are to be expected. Ethics is viewed as central to the contracting process, facilitating functional completion of contracts and helping to reduce residual losses in contracting. Auditing is also demanded (*ex ante*) to reduce the expected contracting residual economic loss resulting from attempts to protect individual property rights. Market participants have incentives to minimise contracting residual losses, and regulatory intervention is valued to the extent that the reforms are more efficient contracting solutions to minimise those losses.

We review fallacies in the market failure arguments used as rationales for regulatory intervention and suggest that the costs of regulation could be underestimated and the benefits could be overstated. The result is that regulatory intervention could increase future bonding and monitoring costs beyond what is optimal, and thus contribute to inefficient allocation of the costs of property rights.

In the same way that ethical behaviour by contracting parties can reduce contracting residual losses, ethical behaviour by politician-regulators in the political process could contribute to lowering the political residual losses and enhancing society's well-being through facilitating the economic outcomes sought by contracting parties.

Introduction

Australia and other countries have been experiencing a new wave of regulatory 'reform' of the institutional arrangements governing audits of company accounts.[1] In Australia, key developments in the regulatory debate are the Ramsay Report (Ramsay 2001), the report of the HIH Royal Commission (HIH Royal Commission 2003) and various reports and submissions at government level, including the CLERP 9 discussion paper (CLERP 2002)[2] and subsequent legislation, the CLERP (Audit Reform and Corporate Disclosure) Act. Internationally, major reforms affecting auditors include the US Sarbanes-Oxley Act (2002).[3] These reforms potentially affect the relationships between statutory regulation and other institutions and actors in the economy and society. As such, they are likely to affect the distribution of costs and benefits in society. It is important to understand these effects when making regulatory changes, including those directed at ethical issues.

In this chapter, we review the role of markets, companies, audit firms and their partners, professional associations, and accounting and auditing standard-setting and statutory regulation. We do so by drawing together the key ideas and findings from research into the economics of the firm, auditing and regulation to outline a framework for understanding these relationships. We argue this current institutional regulatory framework, and the regulatory developments placed within it, reflect an underlying philosophy about the existence of individual property rights and how to protect them. This notion of property rights creates a tension to which auditing is a partial solution. We focus on the economics of auditing as a method of explaining the ethical dimension, because contracting, including for auditing, implicitly and explicitly relies on and influences society's institutions and norms. Ethics and the economics of auditing are interrelated.

Our underlying thesis is that auditing is a social construct based on the current institutional framework in which contracting parties expect some residual (economic) loss. Furthermore, in the absence of regulatory intervention, firms and markets have incentives to minimise contracting residual losses and auditing is demanded (*ex ante*) to do this. Ethics is viewed as central to the contracting process, facilitating functional completion of contracts and helping to reduce residual losses in contracting. We will suggest that it is too easy to put in place crisis statutory regulation solutions without understanding the intricate relation-

---

[1] While many of the arguments in this chapter can be adapted to other types of audits and assurance engagements, the focus here is on corporate audits and reform.
[2] The Australian reform process is summarised in CLERP (2003), p.1.
[3] Overseas developments in auditor independence regulations prior to the release of Ramsay (2001) include the International Federation of Accountants' (IFAC) proposals for updating its ethical requirements on audit independence, the European Commission's release of a consultative paper containing proposals designed to achieve greater uniformity among member states of the European Commission, and the US Securities and Exchange Commission's (SEC) rules on auditor independence, which were released in November 2000.

ships between these institutional features and the roles they can play-out to generate 'reform' in their own right, in the absence of regulatory intervention.

While the demand for auditing predates the demand for regulatory intervention, such intervention, however, can be viewed as a rational response to 'crisis'-solving to protect those individual property rights affected by the residual loss. We review the fallacies in the market failure rationales used for regulatory intervention and stress the concept of political residual loss. We suggest that the costs of regulatory intervention could be underestimated and the benefits overstated, raising questions about whether regulatory solutions really do serve the public interest. We suggest too that, in the same way that ethical behaviour by contracting parties can reduce contracting residual losses, ethical behaviour by politician-regulators in the political process can contribute to lowering the political residual losses and enhancing society's well-being through facilitating the economic outcomes sought by contracting parties.

The chapter is organised as follows. The second section reviews the role of markets and firms and the demand and supply of auditing services. The third and fourth sections respectively address the role of professional societies and the setting of accounting and auditing standards. An evaluation of the regulatory process for audit reform follows in the fifth section, and the sixth section provides concluding comments.

The role of markets and firms in auditing

It was Coase (1937) who gave us a basis for understanding the role of firms in markets and ultimately gave us an economic framework in which to understand the role of auditing. Coase advocated that contracting solutions between parties, such as investors, suppliers and customers, will be demanded and supplied through firms up to the point where it is more efficient to do so than to establish multidimensional contingent claims contracts between the individual parties directly in markets. Firms exist only as efficient contracting mechanisms to lower the costs of contracting between and within the customer markets and factor markets. In the absence of contracting costs, there would be no demand for firms to exist because parties could costlessly contract directly in markets.

As discussed by Jensen and Meckling (1976), and extended by Ball (1989), contracting covers how to search for and bring parties together (e.g., investors with entrepreneurs and customers); how to design, negotiate and execute contracts (e.g., prospectuses to raise equity capital and customer service contracts) to fairly protect the interests of the parties so that they benefit from combining their investment and human capital to provide services/products to customers; how to establish bonding mechanisms such as performance contracts to align the interests of the parties; how to monitor that the parties are contracting fairly (such as agreeing perhaps to have the firm's performance audited); how to arbitrate where there are claims of unfairness of outcomes (e.g., through common law courts dealing with contracts and the tort of negligence); and how to make contract payments and how to *ex post* settle up where there are unfair contractual outcomes (again through, for example, the courts or through negotiation/arbitration). Contracting directly within and between parties in customer markets and factor markets is also aimed at such outcomes, but the combination of relying on market and firm contracting solutions depends upon their relative contracting efficiency, or as Ball (1989) suggests, where there are increasing returns to scale from contracting.

We support a view that ethics is about the exercise of power[4] between contracting parties for the benefit of all the parties brought together under the explicit and implicit contracts that define the firm and the markets in which firms operate. Ethics is central to the contracting process because it contributes to fairness in functional completion of the contracts through the exercise of power held by the contracting parties.[5]

Using a contracting cost framework to examine firms and markets, Watts and Zimmerman (1986) summarise much of the foundation literature of the 1970s and 1980s in the economics of auditing as well as accounting. They emphasise a 'property rights' perspective, with rights established by contracts in which self-interested parties contracting through the firm have incentives to take actions to transfer wealth from other parties associated with the firm, but who recognise that their welfare depends upon the firm's survival as a contracting mechanism relative to other contracting mechanisms. They describe a concept from the literature – 'price protection' through markets; that is, markets charge a higher cost (e.g., for capital) if the parties do not contract to minimise self-interested value-reducing actions in the firm. The process of price protection causes parties to bear the costs of their actions. This incentivises the parties to take any lower-cost contracting solution to bond themselves to the firm to restrict those actions, and to have them monitored through the firm rather than the market's price protecting for the risk.

Some firms bring in an external auditor to monitor and arbitrate on the accounting for firm performance and financial position, in order to meet the demands of customers, investors and suppliers for information about their contracts. Auditors supply an opinion on the accounts' fairness, and where the auditors believe there are unfair revelations of what was expected under the contracts, they provide details to alert parties to what they know about the unfairness. The threat of such audit qualifications can be a discipline mechanism that motivates management to deliver a fair set of accounts. Audits also provide a form of

---

[4]Ethics as an exercise in power is discussed in Howieson (2003).
[5]The notion of functional completion of contracts is described by Ball (1989), drawing upon the work of Cheung (1983).

insurance in that, if some aspect of audit failure can be demonstrated, investors can litigate to recover where their economic losses can be attributed to the audit failure (see, for example, Menon & Williams 1994). This notion of *ex post* settling up with an auditor is a cost of contracting as defined above. It is important to stress that the insurance bond being offered here again facilitates functional completion in contracting, and is in respect of the risk with the quality of the audit and not the total risk with the quality of the investment. Distinguishing audit failure from investment failure is important in the first instance in understanding the focus of regulatory reform in the audit area.

Empirical evidence supports the general price protection argument for contracting through the firm versus markets, and shows the value audits provide in making it cheaper to contract through the firm. Blackwell, Noland and Winters (1998) show that borrowing interest rates are 25 basis points lower for companies that voluntarily choose to be audited than for unaudited firms. This discount is after controlling for other determinants of interest rates. In other words, companies that choose to be audited do so because it lowers the cost of contracting compared to using the market mechanism *ex ante* to price the risk of misleading accounting numbers into interest rates.[6]

The Blackwell, Noland and Winters study is interesting because it demonstrates how the potential for unfair outcomes to be derived by one party over others who contracted through the firm is priced in the relevant markets. In this case, debt-holders priced the potential for management/shareholders to supply an unfair set of unaudited accounting numbers, but lowered the interest rate to recognise the value to them of having an audit carried on within the firm. This firm contracting solution is offered up to the point where it is justified in the lowering of interest rates.

Empirical evidence also supports extending the concept of the effect of auditing on price protection to the effects of choices between auditors with reputations for different quality. Competition for auditors' services informs market prices, allowing the conclusion to be drawn that in the audit market, audit reputations are priced. Research beginning with Simunic (1980), and continuing with a series of Australian and overseas studies, shows that auditors with reputations for higher audit quality are valued highly in the auditmarket.[7]

An audit firm that fails to deliver the expected audit quality (i.e., an audit failure occurs) can expect to find that its services are priced lower in audit markets, their insurance premiums are likely to be higher in insurance markets, and in the extreme, they are unable to hold clients for any fee or attract insurance

---

[6] Fama (1980) makes a case for the relative efficiency of market solutions in situations where firm solutions are less efficient in handling *ex post* unfair outcomes.
[7] For a review of these studies, see Ferguson, Francis and Stokes (2003).

coverage. The failure of an audit firm is an extreme form of *ex post* price protection in markets, and is discussed more fully below in the specific case of Arthur Andersen's collapse. Audit firms that don't survive in markets are evidence of how markets and firms work in tandem to facilitate contracting. A corporate firm's choice (or failure) to put in place quality control over its accounting, or an audit firm's choice (or failure) to put in place quality control over its audit services, is rationally priced in the respective markets. Market pricing of quality forces owner-managers of the respective firms to bear any reduction in firm value. This gives them an incentive to enhance quality by offering contracting cost-reducing mechanisms through their respective firms.

The extent to which such contracting solutions are adopted depends on the costs of the best available solutions associated with reducing or eliminating the problem (i.e., the self-interested value-reducing actions of the relevant party/ies) relative to the costs borne through the price protection mechanisms employed in markets. Even in the absence of an explicit contract to behave fairly, there will be reliance upon the implicit contract conditions that all parties are trusted to act fairly. These implicit contracting terms in part facilitate the completion of the contracting process *ex ante*, and lower contracting costs in preference to contingency contracting for all specific circumstances that can arise. The ethical exercise of power under the contracts by all parties – including shareholders, investors and customers as well as managers, and auditors if appointed – is part of the process of acting fairly in the execution of contractual obligations, and is in the interests of the firm.

Residual losses are the reduction in firm value caused by any remaining divergence between the interests of the parties that cannot be eliminated by contracting through the firm (Jensen & Meckling 1976). Residual losses are to be expected in firm solutions where further contracting solutions (explicit or implicit) cannot be cost-benefit justified. While ethical behaviour can contribute to reducing the residual losses, it cannot eliminate it because implementing fundamental ethical principles is an imperfect process (Howieson 2003, p. 20). There are at least two implications that follow which are relevant here. First, contracting parties expect residual losses; for example, there is some risk of audit failure. Second, regulatory solutions – for example, auditing reforms – are only valued if they are cost-benefit justified in lowering the costs of contracting. In the fifth section of this chapter, on the role of regulation in auditing, we examine in more detail how politician-regulators utilise a focus on any residual losses to create political opportunities or crises, and then 'solve' those crises with so-called 'public-interest' regulatory solutions to 'market failure'. Before so doing, however, we examine further how market participants have incentives to minimise the risk of audit failure.

Variation in audits

A contracting demand for auditing is not contingent on a regulatory demand for audits. Even in the absence of regulatory codification of best contracting practice or regulatory intervention because of market failure, demand for audits is based on the existence of firms as a means of facilitating contracting between parties. Watts and Zimmerman (1983) document a history of the demand for accounting and auditing and show that auditing was in demand long before regulations emerged for audits, and that the survival of auditing suggests it is a part of the efficient contracting technology for organising firms. They also provide evidence that auditors had incentives to be independent long before regulatory requirements to do so.

There is a body of accounting and auditing research that demonstrates that firms exercise discretion in auditor choice consistent with this contracting perspective. Some firms, given the contracting solutions they address, do not demand audits, relying instead on other monitoring mechanisms to report and monitor firm performance. Anderson, Francis and Stokes (1993) provide evidence of a mix of monitoring mechanisms being used in firms dependent upon the types of investments under managers' charge. Other work has shown that, for example, smaller firms have lower demand for audits (Chow 1982). Where there exists demand for an audit, firms can vary in their demand for the quality they require. Firms with more complex operations, for example, and related contracting and accounting issues, demand higher quality audits and are prepared to pay higher audit fees.[8]

Audit quality is defined as consisting of two components – auditor competence to detect errors or irregularities with the accounting, and auditor independence to report their existence in the auditor's opinion (Watts & Zimmerman 1986, p. 314). Auditor independence only exists in the supply of audit services to a client if the client in the market is convinced the auditor has something to lose by never reporting errors or irregularities (Watts & Zimmerman 1986). DeAngelo (1981a, 1981b; and see Watts & Zimmerman 1986, p. 314) argues auditors that are independent are prepared to give up fees associated with incumbency because, while they forego these in respect of one client where the manager switches auditors, they maintain the fees from other clients who are prepared to value independence. Larger audit firms offer a larger bond because they have more clients (with fees at risk for failure to deliver an independent audit).

Audit firms and audit partners

The auditor's reputation acts as a collateral bond in the contracting process with the firms utilising their audit services. Auditors can organise and invest in pro-

[8]See, for example, Simunic (1980), Ferguson, Francis and Stokes (2003), and Godfrey and Hamilton (2005).

cesses to supply higher audit quality in order to capture the higher audit fees that are in evidence where quality is valued. Watts and Zimmerman (1983) argue that with the expansion in the number of companies in the United Kingdom and the United States in the latter half of the 19th century – and, in particular, the enormous growth in foreign companies, with the associated complexity of accounting for the operations – there came a demand for specialisation in auditing (audit competence) and hence the growth of professional accounting firms. The growth in scale of the capital markets increased the fixed cost of an auditor's establishing a reputation that would serve as a bond for the auditor's independence (Watts & Zimmerman 1983, p. 630). Large professional accounting firms emerged as contracting cost-reducing mechanisms for delivering specialisation in auditing (competence) and to establish a reputation that would serve as a bond for auditor independence. A key feature of large accounting firms that enhances the collateral bond is their organisation as unlimited liability partnerships. Unlimited liability partnerships mean that there is more 'skin in the game' for the auditor partners. The partnership form also leads to mutual monitoring (through internal quality controls) by the partners because they are liable for other partners' actions.[9]

As we noted in the second section, on the role of markets and firms in auditing, to the extent that an auditor's reputation is called into question by virtue of problems perceived by the market with the audit firm's internal processes, the contracting process allows parties to engage in *ex post* settling up through the courts and the audit market price-protects by lowering the value of the services being provided. In the extreme case, the audit market can price the services of the audit firm so low, where significant uncertainty about the value of the bond is created, that it is no longer viable. The brand name loses value and the firm goes out of business, as in the case of the Arthur Andersen audit firm. The case of Arthur Andersen's demise demonstrates how audit markets deal with audit failure in this way, and it is important to note too the efficiency with which the market's solution emerged in 2001-02, compared to the ongoing regulatory response to the Arthur Andersen audits called into question in the United States in particular.

In a related case[10], in the early 1990s a US accounting firm, Laventhol & Horwath ('L&H'), went into bankruptcy. Menon and Williams (1994) investigated the effect of the bankruptcy on the share prices of the companies audited by L&H. Consistent with the insurance benefit of the audit in the collateral bond disappearing with the auditor going into bankruptcy, the research showed that the share prices of L&H's clients declined relative to the market. The effect was more

---

[9] Limited liability partnerships have taken away the size of the bond on the auditor's independence and the potential for higher fees (Watts & Zimmerman 1986, p. 317).
[10] The outline of this case, and the implications of the results of its study for Arthur Andersen's disappearance from the market, draw on an analysis by Stokes (2002).

pronounced for those clients who had sustained recent losses, and the extent of security price declines correlated with the size of the sustained losses. In addition, the share price declines were greater for those clients that had recently made initial public offerings and incurred losses relative to those with seasoned equity offerings.

The implication from these findings is that the insurance benefit/bond – which provided the client contracting parties with a right to litigate against the auditors in the event of audit failure – declined with the audit firm going into bankruptcy. This study demonstrates that litigation against auditors is a valued mechanism for *ex post* settlement, and settlements in and out of court are anticipated parts of the contracting process. Auditors carry professional indemnity insurance and self-insurance to meet settlement claims. Furthermore, the mix of insurance from the market versus firm insurance reflects the same principles of costly contracting discussed above. The audit firm will self-insure and contract accordingly up to the point where it is cheaper for all contracting parties that define the audit firm (this includes the client company and its shareholders) to do so, compared to insuring through the insurance market.

So these insurance benefits are valued by shareholders of audit client companies, and they agree to contribute capital on terms that recognise there is not an un-limited pot of insurance benefits to access if there is audit failure (because it would be too costly to have taken out such insurance *ex ante*). That is, they expect there will be some residual losses, whereby any insurance benefit provided may not cover all the costs for them from an audit failure that they knew *ex ante* was a possible contracting outcome. There are no guarantees of a contracting risk-free investment in a world of costly contracting. So audit failures are anticipated and losses due to audit failure are compensated – though perhaps not fully – to the extent that after *ex post* settlement there remains a residual loss. It is important to emphasise that the shareholders who are parties to the contracts that define the client company accept this potential outcome when they contribute their capital. That is how the contracting process works in a world of costly contract-ing.

Combined with the broader empirical evidence that shows how reputations are priced in markets, this suggests audit markets, insurance markets and *ex post* settling up via contracting in the firms can generate a type of 'reform' in their own right, in the absence of regulatory intervention. Auditors bear costs of audit failure as audit and insurance markets revise the value of the reputation of the auditor. This creates incentives for auditor partners to improve the audit quality through internal contracting arrangements (e.g., better quality controls within the firm) in order to reduce the costs of dealing in audit markets (via lower audit fees) and insurance markets (through higher insurance premiums or lower pro-fessional indemnity coverage). As noted, larger firms have more at stake and therefore contribute more to setting best practice, an issue we return to in examining 'reform' through the standard-setting process. And importantly, the 'reform' brings to the audits going forward more efficient contracting solutions, because partners in these firms have been incentivised to be more efficient in contracting to lower residual losses. In other words, the 'reform' focuses on lowering the risk of audit failure in future audits given what is known at this time.

The role of the profession and ethics

As mentioned earlier, professional accounting bodies came into existence in response to the expansion of the number of companies operating in the latter half of the 19th century; Watts and Zimmerman (1983, p. 630) cite evidence of a fourteen-fold increase in the number of companies listed on the London Stock Exchange between 1853 and 1893. Similar rates of growth were also experienced in the United States. The growth created a demand for a low-cost contracting mechanism for accrediting auditors. While the initial impetus for the professional societies in the United Kingdom was to provide information on accountants' reputations for dealing in bankruptcies, this expanded to cover their services in other areas such as auditing (Watts & Zimmerman 1983, p. 631). In the United States, their formation was based on the work of accountants as auditors and investigators.

Professional accounting bodies play an important role in the contracting process by lowering the costs of contracting for parties contracting through firms and in markets. They do this, according to Watts and Zimmerman (1983, 1986), by providing contracting parties with information about an auditor's independence and competence. Watts and Zimmerman (1986, p. 316) argue that professional societies develop brand names such as 'CPA' or 'chartered accountants' by establishing processes for training and qualifying auditors who, as members of the society with the brand name, are assumed by contracting parties to deliver a minimum level of competence and independence. These processes involve maintaining educational entry requirements, completion of 'articles' with an existing member, professional ethics/standards/guidelines, professional year programs, exams, continuing education, quality-control monitoring of members and their firms, and ethics committees and disciplinary mechanisms and publicity of their outcomes.

Membership of the society acts as a collateral bond in the contracting process in the same way as the auditor and audit firm's reputations, in that loss of membership results in loss of fees (Watts & Zimmerman 1986, p. 316). Also, to the extent that the professional society's processes break down and an audit failure occurs, the decline in the member's brand name affects the brand name of the society, and other members' reputations also decline. This decline is more pronounced for fellow members of the same firm because they are liable for the miscreant's actions (Watts & Zimmerman 1986, p. 318).

So in the case of Arthur Andersen's demise, we have seen the other 'Big Four' reviewing their operations in an attempt to protect and repair any damage to their reputation from being members of the same professional society as Arthur Andersen's partners.[11] Also, we have seen the professional societies attempting to repair any reputation damage with initiatives such as publishing opinion pieces and articles designed to lead the debate on accounting and auditing reform and making proposals for tightening their quality-control procedures.[12] Professional societies, as parties to the contracting processes in firms and markets, are incentivised for their own survival, as contracting cost-reducing mechanisms, to engage in reform to minimise the risk of audit failure in future contracts, and thus protect the brand name and ensure their own survival.

Breakdowns in professional society processes are another source of market failure targeted by regulatory solutions. It is arguable that the transfer in the CLERP 9 legislation of the Australian auditing standard-setting authority (the AuASB) from the professional accounting bodies' control to statutory control is related in part to the perceived failure by the profession in setting and enforcing auditing standards in the wake of recent corporate failures. In part, it could also be a matter of Parliament incorporating into law a version of best practice that has been in existence for some time (Watts & Zimmerman 1983, p. 626). These two explanations could equally apply to the earlier transfer of accounting standard-setting authority under statutory law in Australia. However, the issue of codifying accounting and auditing standards under statute versus leaving it to professional accounting bodies, or for that matter being completely unregulated, demands the same attention as any other proposed regulatory reform in auditing. It requires an understanding of the relative efficiency with which these standards are delivered to the contracting process under the alternative regimes. We offer some observations on this issue in the following sections.

The role of accounting and audit standard-setting

In the absence of regulatory coercion, professional accounting bodies have met a demand for codification of accounting choices in accounting standards. Codification possibly assists the process of adaptation of accounting choices that are

[11]Witness PricewaterhouseCoopers Australia establishing the Auditing Standards Oversight Board in August 2002 to assess PwC systems of monitoring quality control. The board provided a report to the PwC board of partners in June 2003 and published this on its website. KPMG Australia commissioned a review by two Australian academics (Keith Houghton and Ken Trotman) of their policies and procedures in respect of independence, conflict resolution and main quality controls. KPMG publicised this report in 2002.
[12]The professional accounting bodies have increased in recent years the running of 'best practice' conferences and seminars in the area of corporate governance and aligning themselves with key self-regulatory initiatives such as the ASX Corporate Governance Council.

used in certain contracting circumstances to new contracting circumstances (Ball 1989, p. 66). Likewise, standards for auditing have evolved from generally accepted best practices and the professional accounting bodies have provided, through their centralised standard-setting processes, scale economies in accounting and auditing to facilitate more efficient contracting (Ball 1989). Auditing standards, like accounting standards, are implicit terms of contracting for the preparation of the accounts. Standard-setters execute the accounting and auditing standards' design, the accounting firms specialise in applying them, and individual audit partners adapt them to the particular contracting circumstances (Ball 1989). The process of application in turn reforms the standards. Concepts like 'fairly present' and 'generally accepted' serve to govern adaptation choices where there are no specific rules, and in a sense provide some functional completion to the contracting process that relies upon codified accounting and auditing standards.

The notion that these standards need to be regulated to remove choice, and that there is an optimal set of accounting and auditing standards, was dispelled by Demski (1973). He argued against the possibility of attaining an optimal set of accounting standards. His arguments could equally apply to auditing standards. Rather, cross-sectional and cross-temporal variation in accounting (and arguably auditing) techniques are to be expected as different contracting circumstances create demand for different techniques (Ball 1989).

The case for the regulatory control of auditing standards through statute is poorly made, as is the case also with other audit regulatory reforms (Culvenor, Stokes & Taylor 2002), and in the next section we turn to analyzing this in more detail.

The role of regulation in auditing

Regulators typically argue that their reforms are in the public interest. If regulators' actions are unbiased, we would expect them to be supported by the existing research literature, and regulators to be actively interested in subsequent research that provides evidence against the proposed regulatory change (Watts & Zimmerman 1979).[13]

Regulations are the result of a political process where self-interested parties such as politicians, regulators and constituents come together for the purpose of creating 'public-interest' outcomes. The political process operates through implied contracts between the parties and in circumstances where firms and markets are less efficient at lowering contracting residual losses. Like the contracting process, the political process entails contracting solutions for bonding (e.g., policies and

---

[13]To claim that regulation can't wait for research to shed light on issues, and to regulate to be seen to solve a crisis, carries a risk of underestimating the costs of the regulatory change and those of undoing poor regulation.

voting at elections) and monitoring of politician-regulators (e.g., through Parliament and the Auditor-General). Political residual losses are to be expected because it is costly to participate in the political process and monitor the actions of politician-regulators.

Watts and Zimmerman (1979) argue that regulators are self-interested, wealth-maximizing individuals who have incentives to employ the powers of the State to make themselves better off, and can do so with legislation that redistributes wealth through welfare benefits for themselves (via their voting public) by imposing costs on firms. Proponents of change need arguments for the positions they advocate, and theories which serve as justifications are useful. Such theories will usually contend that the political action is in the public interest, everyone is (or most are) made better off, and that the action is 'fair'. The typical argument is that there is a market failure which can only be remedied by government intervention (Watts & Zimmerman 1979, p. 282). In other words, regulators imply they have a more efficient solution(s) than that generated by firms and markets to lower the residual losses of future contracting.

The self-interest view of regulators' actions is supported by the high costs of participating in the political process. The expected impact of an individual's vote on the outcome of an election is trivial, and hence the individual voter has very little incentive to incur the costs of becoming informed on political issues. However, economies of scale in political action can encourage group participation, allowing voters to share the fixed costs of becoming informed and increase the likelihood of affecting the outcome of an election by voting as a block (Downs 1957; Stigler 1971; Watts & Zimmerman 1979).

The result of high political costs is that regulators motivated by self-interest will not always act in the public interest to reform with more efficient solutions than those provided by firms and markets, and the best theory is not always accepted (Watts & Zimmerman 1979, p. 284). It is too costly for an individual to take control of the political process, so the market mechanism does not ensure that public interest prevails over the self-interest of regulators. The adoption of regulation motivated by self-interest does not require people to be 'fooled'. An individual will rationally fail to investigate the validity of the proposed regulation because the expected benefits to that person of so investigating are small. So, in a similar way to understanding that contracting parties to the firm incur contracting residual losses because it is costly to contract, voters in effect incur 'political' residual losses because it is costly to take control of the political process.

Watts and Zimmerman (1979) state that they do not intend to disparage the integrity of the researchers supplying the theories which are used as justifications for the regulators' actions. Watts and Zimmerman use economic analysis to show that high political transactions costs create a demand for excuses to use as weapons in the political arena. The effect is that the political process generates theory, not that theory generates political debates. They suggest that we can reject the alternative notion that theories are used to further the public interest (i.e., they assist politicians to produce regulations to further the public interest) if theories do not precede the regulations. Their analysis of several significant regulatory changes, including the US Securities Acts of 1933-34, supports their proposition. The Securities Acts emphasised the use of accounting as information useful for investors' decision-making. The accounting theories that were quoted and promoted after introduction of the Acts prescribed accounting principles consistent with greater priority for users external to the firms at the expense of internal users.

The demand for 'excuses theory' suggests that proponents of regulatory changes affecting auditors have vested interests and use theories and research evidence selectively to provide excuses for their preferred position. The argument that theories are being used as excuses when regulation temporally precedes the research evidence can be tested in the context of the most recent set of regulatory reforms in auditing, which emerged in response to the Ramsay Report on the Independence of Australian Company Auditors released in October 2001 (Ramsay 2001). We have analyzed the report in detail elsewhere (Culvenor, Stokes & Taylor 2002) and draw heavily upon parts of that analysis in this section.

The report was commissioned in mid-2001 because of regulatory developments in auditor independence overseas and publicity surrounding the auditor's role in recent Australian corporate collapses (Ramsay 2001, p. 6). The report reviews overseas auditor independence regulations extensively, and suggests these as appropriate benchmarks. However, although recent Australian events are used as motivators for the review of auditor independence regulations, the report does not discuss them further or use evidence from these events to support the recommendations.

The use of overseas developments as justification for regulatory change is an 'appeal to authority' approach. It implies that the differences between Australian and overseas regulation results in lower auditor independence in Australia. Explicit detailed analysis of expected costs and benefits of adapting overseas regulations to lower the risk of audit failure in Australia is absent from the report. It is also limited by its terms of reference to focus exclusively on auditor independence because it fails to address the other most likely underlying cause of any alleged audit failure, namely auditor competence.

The appeal to authority approach in the report is also revealed by the way it uses the research evidence. For example, while the report cites Pincus, Rubarsky and Wong (1989) as evidence supporting the recommendation for mandatory audit committees, it downplays the key message of that study. Pincus, Rubarsky and Wong suggest that market incentives exist for voluntary audit committee formation. There is evidence of variation in companies' use of audit committees, despite the history of published guidelines for best practice and professional and academic debate about the role and value of audit committees. The report does not acknowledge that the formation of audit committees depends on the company's circumstances. It also overlooks existing theory of the firm (outlined in the second section of this chapter) which argues that differentiation in contracting solutions is the key to firm survival. The recommendation for mandatory audit committees is not supported by the existing research evidence and as such appears to support the demand for excuses theory.

Ramsay (2001) and CLERP 9 (2003) both advocate mandatory audit partner rotation as a solution to audit failure because it is argued to increase auditor independence. The case for mandatory rotation is not explained in the Ramsay Report, except to say that it accepts the conclusion of the Audit Review Working Party and the US and UK practice of rotating partners every seven years. No effort is made to describe the arguments or evidence relied upon by the working party. The report offers no additional insight into why there should be mandatory rotation. There is only one paper cited as support for mandatory rotation, but it relates to auditor tenure (rather than rotation) and is acknowledged as flawed by Ramsay. The recommendation appears to rest on an appeal to authority − that is, overseas regulation − rather than the research evidence, and is also consistent with the selective use of excuses to support preconceived notions described in Watts and Zimmerman (1979).

CLERP 9 (2003) adopts recommendations in Ramsay (2001) and the HIH Royal Commission (HIH Royal Commission 2003) without further comment on the research evidence. The HIH Royal Commission recommends mandatory audit partner rotation despite there being little apparent direct relationship between the HIH failure and the audit partner's tenure. It is possible that mandatory engagement partner *retention,* rather than rotation, could have been beneficial in the HIH situation because it might have prevented the removal of the long-standing engagement partner at Arthur Andersen from the HIH audit, following his decision to meet with some of the non-executive directors of HIH in the absence of management (HIH Royal Commission 2003, vol. 1, p. 36).[14]

Regulations requiring mandatory audit partner rotation appear to be leading the research evidence, supporting the Watts and Zimmerman (1979) argument. However, it is possible that although there is little research on audit partner rotation, related research could provide evidence consistent with the partner rotation recommendation, thereby supporting the public-interest argument. Related research includes the association of audit firm tenure and accounting

---

[14]See also the analysis in Hamilton and Stokes (2003).

and auditing quality. Support for mandatory rotation would be provided by evidence of a decline in financial statement quality as audit firm tenure increases. However, recent studies of audit firm tenure provide evidence of audit quality and earnings quality problems associated with initial engagements or short tenure periods. This suggests this regulatory reform could impose unforseen costs and not generate the anticipated benefits.

Geiger and Raghunandan (2002) find that auditors are less likely to modify audit opinions immediately preceding bankruptcy during the initial years of audit engagements, providing evidence that audit quality increases as tenure increases.[15] Myers et al. (2003) find that the association between audit firm tenure and financial statement restatements is context-specific and could be either positive or negative. They conclude that their evidence provides no clear support for mandatory auditor rotation. Myers, Myers and Omer (2003) show that mean, median and standard deviation of accruals are smaller the longer the auditor-client relationship, suggesting that mandatory firm rotation could lower earnings quality.

In the period between Ramsay (2001) and the CLERP legislation, research into audit partner rotation had been conducted using data on audit partners signing audit reports for listed Australian companies (Daly, Hamilton & Stokes 2003; Bond, Hamilton & Stokes 2003) and publicised in the national press and bulletins (Culvenor & Stokes 2002a, 2002b, 2003). The evidence is of voluntary audit partner rotations and does not provide support for mandatory audit partner rotations. The lack of referencing in the commentary to the draft Bill of these studies leaves open to suggestion that the regulators seek to quote only evidence that buttresses their preconceived notions, as suggested by Watts and Zimmerman (1979, p. 274).[16]

Daly, Hamilton and Stokes (2003) investigate whether audit partner rotation is associated with changes in audit quality as revealed through both audit fees and the audit opinion. They use data from the Big Five/Six accounting firms in Sydney, and show that voluntary partner rotation is associated with an initial 10.9% audit fee discount. Where the rotation leads to a less competent partner (as measured by the market share of audit fees that they command), the magnitude of the audit fee discount is greater, while a partner rotation to a more competent partner is associated with no significant audit fee discount. The study's results also show that a partner rotation is not significantly associated with a change in the audit opinion issued. A partner rotation does not lead to a greater propensity to issue a qualified audit opinion. These results suggest that the

---

[15]Additional evidence of audit failure associated with short audit firm tenure is provided by Elitzur and Falk (1996), Walker, Lewis and Casterella (2001), St. Pierre and Anderson (1984), Stice (1991), and Ragunathan, Lewis and Evans (1994).
[16]An alternative explanation is that the research by Daly, Hamilton and Stokes (2003), and Bond, Hamilton and Stokes (2003), was unpublished and was therefore open to scrutiny as to the veracity of the findings. But not to have even requested a copy of a draft paper to form a view on the quality of the research at all reinforces the selective quotation approach.

practice of partner rotation possibly does not have the desired audit quality benefits that proponents suggest.

Bond, Hamilton and Stokes (2003) investigate whether audit partner industry expertise affects audit fees. They attempt to determine whether it is the audit office or partner expertise that dominates. The 'office-wide' perspective considers an accounting firm's office practice in aggregate, with no differentiation presumed to exist across the partners in the practice office of the firm. The 'partner-level' perspective views each individual partner in the practice office as a unique and relevant unit of analysis in their own right, due to the importance each plays in the audit contracting process. Bond, Hamilton and Stokes' results support the view that market pricing of industry expertise in Australian audit is primarily based on partner-level industry leadership in city-specific audit markets. The study implies that partner rotation within offices of large accounting firms could have significant costs.

If this recent research evidence does not support proposals for regulatory change, the question arises how the proponents convince their opponents of the need for change. It is simpler to point to the apparent costs of the corporate failure as the proxy for the costs of audit failure than to specify the costs and benefits of the proposed change. For example, the HIH Royal Commission report (HIH Royal Commission 2003) begins with a discussion of the harm to individuals, community distress and consequences for the public of HIH's failure. There would be many individuals and organisations willing to provide evidence to such an inquiry of their losses. However, the critical issue is not, as we have noted above, whether a particular corporate failure leads to loss, because there are many factors that add risk to investing in firms that contribute to losses beyond auditing failure, and some residual loss from contracting involving audits is expected. Rather, the issue is whether regulatory intervention for audit reform is more efficient in lowering the costs of contracting from auditing and generates benefits to the contracting parties. The arguments and evidence in this section suggest that the regulatory reform process for auditing and some of the solutions that emerge are not likely to meet this test and therefore be in the public interest. The regulatory audit reforms could increase future costs of contracting and contribute to inefficient allocation of the costs of property rights.

Conclusions and implications

We argue that the onus of proof for regulatory reform of auditing resides with the proponents of change. Their tasks are to measure the relevant loss used as justification for the reform, to identify the causes of the loss, and to justify the reforms as efficient and beneficial solutions. Appreciation of the nature of contracting and markets and the role of research informs the analysis of proposed regulatory reforms.

The theory and empirical evidence of audit contracting suggest that audits are demanded because they reduce contracting costs. Contracting parties search for the lowest cost solution and use auditing to monitor activities within firms to avoid the costs imposed by price protection in markets. Audited financial statements, and contracts based on those statements, are fair to the level determined by societal norms and enforced by courts and other institutions (Ball 1989). The greater uncertainty about norms of 'fairness' and contract enforcement, the greater the likely demand for detailed specification of contract terms: the greater the acceptance of auditors as ethical and fair arbitrators and monitors, the greater the likely reliance placed on auditors in contracting to determine the economic outcomes for contracting parties.

We have drawn on literatures that raise questions about whether the proponents of regulatory reform in auditing have satisfied the onus of proof for the reforms. We have argued that the policy-makers are liable to fall victim to fallacies of thinking and increase future bonding and monitoring costs on firms. The result is an inefficient allocation of the costs of property rights, adversely affecting the conditions that would lead to audit market reform. We have outlined a concept of political residual losses in relying on the political process for regulatory reform. These losses can occur when politician-regulators decree a firm/market failure exists that warrants regulatory intervention, overstate the losses from firm failure, and do not consider contracting residual losses in advocating regulatory reform. The political residual losses can also arise when politician-regulators define the likely cause of the decreed failures and thereby the focus for regulatory reform, as well as specifying the conditions for assessing value in the proposed regulatory reforms. We also show these residual losses can arise when politician-regulators identify the justification (theory) for the selected solutions − 'demand for excuses' − through appeals to authority.

In the same way that contracting parties' ethical behaviour can reduce contracting residual losses, ethical behaviour by politician-regulators in the political process can contribute to lowering the political residual losses and enhancing society's well-being through facilitating the economic outcomes sought by contracting parties. To the extent that philosophical debates contribute to increasing ethical behaviour by all parties in the contracting and political process (not just the auditors and the politician-regulators, but also shareholders, management, directors and the professions), they can contribute to achieving these objectives.

References

Anderson, D., Francis, J. & Stokes, D. 1993, 'Auditing, Directorships and the Demand for Monitoring', *Journal of Accounting and Public Policy*, vol. 12, no. 4, pp. 353-75.

Ball, R. 1989, 'The Firm as a Specialist Contracting Intermediary: Application to Accounting and Auditing', working paper, University of Rochester, NY.

Blackwell, D.W., Noland, T. R. & Winters, D. B. 1998, 'The Value of Auditor Assurance: Evidence from Loan Pricing', *Journal of Accounting Research*, vol. 36, no. 1, pp. 57-70.

Bond, D., Hamilton, J. & Stokes, D. 2003, 'Big 5 Audit Partner Industry Expertise – Audit Pricing Evidence', working paper, University of Technology, Sydney.

Cheung, S. 1983, 'The Contractual Nature of the Firm', *Journal of Law and Economics*, no. 26, no. 1, pp. 1-21.

Chow, C. 1982, 'The Demand for External Auditing: Size, Debt and Ownership Influences', *The Accounting Review*, vol. 57, no. 2, pp. 272-91.

CLERP (Corporate Law Economic Reform Program) 2002, 'Corporate Disclosure: Strengthening the Financial Reporting Framework', Commonwealth of Australia, Canberra. (CLERP 2002)

CLERP (Audit Reform and Corporate Disclosure) Bill 2003, 'Commentary on the Draft Provisions', Commonwealth of Australia, Canberra. (CLERP 2003)

Coase, R. 1937, 'The Nature of the Firm', *Economica*, new series 2, November, pp. 386-405.

Culvenor, J. & Stokes, D. 2002a, 'A Touch of Reform for Its Own Sake', *Australian Financial Review*, 8 October, p. 63.

Culvenor, J. & Stokes, D. 2002b, 'Is There a Case for Mandatory Audit Partner Rotation?', *Butterworths Corporation Law Bulletin*, 20 [432].

Culvenor, J. & Stokes, D. 2003, 'Governance Reforms May Lower Audit Standards', *Australian Financial Review*, 30 April, p. 63.

Culvenor, J., Stokes, D. & Taylor, S. 2002, 'A Review of the Proposals for Reform of Independence of Australian Company Auditors', *Australian Accounting Review*, vol. 12, no. 2, pp. 12-23.

Daly, S., Hamilton, J. & Stokes, D. 2003, 'Audit partner rotation and audit quality effects', working paper, University of Technology, Sydney.

DeAngelo, L. E. 1981a, 'Auditor Size and Audit Quality', *Journal of Accounting and Economics*, vol. 3, no. 3, pp. 183-99.

DeAngelo, L. E. 1981b, 'Auditor Independence, "Low Balling", and Disclosure Regulation', *Journal of Accounting and Economics*, vol. 3, no. 2, pp. 113-27.

Demski, J. S. 1973, 'The General Impossibility of Normative Accounting Standards', *The Accounting Review*, vol. 48, no. 4, pp. 718-23.

Downs, A. 1957, *An Economic Theory of Democracy*, Harper and Row, San Francisco.

Elitzur, R. & Falk, H. 1996, 'Planned Audit Quality', *Journal of Accounting and Public Policy*, vol. 15, no. 3, pp. 247-69.

Fama, E. 1980, 'Agency Problems and the Theory of the Firm', *Journal of Political Economy*, 88, pp. 288-307.

Ferguson, A., Francis, J. & Stokes, D. 2003, 'The Effects of Firm-Wide and Office-Level Industry Expertise on Audit Pricing', *The Accounting Review*, vol. 78, no. 2, pp. 429-48.

Geiger, M. & Raghunandan, K. 2002, 'Auditor Tenure and Audit Reporting Failures', *Auditing: A Journal of Practice and Theory*, vol. 21, no.1, pp. 67-78.

Godfrey, J. M. & Hamilton, J. 2005, 'The impact of R&D intensity on demand for specialist auditor services', *Contemporary Accounting Research*, vol. 22, no. 1 (forthcoming).

Hamilton, J. & Stokes, D. 2003, 'Questioning Audit Reform – The Case of Partner Rotation and the "High Court Judge" Standard of Independence', *Butterworths Corporation Law Bulletin*, 22 [519].

HIH Royal Commission 2003, *The Failure of HIH Insurance*, Commonwealth of Australia, Canberra.

Howieson, B. 2003, 'Can we teach auditors and accountants to be more ethically competent and publicly accountable?', Academy of Social Sciences in Australia Ethics and Auditing Workshop, Australian National University, Canberra.

Jensen, M. & Meckling, W. 1976, 'Theory of the Firm: Managerial Behavior, Agency Costs and Ownership Structure', *Journal of Financial Economics*, 3, pp. 305-60.

Menon, K. & Williams, D. 1994, 'The Insurance Hypothesis and Market Prices', *The Accounting Review*, vol. 69, no. 2, pp. 327-42.

Myers, J. N., Myers, L. A. & Omer, T. 2003, 'Exploring the term of the auditor-client relationship and the quality of earnings: A case for mandatory auditor rotation?', *The Accounting Review*, vol. 78, no. 3, pp. 779-800.

Myers, J. N., Myers, L. A., Palmrose, Z. & Scholz, S. 2003, 'Mandatory Auditor Rotation: Evidence from Restatements', working paper, University of Illinois at Urbana-Champaign.

Pincus, K., Rubarsky, M. & Wong, J. 1989, 'Voluntary Formation of Corporate Audit Committees Among NASDAQ Firms', *Journal of Accounting and Public Policy*, vol. 8, no. 4, pp. 239-65.

Raghunathan, B., Lewis, B. & Evans, J. 1994, 'An Empirical Investigation of Problem Audits', *Research in Accounting Regulation*, 8, pp. 33-58.

Ramsay, I. 2001, *Independence of Australian Company Auditors: review of current Australian requirements and proposals for reform*, Report to the Minister for Financial Services and Regulation, Department of Treasury, Canberra.

St. Pierre, K. & Anderson, J. 1984, 'An Analysis of Factors Associated with Lawsuits Against Public Accountants', *The Accounting Review*, vol. 59, no. 2, pp. 242-63.

Simunic, D. 1980, 'The Pricing of Audit Services: Theory and Evidence', *Journal of Accounting Research*, vol. 18, no. 1, pp. 161-90.

Stice, J. 1991, 'Using Financial and Market Information to Identify Pre-Engagement Factors Associated with Lawsuits Against Auditors', *The Accounting Review*, vol. 66, no. 1, pp. 42-55.

Stigler, G. J. 1971, 'The Theory of Economic Regulation', *Bell Journal of Economics and Management Science*, Spring, pp. 3-21.

Stokes, D. 2002, 'Ripples from Andersen's Dive Limitless', *Australian Financial Review*, 10 April, p. 55.

Walker, P., Lewis, B. & Casterella, J. 2001, 'Mandatory Auditor Rotation: Arguments and Current Evidence', *Accounting Enquiries*, January, p. 209.

Watts, R. L. & Zimmerman, J. L. 1979, 'The Demand for and Supply of Accounting Theories: The Market for Excuses', *The Accounting Review*, vol. 54, no. 2, pp. 273-305.

Watts, R. L. & Zimmerman, J. L. 1983, 'Agency Problems, Auditing, and the Theory of the Firm: Some Evidence', *Journal of Law and Economics*, vol. 26, no. 3, pp. 613-33.

Watts, R. L. & Zimmerman, J. L. 1986, *Positive accounting theory*, Prentice Hall, Englewood Cliffs, NJ.

Chapter 5. True and fair to whom?: a philosophical approach to auditing

Tom Campbell

Abstract

This chapter is a philosophical exploration of auditing ethics through an analysis of the role of the concept of a 'true and fair view' (TFV) in auditing discourse and practice. The chapter examines the meanings and uses of the concept in the context of the contrast between rule-based and principle-based approaches to accounting and auditing standards, concluding that the idea of a TFV is better seen as an objective of auditing regulation than as a basis for overriding or supplementing rules in audit practice, and going on to suggest that there are some difficult ethical issues that arise in determining who constitutes the audiences to which audits ought to be addressed, issues that have bearing on current controversies about auditor independence and probity.

The scope of auditing ethics

The crescendo of interest in auditing (and external accounting generally) arises from the perceived failure of auditors to do what has traditionally been expected of them – to alert shareholders and others with a stake or potential stake in a business to doubts about the published accounts of a company as a representation of the trading position of that company that is sufficiently accurate for them to make rational economic choices in relation to that company.

Critiques of auditing failures range from allegations of technical incompetence (often due to cost-cutting and inadequately trained staff) and lack of diligence in getting beyond the paper figures to the underlying economic realities, to charges of illegality and deception that amount to gross immorality, in particular where the failure to conduct a proper audit is attributed to a conflict of interest whereby auditors do their job in a way that secures their personal careers, their continuing contracts as auditors or promotes the other business interests of their firm, rather than a way that fulfils their legal and moral professional obligations to shareholders and other stakeholders (Bowie 2004, p. 61f).

It is at the point when illegality and immorality are involved that, it may be thought, ethics comes into the picture as a basis for blaming those who put profit before professional duty and personal gain before law-abidingness. Such failings are indeed ethical failings, but the interface of ethics and auditing goes much further and deeper than the critique of such evident sins. Ethics is not just about whether or not people do what they ought to do in their personal or professional lives and how to regulate conduct so that there is greater compliance with agreed norms. Ethics is also about how to determine more precisely what it is that people ought to do in their personal and professional lives. These normative questions include asking what should be the form and content of the laws, codes and standards by which we judge their conduct. What are the norms by which we ought to critique auditors' conduct? How are these norms to be justified? And then, yes, there are the further questions: why is it that auditors ought to conform to these norms and what ought to be done if they fail so to do?

To raise questions as to what auditing norms ought to be is to enter a realm of immense technical complexity with which few ethicists have the minimal competence to engage. In fact few people, other than experienced accountants, have such a capacity and it may be considered a defect of the existing system that company accounts have become so technical as to be incomprehensible to even well-informed members of the public. This certainly makes ethical reflection of accounting and auditing more difficult. The result is that adequately-informed opinion is largely confined to those who have a vested interest in how auditing is evaluated. As in so many fields, specialist knowledge and self-interest go unhappily hand in hand, thus making it problematic to leave the resolution of normative issues entirely to unsupervised experts and the perceived need; for instance, to have a majority of non-accountants on bodies responsible for standard-setting for accounting and auditing practice, as exemplified in the Sarbanes-Oxley Act in the United States and the CLERP 9 proposals in Australia.

Ethics, as well as accounting, has its technical aspects. Certainly, the nature of ethics as applied to phenomena such as auditing is often misunderstood. One common misunderstanding is that ethics is a matter of intuiting that there are certain things we must or must not do as we go about our daily business. These 'intuitions' are assumed to be mainly about normative limitations on how we go about reaching our basically amoral objectives, such as making money. Examples include 'do not lie' or 'be polite'. These moral 'oughts' are perceived to be separate from our legal obligations and may differ from the conduct that other people expect of us. Although they are routinely used to criticise the conduct of other people, such moral imperatives are experienced as binding on each of us as a matter of individual conscience. Irrespective of what the law or other people say, we believe that we should not steal, we should tell the truth and we should be kind and considerate to others, even if we could get away with behaving differently, whatever else we may be doing. This is known as 'deontological' morality.

Yet morality is not always a list of dos and don'ts that mark out the limits of morally correct or acceptable conduct. A great deal of morality is not captured by the deontological model. In practice most ethics is consequentialist; that is, it is a matter of working out what is the most effective means to produce morally desirable results. In the classic utilitarian version of consequentialism, the morally right action (or rule or system) is the one that produces the greatest happiness of the greatest number ('utilitarianism'), although other consequentialists are more concerned with maximising preferences, or other morally valued outcomes. Utilitarianism is, of course, the moral philosophy – deriving from the likes of Thomas Hobbes and coming down to us through Adam Smith, John Stuart Mill and Ricardo – that provides the moral foundations of modern economics.

In so far as consequentialism is an acceptable approach to ethics – and no one says that consequentialist reasoning has *no* place in an acceptable morality – moral questions are crucially dependent on matters of fact. Working out consequences is an empirical question that takes us deep into the factual details of actual and possible economic and political systems.

Of course, there can be morally detached debates about what will happen if you do this or that which have in themselves no moral content, but as soon as you take, or assume, a position about the desirability of the results, then you are on a trail of reasoning that terminates in the acceptance or rejection of some values that we take to be important for their own sake, be they happiness, preferences, wants or satisfactions. Indeed, no technical factual discussion about economics, or accounting or auditing, has legitimating or justificatory force unless it terminates in such ethical or moral evaluations.

It follows that, if the technical auditing experts want us to give moral or political weight to their knowledge and expertise, they must show us how this knowledge and expertise produces morally desirable results and be prepared to consider whether these results are indeed morally optimal. In so doing, whatever accounting technicalities are involved, they are also engaging in a form of moral discourse. It has to be remembered that Adam Smith wrote a book (Smith 1790) about the foundations of morality and the economic role of moral values that is almost as long as *The Wealth of Nations*. This enabled him to assume in his economic works that, for instance, the wealth that he is talking about is constituted by satisfaction rather than by money, and that failure to rectify breach of contract is inefficient and immoral – and to some extent immoral because it is in efficient.

This is to claim that much of what passes for technical accounting and auditing debate is a form of ethical debate about what rules, what standards, what systems we ought to have in place to reach what are accepted as morally desirable results.

Ethics does not start when the deontological intuitions are brought to bear on limiting or channeling such outcomes, but underpins all technical accounting issues that have a bearing on practical outcomes. Conversely, it is a mistake for ethicists to consider the economic and other consequences of accounting practice as morally neutral simply because they do not offend deontological morality. Whatever moral theory is adopted, consequences do – always to some extent and perhaps exclusively – count. Thus, the issue debated throughout this book, as to whether rules designed to increase audit independence impair or enhance the quality of the audit, is, when followed through, a moral issue (Dunfee 2004, pp. 79-85).

The distinctiveness of consequentialism as a moral theory is its claim that *all* morality can be reduced to consequentialist calculations. On this view, the moral 'intuitions' of a deontological sort may feel morally imperative, but they are justified only in so far as they produce morally desirable results. Very often this is so. Theft is wrong because it brings unhappiness to others, it doesn't produce unhappiness because it is wrong.

However, most theorists think there are limits to such consequentialist reductionism. It seems evident to them that there are some things you ought not to do (such as kill an innocent person) and some things you ought to do (such as treat people with respect), whatever the consequences. If it is these features of morality that are taken to delineate the scope of ethics, this is to relegate ethics to the periphery of practical fields such as accounting, with ethics being a constraining framework rather than an internal driving force.

Often these deontological imperatives are dignified with the title of 'rights', perhaps because they are seen as terminating in an affirmation of the value and intrinsic importance of all individual human beings, a grounding that enables them to be professed as moral trumps that take precedence over all other considerations in the moral game (Dworkin 1978). Again, no ethicists would exclude this type of moral consideration – there are some things that it is always wrong to do to other human beings – but a purely rights-based morality over-emphasises deontological morality at the expense of consequentialist moral reasoning. Not only are many such rights themselves evidently justified in part by consequentialist reasoning, but there is scarcely any right that cannot itself be trumped, not only by other rights, but by wider considerations of utility. This means that we cannot read off specific ethical obligations from a list of rights or assume that rights (such as the property rights of shareholders) are in an entirely different moral category from consequentialist morals. Hence we must expect that a lot of consequentialist reasoning, including technical auditing matters, must feature in determining the legitimate rights and duties of those involved in and affected by the outcome of the auditing process.

On the other hand, if accountants are to be fully involved in the process of ethical justification, they can never rest on affirmations, however empirically well-founded they may be, about the way in which things are done or statements about what practitioners and other participants believe ought to be done: the standing norms of the profession, or the respectable parts of it. They may have great epistemic authority on account of their knowledge of what will and what will not work in the real world of auditing, but they cannot justify any preferences within the range of workable alternatives without engaging in ethical debate. The message is, and it is not unfamiliar even if it is often forgotten, that what may be called 'critical accountancy' is routinely involved in ethical contestation, usually consequentialist but often broad enough to take into consideration those moral considerations, such as autonomy, fairness and equality, that escape the consequentialist net.

It follows from all this that both the consequentialist and the deontological dimensions of ethics draw us into deeply technical discussion into which most of us will be ill-equipped to enter. This means that it is impossible to say anything very specific and interesting about the ethical duties of auditors without engaging in at least a measure of such technicalities. It is simply not the case that applied ethics is a matter of insisting that professional groups, for instance, behave ethically and decently with respect to some self-evident deontological rules. Rather, what is needed is detailed and sophisticated discussion about the ethical duties of auditors that derive from what their role is, or ought to be, within a morally justified economic system. This is evidently a very open-ended enquiry.

Thus, in seeking to determine what preparers of external accounts ought to be required to put in their reports, it is hopelessly inadequate just to say that they should record the truth about the accounts – in other words, they should not lie. Even where there are objectively incontrovertible facts that can be ascertained, we are left with the issue of which facts to report, for they cannot all be reported. Where what is at stake is not misleading the reader of a report, the 'lie' cannot be identified without an idea of what it is that the reader wants to know or has a right to know. Without determining the legitimacy of the expectations involved, we do not know what counts as lying by omission, or what is a misleading statement. And, of course, an omission and a misleading statement cannot be considered lies – that is, deliberate falsehoods designed to deceive – unless there is a shared assumption as to what sort of information (and in what institutionalised form) is to be expected of a person in that situation.

So what is the role of the auditor? What service can auditors be legitimately expected to provide? This is a specific ethical question in a larger moral context that extends to a consideration of what constitutes a justified economic system within a justified political system. As such, it is not settled by any factual assertions about what auditors actually do, or about how our economic system actually operates, although any practical recommendations that arise out of such reflection must take off from and return to what is known about how the system currently performs and what sort of reform might work in practice.

This ethical scheme may be applied to the question of what place, if any, there is for the concept of a 'true and fair view' (TFV) in the auditing process and its regulation. The familiar line here is that the object of an external financial audit is to give an opinion that the reported accounts of a business give a true and fair view of its trading position and financial standing. In general terms this is often interpreted by saying that the auditor's role is to tell actual and potential shareholders whether they can trust the published accounts of the company as giving a reasonably accurate picture of its economic performance for the purpose of investment decisions (Mautz & Sharaf 1961, p. 158; Flint 1988).

This conception has its attractions because it presents a readily intelligible and clearly significant purpose for the auditing function: a financial audit is intended to provide reassurance that there is a valid informational basis for shareholders and others with an interest or potential interest in the performance of an organisation to carry out such roles as investors, owners and financial advisers, roles that are considered to be crucial to the performance of a liberal capitalist economic system in which it is important that funds are invested in the most efficient way – that is, the way that best enhances the production of desired goods and services at the lowest feasible price – the assumption being that this requires investors to make their investments on an economically-informed basis.

Interestingly, this gives auditors a dramatic and explicit ethical role, on any definition of 'ethical', since they are in the business of creating or destroying the trust on which business relationships largely depend, something that is generally regarded as, other things being equal, a desirable moral relationship in itself and is, in many circumstances, essential for mutually beneficial human cooperation. It follows that any failure in carrying out the audit role, if due to incompetence or negligence, is morally wrong, and if deliberate, is highly immoral, not only because of its adverse consequences, but also because it destroys a relationship that is valuable in itself. No wonder shareholders who are let down by auditors are angry and resentful as well as hurt: not only have they lost money on their investment but their trust has been betrayed.

Moreover, in creating, sustaining or undermining trust between other parties (the shareholder and the company being audited), auditors are relying on the assumption of others that they themselves are trustworthy, in that they can be relied upon to give an honest and reliable judgment as to the accuracy of the accounts and thus the trustworthiness of the company. Auditors depend on being trusted to sustain trust in others. They must therefore present themselves as honest and capable persons, for if they are not, then their services are valueless in economic terms and hence morally defective as well.

From the economic point of view there is, of course, a market in trust, and in this market, if it is in working order, auditors who are generally believed to be untrustworthy go to the wall, since they will not be hired. The market value of an auditing firm depends on its being trusted (although not necessarily on its being trustworthy). But markets are not perfect, especially in the short term, and many auditing failures never come to light publicly, and in the meantime the market remains, in consequence, less efficient, and the shareholders remain aggrieved or simply duped. Arthur Andersen rode high in reputational terms until their rapid demise following on their part in the Enron scandal (Toffler & Reingold 2003).

And the injury goes wider than that, for any discovered breaches of auditors' trust will make investors less likely to risk their funds in future, thus retarding the effective working of the economic system to the detriment of others who might otherwise benefit from the success of the system. Auditing is thus crucial to the creation and sustenance of trust as a public good, through the stimulating effect of a general belief in an economic community that there is available reliable information as to the performance of public companies.

The systemic need for reliable audits goes some way to explaining the (now tarnished) public image of auditors as reliable and honest people who use their special status as monopolists of accounting legitimation for the benefit of others, and sets the scene for the abuse of such high public esteem of the sort that has been shown in the arrogance and greed of senior partners in the now defunct Arthur Andersen, and is thereby inevitably suspected to occur in other comparable companies.

Leaving to one side, for the moment, whether the TVF is either a necessary or sufficient statement of the justifying objectives of the audit (and there are clearly other objectives and other audiences beyond shareholders that need to be considered), this chapter examines the TFV concept and its different actual and possible interpretations, before going on to consider how it might be deployed and sustained in the auditing process. With this in mind two sorts of question are raised: (1) what are the competing functions of the TFV, and (2) what are the competing meanings of the TFV? This then leads on to topic (3), how might or ought the function and the content of the TFV relate to each other?

Functions and meaning of the TFV

An examination of some of the literature on the TFV reveals a number of distinct but sometimes overlapping uses or functions for the concept. We may label them

(1) *the override function*, (2) *the supplementation function*, (3) *the interpretive function*, (4) *the legitimation function*, and (5) *the justifying function*.

1. *The override function* takes the TFV to be part of a working external accounting and auditing principle that is used to trump accounting and auditing rules or standards in that the preparer of financial statements is permitted (or required) to avoid conformity to such norms if this is necessary in order to present a TFV.[1] This may be applied to preparers, auditors, standard-setting bodies or courts.[2]

The override function represents the legal position in the United Kingdom (although even there accounting standards as set by the Accounting Standards Board do not permit an override with respect to its standards), Hong Kong and Singapore, and perhaps in the European Union (Nobes 1993), but not (any more) in Australia or the United States, where strict conformity to accounting standards, usually expressed in terms of determinate rules, is required. Where the override principle does hold, systems vary as to how far the circumstances of the override are specified and the extent to which an auditor is obliged to draw attention to such departures and give some explanation for them.

2. *The supplementation function* is related to the override function with respect to the circumstances of its use, but instead of overriding the rule in question, it requires that the preparers provide such additional information as will give a true and fair view.[3] This provides an opportunity for the exercise of the responsibility often ascribed to auditors to act as some sort of watch-dog (or even investigator or police) over the accounting practices of companies, drawing attention to 'irregularities' or concerns over practices that may be strictly legal, but are unusual and likely to give rise to a misleading picture of the company's financial situation. It feeds particularly on the idea that an auditor gives an 'opinion' that the prepared accounts give a true and fair view.

---

[1] The UK Companies Act 1948 as amended in 1981 introduced the idea that matters to be included in a company's accounts and notes be overridden if this is necessary to give a true and fair view. For example, Mautz and Sharaf (1961), p. 160: 'Thus the auditor borrows generally accepted accounting principles from accounting but he accepts them with reservations. If they do not meet the needs of the case at hand he must reject them and develop what in his judgment is a proper solution'. And op. cit., p. 167, an auditor 'must decide whether they [accounting presentations] are fair in the circumstances'. In 1983 the Companies Act was amended to require compliance with the accounting standards authorised by the Accounting Review Board, together with an override provision enabling directors to depart from these standards so as to give a true and fair view. The Act was amended in 1991 to permit only the provision of additional information.
[2] See Arden (1997), p. 677, for the TFV as a 'stop gap'. Compare McBarnet and Whelan (1999): 'The true and fair override is an express licence in the Companies Act to depart from, rather than comply with, specific legal requirements in "special circumstances".'
[3] Thus, the Australian *Corporations Act 2001*, s. 296: 'If the financial statements and notes prepared in compliance with the accounting standards would not give a true and fair view, additional information must be included in the notes to the financial statements ...' See also the European Community's Fourth Directive on Company Law, Articles 2.4 and 2.5.

3. *The interpretative function* takes the TFV to be part of a principle or set of principles for use in interpreting the rules and standards laid down for external accounting and auditing when the meaning and import of these are in doubt through ambiguity, lack of specificity or unclarity.[4] This applies particularly to the interpretation of the rule-defined categories that are set by the rules to determine what falls under which heading when using the terms in which accounting standards are expressed – the sphere in which creative accounting flourishes. This function may extend to filling in gaps where there are no existing rules to cover novel situations but not, in theory, to altering rules that are clear and unambiguous.

The interpretive function can be viewed as embodying a certain attitude to rules, seeing them as attempts to give a particular concrete form to the overall objective of presenting a TFV, rather than as formal restrictions that a 'good' accountant should be able to manipulate to best serve the interests of the company whose accounts are under audit. A genuine and good-faith respect for rules, often referred to in terms of following the 'spirit' rather than the 'letter' of the rules, does not mean departing from the rules when it suits those involved, but, when there is doubt as to their meaning, interpreting the rules in the light of their evident purpose, rather than scheming how to get round them by thinking up clever but often dishonest 'misreadings' of the rules in question.

4. *The legitimation function*: this approach sees the TFV as bearing on the duty of an auditor to offer, in addition to assurance that accounting standards have been observed, an opinion that the audited material does represent a TFV of the financial situation of the company. This is seen as having the social function of legitimating the enterprise.[5]

The legitimation function operates independently of (1) to (3) above in so far as it requires that they provide a professional opinion as to whether the proffered accounts provide a broadly accurate view of the company's trading position, although it may be seen as a broad extension of the supplementation function. This legitimating or validating function may involve requiring preparers to make further disclosures or commenting

[4]Nobes (1993), p. 45: 'TFV is used by directors/auditors in interpreting the law and standards or where there is no law or standard ...' This is sometimes put in terms of the TFV being used in the exercise of 'judgment' (Gearin & Khandelwal 1995; Moroney & Sidhu 2001).
[5]Michael Power (1997), p. 9: 'Audit has become a benchmark for securing the legitimacy of an organisational action in which auditable standards of performance have been erected not only to provide for substantive internal improvements and the quality of service but to make these improvements externally verifiable via acts of certification'. Also Peter Miller, cited in Hopwood and Miller (1994), p. 11: 'One could study modern accounting as a ceremonial function that legitimates organizations with the mythical 'users' of accounting information: internal participants, stockholders, the public, and with agencies such as the Securities Exchange Commission'.

on whether conformity to existing accounting standards does provide an accurate enough view of the financial state of the company in question, but it serves primarily to legitimate the financial statements by affirming their general reliability and validity. This function has to do with the social function of the audit as giving assurance not only to investors but to the economic system as a whole, thus contributing to the social and political standing of business.

5. *The justifying function*: unlike the above three functions which take the TFV to be operative within the auditing process, the justifying function sees the TFV to be primarily applicable to determination of what accounting standards and legal rules bearing on such standards and processes ought to be adopted.[6] This is a matter of justifying and criticising the rules, not overriding, interpreting or supplementing them. The justifying function uses the TFV to justify (or not) the rules and standards that are authoritatively adopted as governing the presentation of accounts for audit, either in framing professional accounting standards or in drawing up the legislation within which such standards operate. On this approach, a TFV does not necessarily feature in the working processes of these rule-governed processes but provides the basis for a justification or critique of the processes and the rules that are involved in them.

Rather misleadingly, the justificatory function is sometimes identified in the literature with the override function, perhaps because standard-setters can use the TFV to establish standards that are in conflict with (but in practice 'override') existing legal requirements.[7] This conflict as to whose rules should take priority in practice is quite a distinct matter from the use of discretion by preparers and auditors with respect to departing from authoritative accounting rules, whatever the origin of these rules might be. Clearly, the use by standard- or rule-setters of the TFV to create auditing standards and laws is a justificatory function of a TFV very different from the function of enabling preparers and auditors to depart from such standards and rules as have been made.

Turning to the contending contents or meanings of the idea of a TFV, a sample of these would have to include:

---

[6]Nobes (1993), p. 47: 'In particular, in some countries (e.g. France and Spain) it (TFV) seems to have been used by regulators as a philosophy to accompany reform to the rules'. See also Alexander (1999), p. 252, and CLERP 9, Proposal 16.

[7]Thus Alexander (1999), p. 250: '... if the regulation is going to be changed – as it must and will be – then some overriding criterion greater than that enshrined within the regulation itself must, as a matter of logical necessity, be employed in order to decide on the changes and developments needed'.

1. *The positivist meaning*: the positivist approach to the meaning of the TFV equates the content of the TFV with conformity to existing authoritative (or 'positive') accounting norms, legal and otherwise.[8] Here the TFV is a summation of all the rules and standards that are authoritatively required.[9] It is a TFV if the accounts are in compliance with accepted auditing standards. The term 'positivist' is less applicable when these norms consist of general principles couched in evaluative terms and more applicable when they consist of rules, conformity to which can be objectively determined. As with respect to the idea of 'positive law', the model here is of rules with empirical content that can be scientifically applied to observable situations, rather than unspecific standards which require those who use them to make subjective judgments in order to understand and follow them.

2. *The economic reality meaning*: the economic reality approach assumes that the external financial statements are intended to be an accurate, or at least not misleading, picture or representation of the economic position of the company.[10] In a weaker form, the TFV is one that reflects 'economic relevance' (Tweedie & Whittington 1990, pp. 87-8).

Drawing primarily on 'true' rather than 'fair', an economic reality TFV is one that makes no demonstrably false factual claims about the economic circumstances of the company, and does not mislead the reader by giving an erroneous impression concerning the profitability, economic performance and, by implication, the prospects of the company. While the facts involved in accounting are largely institutional facts whose existence is dependent on social meanings and institutions, the idea here is that a TFV is one that is in accordance with such institutional facts as are relevant to a clear understanding of the company's economic position. This involves going behind the accounts to check their external rather than their internal validity and reliability as representations of economic

---

[8]Thus, in the United States financial statements are required to 'present fairly in conformity with generally accepted accounting principles'. The assumption is that the rules and principles adopted by standard-setting bodies that are independent of the accounting and auditing professional associations have a quasi-legal status in that they are routinely used by the professions and the courts as determining the legal responsibilities of accountants and auditors.
[9]McBarnet and Whelan (1999), p. 88: 'When and how should a true and fair view be equated with specific rules, when and how should it override them?'
[10]Thus, Fourth EC Directive on Company Law, Article 2:

> 3.The annual accounts shall give a true and fair view of the company's assets, liabilities, financial position and profit or loss.
> 4. Where the application of the provisions of this Directive would not be sufficient to give a true and fair view within the meaning of paragraph 3, additional information must be given.
> 5. Where in exceptional cases the application of a provision of the Directive is incompatible with the obligation laid down in paragraph 3, that provision must be departed from in order to give and true and fair view within the meaning of paragraph 3. Any such departure must be disclosed in the notes on the accounts together with an explanation for the reasons for it and a statement of its effect on the assets, liabilities, financial position and profit or loss. The Member States may define the exceptional cases in question and lay down the relevant special rules.

realities. On this approach, a TFV is one that correctly reflects economic reality.

3. *The ordinary and natural meaning*: this approach treats the TFV as an abstract legal term that gains such meaning as it has from its general intelligibility and use amongst ordinary speakers of the language, outside of any technical definitions or attempts to fasten it to specific criteria of meaning. This is the meaning that can be derived from the ordinary and natural meaning of the words 'true and fair', either construed separately or together. In practice this involves courts drawing on, but not being determined by, the way in which the concept is operationalised by those involved in the processes of accounting and auditing.[11] This may be described as a 'contextual plain meaning' in that it is plain to those with some knowledge and experience of accounting and auditing practice.

Some of these functions and meanings might be struck out as manifestly inadequate or insufficient. Thus, we might seek to exclude the override function as being incompatible with the rule of law in that it gives unacceptable discretion to accountants and auditors, permitting all sorts of unfairnesses, uncertainties and biases (unless, that is, one of the other alternative meanings can be used to provide an objective and precise way of determining the proper use of the override function according to specific rules: none would seem to be convincing candidates for this role). This is the prime reason why the override function was removed from the corporate law of Australia.

However, there is a lively debate about the rival attractions of precise rules and general principles in governing conduct generally. It would be unwise to exclude the provision of extensive discretion in auditing. There are many well-rehearsed reasons for encouraging flexibility with respect to rules in areas where there is difficulty in formulating rules that are adequate to meet all the circumstances that arise. This is particularly the case when participants have strong incentives to find ways around rules that are put in place to guide and control their conduct (Griffiths 1986).

The familiar paradox here is that an override function makes it more feasible for honest preparers and auditors to give an accurate picture of the economic position of a company by looking to the substance rather than the form of economic transactions, but, at the same time, it makes it much easier to indulge in the sort of creative accounting that is concerned to present a more favourable economic picture than is actually warranted (McBarnet & Whelan 1999, Chapter 9). Here

---

[11]Arden (1997), p. 676: 'I will now make some general points about the true and fair view. I believe that it cannot be defined and that synonyms cannot be found for it. However I can define a number of features of the true and fair view'. Justice Arden then goes on to say how courts use the concept by drawing on its contemporaneous meaning and take account of the 'authoritative and generally accepted views of expert accountants and the views of the UK Accounting Standards Board'. The lack of a legal definition of TFV in the Australian context has been used to explain the difficulty of taking legal action on the grounds that accounts do not represent a TFV (Deegan, Kent & Lin 1994).

one thing is clear: the override function places proportionately greater reliance on the honesty of those involved than does a tighter, more rule-based regime. This does not, of course, in itself determine which approach is the more effective.

As regards the meaning alternatives, it may be possible to exclude (4) (the ordinary and natural meaning) as leading to contents so vague and indeterminate as to be useless for any of the functions listed. But this also may be thought to show an as yet unjustified bias towards an ideal of rule-governance that neglects the interacting impacts of ideology, authority and discretionary power. Thus on one view of the legitimating function of the audit, there is need for a grand-sounding ideal through which to affirm that people can have confidence to participate eagerly in and politically endorse an economic system that requires their support. Similarly, the capacity of the courts to intervene where things seem to have gone wrong in the business world is enhanced, not diminished, by the existence of an ill-defined concept on which they can draw to justify whatever decision they consider it best to make.[12] Indeed, some may argue that an ordinary and natural meaning is best suited to enabling the wisdom of experienced auditors to exercise their discretion in respect to the override function.

Assuming, then, that all the functions and meanings are at least feasible alternatives, we may note that some of the competing functions go better with some of the competing meanings of the TFV. Thus, the override function does not go well with positivist meaning (conformity to accounting standards). If a TFV is a summary of the norms that apply, it can hardly be used to trump those norms. In fact, it can be argued that positivist meaning cannot serve any of the possible functions, except perhaps a limited interpretive one in which some authoritative norms interpret others analogically. For this reason, positivist meaning might be discarded as tantamount to a declaration of redundancy for the TFV. And, indeed, strict adherence to current rules and standards is often opposed to a TFV approach.

However, to discard the positivist meaning entirely fails to recognise the different meanings that the TFV may have with respect to its different functions and how the positive meaning may feature in a more complicated scenario. Thus, the positivist meaning may have a subordinate role with respect to the uses to which the economic reality sense of the TFV is put. For instance, the economic reality meaning for the TFV is a good starting point for the justificatory function, since accounting standards and auditing criteria should, it may seem evident, be designed so that conformity to them will make the economic reality of the company concerned transparent. Further, having a set of such agreed rules to which all

[12]Alexander (1999), p. 246:

> One of the perceived problems with the Type A approach in general, and with TFV in particular, is the lack of any formal definition. It can be argued, persuasively in the author's view, that the indefinable nature of such a concept is its strength. Like 'justice', for example, it is a concept inherently greater than its precision in terms of any one particular time and place could possibly encapsulate.

companies must conform is a necessary requirement for making comparisons between companies, thus fostering efficiency and fairness in financial market competition. A positivist meaning of the TFV plays a necessary part in a justificatory function that includes the provision of information in a form in which the economic realities of companies can be compared.

If accounting standards do in fact serve to provide a TFV in the sense of economic reality, then it follows that an auditing process that requires these standards to be met is thereby serving the achievement of a TFV in the economic reality sense. In these circumstances, the positivist meaning indirectly serves the goals expressed through the economic reality meaning.

It may appear that the economic reality meaning is in general central and pervasive in that it features in all the listed functions. It seems particularly appropriate for use in the override function, which serves to meet the difficulty that no set of rules can always work out as their designers expect, so that exceptions have to be made if the justificatory aims are to be achieved. Similarly, the generally favoured purposive approach to interpretation enables rules to be read in a way that best serves the justificatory aims of the accounting standards. Legitimation, it may be argued, is best achieved by an affirmation in terms of economic reality. And we have already seen that it is a plausible basis for the justificatory function.

Yet this apparent clean sweep for the economic reality approach to the meaning of the TFV comes up against several difficulties. The chief of these difficulties is that, if the justificatory function is best served by creating appropriate rules, it makes little sense to undermine the role of these rules by allowing for overrides and interpretations that have the effect of making conformity to such rules optional. This is to invite open season for the creative accounting that positive standards are meant to control. In this situation, we need a much more precise meaning for the TFV with respect to the override and interpretive functions than is useful in stating the values and objectives of having the standards and rules in the first place. Indeed, accounting standards cannot simply be seen as having an instrumental role in requiring the provision of information relevant to exhibiting a pre-existing economic reality, for they serve in part to determine what economic reality is taken to be. Accounting standards partly constitute what counts as the real economic position of the company.

This line cannot be taken too far. Any feasible conception of economic reality has to include reference to empirically verifiable and unavoidable realities, such as the capacity of an enterprise to meet its liabilities and provide dividends to its shareholders, but there is considerable scope for identifying softer constituents of 'economic reality' that depend on little more than the general acceptance that certain criteria have a bearing on the sort of economic standing that leads investors to invest.

To the extent that accounting standards determine what counts as economic reality, the idea of justifying these standards by reference to their usefulness for reflecting an independent economic reality undermines the idea that the economic reality meaning of the TFV can operate in the justifying function. However, it also undermines the override function in the same way, in that what would then be happening is a redefinition of economic reality, not a judgment that observance of the standards does not in this instance serve to exhibit that reality.

However, both functions are not undermined to the same extent. The justifying function includes a requirement to make to some extent arbitrary decisions about what standards are to be authoritative in order to achieve the conceptual order required for judging performance and making inter-company comparisons. The override function has no such goal, even though it may actually be used to foster a change in what counts as economic reality.

One way out of this conundrum is to develop the economic reality meaning of a TFV into a more specific theory about what constitutes acceptable indicators of economic reality and how this can be reflected in accounting standards. While I doubt whether this can be refined with a degree of precision that will render the override and interpretive function safe from the dangers of special pleading and self-serving manipulation, it is a task that has to be undertaken anyway for the justificatory function to work.

Making a justifying theory out of the TFV concept is clearly an immense task of great technical and moral complexity, but it is one that must be undertaken if the justificatory function of the TFV has credibility, and it would seem that this function is the only one that will save the TFV from association with a purely rhetorical form of legitimation which does no more than invite the public to 'trust us' (the auditors), or provide courts with a vague principle to legitimate their discretionary power to deal with what they see as unacceptably creative accounting on the grounds that this does not provide a true and fair view in the ordinary and natural meaning of those words. (In practice, courts take the easy way out and fill in the content of the TFV by reference to current accounting practice.)

For whom?

This final section of the chapter is directed at just one aspect of what is involved in developing the idea of a TFV into a justificatory theory of external accounting and auditing: if external accounts should provide a TFV, from whose perspectives are we to consider whether the view in question is true and fair? (See Gaa 1986.) The answer suggested is that the public interest served by auditing must be mediated through considering the interests of a much wider range of users than the traditional investor/shareholder model suggests.

The standard line is that audits are for users (Tweedie & Whittington 1990, p. 87) and these are equated primarily with shareholders, actual and potential. Theory of the audit centres around what these shareholders either want to know or – not the same thing – what they have a right to be told. This assumption is sometimes grounded in the fact that the shareholders are the owners of the company, and are therefore ultimately the persons who are paying the auditors and with whom the auditors have a contract. In short, the audit is one way in which the owners of a company check up on how its managers and workforce are making use of the shareholders' investments. It is a matter of accountability of the agent to the principal.[13]

Given such property and contractual rights, it would certainly seem difficult to deny that shareholders are one major audience for an audit. However, it would be a dubious deontological intuition concerning property rights to say they are the sole group with a legitimate interest in the nature and content of an audit. Ownership does readily imply that there is a right of the owner to exclude others from accessing that property, but this is a right that is routinely qualified by the interests of others in what happens in and with that property.

Nor is the situation necessarily changed by the fact that the shareholders are ultimately paying the auditors. Again, it is a familiar feature of a polity characterised by the rule of law that people can be required to pay for services that are in and for the public interest, such as third-party insurance. It may be the case that companies are required to conduct and pay for audits because of their wider social and economic significance. Indeed, this would seem to be the case, as shareholders are not legally entitled to waive their right to an audit.

This is also clear from the fact that an acceptable theory of the audit cannot terminate in finding out what shareholders want from an audit. Rather, the theories concentrate on what shareholders have the right to get from an audit. But this is not an intuited right, rather it is a deduction from a view of the proper role of the shareholder in a liberal market economy. This is captured in the theory of the rational investor: the person who is committed to investing her money in whatever enterprise will return most by way of dividends and share value.

The model of the rational investor is capable of being interpreted in terms of deontological rights. It can be seen as a fundamental liberty that a person can invest their funds in any way and on any terms they choose and others voluntarily accept, and that right may be seen as including the right to commission an audit for such purposes as they desire. This may indeed be accepted at least as a prima facie right – that is, a right that stands unless good reason is given for its limitation – and harm to others is a standard reason that may be used to

---

[13]David Flint (1988): 'An audit is a form of checking which is demanded when agents expose principals to "moral hazards", because they may act against the principals' interests, and to "information asymmetrics" because they know more than the principals'.

limit such prima facie liberty rights. But it is, at the very least, also an instrumental or consequentialist right due to the role of shareholder investment in the model of an efficient capitalist market economy, which works at its best only when resources are utilised efficiently. On this approach not only are shareholder rights determined by what the rational shareholders need to know to play their part, but the required audience is at the same time extended to include potential investors whose decisions are equally significant for the efficient capitalist economy. And this, of course, explains, or is at least one reason, why audits of public companies are not private documents. This in itself is enough to free up the normative definition of the audit from the determination of shareholders' interests alone. The clients of the audit are at least the investing community as a whole. This is the current orthodoxy.

However, once we allow this extension of audience to potential shareholders and include in the articulation of 'entitlement' what they need to know in order to fulfil a specific role in a market capitalist economy, then we are on a slippery slope towards the inclusion of multiple audiences. Creditors and suppliers can hardly be excluded, given their part in the underwriting of any business activity. Employees too have a role in such economies, in that they should take up and leave employment in the light of their rational calculation of where they can make most money for least work. This leads to the efficient deployment of labour. Employees also require, to play their role, information that is relevant to their determination of what sort of contract to enter into with their employer or potential employer, even if they are not also interested parties through the share ownership they have through their company pension schemes.

Indeed, managers themselves have a legitimate economic interest in an audit that alerts them to inefficiencies or dishonesty in the organisation. Although some of these may be matters more of internal than external audit, others relate to the more personal market decisions that managerial employers have to make, especially when they have artificial incentives to maximise the company's profitability, as is increasingly the case with performance-based pay.

On the other hand, it is clear that one of the major economic and moral issues of corporate governance today is curbing the way in which senior managers are able to treat the resources of their company as if they owned them. Thus, senior management, themselves often without a major investment stake in a company, seem able to reward themselves to excess in the often brief period in which they are effectively in charge of the organisation. Clearly, senior management has an illegitimate interest in disguising the extent of their personal gain as it might emerge in the company's accounts and exaggerating its profitability.

Going in the other direction, towards external interests in the audit – that is, the interests of those who have a particular commercial relationship to the company in question – there are many facets of a public interest in the nature of the economic competition between businesses. The health of the capitalist system depends not only on the existence of competition between manufacturers and service providers, but competition based on adequate information being available to the competitors as well as to the shareholders and potential shareholders.

This model of market efficiency is closely linked to the associated ideal of fair equality of opportunity. It is considered not only inefficient but unfair if opportunities are given to some players in the market economy but not to others, perhaps as a result of insider-trading, selective release of market-related information, legal restrictions on ownership rights or non-discriminatory hiring practices.

Further, given that the profitability of business depends on shareholder confidence in the system generally, this means that all those with a stake in the productivity of an economy have a stake in the prevalence of audits that investors can trust. This is clearly of most direct relevance to financial institutions, including stock exchanges, merchant bankers and investment services generally. And this extends to the interests of the State as regulator of an economy with respect to protecting and fostering economic competition. That interest has economic legitimacy in so far as such regulation is necessary for a free market, and is politically justified to the extent that the State provides infrastructure for business operations and grants privileges to companies with respect to such matters as limited liability.

Fairness may feature here as no more than a synonym for the sort of formal equality of opportunity that maximises market efficiency. Or, more powerfully, fairness may be used to bring in issues of the just distribution of the wealth that is to be maximised, in proportion, for instance, to the value added by the work of those involved. In the latter case, society as a whole has a legitimate interest in the sort of audit that public companies are required to undergo.

In canvassing the range of audiences that might reasonably claim to have a right to true and fair financial reports and trustworthy audits, I have endeavoured to remain within the parameters of a financial audit and to economic justifications that are incontrovertible and draw on purely economic criteria. Clearly, still further audiences enter the picture when we broaden the scope of the audit to take in other social and environmental responsibilities, many of which have, of course, financial implications, for both the business being audited and the financial sustainability of an economy as a whole. As triple bottom lines overlap, so do potential audit audiences, particularly if we depart from the rational investor model to a 'what the actual investor wants to know' model, since actual investors have non-economic as well as economic interests.

It is not possible to follow through all the ramifications of what follows from the admission of multiple audit audiences. All will have different actual expectations and different justified entitlements. This in turn means that what is relevant for one audience may not be so relevant to another, and what one audience needs to know for reasons of economic efficiency may not be necessary for another audience. To some extent this could be met by extending the scope of the information required, or even multiplying the types of audits to suit the different audiences and their roles.

Yet the interests and needs of the audiences are not only different, they are actually in conflict, at least with respect to some matters. Thus, it is in the interests of current shareholders to have a rosy picture of the company's performance made public and legitimated, since this will enhance the value of their shares. But potential investors have an interest in a more accurate picture or they may lose money by investing in the company in the light of its financial reports. Potential creditors may have a similar point of view, but actual creditors may have an outlook similar to existing investors. Employees are likely to have more of an interest in long-term profitability over short-term gain than either shareholders or senior management. And so on.

Of course, these may be conflicts of wants rather than legitimate requirements, and a neutral economic efficiency standpoint might serve to harmonise their legitimate interests in the audit. Thus, actual shareholders may want inside information about the company in which they have invested, but to give them that might render the economy less efficient by distorting the market in those shares. However, it is clear that not all differences between even legitimate audience requirements can be so harmonised, in which case we have a standard political situation in which there is a need to resolve conflicting points of view in a morally acceptable manner − in other words, an issue of fairness, and one to which a TFV may be considered at least linguistically relevant.

This is where we might draw on the ordinary and natural meaning of a TFV, according to which accounts should be presented so as to foster fair equality of opportunity. Here we enter a realm where we cannot simply interpret such terms in a purely aggregative economic dimension that ignores the distributional consequences of any favoured solution.

Applied philosophy can suggest various devices at this point. One of these derives from the famous theory of justice expounded by John Rawls, according to which justice is a form of fairness in which the basic institutions of our society are justified in so far as they approximate to those arrangements that all persons would agree to behind a veil of ignorance − that is, without the knowledge of what particular role or position they would have in society. This is a decision-procedure designed to give equal weight to the preferences of each individual and at the same time to exclude the bias that derives in actual contracts from inequalities and calculations of individual benefit (Rawls 1971).

Applying this model of justice to the fairness between auditing audiences, the decision-procedure would be for representatives of all relevant groups (or stakeholders), who would not know which group they represent. Given that they do not know whether they will be a shareholder, a potential investor, a manager, an employee or an auditor, what would they choose in the light of their general knowledge of how economies and polities work? Would that provide a fair balance on whether preparers are justified in manipulating the rules to minimise the extent of their apparent assets?

Such a model is, however, persuasive principally with respect to the determination of basic universal rights and duties, something in which each individual has an equal legitimate interest. This does apply to the general principles of fair or impartial equality of opportunity and these are not without relevance to the function of a financial audit in a capitalist system. There may indeed be grounds for arguing that, within such a system, individuals have a right to an equal opportunity to make informed investment decisions. But this method of reasoning is not so powerful with respect to the special interests of other players in such economic systems. How do we weigh the (perhaps legitimate) interests of a company not to reveal its commercial secrets and corporate plans, even to its own employees? How do we weigh the (perhaps legitimate) interests of institutional investors with special duties relating to the superannuation rights and hence the basic welfare of large numbers of citizens?

At this point a number of strategies can be adopted. One would be to apply the concept of stakeholders, now widely used in the field of business ethics (Roberts & Mahoney 2004). This has the advantage of pointing us towards the identification of those who have a stake in an enterprise in the sense that they are dependent on its success. We may consider the legitimacy of interests with respect to auditing information as related to the vulnerability of different groups to serious adverse consequences. This tends to shift our focus towards the interests of employees, and investors whose basic material well-being is crucially dependent on the success of their investments. However, the connotations of the idea of 'stakeholders' also points us towards the extent of financial commitment to an enterprise, suggesting that those with larger investments have larger rights to a greater say in all aspects of the company's affairs.

In fact, stakeholder theory is not sufficiently developed to take the issues much further than this. There are radically different relationships between a company of different sorts of 'stakeholders'. The usage of the term is such that it can cover those on whom a company is dependent rather than those who are dependent on the company. And the concept is flexible enough to take in the State, or even the public, amongst those with a legitimate interest in the organisation in question, thus making stakeholders of us all. This may be sound enough in view of the public interest in maintaining the operations of an efficient and fair economy, but it leaves us largely without specific guidance as to who counts when we are deciding what constitutes a TFV.

Another tack is to draw on the developing ideology of human rights as a system of thought that is designed to identify those interests that ought to be overriding in contentious situations of social, economic and political conflict and cooperation. To some extent, this simply takes us back to the question of how far basic rights enter into the identification of specific economic relationships, something which I raised in relation to the application of Rawls' methodology. But it may suggest the need to reconsider some of the priorities that are given to different perspectives, not only those of current and prospective employees, those affected by the operations of multinational corporations in developing countries, and consumers whose health and safety may be at risk as a result of buying or not having access to a company's goods or services.

All this may be viewed as taking us way beyond the scope of financial audits towards ideas of triple bottom lines and wider corporate responsibility for the social and political impact of their activities. Yet it is hard to see how these matters can be divorced from the availability of accurate information as to the financial operations of companies, and what is and what is not to be viewed as an externality from the financial point of view. Does a fair view of a company's financial operations omit the environmental damage that it does not itself have to pay for?

Conclusion

This normative discussion of the legitimate audiences to whom public audits ought to be addressed brings out both the potential and the challenge of developing the idea of a TFV into a comprehensive normative theory of the audit. Whatever the drawbacks of the concept when used for other purposes, it provides perhaps the best starting point for any comprehensive study of the ethics of auditing to draw on the TFV as an outline theory to be used by regulators and by standard-setters.

That said, the justificatory role is not incompatible with using a positivist conception of the TFV as the basis for a presenters' and practicing auditors' ethic that is focused on the accurate implementation of the rules prescribed by the relevant authorities with the objective of generating reliable and comparable measures of a TFV. This excludes using the TFV as a basis for departing from such standards on the basis of broad principles, and probably also excludes requiring auditors to exercise strong discretion by supplementing their reports on the basis of very general principles. But it requires an approach to accounting rules and standards that interprets them as instruments of achieving a TFV.

If accounting standards are well-thought out in terms of the justifying TFV and if they are approached by preparers, auditors and users in the spirit rather than the letter of such standards, then there can be a systemic basis for building trust in a practice that can no longer sustain such trust simply through appeals to the honesty and integrity of the individual auditor. An abandonment of pure commercialism and a return to the 'professional man' model (Reiter & Williams 2004) of the individual auditor cannot by itself restore trust in audits: that is something the system as a whole must regenerate. Yet at the core of the ethics of the audit practitioner must be a respect for and understanding of rules as part of a coordinated effort to provide a systematic approach to achieving the broad public interest objectives of the audit, something that is best captured by the idea of a TFV.

References

Alexander, D. 1999, 'A benchmark for the adequacy of published financial statements', *Accounting and Business Research*, vol. 29, no. 3, pp. 239-53.

Alexander, D. & Archer, S. 2003, 'On economic reality, representational faithfulness and the 'true and fair' override', *Accounting and Business Research*, vol. 33, no. 1, pp. 3-17.

Arden, Hon. Mrs Justice 1997, 'True and fair view: A European perspective', *The European Accounting Review*, vol. 6, no. 4, pp. 675-79.

Bowie, N. E. 2004, 'Why Conflicts of Interest and Abuse of Information Asymmetry Are Keys to Lack of Integrity and What Should Be Done About It', in G. G. Brenkert (ed.), *Corporate Integrity and Accountability*, Sage, London, pp. 61-71.

Deegan, C., Kent, P. & Lin, C. J. 1994, 'The True and Fair View: A Study of Australian Auditors' Application of the Concept', *Australian Accounting Review*, vol. 4, no. 1, pp. 2-12.

Dunfee, T., Glazer, A. S., Jaenicke, H. L., McGrath, S. & Siegel, A. 2004, 'An Ethical Framework for Auditor Independence', in G. G. Brenkert (ed.), *Company Integrity and Accountability*, Sage, London, pp. 72-86.

Duska, R. F. & Duska, B. S. 2003, *Accounting Ethics*, Basil Blackwell, Oxford.

Dworkin, R. M. 1978, *Taking Rights Seriously*, Duckworth, London.

Flint, D. 1988, *Philosophy and Principles of Auditing*, Macmillan, London.

Gaa, J. 1986, 'User primacy in corporate financial reporting: a social contract approach', *The Accounting Review*, vol. 61, no. 3, pp. 435-54.

Gearin, M. & Khandelwal, S. 1995, 'A True and Fair View of Mandatory Standards?', *Australian Accountant*, June, pp. 12-16.

Griffiths, I. 1986, *Creative Accounting: How to Make your Profits What you Want Them to be*, Sidgwick & Jackson, London.

Hopwood, A. G. & Miller, P. (eds) 1994, *Accounting as social and institutional practice*, Cambridge University Press.

Leibler, M. 2003, 'True and Fair – An Imaginary View', *Australian Accounting Review*, vol. 13, no. 3, pp. 61-6.

McBarnet, D. & Whelan, C. 1999, *Creative Accounting and the Cross-Eyed Javelin Thrower*, John Wiley & Sons, Chichester.

Mautz, R. K. & Sharaf, H. A. 1961, *The Philosophy of Auditing*, American Accounting Association, Sarasota, FA.

Moroney, R. & Sidhu, B. K. 2004, 'The Reformed 'True and Fair' Test: How Often does it Trigger Additional Disclosure', *Accounting Research Journal*, vol. 145, no. 1, pp. 6-16.

Nobes, C. W. 1993, 'The true and fair requirement: impact of the fourth directive', *Accounting and Business Research*, vol. 24, no. 93, pp. 35-48.

Power, M. 1997, *The Audit Society: Rituals of Verification*, Oxford University Press.

Rawls, J. 1971, *A Theory of Justice*, Oxford University Press.

Reitner, S. & Williams, P. F. 2004, 'The Philosophy and Rhetoric of Auditor Independence Concepts', *Business Ethics Quarterly*, vol. 14, no. 3, pp. 355-76.

Roberts, R. W. & Mahoney, L. 2004, 'Stakeholder Conceptions of the Corporation: Their Meaning and Influence in Accounting Research', *Business Ethics Quarterly*, vol. 14, no. 3, pp. 399-431.

Smith, A. 1790, *The Theory of Moral Sentiments*, 6th edn, Cadell, London.

Toffler, B. L. & Reingold, J. 2003, *Final Accounting: Ambition, Greed and the Fall of Arthur Andersen*, Broadway Books, New York.

Tweedie, D. & Whittington, G. 1990, 'Financial Reporting: Current Problems and Their Implications for Systematic Reform', *Accounting and Business Research*, vol. 21, no. 81, pp. 87-102.

Part II. Auditor independence

Chapter 6. Conflicts of interest in auditing: are they conducive to corruption?[1]

Edward Spence

Abstract

This chapter will examine and discuss the question whether conflicts of interest in the accountancy and auditing profession are conducive to corruption. In undertaking this enquiry, I will first define what a conflict of interest is and under what type of circumstances and conditions it can arise. The types of circumstances and conditions in which a conflict of interest arises will be illustrated through an examination and discussion of the financial collapse of Enron. In the second part of the chapter I will offer a conceptual account of corruption through an examination of its key features; features that are normally, if not always, present in typical cases of corruption. Through the use of this conceptual account of corruption, I will demonstrate how conflicts of interest in auditing and accounting, as illustrated by the case of Enron, can potentially lead to and result in corruption. Finally, I will discuss ways by which conflicts of interest can be dealt with. Ultimately, the best ethical and governance policy for dealing with conflicts of interest in auditing is to avoid them altogether, as mere disclosure does not eliminate a conflict of interest and its continuing presence thus remains a potential risk that might contribute to corruption.

Introduction

One of the most important facilitators of corruption is conflict of interest. A conflict of interest occurs when a person or group's self-regarding interest comes into conflict with their fiduciary duties, or when a person or group has two fiduciary roles and the duties of one compete with the duties of the other. For example, if a member of the Tax Office decided to adjudicate his own tax return, he would have a conflict between his personal self-interest and his fiduciary duty. Again, if an accountant happened also to be the manager of a football club,

[1]Some of the material in this paper has appeared previously in a different context and format in Miller, S., Roberts, P. and Spence, E. 2005, *Corruption and Anti-Corruption: An Applied Philosophical Approach*, Prentice Hall, Englewood Cliffs, NJ.

and as an accountant he was asked to audit the club's financial statements, he would have a conflict of interest.

Conflicts of interest are conducive to corruption in a variety of ways, depending on the nature of the role of the person or group that has the conflict of interest. For example, a magistrate or police officer with a conflict of interest may fail to apply the law impartially, or a businessman who is a member of a local government body might vote to award himself a contract.

Conflicts of interest can be hard to determine, and sometimes an apparent conflict of interest might turn out on closer inspection to be more of an instance of role ambiguity or confusion rather than a genuine conflict of interest. However, because appearances of impropriety can be harmful to reputations and to trust, it is important to clarify and resolve apparent conflicts of interest as well as to avoid real ones. It is also important to ensure that the precise nature and boundaries of fiduciary and other roles are clearly delineated and rendered perspicuous. For if this is not done, role confusion can arise, and with it the possibility of intended or unintended conflicts of interest.

What is a conflict of interest?

Before we proceed further, let us first determine what a conflict of interest is.

According to the 'standard view' (Davis 1998, p. 590):

> A conflict of interest is a situation in which some person P (whether an individual or corporate body) has a conflict of interest. P has a conflict of interest if and only if (1) P is in a relationship with another requiring P to exercise judgement in the other's behalf and (2) P has a (special) interest tending to interfere with the proper exercise of judgement in that relationship. The crucial terms in this definition are 'relationship', 'judgement', 'interest' and 'proper exercise'.

The 'relationship' required must be fiduciary; that is, it must involve one person trusting (or at least being entitled to trust) another to exercise judgment in his service. 'Judg(e)ment' is the ability to make certain kinds of decisions that require knowledge or skill correctly and reliably. 'Interest' is any influence, loyalty, concern, emotion or other feature of a situation tending to make P's judgment (in that situation) less reliable than it would normally be. 'Proper exercise' of judgment is normally a question of social fact and includes what people ordinarily expect, what P or the group P belongs to invite others to expect, and what various laws, professional codes or other regulations require (Davis 1998, p. 590).

What is generally wrong with a conflict of interest is that it renders one's judgment less reliable than it normally should be and results in a failure or abuse of a fiduciary duty.

Types of conflicts of interest

Generally, a conflict of interest can arise in at least one of two ways:

1. One has a self-regarding interest that is in conflict, or at least potentially so, with one's fiduciary duty, having the tendency to interfere with the proper exercise of one's judgment with regard to that duty.
2. One has two potentially competing fiduciary duties or roles that are in conflict with each other, or at least potentially so, having the tendency to interfere with the proper exercise of one's judgment with regard to one or the other of the two competing duties or roles so that one is not able to properly exercise both.

So, for example, there is a clear conflict of interest in the case of an accountant who is also the manager of a football club and audits the financial statements of his club. For his special interest in the club as manager would have a tendency to make his judgment as auditor less reliable than what it ordinarily should be, because it would be less objective and independent than what would normally be expected of a disinterested auditor. The conflict of interest arises as a direct result of the conflict between the two competing roles in which the football club accountant-cum-manager is engaged, such that it has a tendency to interfere with one or the other of those two competing roles and the respective fiduciary duties associated with each.

Crucially, for the purpose of this chapter, conflicts of interest are conducive to corruption. So, for example, a police officer who also moonlights for a security firm faces a conflict of interest when called upon to investigate criminal allegations against the manager of the security firm. The police officer's personal interest in keeping his additional job conflicts with the requirements of his role as a police officer, and may interfere with the proper exercise of his judgment in fulfilling his fiduciary duty of upholding the law. Again, a judge who presides over a criminal trial which involves his daughter as defendant in a rape case has a conflict of interest. Notice that the police officer in the first case, and the judge in the second, may not in fact necessarily be acting corruptly; each may well intend to do his duty – by investigating the criminal allegation thoroughly (in the case of the police officer) or conducting the trial fairly (in the case of the judge). However, in each case the conflict of interest remains, and therefore there is a real or apparent inability to properly discharge their role requirements.

The above examples illustrate that although a conflict of interest might not in the first instance necessarily involve or result in corruption, it can nevertheless provide the conditions which might facilitate corruption. Thus, it is better for all concerned if the conflict of interest is avoided; for example, another judge with no familial connections to the defendant is appointed to the trial. In cases in which the conflict of interest is not too severe and is not avoidable, it may be possible for the person with the conflict of interest to carry on, if the conflict is disclosed and managed in an apparent and accountable way.

In sum, many conflicts of interest involve a conflict between one's self-interest and the requirements of the role one occupies. Others involve a conflict between two different roles one occupies. Still others involve a role confusion which serves to mask a conflict of interest.

Conflicts of interest involving self-interest are reasonably obvious, but what of role conflicts? By way of illustration, consider the fact that some professions or occupations or businesses impose a restriction under which one could not be, for example, both judge and advocate, or editor and manager of advertising revenue of a newspaper, or cashier and accounts payable/receivable manager of a large corporation. Underlying this institutional division of potentially conflicting roles is the principle of the division and separation of responsibilities, so that the proper exercise of one's judgment cannot be adversely affected by allowing one to occupy two potentially conflicting roles or functions. The role conflicts primarily involve a conflict between two roles, offices or institutions. Traditionally, a Western democratic state is divided into distinct institutional 'estates' — for example, the government and the judiciary — whose functions are by design supposed to remain separate and independent, at least in theory. The separateness and independence of these institutions from one another is designed to ensure the division of power, and also to ensure that potentially harmful conflicts of interest are avoided.

Conflicts of interest in the accounting and auditing profession

Let us now examine the different types of conflicts of interest that may and do arise in the accounting and auditing profession through an examination of the Enron case. As indicated earlier, conflicts of interest may involve a conflict between one's self-interest and the requirements of the role one occupies, or a conflict between two different roles one occupies, or further, they may involve a role confusion which serves to mask a conflict of interest. In order to place the auditors' conflict of interest involved in the Enron case within a practical and professional context, it is important to provide in outline the general financial climate that was prevalent within Enron prior to its collapse. It was indeed this general financial climate which contributed to and precipitated the fall of Enron and it auditors, Arthur Andersen.

The chief financial officer (CFO)

The CFO traditionally is the executive officer within an organisation entrusted with enuring that the company operates with financial discipline and propriety and not excess and impropriety. However, in a business environment where investors are expecting and demanding ever-increasing earnings every financial quarter, CFOs come under constant pressure to 'cook the books' and make them look better than they are (Lindorff 2002, p. 2). This places CFOs in two potentially conflicting roles; the traditional role of policing the integrity and accuracy of the accounts and financial statements of a company, and the contemporary 'role' of making sure that the quarterly earnings of the company look the best that they can, even at times assisting this outcome by recourse to some 'creative' accounting. This conflict of roles creates, in turn, a conflict of interest that has the tendency, at least potentially, of interfering with the proper exercise of the CFO's fiduciary duty of ensuring the integrity and accuracy of the company's financial statements – a duty entrusted to them by the board of directors and the shareholders of the company, as well as prospective investors who require true and fair financial statements on which to base their informed investment decisions.

Andrew Fastow's dual role as both CFO of Enron and manager of the Special Purpose Entities (SPEs) involved a serious conflict of interest, one which Fastow, as the company's financial watch-dog in his role of CFO, should have avoided. Andrew Fastow joined Enron in 1990 as a banking expert and quickly rose to power to become CFO, which, after Ken Lay and Jeffrey Skilling's positions as Chairman and CEO respectively, was the third most influential position within Enron. At the daily financial operational level, it was perhaps the most influential, which might help explain why Fastow, who masterminded a web of very complex off balance sheet partnership arrangements (the SPEs) that had the effect of hiding debt and inflating earnings, is considered to be one of the primary architects behind Enron's spectacular collapse.

Special Purpose Entities, which were Fastow's specialty, were initially introduced by banks and law firms as 'structured finance', complex financial deals intended to enable companies to generate tax deductions and move assets off a company's books (Behr & Witt 2002). With names such as Cactus[2], Braveheart, Whitewing, JEDI, Chewco, LJM 1 and 2 (the initials standing for Fastow's wife Lea and his two children) and Raptors, Enron used SPEs for various purposes. The primary purpose was for financing new projects in Enron's ever-expanding trading business – which continually needed new injections of cash funds to sustain the expansion – as well as providing insurance-hedging for those projects whilst

---

[2]Not a name that Fastow would have chosen if the SPE was launched in Australia, due to the adverse connotations of the term 'cactus' in the Australian vernacular, as used in the phrase 'It's cactus!', meaning that something has flopped or gone belly-up, or it's gone bad and is no good.

managing, sometimes legally but mostly illegally, to keep debt related to them off its balance sheet and taking up earnings relating to those projects in its income statements. For his role in those SPEs, Andrew Fastow reportedly made more than $45 million (all amounts in US dollars). In the wake of the revelations concerning Fastow's key role in the Enron SPEs, especially Chewco and the LJMs, and just one month prior to Enron's final collapse and bankruptcy on 2 December 2001, the company was forced to restate its earnings from 1997 through to 2002, which required a $1.2 billion equity write-down.

Chewco alone accounted for the inflation of earnings by $405 million from 1997 through to 2000, which Enron was not entitled to have on its books, and the concealment of a $600 million-debt which, by contrast, Enron was required to show on its books. Named after Chewbacca, the character from *Star Wars*, Chewco was set up to buy out the share of equity of the California Public Employees' Retirement System (Calpers) in JEDI 1 (another Enron SPE alluding to *Star Wars*).

The main problem with Chewco, it seems, was that Enron did not meet the 3% investment rule, which required that at least 3% of equity in the SPE be held by an independent investor not associated with the company. Because this rule was not met in the case of Chewco, Enron was not legally allowed to keep the SPE off its balance sheet.

Given the complexity of the Enron SPEs – and the complexity seems now to have been intended as a deliberate ploy to obfuscate and render opaque the real purpose to outsiders – it is difficult to explain in great detail their intricate financial mechanisms. However, by focusing on one of the SPEs, LJM, which together with Chewco proved to be the catalyst that brought down the Enron empire, this much seems clear: whilst Chewco was at the periphery of financial impropriety, LJM proved to be its very nucleus.[3]

LJM and its successor LJM 2 were set up to finance an array of deals. The original LJM was set up to finance the Rhythms deal in March 1998, a deal that saw Enron invest $10 million for a block of shares in Rhythms NetConnections, a high-speed Internet service provider. As is usual with dot.com companies, Rhythms went public (in April 1999) and its shares climbed rapidly, making Enron's investment worth $300 million. Because Enron's accounting rules required the company to mark the shares to market on a daily basis – 'mark-to-market' – it meant that Enron had already booked $290 million in profits on the transaction. Concerned, however, that the profit might be reduced or turn to a loss in the future – which would require Enron to take into account substantial losses – the company had to cover for that contingency. Not allowed to sell the

---

[3]My account of the LJM SPEs refers primarily to the account given of those deals in Fusaro, P. C. and Miller, R. M. 2002, *What Went Wrong with Enron*, John Wiley & Sons, Hoboken, NJ, pp. 132-5.

shares for several months, until the end of 1999, Enron wanted to get insurance against a fall in the value of those shares. Traditionally, the way to acquire insurance is through the purchase of a 'put option'. A put option locks in a specific sale price for the shares for the life of the option. So, for example, with Rhythms trading at $65 per share, Enron might have wanted to purchase a put option until it could sell them at the end of 1999 at a lock-in price of $60. The option would not cover the first $5 of loss, but it would cover any remaining loss that might arise dollar for dollar.

The problem for Enron, however, was that its block of shares in Rhythms was so large, and the company so risky, that no one would be willing to provide insurance at a price that Enron considered reasonable. Fastow's solution was to create a company he would manage that used Enron stock as its capital to sell the insurance on Rhythms stock to Enron. Essentially, this amounted to Enron insuring itself! If the insurance was never needed, no one would be the wiser, and Fastow and his partners in the scheme, who were chosen from among his subordinates within the company, could pocket most of the premium that Enron paid, making them quite wealthy. If the Rhythms stock fell dramatically, then the Enron stock that hedged the company would cover the losses. However, if both Rhythms and Enron stocks suffered a significant fall, the company would go broke unless someone bailed it out. However, because Enron was in effect insuring itself, there really was no insurance.

What defies understanding was that such a scheme passed Enron's board, its auditors Arthur Andersen, and its law firm Vinson and Elkins. According to the Powers Report[4], the Enron board approved a waiver of its code of ethics to allow Fastow to set up LJM, which covered the Rhythms deal. As we shall see, it wouldn't be the first time that the ethics of the company and its corporate governance regulations were compromised by Fastow's SPEs. Though committed to ethics on the surface, Enron's cut-throat corporate culture was not designed to allow ethical niceties and sensibilities to get in the way of its trading and financial activities. The cultural ethos at Enron, from the employees to the executives, had a lot more to do with profits – the more the better – and the share value of Enron stock – the higher the better – and very little to do with ethics. The profit incentives at Enron that ruled supreme, and which favoured self-interest gain above all, could not allow ethical considerations to take hold. It was only as a result of people killing the goose that laid the golden eggs, even if those eggs were made of paper, that those both within and outside Enron started taking ethics more seriously.

---

[4]The Powers Report was a 218-page report on Enron's SPEs prepared by the Powers Committee. The committee was formed by Enron's board of directors at the same time that Fastow was fired from Enron. Its mission was to investigate Fastow's dealings. William Powers, the dean of the University of the Texas Law School, led the committee. Powers was recruited as a board member in October 2001 to give Enron and the committee much needed credibility.

The sequel to LJM, LJM 2, took Fastow's ingenuity in coming up with ever more complex and ethically and legally dubious SPEs to new heights. Whilst LJM 1 was used to provide a faulty hedge in a profitable investment in the Rhythms deal, the deals which LJM 2 helped finance, and which were named 'Raptors' after the cunning dinosaurs in the film *Jurassic Park*, were used to hide the losses of unprofitable projects. In total, LJM 2 was used to conceal $1.1 billion of Enron losses. Fastow's secret profit from LJM 1 and the Rhythms deal alone was a staggering $22 million – from a $1 million investment in little less than a year! When such profits are to be had, with the incentives for fraud and corruption existing under such favourable conditions as secrecy, power and greed that feeds self-interest to the detriment of the interest of others, as well as a total disregard for fiduciary duty abetted by a corporate culture that encourages greed and the pursuit of self-regarding gain, it's no wonder that corruption was allowed to thrive within Enron. Add to that an array of conflicts of interest involving Enron's board of directors, its executive officers like Fastow and Skilling, its auditors and lawyers, the media, the investment banks, and generally the ethos of generating and claiming ever new profits for the company by Enron's trading whiz kids always seeking to increase their yearly profit-linked bonuses, and what emerges is a case of corruption waiting to happen. That it happened is not surprising, given that all the usual conditions and causes for corruption were present within the Enron organisation. What is, however, surprising is that it took so long, and required the collapse of the seventh-largest company in the United States, to uncover it.

When Jeffrey McMahon, the company's treasurer, complained to Skilling about the conflict of interest regarding Fastow and his management of the SPEs, he was at first confronted by Fastow (who was told of the complaint by Skilling) and a week later was transferred to another part of the company and replaced by Ben F. Glisan, a close aid and associate of Fastow. It seems that if you can't get rid of a conflict of interest, the next best thing is to get rid of those that issue warnings and complain about it!

The dealmakers

The practice of Enron's in-house dealmakers, or 'developers', of launching new deals irrespective of the risks involved, so they could immediately claim huge profits for the company and collect lucrative bonuses for themselves whilst postponing the problems for later, may be viewed as involving another conflict of interest. Their interest in earning immediate big bonuses for themselves through risky deals was potentially in conflict with their fiduciary duty of enhancing the earnings of the company in the long term, not simply by means of quick paper profits but in real terms. This may have had the tendency to interfere with the proper exercise of their judgment concerning the prudence and financial viability of those deals with regard to the company's long-term interests.

The auditors

In so far as the role of an auditor is potentially in conflict with the role of a financial adviser, when one accountant performs both roles for the same client there is a conflict of interest. Thus we have potential conflicts of interest in accounting firms that perform audits for the companies for which they also provide lucrative financial consultancy and other financial management services. Here the latter role has a tendency to curtail the auditor's independence, and can thus potentially interfere with the proper exercise of an auditor's fiduciary duty of ensuring that a company's financial accounts present a true and fair view of the company's operations. The role of Arthur Andersen in Enron's collapse is a case in point, and crucially highlights this conflict as potentially conducive to corporate corruption.

In 2000, General Electric paid KPMG $23.9 million for audit work and $79.7 million for consultancy work. Similarly, J. P. Morgan Chase paid PricewaterhouseCoopers $21.3 million in audit fees, but $84.2 million for other management services including consultancy. These examples inevitably invite the question as to whether the 'independent auditor' might only be an illusion (Drummond 2002, p. 6).

The ethically problematic nature of the practice of providing both consultancy and auditing services for clients by accountancy firms, as exemplified in the Enron case, also illustrates an important conceptual distinction between *external instrumentalism* on the one hand, and *internal instrumentalism* on the other. According to Alan Gewirth (1986, p. 295):

> In an external instrumentalism, the means or instrument is external to the end, in that it need not have any of the distinctive characteristics of the end. In internal instrumentalism, on the other hand, the means or instrument is internal to the end: it is instrumental to the end not only causally but also conceptually in that its features are also constitutive of the end. It serves as an instrument to the end by enforcing, reinstating, or in some other way bringing about a certain result, while at the same time it embodies distinctive characteristics of the result.

As an example of the two types of instrumentalism, Gewirth refers to a university lecture. If the lecture is given simply for the purpose of earning money, then the lecture, as a means or instrument, is external to the end of spreading enlightenment or understanding on the lectured topic, which are conceptually distinct from financial gain. By contrast, in the case of a lecture given for the purpose of spreading enlightenment and understanding on the lectured topic, the lecture, as means or instrument, is internal to the end: both the means and the end of lecturing conform to the same intellectual criteria of spreading enlightenment or improving understanding of the subject matter.

In the case of the practice of providing both consultancy and auditing services (for easy reference I will refer to this practice as 'conauditing'), there is a conflict between the dictates of internal instrumentalism and those of external instrumentalism. In the case of auditing, the purpose is to provide independent public assurance, by way of the certification offered in the auditors' report, that the financial statements of a corporate entity, whether private or public, present a true and fair view – one that can be relied upon with regard to accuracy and completeness by all relevant stakeholders. As such, both the means and the end of providing that type of independent public assurance must conform to the same conceptual and professional criteria of providing reliable certification as to the true and fair view of a corporate entity's financial statements. By contrast, the primary purpose of offering accounting and consultancy services to a corporation is to provide the corporation with the best financial planning, so as to facilitate the successful application and implementation of financial accounting practices and policies for maximising the corporation's profits and assets and minimising its losses and liabilities. Moreover, such financial consultancy is designed to enable the corporation to present its financial statements in the best light possible within the law so as to enhance its market profile, thus rendering it attractive to prospective investors. As such, the strategies of financial consultancy are external to the concern of ensuring that the corporation's financial statements are true and fair – not merely from the corporation's internal subjective perspective, but equally from the independent external and objective perspective of all relevant stakeholders. As the case of Enron illustrates, creative accounting policies employed to make the accounts look good, even when conforming to corporate law, need not reflect a true and fair view, especially as regards the interests of the shareholders – prospective investors as well as other relevant stakeholders that have an interest that the information provided in a corporation's financial statements is actually, and not merely cosmetically, true and fair.

Conauditing practices seek to have it both ways: with regard to auditing they conform to a principle of internal instrumentalism, but with regard to consultancy they conform to a principle of external instrumentalism that seems to be inherently incompatible with the internal instrumental auditing function of providing public assurance that a corporation's accounts are true and fair.

Conflicts of interest and corruption

What is wrong with conflicts of interest?

In the first place, what is generally morally wrong with conflicts of interest? There are at least three reasons why conflicts of interest may be considered morally wrong:[5]

1. A person, P, involved in a conflict of interest may be negligent in allowing himself to get involved in the conflict, and also negligent in not responding to it. For in so far as P is unaware of the conflict of interest in which he is involved, he has failed to exercise proper duty of care and judgment for the benefit of those to whom he owes a fiduciary duty, and thus he has acted negligently, which is morally wrong.

2. If those to whom P owes a fiduciary duty are unaware of the conflict of interest in which P is involved and P knows this (or at least should know it), and does not reveal the conflict to them, then he has acted deceptively, and deception for one's self-gain at the expense of others is morally wrong.

3. Notwithstanding that P has disclosed his conflict of interest, the conflict of interest still remains, if not as a moral problem then at least as a technical problem which can still be ethically problematic if it harms the reputation of P's profession or institution. This goes to show that the best remedy for resolving conflicts of interest is to avoid them in the first place whenever possible.

With regard to corruption, it is the conflicts of interest in the second category of moral wrongness that is relevant, as it is the only one of the three categories that involves deception or the intention to deceive, which together with concealment is usually, if not always, one of the characterising features of corruption. Negligence in responding to conflicts of interest or disclosure of them that results in harm to one's profession or institution would still count as morally wrong, but not as a moral wrong that qualifies as corruption due to the absence of deception and concealment.

In so far as corruption is morally wrong, conflicts of interest which facilitate or result in corruption are also morally wrong. And to the extent that they do actually or potentially contribute to corruption, they should be avoided. How do they in fact facilitate corruption? Before we attempt to address that question, let us first briefly determine what corruption is.

---

[5]For what is wrong with conflict of interest, see Davis (1998), p. 590. To the extent that conflict of *interests* usually also involve conflict of interest, the same reasons regarding the moral wrongness of conflict of interest apply also to conflict of interests.

What is corruption?

Let me say at the outset that, although related, corruption and immorality are not the same thing. Though corruption is always immoral, not all immoral acts qualify as corruption. Though immoral, the actions of a house burglar or bank robber, for example, are not what we would normally describe as corrupt. The missing condition is a socially, professionally or institutionally pre-established fiduciary relationship of trust between the corrupt person or group and the person or group who are harmed in some way by the corrupt person or group's actions. The reason why house burglars or bank robbers, though typically deemed immoral, are not deemed corrupt is because there is an absence of a prior fiduciary relationship of trust between the burglar or bank robber on the one hand, and those who are harmed by their actions on the other; namely, the householders or the banks and their customers. By contrast, typical cases of corruption, and its sub-species fraud, involve a breach of a socially, professionally or institutionally pre-established fiduciary relationship of trust between the corrupt agents and their victims. The addition of the condition of a fiduciary duty is in keeping with one of the traditional dictionary definitions of corruption; namely, 'the changing from the naturally sound condition' or 'the turning from a sound into an unsound impure condition' or ' the perversion of anything from an original state of purity'.[6] The fiduciary relationship can be articulated in political, professional, social or familial, or corporate terms.

Typical cases of corruption will normally involve the abuse of a socially, professionally or institutionally pre-established fiduciary duty of trust for self-interest, that may involve individual or group interest under concealment and the absence of transparency that is conducive to an absence of accountability.

How are conflicts of interest conducive to corruption?

First and most obviously, conflicts of interest involving a conflict between self-interest and the requirements of one's role can lead to one pursuing one's self-interest at the expense of the role requirements. So these sorts of conflicts of interest are a direct threat to the proper performance of institutional and professional roles.

Role conflicts can lead to corruption when the conflicts interfere and subvert or pervert the proper function of a process, profession, practice or institution. Crucially, cases of corruption will usually and typically involve a conflict of interest, especially those that involve role conflicts, though a conflict of interest of itself would not necessarily amount to corruption, as some other key features of corruption might be absent. So, for example, a police officer who accepts a

---

[6]See the *Shorter Oxford Dictionary* (1973).

bribe to drop a criminal charge is corrupt and his corruption involves a conflict of interest; his interest in money conflicts with his duty as a police officer to uphold the law. However, a judge who merely presides over a rape trial which involves his daughter as defendant has a conflict of interest, though the judge is not acting corruptly if his intention is to conduct the trial fairly. His problem won't be one of corrupt activity, but simply a case of a perceived and real inability to properly exercise his judgment as a judge impartially. He would, on the other hand, be acting corruptly if he arranged to have false evidence presented against the person charged with his daughter's rape so as to secure a guilty verdict and the suspect's imprisonment. Thus, in the former case, mentioned earlier in this chapter, of the judge who merely presides over a trial that involves his daughter, and which he intends to conduct fairly and impartially, there is a conflict of interest but no corruption. In the latter case, however, there is both corruption and a conflict of interest. Moreover, the conflict of interest has facilitated the corrupt activity of the judge in allowing him the opportunity to exercise his power to secretly engineer false evidence against the accused for the sole purpose of securing a guilty verdict and the suspect's punishment. In the latter case but not the former, some of the key characterising features of corruption, such as the abuse of public office for self-interest under concealment and lack of transparency, are present. Therefore, although a conflict of interest is necessary for corruption, it is not sufficient.

The above example illustrates that although a conflict of interest might not in the first instance necessarily involve, or result in, corruption, it can nevertheless provide the conditions, and perhaps one of the necessary conditions, which might facilitate corruption. Thus, it is better for all concerned if the conflict of interest is avoided (another judge with no familial connections to the defendant is appointed to the trial), or if that is not possible (the defendant's father is the only judge in town), the conflict is disclosed and managed in an apparent and accountable way where strict procedures of due course are followed and recorded throughout the trial.

In the case of Enron, for example, the potentially conflicting roles and interests of Arthur Andersen, in their dual capacity as both financial consultants and auditors of the company, may have created the conditions that facilitated the corrupt activities of which Enron now stands accused. That is, the conflict between Arthur Andersen's dual role as auditors and financial consultants may have been a major contributing factor in their failure to exercise proper diligence and care in auditing Enron's financial statements. This was a care which Arthur Andersen owed to Enron's shareholders, which included a large number of the company's employees, a stakeholding group to whom Arthur Andersen owed a fiduciary duty in their capacity as auditors. That fiduciary duty was, however, undermined by their role as financial consultants of Enron. By virtue of that role, Arthur Andersen owed a fiduciary duty to Enron's management, which undermined their role as independent auditors and made them complicit, by association if not by direct involvement, in dubious accounting practices that had the effect of concealing debt and inflating earnings. If the Arthur Andersen auditors knew of those accounting practices (or should have known about them) and did not inform those to whom they owed a fiduciary duty – that is, all the Enron shareholders, and not just the company directors who held large numbers of Enron shares – then they were responsible for deception, by omission if not commission, and thus responsible for the corrupt activities of which Enron stands accused.

Deception or the intention to deceive is crucial in determining the level of moral responsibility of the Arthur Andersen auditors in relation to Enron's corrupt activities. It is hard to imagine that the level of corruption at Enron would not have been known to the auditors and that their moral failure was merely one of negligence. However, whether it turns out to be complicity in corruption or mere negligence of care, the role of the Arthur Andersen auditors with regard to Enron highlights one of the core problems concerning conflicts of interest: role conflicts that involve a conflict of interest relating to outcomes concerning stakeholder groups, to whom one has conflicting fiduciary duties, can potentially facilitate or result in corruption.

In sum, in their role as auditors Arthur Andersen may have participated in, or at least tolerated, the concealment and later destruction of evidence that revealed deceptive and misleading accounting practices and policies in the financial reporting of Enron's accounts which no doubt contributed to the corruption within the company, and thus are indirectly if not directly partly responsible for the corrupt accounting practices within Enron.

How to deal with conflicts of interest

Avoidance

The most obvious way to deal with conflicts of interest that actually or potentially facilitate or result in corruption is to avoid them whenever possible.

Potential role conflicts can best be avoided through a strict division of duties and responsibilities that does not allow one of the opposing roles to exert undue influence over the other. For example, the division of accounting responsibilities between the cashiering and banking functions on the one hand, and the accounts payable and receivable functions on the other hand, reduces the risk of a conflict of interest between those two functions that may otherwise facilitate potential corruption.

A further way of reducing conflicts of interest arising from conflicting role obligations is to institute a strict division and separation of roles between members of professions or other institutions that owe fiduciary duties to different groups of stakeholders with potentially conflicting interests. For example, in the case of accountants, conflicts of interest can best be avoided through the strict division and separation of the auditing and financial consultancy functions within an accounting firm. However, this control may not be adequate to avoid conflicts of interest in situations, as the ones at present, where fees from financial consultancy services far exceed auditing fees. One possible solution to this problem is to increase audit fees substantially to at least match those from financial consultancy services, or, if that is not possible, require accounting firms to choose to undertake one but not both of the two potentially conflicting roles. Under this envisaged scheme, accounting firms that specialise in auditing would be precluded from acting as financial consultants to their clients, or alternatively, from auditing the accounts of their financial consultancy clients. The problem, of course, with either suggestion is that they might not prove to be feasible or practical for implementation.

The overall problem with this type of conflict of interest is that sometimes either the role or the stakeholding groups to whom one has fiduciary duties are not clearly defined or delineated. This allows the ambiguity of roles and fiduciary duties to render this type of conflict of interest opaque, if not entirely concealed. In the case of auditors, to whom do they owe their primary fiduciary duty? If it is to the majority of the shareholders, then their role as financial consultants to a client, as in the case of Arthur Andersen and Enron, can compromise that role and might, under certain circumstances, lead to corruption – to the overall detriment of the shareholders.

Disclosure

It may not, however, always be possible to avoid conflicts of interest, so the next best solution is to disclose them. One of the main conditions conducive to corruption is concealment or secrecy, which enables the agency of the corrupt person or group to remain undetected, thus allowing the corrupt person or group to engage in corruption with impunity and without fear of retribution. Accordingly, disclosure of conflicts of interest, if exercised stringently and properly, can be an effective control measure against corruption by eliminating or at least reducing one of its contributing factors, namely concealment or secrecy.

Apparent conflicts of interest can be as ethically problematic as actual conflicts of interest, because of their tendency to mislead people and create in their minds uncertainty concerning the reliability and integrity of the judgment of those from whom they have a legitimate expectation of a fiduciary duty of trust. The best way to avoid such apparent conflicts of interest is by disclosing sufficient information to demonstrate that there are no actual or potential conflicts of interest.

This is important because a suspicion of corruption regarding a person or institution created by merely apparent conflicts of interest can be as damaging to public confidence in that person or institution as actual or potential conflicts of interest. It is precisely for this reason that transparency as an anti-corruption measure is important, not only as a way of preventing corruption through eliminating or reducing one of its key contributing conditions – namely, concealment or secrecy – but also for preserving and maintaining public confidence in persons, professions, practices, processes and public institutions by eliminating or at least reducing the appearance of conflicts of interest.

Conclusion

Are conflicts of interest in auditing conducive to corruption? In so far as the role of auditor is potentially in conflict with the role of financial adviser when the same person performs both roles for a client, there is a conflict of interest. Thus we have conflicts of interest in accounting firms that perform audits for the companies for which they also provide lucrative financial consultancy and other financial management services. Here the latter role has a tendency to curtail or diminish the auditor's independence, and can thus potentially interfere with the proper exercise of an auditor's fiduciary duty of ensuring that a company's financial statements present a true and fair view of the company's operations. The role of Arthur Andersen in Enron's collapse is a case in point, showing how conflicts of interest in auditing can contribute to and result in corruption. Conflicts of interest in auditing should thus be avoided wherever possible, as their mere disclosure does not remove the conflict of interest and hence does not remove its capacity to cause corruption, as in the Enron case.

References

Behr, P. & Witt, A. 2002, 'Visionary's Dream Led to Risky Business', *Washington Post*, 28 July. (Behr and Witt are *Washington Post* staff writers.)

Davis, M. 1998, 'Conflict of Interest', in R. Chadwick (ed.), *Encyclopedia of Applied Ethics*, Academic Press, Orlando, FA, vol. 1, A-D, p. 590.

Drummond, M. 2002, 'Class action warrior', *Salon*, 28 January, p. 6, viewed 27 February 2003, http://www.salon.com.

Gewirth, A. 1986, 'Professional Ethics: The Separatist Thesis', *Ethics*, 96, pp. 282-300.

Lindorff, D. 2002, 'Chief fudge-the-books officer', *Salon*, 20 February, p. 2, viewed 27 February 2003, http://www.salon.com.

Chapter 7. Attachments between directors and auditors: do they affect engagement tenure?

Nicholas P Courtney
Christine A Jubb

Abstract

Auditors and directors may develop personal attachments over time based on trust and familiarity, and these personal ties seem important for the maintenance of long-term auditor-client relationships. This study examines the tenure of the audit engagement in the presence of these links, which is expected to be longer than auditor-client relationships not so linked. Results indicate director-auditor links are positively associated with auditor tenure and the retention of auditors beyond the critical four-year period identified by Levinthal and Fichman (1988).

Introduction and motivation

It has been argued that auditing is a service that is difficult to evaluate without being experienced, since its quality is not easily discernible (Pennings, Lee & van Witteloostuijn 1998; Craswell & Francis 1999). In such a circumstance, relationships between individuals are likely to influence the decision to select, or continue, relationships with service providers (Koreto & Harding 1996).

The impact of personal connections in exchange relationships has been well-established (e.g., Pfeffer 1994), and these ties have been examined in the context of auditing service provision. One of these studies, Davison, Stening and Wai (1984), investigates the impact of personal attachments (captured by interlocking directorates)[1] on choice of auditor. Davison, Stening and Wai report a positive and significant association between the number of director interlocks attributable to a company and the probability that the interlocked companies are audited by the same public accounting firm. Jubb (2000), employing a more robust and

---

[1] The terms 'interlocking directorate', 'interlocking directorship', 'multiple directorship' and the more generic term 'interlocks' are used interchangeably throughout this chapter to describe the phenomenon of a director sitting on the board of directors of more than one company.

detailed empirical analysis, finds results consistent with those of Davison, Stening and Wai.

The primary purpose of this study is to investigate the association of director-auditor links with auditor tenure. That is, where companies with interlocking directors are audited by the same public accounting firm, it is expected that the tenure of that auditor is significantly longer than for that in respect of companies not so linked.

A secondary purpose of this study is to investigate whether the personal attachments measured by director-auditor links are associated with mitigation of the pressure for an auditor switch during the critical initial four-year period found by Levinthal and Fichman (1988).

The next section examines the relevant literature surrounding the relationship between interlocking directorates and the selection and retention of auditors.

Previous literature

For some time the incidence of interlocking directorates has been acknowledged and studied (for example, Dooley 1969; Allen 1974; Alexander, Murray & Houghton 1994) and explanations have been offered for this phenomenon (Mizruchi 1996; Allen 1974). One of the main reasons suggested for the existence of interlocking directorates is that these associations reflect corporate strategies to reduce or control important sources of uncertainty in companies' environments (Allen 1974; Schoorman, Bazerman & Atkin 1981). In addition, interlocking is seen as a means of exchange of information and expertise between companies. It is therefore surprising that more research has not been focussed on the relationship between interlocking directorates and the selection and retention of auditors, especially since auditing is a relatively complex service performed in an uncertain environment (Crosby, Evans & Cowles 1990).

As noted earlier, the primary paper addressing this issue thus far is by Davison, Stening and Wai (1984), who provide evidence that the presence of interlocking directorates is important to the choice of auditor, creating significant links between directors and auditors. Another study, Seabright, Levinthal and Fichman (1992), investigated the effect of attachment of individuals primarily responsible for the auditor-client exchange on the likelihood of auditor switching. The study showed that while changes in resource requirements (of the client) and resource provisions (of the auditor) increased the likelihood of an auditor switch, the development of attachments between boundary spanners[2] attenuated this effect on auditor change. Seabright, Levinthal and Fichman suggest that the auditor-

---

[2] Boundary spanners are defined by Seabright, Levinthal and Fichman (1992, p. 124) as 'organisational members whose role requires both intra- and inter-organizational relationships'.

client relationship relies largely on personal knowledge and trust, and that these act as disincentives for clients to change auditors.

This current study provides a more direct and arguably more meaningful measure[3] of the impact of personal attachments on exchange relationships than that employed by other researchers, especially Seabright, Levinthal and Fichman, who operationalised their individual or personal attachment variables through tenure of company officers (that is, CEO, CFO, etc.). Those authors noted that there might be other consequential attachments within a larger network of relationships in which an auditor and client are involved (Seabright, Levinthal & Fichman 1992, p. 155). The current study responds to this call by using director-auditor links as a measure of personal attachment in testing an hypothesised association between director-auditor links and auditor tenure. As such, it is related to studies examining board and board committee composition and audit-related phenomena (e.g., Beasley 1996; Carcello & Neal 2000).

It can be argued that factors increasing the likelihood of a company changing its auditor (see, for instance, Williams 1988) can be seen also as factors reducing the likelihood of continued tenure. While this is true, such an 'auditor change' approach risks ignoring variables impacting specifically on the length of auditor tenure rather than on auditor change. Further, examination of the determinants of tenure length may be as important, if not more so, than the determinants of auditor change to accounting firms and to concerns over corporate governance. Both the US Sarbanes-Oxley Act 2002 and Australia's proposed reforms discussed in the Corporate Law Economic Reform Program (CLERP 9) address partner rotation rather than firm rotation, but the issue of firm rotation has received much public comment in the aftermath of Enron and WorldCom in the United States and HIH in Australia. As much as it may be useful to explain why auditor-client relationships end, an indication as to what might make them last is arguably of greater practical significance to firms engaged in these relationships.

Additionally, this study potentially informs the debate concerning mandatory auditor rotation. Concerns have been raised about the impact on audit quality and auditor independence when auditor tenure is for particularly short or long periods (e.g., Geiger & Raghunandan 2002; Latham, Jacobs & Roush 1998; Raghunathan, Lewis & Evans III 1994; Aldhizer III & Lampe 1997) because of the impact on familiarity with the client. While audit quality is not specifically tested in the context of this study, any association between director-auditor links and longer auditor tenure may accentuate concerns over auditor independence, an issue of major concern to the accounting and auditing professions and those who regulate them (e.g., Levitt 1998). In fact, auditing standards and ethics

---

[3] Other researchers, such as Seabright, Levinthal and Fichman (1992), use proxies for personal attachment such as tenure of office holders.

statements, regardless of the jurisdiction in which they are based, generally include commentary on tenure length.

Where an interlocking director comes into contact with the same auditor across other companies on whose boards (s)he sits, and auditor tenure is relatively long, the potential impact on auditor independence is unclear. Longer tenure has been criticised in its own right as potentially reducing independence (Raghunathan, Lewis & Evans III 1994; Aldhizer & Lampe 1997). Interlocking directorates (regardless of their links with auditors) have also attracted criticism.[4] It is therefore likely that any significant positive association between director-auditor links and auditor tenure will heighten concerns with respect to auditor independence. The aim of this chapter is to investigate whether such a positive association exists.

The remainder of this chapter is presented as follows. The next section discusses the prior literature and develops the hypotheses to be tested. The variables selected for the testing of the hypotheses and their measurement are discussed, and an outline of the research design and sample data is then provided. Finally, the results are presented and discussed, and limitations and opportunities for future research are outlined.

Literature review and hypotheses development

Interlocking directorates

An interlocking directorate[5] arises when a director sits on two or more company boards.[6] Many explanations have been offered for the existence of interlocking directorates, covering a range of theoretical prescriptions. These perspectives have included transaction costs (Williamson 1991), agency theory (Eisenhardt 1989) and class theories (Koenig & Gogel 1981). However, the most relevant explanation for their existence, in terms of the context relevant to this study, is that they serve to reduce or control uncertainty in business environments (Allen 1974; Schoorman, Bazerman & Atkin 1981; Mizruchi 1996). Allen (1974, p. 395) specifies three main ways in which interlocking directorates attempt to reduce environmental uncertainty. These are (1) by the exchange of information and expertise between companies, (2) by providing a stable means of communication and liaison between companies, and (3) by advising management concerning the relationship of the company to its external environment. However, when interlocking directors are systematically associated with a common auditor across

[4]For instance, Judge Louis Brandeis in the United States was once quoted as labelling interlocking directorates 'the root of many evils'. He claimed that they 'tend(s) to the suppression of competition' and that they violated the fundamental law that 'no man can serve two masters' (Carroll, Stening & Stening 1990, p. 290).
[5]In Australia, a legal limit on the number of directorships that can be held does not exist, nor does any formal mechanism to suggest limits (Alexander, Murray & Houghton 1994). Alexander, Murray and Houghton observe that the concentration of multiple directorships increased between 1986 and 1991.
[6]'Board' here includes alternate directors.

their various board holdings, it is not clear that benefits exist for all stakeholders. The objectivity of the auditor may be compromised if the relationship is 'too cosy', and/or if the loss of several rather than a single client is the feared consequence of the auditor remaining non-compliant with the auditee's preferred reporting.

Interlocking directorates and auditors

Unlike other products or services, the quality of an audit is not readily discernible. It cannot be judged from the outside and must be experienced to be evaluated (Pennings, Lee & van Witteloostuijn 1998; Craswell & Francis 1999). Interlocking directors holding multiple board positions are in one of the best positions to judge the relative quality of audits due to their experience with various service providers. Their experience gives them the ability to advise on, and perhaps contribute to, selection of the most appropriate auditor for companies on whose boards they sit. Sharing this knowledge with boards of other companies on which they sit reduces the costs of evaluating the strengths and weaknesses of potential auditors.

Zajac (1988) indicates that multiple directorships allow directors to view a panorama of their companies' environments within which to monitor and control uncertainties. Sharing this outlook with auditors, who may be knowledgeable about their clients' business environments, creates synergies that potentially enable difficulties to be overcome more smoothly.

In the accounting literature, little attention has been paid to the relationship between interlocking directors and auditors. From the research that does exist, it appears that there is a tendency for interlocking directors to employ the same auditor across the group of companies through which they are interlocked (Davison, Stening & Wai 1984; Jubb 2000).

Auditor tenure

Director-auditor links and tenure

Many factors have been found to influence the length of auditor tenure. However, the focus of this section is the expected positive association of the hypothesis variable – director-auditor links – with auditor tenure.

As noted, director-auditor links develop, in part, due to the building of attachments and personal ties between directors (in their roles as boundary spanners) and auditors. Literature in the field of management and marketing would suggest that the development of personal ties is important to the development and continuance of corporate relationships. De Ruyter and Wetzels (1999) found that trust and pleasant business partnerships increase the commitment of clients to the relationship and their intention to continue it. Similarly, numerous researchers have concluded that the choice of continuing business relationships depends on the trust that emerges between organisations due to repeated personal attachments and ties (e.g., Cook 1977; Levinthal & Fichman 1988; Gulati 1995).

With respect to the impact of personal ties on auditor tenure specifically, Seabright, Levinthal and Fichman (1992) examined the effect of personal attachments on the dissolution of the auditor-client relationship. They found that attachments between client and auditor organisations occur mainly at the individual level, and their findings suggest that while other factors may act as pressures for auditor change, it is personal attachments that attenuate the impact of these influences and are critical to the maintenance of the relationship.

Relationships generated in the presence of director-auditor links are argued to allow the development of mutual dependence due to the greater stability of the alliance. This dependence relies on trust as an integral ingredient in the relationship. Therefore, it is posited that the trust and dependence manifested in the auditor-client relationship will be influential in client decisions to retain the auditor, and that the development of personal ties or attachments over time resulting from director-auditor links will be positively associated with auditor tenure.

> H_1 *A positive association exists between director-auditor links and auditor tenure.*

The results of Levinthal and Fichman (1988) provide the basis for the second hypothesis. Those authors found that the likelihood of auditor change increased up to the fourth year of tenure before reducing. They posited that since the client receives feedback about the desirability of the auditor-client attachment only on an annual basis, it might take a number of years (up to four) for initial favourable beliefs to change sufficiently for the attachment to be ended. Given this result, Hypothesis 2 examines the impact of director-auditor links on the realisation of auditor tenure surrounding what appears to be the critical four-year period. That is, it is hypothesised that personal attachments between directors and auditors will ameliorate the pressure for an auditor switch within the first four years of auditor tenure.

> H_2 *There is a positive association between director-auditor links and the retention of the auditor for the critical[7] four-year period and longer but not for a lesser period.*

---

[7] As found by Levinthal and Fichman (1988).

Selection and measurement of variables

Dependent variables

Auditor tenure is the dependent variable for the testing of Hypotheses 1 and 2. However, a different measure of tenure is employed in each as appropriate. For Hypothesis 1, a continuous (but capped) measure of tenure is used (AUDTEN). Auditor tenure can, and often does, last for many years. Given the findings of Levinthal and Fichman (1988), that the majority of auditor switches occur in the first four years of the auditor-client relationship, the limit on tenure should be greater than four years but short enough to maximise company survival over the examined period. In this study, auditor tenure is measured continuously and is censored at seven years.[8] While accepting the survivorship bias that any censoring of tenure may induce[9], a trade-off must be made between the logistics of data collection and adequately capturing the length of auditor engagement of the companies in the sample.[10]

For Hypothesis 2, which involves examination of auditor tenure surrounding the critical four-year period in the auditor-client relationship, a dichotomous variable is used to represent periods either side of the four-year period. As discussed earlier, Levinthal and Fichman (1988) found that the likelihood of auditor switching increases up to the fourth year of auditor tenure, where it peaks before declining. Therefore, the dependent variable for Hypothesis 2, a categorical measure of auditor tenure (CATTEN), takes the value 1 if the tenure of the incumbent auditor is greater than four years and 0 otherwise.

Independent variables

Hypothesis variable

Director-auditor links (ALOCKYRS)

The preceding discussion indicates the rationale behind the presence of director-auditor links as the hypothesis variable. This variable represents the cumulative total of director-auditor links per company observation over the measurement period, which commences in 1995 and is traced retrospectively for seven years inclusive. That is, ALOCKYRS measures the total number of years that an observed company's interlocking directors have had a personal attachment link with a particular audit firm. This is appropriate given that the hypothesis is concerned with personal attachment links over the observed length of auditor tenure. Furthermore, it is likely to be the endurance of these director-auditor

---

[8]Levinthal and Fichman (1988) also left- and right-censor (at 0 and at 13 years respectively) auditor tenure in their study on interorganisational attachments.
[9]Nevertheless, not censoring auditor tenure is likely to induce a larger survivorship bias.
[10]The variable auditor tenure in itself (whether censored or not) creates a bias, given that if a client ceases to exist it is not possible for an auditor to be engaged.

links that will most affect auditor tenure, not the occurrence of a link at any particular point in time.

Director-auditor links are measured over their existence and capped at seven years. ALOCKYRS is measured as the total number of director-auditor links for each focal or observed company (regardless of the number of directors interlocking with another company) for each given year, summed over the seven-year period.[11]

Table 7.1 provides an example of the calculation of ALOCKYRS and is based on a hypothetical sample of three companies over three years. ALYRS represents the number of total director-auditor links for any given year which, when summed across the potential seven-year period, gives ALOCKYRS. The measurement of this variable over a potential seven-year period is consistent with the measurement of auditor tenure, the dependent variable.

Table 7.1. Example of measurement of ALOCKYRS

Co. no.	Year 1			Year 2			Year 3			ALOCKYRS
	Directors	Auditor	ALYRS	Directors	Auditor	ALYRS	Directors	Auditor	ALYRS	
1[a]	A, B, C	Y	3	A, B, C	Y	3	A, B, C	X	1	7
2[b]	B, C, D, E	Y	3	A, C, D, E	Y	4	A, C, D, E	Y	0	7
3[c]	E, F, G, A	Y	2	E, F, G, A	Y	3	E, F, G, A	X	1	6

Explanation:

[a]Co. 1 ALOCKYRS = (Yr 1 ALYRS) + (Yr 2 ALYRS) + (Yr 3 ALYRS) = (Co. 2 Dir's B + C; Co. 3 Dir A) + (Co. 2 Dir's A + C; Co. 3 Dir A) + (Co. 3 Dir A) = 3 + 3 + 1 = 7

[b]Co. 2 ALOCKYRS = (Co. 1 Dir's B + C; Co. 3 Dir E) + (Co. 1 Dir's A + C; Co. 3 Dir's A + E) + (Nil) = 3 + 4 + 0 = 7

[c]Co. 3 ALOCKYRS = (Co. 1 Dir A; Co. 2 Dir E) + (Co. 1 Dir A; Co. 2 Dir's E + A) + (Co. 1 Dir A) = 2 + 3 + 1 = 6

For a director-auditor link (ALYRS) to be included in the calculation of ALOCKYRS, two conditions must be met. Firstly, a given director must sit on at least one board amongst the sample companies other than that of the observed or focal company, and secondly, the observed and 'other' company/ies must engage the same auditor. Note that failure to meet the second condition reveals why, in the above example, there are no director-auditor links (ALYRS) for Company 2 in Year 3. Although some Company 2 directors sit on other sample company boards, Company 2 does not share the same auditor in Year 3 as either Company 1 or Company 3.

---

[11]Or as long as the company has survived within those seven years.

Working through the calculation for Company 1 in Table 7.1 provides the following; Year 1 ALYRS are equal to 3, and Year 2 ALYRS are also equal to 3. However, because of the change in auditor, Year 3 ALYRS equals only 1, giving a total of 7 ALOCKYRS.

Control variables

The control variables used in the testing of Hypotheses 1 and 2 are based primarily on those used in prior research that has examined auditor tenure or auditor switching. Table 7.2 provides a summary of the relevant auditor tenure and change studies that have influenced the models used in the current study. The study by Seabright, Levinthal and Fichman (1992) is the source of the majority of variables. The variables used in a number of auditor change models (e.g., Haskins & Williams 1990; Levinthal & Fichman 1988) are relevant also because of the aforementioned link between auditor tenure and change.

Table 7.2. Summary of auditor tenure and auditor change models used in prior literature

Study	Dependent variable	Independent variables	Significant variables
Chow and Rice (1982)	Auditor change (dichotomous) $R^2 = 0.104$	• Qualified opinion (dichotomous) • Management change (dichotomous) • Merger between companies (dichotomous) • New financing arrangements (dichotomous) • Other (dichotomous)	• Qualified opinion (+ve)

Levinthal and Fichman (1988)	Auditor change hazard rate	• Client size (assets)
		• Complexity
		  • inventories to assets
		  • receivables to assets
		• Qualified opinion (dichotomous)
		• Segmented sales
		• Foreign activities (dichotomous)
			• Client size (−ve)
			• Inventories to total assets (−ve)
			• Qualified opinion (+ve)

Seabright, Levinthal and Fichman (1988)	Auditor change (dichotomous) $U^2 = 0.24$	• Auditor tenure • Financial health • Resource requirement of client • Change in auditor market share • Age • Qualified opinion • Age • Big Eight • Industry specialist • Individual attachments	• Retained earnings to assets (−ve) • Earnings to assets (−ve) • Equity to liabilities (+ve) • Sales to assets (+ve) • Big Eight (−ve) • Tenure of CFO (−ve) • Tenure of audit committee (−ve)
Haskins and Williams (1990)	Auditor change (dichotomous)	• Financial distress • Client size (sales) • Qualified opinion (dichotomous) • Change in ownership • IPO (dichotomous) • Client growth • Perceived Big Eight expensiveness • Industry specialist • Auditor litigation • Fees per partner	• Industry specialist • Financial distress[6] • Client size[6] • Client growth[6]

Study	Dependent variable	Independent variables	Significant variables
Raghunathan, Lewis and Evans III (1994)	Problem audits (dichotomous) pseudo R^2 = 0.36	• Auditor tenure (dichotomous) • 1 year • 2-5 years • > 5 years • Client fees (both audit and NAS) • Management controlled (dichotomous) • Financial health	• Auditor tenure • 1 year (+ve) • > 5 years (+ve) • Client fees (+ve) • Financial health (+ve)
Krishnan and Krishnan (1997)	Auditor resignation (1) v. auditor dismissal (0) (dichotomous) pseudo R^2 = 0.208	• Probability of bankruptcy • Auditor change due to: • reportable event (dichotomous) • disagreement (dichotomous) • Total accruals to assets • Growth in sales from prior year • Probability of acquisition • Auditor tenure (> 3 yrs prior to switch – dichotomous) • Client sales/total sales of all clients of the auditor • Modified audit opinion (dichotomous) • Modification for going concern (dichotomous) • Modification for other material concerns (dichotomous) • Client size • Variance of client abnormal returns	• Probability of bankruptcy (+ve) • Auditor change due to: • reportable event (+ve) • disagreement (+ve) • Auditor tenure (–ve) • Client sales/total sales of all clients of the auditor (–ve)
Latham, Jacobs and Roush (1998)	Appropriateness of audit opinion pseudo R^2 = 0.51	• Auditor tenure • Loss status (dichotomous) • Risk (debt/assets)	• Auditor tenure (+ve) • Loss status (+ve)
Walker, Casterella and Moet (1998)	Auditor changes with audit failures (dichotomous) Model Chi-square = 21.943 Sig. = 0.0005	• Fraud • Industry specialist • Complexity • Distress	• Fraud (+ve) • Industry specialist (+ve) • Complexity (+ve)
Geiger and Raghunandan (2002)	Going concern opinion prior to bankruptcy pseudo R^2 = 0.33	• Size (log sales) • Probability of bankruptcy (Hopwood et al. 1994) • Default (dichotomous) • Number days between audit report and bankruptcy • Auditor tenure (log)	• Size (log sales) (–ve) • Probability of bankruptcy (Hopwood et al. 1994) (+ve) • Default (dichotomous) (+ve) • Number days between audit report and bankruptcy (–ve) • Auditor tenure (log) (+ve)

Auditee Characteristics

Complexity (COMPL)

Simunic's (1980) work indicates that providing assurance on financial statements is more demanding where an audit is more complex. Further, auditees are more likely to choose the auditor most capable of dealing with such complexities. The inclusion of complexity recognises the positive significance of this variable found by Walker, Casterella and Moet (1998).

Consistent with Simunic (1980), and Walker, Casterella and Moet (1998), complexity is measured as the proportion of inventory and receivables to total assets, given that both studies find these areas to add to the complexity of an audit.

Distress (DISTRESS)

Previous studies have identified the importance of financial distress for the likelihood that a company will change auditor (for example, Schwartz & Menon 1985; Haskins & Williams 1990). In addition, distressed companies are more likely to be associated with damage to the reputation of auditors in the event of litigation (Krishnan & Krishnan 1997), and shareholders of distressed companies are likely to seek compensation for losses in the event of failure (Menon & Williams 1994). For these reasons, auditors may be less likely to retain such clients (DeFond, Ettredge & Smith 1997; Krishnan & Krishnan 1997).

Distress is measured using re-estimated parameters of Altman's (1968) model (the original model has been used in prior literature, e.g. Seabright, Levinthal & Fichman 1992; Schwartz & Menon 1985). This revised model[12] was re-estimated by Constable and Woodliff (1994) based on Australian company data and was found to improve the original model's predictive ability.

Risk (RISK)

Similar to distress, risk (in the context important to this study) is a measure of the attractiveness of a client to an auditor. Highly leveraged companies have a greater chance of failure than do those with less debt. Since auditors are perceived to have 'deep pockets' (Wallace 1987), the stakeholders of failed companies (such as shareholders or creditors) may seek compensation from the auditor for losses incurred. This acts as a disincentive to auditors for continuance of the auditor-client relationship and is predicted to result in lower auditor tenure.

Risk is measured as the proportion of debt to total equity. While other factors may influence the risk of a company, leverage has the advantage of explanatory power and parsimony.

Qualified opinion (PRIORQUAL)

Chow and Rice (1982), and Schwartz and Menon (1985), found that clients in receipt of a qualified audit opinion in the prior year have a higher tendency to switch auditor. This may be because the directors seek to engage an auditor whose views are more in line with those of management. These new auditors are therefore assumed less likely to qualify.

---

[12]Altman's z-score, re-estimated by Constable and Woodliff (1994), is calculated as:

$$Z = -0.939 + 1.688 \text{ WC/TA} + 0.465 \text{ RE/TA} + 0.102 \text{ EBIT/TA} + 0.013 \text{ MVE/TL} + 1.010 \text{ S/TA}$$

where WC/TA = working capital/total assets, RE/TA = retained earnings/total assets, EBIT/TA = earnings before interest and tax/total assets, MVE/TL = market value of equity/total debt, and S/TA = sales/total assets.

A dichotomous (dummy) variable is used to operationalise a qualified opinion, coded 1 if the audit report of a company was qualified in the prior year, and 0 otherwise.

Auditee age (AGE)

Auditor tenure may depend on the longevity of companies in the sample. If an audit client has been in existence only for a limited period, it would follow that the tenure of its auditor cannot exceed the client's age (although it may be less than this). Further, older companies have had the time, and therefore the opportunity, to build personal attachments of the nature tested by the hypothesis variable in this study. Thus, the age of the client is predicted to positively influence auditor tenure and needs to be controlled for.

Age is measured continuously as the number of years a company has been listed on the Australian Stock Exchange (ASX).

Audit fee (AUDFEE)

Audit fees that are perceived to be excessively high have been found to influence auditor change (Haskins & Williams 1990; Eichenseher & Shields 1983; Shockley & Holt 1983). Thus, the higher the audit fee, *ceteris paribus*, the lower the expected tenure.

Audit fees are measured as the dollar amount paid to the principal auditor only for the auditing of a client's financial statements as disclosed in the company's annual report.

Auditee growth (GROWTH)

The resource requirements of a company change throughout its existence. Thus, growth may influence the decision to change auditor due to a difference between current resource requirements of clients and the ability of an audit firm to provide these resources (Seabright, Levinthal & Fichman 1992). Indeed, Haskins and Williams (1990) found growth to be a significant determinant of auditor change. Consequently, auditor tenure is expected to be lower for companies experiencing growth.

Consistent with previous studies (for instance, Haskins & Williams 1990), growth is operationalised as the percentage change in revenue from the prior year.

Director tenure (DIRTEN)

This study proposes that directors may gain a familiarity with, and attachment to, an auditor over time. Furthermore, Seabright, Levinthal and Fichman (1992) found the tenure of the CFO and audit committee members are negatively associated with auditor changes. Thus, auditor tenure is predicted to increase with the average tenure of directors on a company's board, given that longer director tenure provides a greater time frame for an attachment to develop.

Director tenure is measured as the average number of years' tenure (capped at seven years) for a focal company's board members.

Non-audit services purchased (NAS)

Beck, Frecka and Solomon (1988) report that companies that purchase high levels of recurring NAS from their auditor tend to have longer auditor tenure. In an Australian context, Butterworth and Houghton (1995) report findings consistent with this result. NAS is measured as the remuneration paid to a company's principal auditor for non-audit services as disclosed in the company's annual report.

Auditee size (SIZE)

Prior research by De Angelo (1981) found that as the size of clients increases, they are more likely to select larger auditors. Thus, it is expected that as the auditee size increases, companies will tend to select Big Six (now Big Five) auditors. Additionally, Levinthal and Fichman (1988) found that auditor size is highly significant in explaining the expected duration of the auditor-client relationship.

Consistent with prior research (e.g., Francis & Wilson 1988; Levinthal & Fichman 1988), client size is measured as total assets.

Auditor characteristics

Big Six (BIG6)

The size of audit firms has been shown to have a systematic effect on the duration of the auditor-client relationship. For instance, prior research (Levinthal & Fichman 1988) has shown that client relations with Big Eight (Big Six in this sample) firms are likely to last longer than those with non-Big Eight (non-Big Six) auditors.

BIG6 is captured by a dichotomous variable taking the value 1 if a company's auditor is a member of the Big Six, and 0 otherwise.[13]

Industry specialist (SPECAUD)

The existence of an industry premium specialist has been shown to result in fee premia attributed to the expertise and quality that such an auditor exhibits (Craswell, Francis & Taylor 1995; DeFond, Francis & Wong 2000). Further, research by Haskins and Williams (1990) indicates that auditor switches can be

---

[13]Where audit firms have merged during the period examined, as long as a company audited by one of the separate firms stays with the merged audit firm, tenure is taken as continuous, consistent with Levinthal and Fichman (1988).

explained partly by clients preferring to choose a specialist auditor. Thus, auditor tenure for industry specialists is likely to be longer than that for non-specialists.

An industry specialist auditor is deemed to exist if at least one audit firm within an industry receives at least 15% of the total industry audit fees.[14] Consistent with Craswell and Taylor (1991), and Craswell, Francis and Taylor (1995), at least 30 companies must exist in an industry for a specialist to be deemed to exist. Auditor specialisation is measured in the prior year, because the decision to retain or change auditor may depend, in part, on a company's perception of which audit firm(s) is a specialist auditor in its market. If an auditor meets the aforementioned criteria in the prior year, the dichotomous variable is coded 1, and 0 if it does not.

Therefore, the model to be tested takes the following form:

$$\text{Auditor tenure} = \alpha + \beta_1 \text{ALOCKYRS}_t + \beta_2 \text{COMPL}_t - \beta_3 \text{DISTRESS}_t - \beta_4 \text{RISK}_t - \beta_5 \text{PRIORQUAL}_{t-1} + \beta_6 \text{AGE}_t - \beta_7 \text{AUDFEE}_t - \beta_8 \text{GROWTH}_{(t-1)-t} + \beta_9 \text{DIRTEN}_t + \beta_{10} \text{NAS}_t + \beta_{11} \text{SIZE}_t + \beta_{12} \text{BIG6}_t + \beta_{13} \text{SPECAUD}_{t-1} + \varepsilon$$

The variable definitions and their expected direction are summarised in Table 7.3.

Table 7.3. Variable measures

Dependent variable	Pred. dir.	Operationalisation
AUDTEN		The number of years of the auditor's incumbency from a base year for company$_i$ up to a maximum of seven years.
or		
CATTEN		Dichotomous variable taking value 1 if the number of years of the auditor's incumbency is greater than 4, 0 otherwise.
Independent variables		
ALOCKYRS	+	The total number of director-auditor links for company$_i$ in a given year summed over a potential seven-year period.
DIRTEN	+	The number of years' tenure (capped at seven years) of all board members, averaged, for each company$_i$.
COMPL	+	The proportion of inventories and receivables to total assets.
DISTRESS	−	A continuous z-score measure (Constable & Woodliff 1994) of auditee's financial health in the current year.
RISK	−	The proportion of debt to equity.
PRIORQUAL	−	A dichotomous variable taking the value 1 if auditee$_i$'s financial report is qualified in the prior year, 0 otherwise.
AGE	+	The number of years (rounded to the nearest whole year) since company$_i$ listed on the ASX.
AUDFEE	−	The dollar amount of audit fees received by the incumbent auditor for auditing the accounts of company$_i$.
NAS	+	The dollar amount of NAS earned by the incumbent auditor in the current year.

[14]Craswell and Taylor (1991) classified a specialist as an auditor in receipt of 10% of the national audit fees for that ASX two-digit industry. However, this chapter uses 15% of total fees to account for the influence of the reduction from the Big Eight to the Big Six.

SIZE	+	The total assets of company$_i$ in the current year.
BIG6	+	A dichotomous variable taking the value 1 if company$_i$'s incumbent auditor is a Big Six firm, 0 otherwise.
SPECAUD	+	A dichotomous variable taking the value 1 if company$_i$'s auditor receives at least 15% of the total industry audit fees and at least 30 companies exist in that client's ASX (2-digit) industry code.
GROWTH	–	The percentage change in auditee$_i$'s sales since the prior year.

Methodology

Hypothesis 1

Hypothesis 1 examines the association of director-auditor links with auditor tenure (measured continuously). Rather than using an ordinary least squares (OLS) regression, multivariate Tobit analysis is used due to the censoring of auditor tenure.

Hypothesis 2

Hypothesis 2 examines the potential impact of director-auditor links in influencing the extension of auditor tenure past the four-year barrier argued to be critical by Levinthal and Fichman (1988). Given that the dependent variable for the testing of this hypothesis is dichotomous, logistic regression is used.

Sample and data

The same sample companies are used for the testing of both hypotheses. The sampling frame consists of the top 242 companies by total assets listed on the ASX in the year 1995, and meeting the required data considerations. Hence, variables measured at t-1 relate to 1994. To be included, companies had to be audited by a single (3 deletions) private-sector auditor (2 deletions) and have been listed for at least two years (16 deletions). In addition, only companies with financial statements denominated in Australian dollars (19 deletions) and all data (2 deletions) were included. The final sample size was set at the largest 200 companies meeting all the data requirements. To achieve this, the largest 242 companies by total assets in 1995 were the initial starting point. Table 7.4 explains the sample size at each step of determining the presence of the requisite data.

Table 7.4. Sample criteria

Criterion (base year 1995)	Deletions	Balance
Largest companies by total assets		242
Must have one auditor only	3	239
Financial statements denominated in AUD$	19	220
Private-sector auditor	2	218
Must be listed at least two years	16	202
Other	2	200

It was necessary to delete companies with more than one auditor (2 deletions) because of the inherent difficulty this would cause in the calculation of auditor tenure and ALOCKYRS. Similarly, the inclusion of companies listed for at least two years enabled the collection of prior year data for the growth, auditor industry specialist and qualification variables. The 'other' category consists of companies for which not all data was currently available.

The data was hand-collected from a variety of sources including *Who Audits Australia?* (Craswell 1996), the *Australian Financial Review Shareholder* handbook, *Jobson's Year Book of Australian Listed Companies* (1989-96), *Jobson's Year Book of Mining Companies* (1989-96), the *Australian Stock Exchange Datadisc*, the *Australian Graduate School of Management (AGSM) Annual Report Microfiche File* and *Connect4*.

Results

Hypothesis 1

Univariate results

Hypothesis 1 examines the association of director-auditor links with auditor tenure measured continuously over a maximum seven-year period up to 1995 inclusive, left-censored at two years and right-censored at seven years. The descriptives reported in Table 7.5 show that the mean tenure for all companies in the sample is 5.4 years. This indicates that the average company observation has an audit relationship that has lasted for more than five years.

Table 7.5. Descriptive statistics

Variable	OVERALL SAMPLE N = 200				AUDITOR TENURE > 4 YRS N = 134				AUDITOR TENURE ≤ 4 YRS N = 66				t-test or Chi square	p-value
	Max.	Min.	Mean	Std dev.	Max.	Min.	Mean	Std dev.	Max.	Min.	Mean	Std dev.		
TENURE	7	1	5.435	2.092										
ALOCKYRS	68	0	9.190	14.606	68.000	0.000	11.948	16.732	38.000	0.000	3.591	5.727	5.197	0.000
DIRTEN (YRS)	7	1	3.838	1.278	7.000	1.938	4.324	1.046	6.286	1.000	2.851	1.133	8.864	0.000
COMPL (%)	0.85	0	0.221	0.199	0.841	0.001	0.239	0.204	0.848	0.000	0.185	0.186	1.890	0.061
DISTRESS (z-score)	3.68	-3.59	0.036	0.916	2.141	-3.589	0.059	0.821	3.676	-2.198	-0.010	1.090	0.454	0.651
RISK (debt/equity)	2.6	0.02	0.478	0.292	2.599	0.015	0.489	0.307	1.150	0.021	0.455	0.257	0.810	0.419
PRIORQUAL(0/1)	1	0	0.035	0.184	1.000	0.000	0.045	0.208	1.000	0.000	0.015	0.123	1.149	0.284
AGE (YRS)	92	2	20.920	20.324	92.000	4.000	25.306	20.520	71.000	2.000	12.015	16.818	4.877	0.000
AUDFEE ($'000)	5542	3	507.20	836.326	5542.000	10.000	657.231	977.232	1233.000	3.00	202.576	216.097	5.251	0.000
NAS ($'000)	6,356.00	0	419.25	811.027	6356.000	0.000	537.828	946.862	1443.000	0.000	178.485	302.409	3.563	0.001
SIZE ($m)	147.077	0.159	3.035	13.391	147.077	0.159	4.041	16.206	17.578	0.160	0.993	2.300	4.051	0.000
BIG6 (0/1)	1	0	0.885	0.320	1.000	0.000	0.910	0.287	1.000	0.000	0.833	0.376	2.584	0.108
SPECAUD (0/1)	1	0	0.175	0.381	1.000	0.000	0.201	0.403	1.000	0.000	0.121	0.329	1.974	0.160
GROWTH (% change)	1349.490	-91.85	41.766	127.952	1349.490	-91.850	32.503	132.057	610.140	-38.390	60.573	117.916	-2.751	0.007

The majority of companies (59.5%) exhibit auditor tenure of at least seven years. This is interesting, given the findings of Levinthal and Fichman (1988) that auditor switches are most likely to occur in the first four years of the auditor-client relationship. These findings suggest two possible alternatives. Firstly, average auditor tenure[15] (since the study by Levinthal and Fichman) has tended to increase. Alternatively, given that Big Six auditors generally have longer tenure than non-Big Six auditors (Fichman & Levinthal 1991), the incidence of auditor switching among the largest 200 companies (which tend to be audited by Big Six) may be so low as to have no significant impact on average auditor tenure. The latter explanation appears most pertinent, given that auditor switching in Australia is relatively rare in any given year.[16]

The descriptive statistics for the overall sample (Table 7.5) show that the mean number of director-auditor links (ALOCKYRS) is 9.19, with a maximum of 68. This indicates that on average, over the seven-year measurement period, there are 9.19 links created where the directors of a sample company encounter the same auditor at other companies where they have board membership. The mean number of years that the sample companies have been listed on the ASX (AGE) is 21, indicating that on average the companies are well-established. This is to be expected since the sample is comprised of large, and generally stable, companies. In addition, the mean tenure of directors on the sample companies' boards (DIRTEN) indicates that on average directors in the sample were on those boards for almost four years.

In terms of financial characteristics, the mean level of leverage (RISK), 0.478, suggests that on average the companies in this sample do not have overly high debt-to-equity ratios. The mean distress score is 0.036, indicating that the sample companies have relatively sound financial health. The dichotomous variables show that on average only 3.5% of companies were issued a qualified opinion in the prior year (which is expected, given that the sample includes large companies), 89% of companies are audited by a Big Six auditor, and 18% of companies engage a specialist Big Six auditor.

The Pearson's correlation matrix is reported in Table 7.6. Only two instances exist where independent variables have correlations over 0.5 (LOGFEES has a 0.555 correlation with LOGNAS and a 0.729 correlation with LOGSIZE).

[15] While Levinthal and Fichman (1988) did not report the average duration of auditor tenure in the descriptive statistics for their study, their finding that most auditor switches occur in the first four years of tenure indicates that average tenure in their sample was less than in the current study.
[16] In 1995, the switching rate was 6.5% of all listed companies and in 1994 6.3% (Craswell 1996).

Table 7.6. Pearson correlation coefficient matrix (N = 200)

	AUD-TEN	ALOCKYRS	DIRTEN	COMPL	DISTR	RISK	PRIOR-QUAL	AGE	BIG6	SPEC-AUD	LOG-NAS	LOG-FEES	LOG-SIZE
AUDTEN	1.000												
ALOCKYRS	0.275**	1.000											
DIRTEN	0.551**	0.138	1.000										
COMPL	0.107	0.042*	0.155*	1.000									
DISTRESS	0.024	-0.100	0.111	0.473**	1.000								
RISK	0.067	0.036	0.007	0.423**	0.055	1.000							
PRIORQUAL	0.091	0.007	0.020	-0.009	-0.111	0.196**	1.000						
AGE	0.334**	0.193**	0.250**	0.139*	0.263**	0.086	0.242**	1.000					
BIG6	0.105	0.083	-0.080	0.038	0.052	-0.021	-0.187**	-0.114	1.000				
SPECAUD	0.074	0.100	0.083	0.050	0.113	0.017	-0.088	0.102	0.166*	1.000			
LOGNAS	0.254**	0.113	0.082	0.259**	0.137	0.154*	-0.011	0.205**	0.242**	0.095	1.000		
LOGFEES	0.355**	0.304**	0.190**	0.329**	0.160*	0.330**	0.066	0.314**	0.143*	0.060	0.555**	1.000	
LOGSIZE	0.257**	0.339**	0.050	0.097	-0.203**	0.293**	0.134	0.187**	0.121	-0.111	0.359**	0.729**	1.000
LOGGROWTH	-0.205**	-0.051	-0.059	-0.056	-0.002	-0.075	-0.054	-0.104	-0.067	-0.099	-0.100	-0.068	-0.116

** Correlation is significant at the 0.01 level (2-tailed). Refer to Table 7.3 for variable definitions.
* Correlation is significant at the 0.05 level (2-tailed).

Multivariate results

The multivariate results for testing Hypothesis 1 are shown in Table 7.7. The model is significant with an adjusted R^2 of 43%. Robust analysis that applies the Huber-White technique is used, since testing reveals the presence of heteroscedasticity. [17] These results show that six of the 13 independent variables are significant with respect to auditor tenure.[18] The coefficient of the hypothesis variable, ALOCKYRS, is positive and highly significant (p-value = 0.005 (one-tailed)), indicating that director-auditor links are significantly associated with the length of auditor tenure. This finding supports the results of Seabright, Levinthal and Fichman (1992), who found that personal attachments between those integral for the auditor-client relationship decreased the likelihood of auditor switching.

Table 7.7. Hypothesis 1 – Auditor tenure as a continuous measure Tobit regression (dependent variable = AUDTEN)

Variable	Pred. dir.	Coefficient	S.E.	z-Statistic	Prob.
ALOCKYRS	+	0.076	0.030	2.578	0.010
DIRTEN	+	1.543	0.247	6.256	0.000
BIG6	+	1.767	0.860	2.054	0.040
AGE	+	0.032	0.018	1.761	0.078
LOGGROWTH	−	−1.086	0.522	−2.083	0.037
LOGFEES	−	2.048	1.028	1.993	0.046
RISK	−	0.171	1.093	0.156	0.876
COMPL	+	−1.398	1.865	−0.750	0.454
DISTRESS	−	−0.409	0.384	−1.066	0.286
PRIORQUAL	−	2.130	2.150	0.991	0.322
SPECAUD	+	−0.543	0.809	−0.671	0.502
LOGSIZE	+	−0.839	0.887	−0.946	0.344
LOGNAS	+	0.569	0.391	1.457	0.145
Constant		3.158	4.938	0.640	0.522
N R^2 Adjusted R^2	200 0.4716 0.4316				

Refer to Table 7.3 for variable definitions.

A number of control variables were also significantly associated with auditor tenure (AUDTEN). Director tenure (DIRTEN) (p-value = 0.000 (one-tailed)) is highly significant in the direction hypothesised, suggesting that the average tenure of directors on the board is positively associated with auditor tenure. The number of years since listing (AGE) is also significant (p-value = 0.039 (one-

---

[17] Pre-testing for multicollinearity was also performed under OLS assumptions. Again, although this is not the optimal method of analysis, the available statistical packages are limited in testing for violation of Tobit estimates. Variance Inflation Factors (VIF) indicate multicollinearity is not a significant problem using OLS.
[18] Further testing for outliers indicated that none were present.

tailed)) and positive as hypothesised, as is BIG6 (p-value = 0.020 (one-tailed)), while LOGGROWTH is significantly negatively associated with auditor tenure (p-value = 0.019 (one-tailed)). The significance of LOGGROWTH further supports the hypothesis and findings of Seabright, Levinthal and Fichman (1992), that changes in resource requirements of clients increase the likelihood of auditor switches.

The other control variable significant in the model is LOGFEES (p-value = 0.023 (one-tailed)), although in the opposite direction to that hypothesised. The results indicate that audit fees are positively associated with auditor tenure, suggesting that fee expensiveness is not associated with auditor change. This is consistent with Simon and Francis (1988), who found that any lowballing is fully recouped within four years. In addition, given that larger audit firms predominate in the sample and are generally considered to provide a higher quality audit (De Angelo 1981), presumably companies are willing to pay a premium (Craswell, Francis & Taylor 1995; DeFond, Francis & Wong 2000). The positive direction of this variable therefore seems to reflect the hypothesised positive, significant relationship between BIG6 and auditor tenure.[19]

Interestingly, RISK, DISTRESS and complexity (COMPL) are all insignificant, suggesting that the financial health of clients, and difficulty of the audit task, do not significantly influence auditor tenure. However, given that the sample consists of large companies tending to be well-established, there is likely to be little variation in these variables. Qualification in the prior year (PRIORQUAL) is insignificant in this study. Levinthal and Fichman (1988) suggest that where relationships have survived for several years, there is likely to be less conflict between client and auditor, and hence a low frequency of qualified opinions. Given that the companies in this sample predominantly have incumbent auditors with at least seven years' tenure and are healthy financially, a low incidence of qualified opinions may be expected.

The significance of the hypothesis variable, director-auditor links (ALOCKYRS), provides strong support for Hypothesis 1.

Hypothesis 2

Univariate results

The explanatory variables used in the estimation of Hypothesis 1 are included also for the testing of Hypothesis 2.[20] However, a categorical measure of auditor tenure is used to test Hypothesis 2, which proposes a positive association between

---

[19]Given its multicollinearity with LOGNAS, LOGFEES was omitted from the model. Interestingly, this resulted in LOGNAS becoming highly significant (p = 0.007 (one-tailed)), also in the opposite direction to that hypothesised. The removal of LOGFEES or LOGNAS (given correlation with LOGSIZE) had no impact on the significance of LOGSIZE.
[20]As for the Tobit case, the transforming of some of the variables improved the normality of the disturbances under a logistic regression in pre-testing.

director-auditor links and the retention of the auditor for more than the critical four-year period noted by Levinthal and Fichman (1988). Based on the findings of Levinthal and Fichman, the dependent variable takes the value 1 if auditor tenure is greater than four years and 0 if tenure is less than, or equal to, four years. Of the observations, 67% exhibit auditor tenure longer than four years.

The descriptive statistics in Table 7.5 show that the mean level of director-auditor links is greater for companies where the incumbent auditor has tenure for more than four years as opposed to less than, or equal to, four years. This trend is evident for most of the explanatory variables in Table 7.5. Companies with auditors exhibiting more than four years' tenure tend to have longer director tenure, are more complex and riskier, have higher fees, and are more likely to be audited by a specialist auditor than those companies where the auditor does not have tenure greater than four years. The only exception is company growth, which suggests companies whose auditors have less than, or equal to, four years' tenure (61%) grow more quickly than those companies whose auditors have greater than four years' tenure (33%).

The univariate results are presented in Table 7.5. The independent samples t-tests for the continuous variables (Table 7.5, Panel A) indicate that most of the means in the two groups (tenure greater than four years and tenure less than, or equal to, four years) are significantly different from each other (two-tailed test). The only exceptions are complexity (COMPL), DISTRESS and RISK, where the means for the two groups are insignificantly different from each other. The significant result for ALOCKYRS ($p = 0.000$ (two-tailed)) indicates that the mean incidence of director-auditor links is greater for those company observations with auditor tenure longer than four years on a univariate basis.

Univariate Chi-square tests conducted on the categorical variables (Table 7.5, Panel B) suggest that there is no significant difference in the incidence of prior year audit qualifications ($p = 0.284$), BIG6 ($p = 0.108$) or use of a specialist auditor (SPECAUD; $p = 0.160$) between the two tenure groups.

Multivariate results

Table 7.8 (Panel A) presents the results of the logistic regression. Overall, the model is significant, with a Chi-square statistic of 102.138 ($p = 0.000$), and has a McFadden-R^2 of 0.413. The Hosmer and Lemeshow 'goodness of fit' test calculates a Chi-square value of 6.859 ($p = 0.552$), indicating that the model provides a good fit. Furthermore, the classification table, another indicator of the goodness of fit comparing predictions to the observed outcomes (Table 7.8, Panel B), shows that the model overall correctly predicts 83% of the observed cases. No other studies of auditor tenure known to the author have published this information.

Consequently, these results are difficult to compare.[21] However, the findings indicate that approximately 35% of the time the model predicts auditor tenure greater than four years when it is less than, or equal to, four years (Type II errors). Furthermore, approximately 9% of the time the model predicts that tenure is less than, or equal to, four years when it is actually greater than four years (Type I errors).

Regulators and professional bodies are likely to be more concerned with longer auditor tenure in the presence of links between directors and auditors. Hence, regulators are likely to be interested in a model that more accurately predicts tenure greater than four years than tenure less than, or equal to, four years. While overall predictive accuracy is important, this implies that a model that minimises Type I errors would be of more value than a model minimising Type II errors.

Table 7.8. Hypothesis 2 – Logistic regression (dependent variable = CATTEN) (N = 200)

Variable	Panel A				Panel B				Panel C			
	Coef.	S. E.	Wald	Prob. (2-tail)	Coef.	S. E.	Wald	Prob. (2-tail)	Coef.	S. E.	Wald	Prob. (2-tail)
	CATTEN coded 1 if tenure > 3 Years				CATTEN coded 1 if tenure > 4 Years				CATTEN coded 1 if tenure > 5 Years			
ALOCKYRS	0.046	0.032	1.417	0.156	0.049	0.025	3.880	**0.049**	0.052	0.022	2.375	**0.018**
DIRTEN	1.452	0.268	5.424	**0.000**	1.262	0.234	29.070	**0.000**	0.884	0.191	4.634	**0.000**
BIG6	1.329	0.715	1.859	**0.063**	1.203	0.675	3.172	**0.075**	1.359	0.635	2.139	**0.032**
AGE	0.002	0.015	0.125	0.901	0.016	0.014	1.438	0.230	0.025	0.013	1.983	**0.047**
LOGGROWTH	–0.315	0.378	–0.833	0.405	–0.327	0.383	0.729	0.393	–1.115	0.550	–2.028	**0.043**
LOGFEES	0.601	0.892	0.674	0.500	0.152	0.761	0.040	0.842	0.668	0.666	1.002	0.316
RISK	–0.413	0.780	–0.530	0.596	–0.160	0.759	0.045	0.833	0.032	0.737	0.043	0.966
COMPL	0.328	1.839	0.178	0.858	0.765	1.630	0.220	0.639	0.021	1.334	0.016	0.987
DISTRESS	–0.211	0.346	–0.610	0.542	–0.260	0.333	0.610	0.435	–0.406	0.313	–1.298	0.194
PRIORQUAL	0.791	1.723	0.459	0.646	1.044	1.522	0.471	0.493	0.920	1.384	0.664	0.507
SPECAUD	–0.151	0.659	–0.229	0.819	0.200	0.611	0.107	0.743	–0.151	0.557	–0.272	0.786
LOGSIZE	0.789	0.834	0.945	0.344	0.520	0.722	0.519	0.471	–0.381	0.611	–0.623	0.533
LOGNAS	0.098	0.344	0.286	0.775	0.390	0.296	1.742	0.187	0.363	0.272	1.333	0.182
Constant	–9.764	4.826	–2.023	0.043	–5.785	4.175	1.920	0.166	0.406	3.937	0.103	0.918
Chi²(13)	94.110				102.14				94.770			
p-value	0.000				–75.766539				0.000			
Log likelihood	–65.413				0.000				–85.426			
Pseudo R²	41.84				40.26				35.68%			
Classification Accuracy	Tenure < 4 years 66% Tenure > 4 years 94% Overall 87%				Tenure < 4 years 65% Tenure > 4 years 91% Overall 83%				Tenure < 4 years 68% Tenure > 4 years 86% Overall 80%			

[21]Nevertheless, this outcome compares favourably with other studies, such as the auditor change model estimated by Williams (1988), which correctly predicted 66.13% of switches.

Dependent variable: CATTEN = A dichotomous variable taking the value 1 if auditor tenure > 3, 4, 5 years in Panels A, B and C respectively, 0 otherwise. Refer to Table 7.3 for variable definitions.

The hypothesis variable, ALOCKYRS, is positive and significant ($p = 0.025$ (one-tailed)), as hypothesised. This supports Hypothesis 2, which predicts that director-auditor links are positively associated with auditor tenure greater than four years. As distinct from the interpretation of the findings for Hypothesis 1, the results of Hypothesis 2 suggest that director-auditor links may alleviate the pressure for an auditor switch within the critical first four years of auditor tenure (when an auditor switch is most likely; see Levinthal & Fichman 1988).

Two control variables are also significantly positively associated with auditor tenure over four years in duration. Director tenure (DIRTEN) is highly significant ($p = 0.000$ (one-tailed)), as is BIG6 (p-value $= 0.038$ (one-tailed)). No other independent variables are found significant in this logistic regression. Many control variables important to a continuous measure of tenure are not associated with this dichotomous measure, which partitions the sample according to whether or not auditor tenure lasts beyond the critical four-year stage.

Discussion and conclusions

The purpose of this chapter is to investigate the impact of director-auditor links (a personal attachment where interlocking directors engage the same audit firm across their company directorships) on auditor tenure. Motivation is provided not only by the paucity of empirical analysis in the auditing literature on the relationship between interlocking directorates and auditors, but also by potential policy implications of any findings for the debate surrounding mandatory auditor rotation.

The results provide support for the findings of Seabright, Levinthal and Fichman (1992) that personal attachments between directors and auditors diminish the pressure for auditor switches, considering the significant, positive relationship between director-auditor links (ALOCKYRS) and auditor tenure. The results also suggest that director-auditor links facilitate continuance of the relationship beyond the first four years of tenure. This four-year period was demonstrated by Levinthal and Fichman (1988) to be important to the likelihood of auditor switching.

The findings may also inform the debate over mandatory auditor rotation. For example, the existence of director-auditor links in an environment of longer auditor tenure could arguably appear to be an example of the nurturing of 'close personal or professional relationships with clients' by auditors proscribed under the auditing standards and codes of professional conduct in many jurisdictions.

The results show that over half of the largest 200 Australian listed companies in the sample engaged the same auditor for at least the last seven years prior to and including 1995. However, this study does not investigate whether the same engagement partner was present in each of the years of incumbency. Nevertheless, the pressure for mandatory auditor rotation, on the grounds of ensuring actual or perceived independence, may gain momentum if auditor tenure is accompanied by director-auditor links. As noted earlier, longer auditor tenure has been criticised for impairing independence regardless of any attachments between directors and audit firms. Such attachments may heighten these independence concerns.

This study is further motivated by the implications it may have for public accounting firms. As mentioned earlier, many studies have focussed on the determinants of auditor change as opposed to auditor tenure. This study could provide guidance to accounting firms by indicating some of the factors that are associated with longer auditor tenure. Nevertheless, this guidance should be acknowledged with regard to the possible independence concerns noted above.

While the findings of this research do have some interesting policy implications, they must be considered in the light of the limitations of the study. Given that the study includes data on only the largest 200 Australian listed companies, it is questionable whether the results generalise to the population of Australian companies (including smaller and private companies). In addition, the strict criteria for the inclusion of companies in the sample may detract from the study's generalisability. Nevertheless, the sample used here is comparable to that used by Davison, Stening and Wai (1984) and Jubb (2000). The capping of auditor tenure also creates a limitation in this chapter. However, a measure of tenure over longer periods is accompanied by non-trivial survivorship bias issues.

Even capping tenure at seven years, the study may suffer from survivorship bias because some of the companies included in the sample may not have existed for the seven-year measurement period. However, the inclusion of the variable AGE attempts to control for this potential limitation.

This study also assumes that ALOCKYRS captures accurately the explanatory power of personal attachments. However, other types of personal attachment may exist that are not captured by director-auditor links (for instance, managerial links with auditors). In addition, the effect of partner turnover, and its potential impact on auditor tenure due to the loss of personal attachment, is not considered. This study also assumes that where an audit firm merger occurs, auditor tenure is continuous if a client of either of the two firms continues to engage the merged audit firm. As noted earlier, companies choosing to measure an end to the auditor-client relationship due to a merger between audit firms may confound the study's results.

Nevertheless, the findings also provide interesting avenues for future research. This study raises the potential concern over auditor independence when director-auditor links and long auditor tenure occur concurrently. Future studies could investigate the impact of auditor-director links, in conjunction with longer auditor tenure, on audit quality as measured by, for instance, litigation against auditor. The impact on tenure of director-auditor links and other types of relationships (e.g., at the audit partner level) could be investigated over longer periods. Researching the impact of changes in the number of links or participants to the links in their association with auditor changes might be of benefit to the auditor change literature. Finally, examining whether the purchase of non-audit services from the incumbent auditor is contingent on the relationship between director-auditor links and tenure might add insight to the independence debate in the context of joint provision of services.

Auditors, audit firms, regulators, professional accounting bodies and purchasers of assurance services are likely to find the results of this study useful in informing the debate over both auditor independence, when audit firms are associated repetitively with directors, and rotation of auditors.

References

Aldhizer, G. R., III & Lampe, J. C. 1997, 'Competitive Bidding, Auditor Tenure and the Extent of Single Audit Findings', *Government Accountants Journal*, vol. 46, no. 4, pp. 45-9.

Alexander, M., Murray, G. & Houghton, J. 1994, 'Business Power in Australia: The Concentration of Company Directorship Holding Among the Top 250 Corporates', *Australian Journal of Political Science*, vol. 29, no. 1, pp. 40-61.

Allen, M. P. 1974, 'The Structure of Interorganizational Elite Cooptation: Interlocking Corporate Directorates', *American Sociological Review*, vol. 39, no. 3, pp. 393-406.

Beasley, M. S. 1996, 'An Empirical Analysis of the Relation Between the Board of Director Composition and Financial Statement Fraud', *The Accounting Review*, vol. 71, no. 4, pp. 443-65.

Beck, P. J., Frecka, T. L. and & Solomon, I. 1988, 'An Empirical Analysis of the Relationship between MAS Involvement and Auditor Tenure: Implications for Auditor Independence', *Journal of Accounting Literature*, 7, pp. 65-84.

Butterworth, S. & Houghton, K. A. 1993, 'Auditor Switching and the Pricing of Audit Services', *Journal of Business Finance and Accounting*, vol. 22, no. 3, pp. 323-34.

Carcello, J. V. & Neal, T. L. 2000, 'Audit Committee Composition and Auditor Reporting', *The Accounting Review*, vol. 75, no. 4, pp. 453-68.

Carroll, R., Stening, B. & Stening, K. 1990, 'Interlocking Directorships and the Law in Australia', *Company and Securities Law Journal*, vol. 8, no. 5, pp. 290-302.

Chow, C. W. & Rice, S. J. 1982, 'Qualified Audit Opinions and Auditor Switching', *The Accounting Review*, vol. 57, no. 2, pp. 326-35.

Constable, J & Woodliff, D. 1994, 'Predicting Corporate Failure Using Publicly Available Information', *Australian Accounting Review*, vol. 4, no. 1, pp. 13-27.

Cook, K. 1977, 'Exchange and Power in Networks of Interorganizational Relations', *Sociological Quarterly*, vol. 18, no. 1, pp. 62-82.

Craswell, A. T. 1985, 'Studies of the Information Content of Qualified Audit Reports', *Journal of Business Finance and Accounting*, vol. 12, no. 1, pp. 93-115.

Craswell, A. 1996, *Who Audits Australia*, University of Sydney.

Craswell, A. T. & Francis, J. R. 1999, 'Pricing Initial Audit Engagements: A Test of Competing Theories', *The Accounting Review*, vol. 74, no. 2, pp. 201-16.

Craswell, A. T., Francis, J. R. & Taylor, S. L. 1995, 'Auditor Brand Name Reputations and Industry Specializations', *Journal of Accounting and Economics*, vol. 20, no. 3, pp. 297-322.

Craswell, A. T. & Taylor, S. L. 1991, 'The Market Structure of Auditing in Australia: The Role of Industry Specialization', *Research in Accounting Regulation*, 5, pp. 55-77.

Crosby, L. A., Evans, K. R. & Cowles, D. 1990, 'Relationship Quality in Services Selling: An Interpersonal Influence Perspective', *Journal of Marketing*, vol. 54, no. 3, pp. 68-81.

Davison, A. G., Stening, B. W. & Wai, W. T. 1984, 'Auditor Concentration and the Impact of Interlocking Directorates', *Journal of Accounting Research*, vol. 22, no. 1, pp. 313-17.

DeAngelo, L. E. 1981, 'Auditor Size and Audit Quality', *Journal of Accounting and Economics*, vol. 3, no. 3, pp. 183-99.

DeFond, M. L., Ettredge, M. & Smith, D. B. 1997, 'An Investigation of Auditor Resignations', *Research in Accounting Regulation*, 11, pp. 25-45.

DeFond, M. L., Francis, J. R. & Wong, T. J. 2000, 'Auditor Industry Specialization and Market Segmentation: Evidence from Hong Kong', *Auditing: A Journal of Practice and Theory*, vol. 19, no. 1, pp. 49-66.

De Ruyter, K. & Wetzels, M. 1999, 'Commitment in Auditor-Client Relationships: Antecedents and Consequences', *Accounting, Organizations and Society*, vol. 24, no. 1, pp. 57-75.

Dooley, P. C. 1969, 'The Interlocking Directorate', *American Economic Review*, vol. 59, no. 3, pp. 314-23.

Eichenseher, J. W. & Shields, D. 1983, 'The Correlates of CPA-Firm Change for Publicly-Held Corporations', *Auditing: A Journal of Practice and Theory*, vol. 2, no. 2, pp. 23-37.

Eisenhardt, K. M. 1989, 'Agency Theory: An Assessment and Review', *Academy of Management Review*, vol. 14, no. 1, pp. 57-74.

Fichman, M. & Levinthal, D. A. 1991, 'History dependence in professional relationships: The ties that bind', in S. B. Bacharach, S. Barley & P. S. Tolbert (eds), *Research in the Sociology of Organizations*, 8, pp. 119-53.

Francis, J. R. & Wilson, E. R. 1988, 'Auditor Changes: A Joint Test of Theories Relating to Agency Costs and Auditor Differentiation', *The Accounting Review*, vol. 63, no. 4, pp. 663-82.

Geiger, M. A. & Raghunandan, K. 2002, 'Auditor Tenure and Audit Reporting Failures', *Auditing: A Journal of Practice and Theory*, vol. 21, no. 1, pp. 67-78.

Gulati, R. 1995, 'Does Familiarity Breed Trust? The Implications of Repeated Ties for Contractual Choice in Alliances', *Academy of Management Journal*, vol. 38, no. 1, pp. 85-112.

Haskins, M. E. & Williams, D. D. 1990, 'A Contingent Model of Intra-Big Eight Auditor Changes', *Auditing: A Journal of Practice and Theory*, vol. 9, no. 3, pp. 55-74.

Jubb, C. A. 2000, *Choosing an Auditor: Corporate Governance, Interpersonal Associations and Investor Confidence*, unpublished Ph.D., University of Melbourne.

Koenig, T. & Gogel, R. 1981, 'Interlocking Corporate Directorships as a Social Network', *American Journal of Economics and Sociology*, vol. 30, no. 1, pp. 37-50.

Koreto, R. J. & Harding, F. 1996, 'How to Build a Network', *Journal of Accountancy*, vol. 181, no. 5, pp. 79-82.

Krishnan, J(agan) & Krishnan, J(ayanthi) 1997, 'Litigation Risk and Auditor Resignations', *The Accounting Review*, vol. 72, no. 4, pp. 539-60.

Latham, C. K., Jacobs, F. A. & Roush, P. B. 1998, 'Does Auditor Tenure Matter?', *Research in Accounting Regulation*, 23, pp. 165-77.

Levinthal, D. A. & Fichman, M. 1988, 'Dynamics of Interorganizational Attachments: Auditor-Client Relations', *Administrative Science Quarterly*, vol. 33, no. 3, pp. 345-69.

Menon, K. & Williams, D. 1994, 'The Insurance Hypothesis and Market Prices', *The Accounting Review*, vol. 69, no. 2, pp. 327-42.

Mizruchi, M. S. 1996, 'What Do Interlocks Do? An Analysis, Critique, and Assessment of Research on Interlocking Directorates', *Annual Review of Sociology*, 22, pp. 271-98.

Pennings, J. M., Lee, K. & van Witteloostuijn, A. 1998, 'Human Capital, Social Capital, and Firm Dissolution', *Academy of Management Journal*, vol. 41, no. 4, pp. 425-40.

Pfeffer, J. 1994, *Competitive Advantage Through People*, Harvard Business School Press, Boston.

Raghunathan, B., Lewis, B. L., & Evans, J. H., III 1994, 'An Empirical Investigation of Problem Audits', *Research in Accounting Regulation*, 8, pp. 33-58.

Schoorman, F. D., Bazerman, M. H. & Atkin, R. S. 1981, 'Interlocking Directorates: A Strategy for Reducing Environmental Uncertainty', *Academy of Management Review*, vol. 6, no. 2, pp. 243-51.

Schwartz, K. B. & Menon, K. 1985, 'Auditor switches by failing firms', *The Accounting Review*, vol. 60, no. 2, pp. 248-61.

Seabright, M. A., Levinthal, D .A. & Fichman, M. 1992, 'Role of Individual Attachments in the Dissolution of Interorganizational Relationships', *Academy of Management Journal*, vol. 35, no. 1, pp. 122-60.

Shockley, R. A. & Holt, R. N. 1983, 'A Behavioral Investigation of Supplier Differentiation in the Market for Audit Services', *Journal of Accounting Research*, vol. 21, no. 2, pp. 545-64.

Simon, D. T. & Francis, J. R. 1988, 'The Effects of Auditor Change on Audit Fees: Tests of Price Cutting and Price Recovery', *The Accounting Review*, vol. 63, no. 2, pp. 225-69.

Simunic, D. A. 1980, 'The Pricing of Audit Services: Theory and Evidence', *Journal of Accounting Research*, vol. 18, no. 1, pp. 161-90.

Walker, P. L., Casterella, J. R. & Moet, L. K. 1998, 'An Investigation of Audit Failures in New Audit Engagements', *Research in Accounting Regulation*, 12, pp. 61-75.

Wallace, W. A. 1987, 'The Economic Role of the Audit in Free and Regulated Markets: A Review', *Research in Accounting Regulation*, 1, pp. 7-34.

Williams, D. D. 1988, 'The Potential Determinants of Auditor Change', *Journal of Business Finance and Accounting*, vol. 15, no. 2, pp. 243-61.

Williamson, O. E. 1991, 'Comparative Economic Organization: The Analysis of Discrete Structural Alternatives', *Administrative Science Quarterly*, vol. 36, no. 2, pp. 3-37.

Zajac, E. J. 1988, 'Interlocking Directorates as an Interorganizational Strategy: A Test of Critical Assumptions', *Academy of Management Journal*, vol. 31, no. 2, pp. 428-38.

Chapter 8. Where were the gatekeepers? Corporate collapses and the role of accountants

Barry J Cooper

Abstract

While it is generally acknowledged that the key to the recent spate of corporate collapses lies in the lack of effective corporate governance, there are a number of other factors that need to be considered in understanding this phenomenon. These include the new age of materialism that developed during the 1990s and the consequent corporate and investor greed, which contributed to the spiral that led to the demise of corporations such as Enron, WorldCom, HIH, One.Tel and the global accounting firm Arthur Andersen. Compounding these developments in the corporate environment was the behaviour of the traditional gatekeepers, including accountants in particular, who betrayed the public trust. The accounting profession is now paying the price, with increased government regulation and a credibility crisis that will take many years to resolve.

A fairytale

> The day Arthur Andersen loses the public trust is the day we go out of business.
> *Steve Samek, Country Managing Partner, Arthur Andersen US (Independence and Ethical Standards 1999).*

Looking back to 1999, it was inconceivable at the time that probably the world's most respected accounting firm was predicting its demise; the stuff of fairytales — which leads us to the well-known 'fairytale' of Alice in Wonderland:

> There was a table set out under a tree in front of the house, and the March Hare and the Hatter were having tea at it: a Dormouse was sitting between them, fast asleep, and the other two were using it as a cushion, resting their elbows on it, and talking over its head. 'Very uncomfortable for the Dormouse,' thought Alice; 'only, as it's asleep, I suppose it doesn't mind.' The table was a large one, but the three were all crowded together

at one corner of it: 'No room! No room!' they cried out when they saw Alice coming. 'There's plenty of room!' said Alice indignantly, and she sat down in a large arm-chair at one end of the table (from *Alice in Wonderland*, by Lewis Carroll).

As observed by Leung and Cooper (2003), the tea party of corporate greed has been exposed with a vengeance in recent times, with the CEOs and directors (the March Hare and the Mad Hatter) having their fill, the regulators (the Dormouse) caught sleeping, and the accountants and auditors (Alice) joining the fray at the surreal event. Hewitt (2002) argues that the party seems to come around every decade or so, until the bubble seems to expand another size in absurdity and cost to the community, before it finally implodes once again. Whatever the reasons, this time an increasingly angry public have seen their superannuation and pension savings savagely mauled, and respect for corporate managers, regulators and the accounting profession has arguably sunk to an all-time low (Leung & Cooper 2003). Fairytales are fun for children, but the story of Alice in Wonderland takes on a new dimension when viewed in the analogous context of the recent corporate collapses, and the actions of those responsible for this sorry period of business and professional greed in the United States, Australia and elsewhere.

Back to the future

The corporate greed and consequent collapses have been categorised by Gittins (2002a) as arising from a 'new age of materialism', researched by the leading American social psychologist, David Myers, in his recent book on the American paradox of spiritual hunger in an age of plenty (Myers 2000). Support for this view is offered by the Australian social researcher Hugh Mackay, who observes that corporate greed in recent times is as much about morality and culture as about economics (Mackay 2002). More recently, the Hon. Justice Owen, HIH Royal Commissioner, lamented that for all the breaches of law and flaws of the system he identifies, for all the thoughtful remedies he advances, the core problem is something he simply cannot fix. Australia's worst corporate disaster, Owen suspects, was at heart a profound failure of morality (Brearley 2003).

Before examining this recent spate of collapses, and the role played in them by the accounting profession, it is probably useful to look briefly at the history of Australian corporate collapses in the last few decades (including, again, the role played by accountants) to see what, if anything, we can learn from the past. These have been categorised by Clarke, Dean and Oliver (1997) as the dubious credit and tangled webs of the corporate 1960s, going for broke in the 1970s, and the 1980s decade of the deal.

The corporate '60s, '70s and '80s

The 1960s saw the collapse of well-known corporations including Latec Investments, Stanhill Development Finance, Reid Murray and H. G. Palmer. The common threads in all these collapses, impacted by a tight credit squeeze, were valuations of receivables and investments, treatment of unearned income, and intermingling of private and public companies. Directors were jailed, as was one auditor. In the then still developing accounting profession, there was much hand-wringing and finger-pointing at bad management practice, but not much introspection about the role of accountants themselves, and their lack of understanding about the need to properly account for the market value of investments and the collectability of receivables. As observed by Clarke, Dean and Oliver (1997, p. 43), 'those events of the 1960s (and the succeeding decade) are instructive for a considered assessment of professional ethics and business techniques, transactions, structures and accounting employed by the 1980s entrepreneurs' – including Bond, Spalvins, Herscu and Skase, the aggressive and flamboyant corporate dealers of that time.

Following the collapse of Mainline, Cambridge Credit, Minsec and Gollins Holdings in the early 1970s, the public outcry lead to a search for scapegoats. A number of directors were charged and criminal actions against two directors of Gollins Holdings saw them both jailed for more than 10 years. Unfortunately for the accounting profession, a civil action by the debenture holders in Cambridge Credit against the auditors resulted in a then unprecedented out-of-court settlement of $20 million, followed a couple of years later by a $6 million settlement for debenture holders in Gollins Holdings. These settlements have since been dwarfed by others, including $136 million in the Tricontinental case, amongst the largest audit settlements in Australian history (Sykes 1994).

In the early 1970s, Professor Ray Chambers was warning the accounting profession of the dangers lying ahead. He opined at the time that, 'if due to the optional accounting rules available to them, the company managers and directors are able to conceal the drift (in financial position), shareholders and creditors will continue to support, and support with new money, companies that are weaker than their accounts represent them to be' (Chambers 1973, p. 166). Following the collapses of the early '70s, the NSW Government formed the Accounting Standards Review Committee in 1978, chaired by Professor Chambers. The report was critical of the standards applied by the profession, and the then NSW Attorney-General threatened intervention in the accounting standard-setting process. The accounting profession publicly opposed the committee's recommendations and inertia set in; little did the profession realise then that the day of judgment would finally arrive when government intervention would dramatically occur, even though it was to take nearly another 30 years.

The 1980s was a return to the excesses of the '60s and '70s, but on a grander scale. Green (1991) noted that everyone — bankers, lawyers, accountants, regulators and directors — had their eyes closed, and some directors fraudulently abused their trust. It is now apparent that the greed and cavalier attitudes of business and the professions in the 1980s were to return with a vengeance in 2001-02. Many of the accounting issues unresolved in the 1980s, including practices such as interest expenditure being capitalised, formation expenditure being treated as an asset, and related party transactions, came back to haunt the profession in the years 2001-02.

The comments by Clarke, Dean and Oliver (1997, p. 148) in respect of the practices in the accounting profession in the 1980s are insightful:

> ... our conventional standard accounting practices were unable to cope with the complexities. Primarily they failed because of their ad hoc, one-off orientation — methods drummed up as a quick fix for a current anomaly, the current object of complaint, the subject of current pressure on the accounting, irrespective of whether they meshed or conflicted with other practices or financial common sense ...

And:

> ... the use of Urgent Issues Groups to come up with a speedy fix to urgent accounting problems ... the old reductionist approach and its one-off solutions continues, with as little hope of success in improving accounting data generally as the well-intentioned efforts in the past.

These sentiments do underline some of the problems that were in fact still facing the profession when the collapses of 2001-02 came. The consequences have impacted on one of the fundamental attributes of a profession, namely that of self-regulation. The upshot is that, in Australia, the profession has now lost its self-regulatory status, with the Australian Accounting Standards Board now under the government-sponsored Financial Reporting Council, and with the Auditing and Assurance Standards Board soon to follow under the CLERP 9 draft legislation.

The recent corporate collapses

The recent collapses in Australia of companies such as HIH Insurance, Harris Scarfe and One.Tel clearly demonstrate similarities to many of the factors surrounding the corporate collapses in the '60s, '70s and '80s. However, there are also important differences. In the 1980s, there was the impact of a severe credit squeeze with the consequent high interest rates, unlike the very low interest-rate regime in 2001-02. There was also virtually no inflation as occurred in the early 1970s. So where was the problem?

The new age of materialism

During the 1990s, there were fundamental changes occurring in Australian society, including changes in corporate and professional culture. As noted above, Gittins (2002a) refers to this as the 'new age of materialism'. He observes that the rise of economic rationalism in the 1980s, which gathered pace in the 1990s, had been the politicians' response to the electorate's increased materialism and the higher living standard that a more efficient economy could deliver. The advice by economists to politicians on the need to cut protection and reduce government regulation was straight out of Economics 101, and had been doctrinaire and politically unpopular until the 1980s. The reforms have worked, but an ancillary development has been the way money has invaded our lives where it formerly played a lesser role (Gittins 2002b). Consider how sport has been taken over by media companies and professionalised; how the weekend has been commercialised, which means more of us now have to work on weekends; how we are now more litigious, so that after an accident we think about how we can turn misfortune into cash; how school fêtes are cancelled because public-risk insurance is too expensive; how houses are getting bigger as families shrink. So it is okay to attack evil economic rationalists, greedy businessmen or stupid politicians, but it's just not done to attack materialism – that would come altogether too close to home (Gittins 2002b).

However, this age of materialism is not a peculiarly Australian phenomenon. Myers (2000) has provided impressive evidence for similar changes in values in the United States. The American psychologist observes that average Americans have doubled their real incomes and have access to relatively cheap goods and services such as espresso coffee, mobile phones, four-wheel drive vehicles and the world-wide web. And yet Myers also observes that Americans have less happiness, more depression, more fragile relationships, less communal commitment, less vocational security, more crime and more demoralised children. Through a series of polls, Myers noted, for example, that the proportion of students going to college believing it essential they 'become well-off financially' rose from 39% in 1974 to 74% in 1990, and that over the same period the proportion that hoped to 'develop a meaningful philosophy on life' slumped from 76% to 43%, and that this reversal stayed unchanged throughout the 1990s.

The point is that once you appreciate the way our values have changed, the reason for a lot of developments becomes clear (Gittins 2002b). The new age of materialism could also help explain why, in recent years, Australian CEOs have been awarding themselves unprecedented – and to many, unbelievable – pay rises, and have become much more ruthless in their attitudes to customers and employees. Corporate boards often justify astronomical salary and bonus payments by the need to compete on the international market and to reward CEOs for the positive impact they can have on the share price. However, with the average wage for Australians with full-time jobs being $45 000 per year in 2002, Hugh Mackay observes that the community perception of employee exploitation is heightened by revelations of multimillion-dollar salaries and perks for senior executives (Mackay 2002). Even after the criticism of the excesses of 2001-02, the governance débâcle relating to rogue trading at the National Australia Bank (NAB) during 2004, which resulted in the resignation of the CEO Frank Cicutto, meant he walked away from the bank with a reported $3.27 million-payout, including a payment in lieu of six months' notice. However, he had to forgo almost $1.3 million in shares. All of this was cold comfort, however, for NAB's shareholders and the bank itself, which has endured a substantial loss of reputation along with the money (AAP 2004).

As discussed above, this heightened materialism also provides a context for the arguably declining ethical standards among company directors, accountants and auditors. David Knott, the former chairman of corporate regulator the Australian Securities and Investment Commission (ASIC), has strongly criticised the outbreak of management greed, the failure of boards to put a brake on excessive and structurally unsound remuneration practices, the focus on short-term pay-offs, and the behaviour of analysts – and at least some auditors – in foregoing their ethics in return for record-level fees and commissions (Knott 2002). At the same time, others have lamented that the regulators were caught sleeping. The insurance industry regulator, the Australian Prudential Regulation Authority (APRA), was criticised in respect of the HIH Insurance collapse, with politicians and leading insurance executives claiming the regulator was not adequately staffed to identify the weaknesses in the company's systems (Kemp 2001; Elias 2001).

The concept of corporate greed is also illustrated by the work of Toms (2002), who, in an historical analysis of the Lancashire cotton mills from 1870 to 1914, concluded that the collapse of a system of open corporate accountability was due to the rise of a clique of shareholder-entrepreneurs who instigated accounting manipulation. Toms' detailed analysis of the cotton mills shows that social capital (namely, the capital contributed by workers) demanded accurate financial information, with the support of cooperative governance. But systematic wealth transfers in favour of cliques of promoters, directors and institutions narrowed the social base of share ownership, increasing the power of the cliques and reducing proper accountability. This cyclical effect can be seen also in agency compensation, a mechanism to minimise agency costs by aligning individual agents' interests with those of the organisation. But as such a mechanism becomes the tool for wealth transfers, and prey to power and materialism, agency compensation can become the rationale for creative accounting and ultimately the demise of corporations. Also, accounting and auditing rules develop according to the accountability demanded by collective capital, which is in turn the subject of manipulations by managerial agents, resulting in a failure to produce transparent information.

Toms also noted that individual financial status and capital maintenance reputation were secured through accounting manipulations and dividend announcements and little reliance was placed on the publication or auditing of financial statements. In examining past history, Toms has successfully provided a portrait of how an open corporate accountability system collapsed, with features of shareholder-entrepreneurs, accounting manipulation and the failure of a reliable audit function. The Toms analysis revolves around events that occurred over 100 years ago, but it all sounds very familiar. Other authors have also highlighted the significant pay-outs of under-performing directors and managers (Gordon, Salmons & FitzGerald 2003; Gray 2000), and there has been plenty of evidence of this, particularly in the United States and Australia in recent years.

The collapse of Enron and the implosion of Arthur Andersen

> I also experienced a culture rife with conflict and an organization consumed by never-ending financial and political pressures. I worked with people so in thrall to the great bull market of the 1990s and the power and wealth of their corporate benefactors that they completely forgot that the true purpose of their job was to protect the investing public.
> *Barbara Toffler, former partner-in-charge of Arthur Andersen's Ethics and Responsible Business Practices division (Toffler & Reingold 2003).*

The implosion in 2002 of Arthur Andersen (one of the then 'Big Five' global accounting firms) following the collapse of Enron was arguably the defining moment when public trust was lost in the accounting profession and when the gatekeeping role was clearly breached. It is therefore useful to consider the implosion in the context of the new age of materialism as articulated by Gittins (2002a, 2002b), Myers (2000) and Mackay (2002). In this way, it is possible to provide an enlightening illustration of the link between the new religion of materialism and the loss of integrity and independence by the accountants who prepared the accounts and, in particular, those who audited them.

Enron is a classic case of corporate collapse caused by the failure of the board, a series of accounting frauds, lack of independence and objectivity by the auditor, and poor corporate ethics. Enron was a giant energy trading company listed on the New York Stock Exchange. It had one of the largest audit firms as auditor, namely Arthur Andersen, and a 'blue ribbon' board of directors. Its share price rose from US$20 in 1999 to peak at US$90 in August 2000. However, by December 2001 it dropped to being worthless when Enron filed for bankruptcy protection under Chapter 11 of the US Securities Act.

Much has been written about the collapse of Enron, and the Senate Sub-Committee Report, known as the Powers Report (Powers 2002), is an authoritative investigation of what went wrong. In summary, the issues uncovered by the Powers investigation included substantial and unapproved employee bonuses paid to managers and executives; partnerships (Special Purpose Entities, or SPEs) established to accomplish favourable financial results without bona fide economic objectives, and which did not conform with accounting rules; other improper transactions entered into to disguise US$1 billion in losses; and wrong accounting treatments, despite the auditors' involvement. Arthur Andersen was paid US$5.7 million above audit fees for advice on the accounting treatments. Account restatements were necessary because the SPEs failed to satisfy conditions required for treatment as independent entities. The result was that the financial statements for the financial years 1997 through to 2001 had to be restated. The magnitude of losses was so great that, for example, Enron was found to have lost US$618 million in the third quarter of 2001, and another US$1.2 billion in its SPEs that had not been accounted for. The Powers Report also found failures of the Enron board of directors in their fiduciary duties, high-risk accounting practices, inappropriate conflicts of interest, extensive undisclosed off-the-books activities, and excessive compensation. It was also noted that there was a lack of independence by the board and the auditors. And yet it wasn't just Enron that brought Arthur Andersen down. Toffler and Reingold (2003) observe that Enron was simply the final straw for Arthur Andersen, which was a respected firm before its culture began to decay. They also observe that the downfall of Arthur Andersen and the loss of public trust in the accounting profession could have been avoided had people paid attention to the danger signs flashing everywhere in the late 1990s.

Co-founded by 28-year-old Arthur Andersen, an accounting professor, in 1913, the firm quickly built up a significant reputation for integrity. In 1954, the company began consulting services, and by 1978 it had become one of the largest professional services firms in the world. In 2000, the Arthur Andersen consulting division underwent an acrimonious split from the Arthur Andersen auditing practice and became Accenture. Arthur Andersen continued with its auditing and limited related services until its demise in 2002. In many ways, the company had been seen as a leader in its field. For example, it was first in the use of sophisticated training facilities, set up in St. Charles, Chicago, for its world-wide staff. It recognised the need for formal professional ethics training, and developed ethics cases and educated scores of accounting professors to teach ethics; and yet it was to become the first large international accounting firm to be convicted on criminal charges.

It has been argued that Arthur Andersen's changed culture accounted for its demise (Toffler & Reingold 2003). When the consulting practice surpassed the audit function and became the most profitable division, the generation of revenue took priority. As observed by Toffler and Reingold, Arthur Andersen came down from its lofty perch to wrestle in the mud in search of more fees, more power, more political clout – more everything: Arthur Andersen had embraced the new age of materialism. A number of issues were soon to become evident. The auditors in the firm were identified with large audit clients and hence the strong desire to maintain clients; audit personnel even looked forward to joining clients as a possible future career path. A number joined Enron and other high-profile clients such as WorldCom and HIH Insurance in Australia. An innovative business audit approach was devised to perform an audit with minimum time but which required a higher level of analysis. Judgment sampling gave way to statistical sampling, and then to strategic risk auditing. Tighter time budgets with a broadened focus on other non-audit outcomes were leading to services that helped to advise on business processes. Growing conflicts between serving the client management team and the interests of the shareholders were recognised by some partners but not reinforced with ethical principles. It became apparent that a good ethical culture amongst top management was lacking.

The final demise of Arthur Andersen was inextricably linked with Enron, where it had multiple roles. These included the role of external auditor, consultant on accounting and other matters, internal auditor, tax advisor, and advisor and reviewer of financial disclosure. In its last year at Enron, Arthur Andersen earned audit fees of US$25 million and other fees of US$27 million, and Enron was one of its largest clients. Arthur Andersen's conflicts of interest included effectively self-audit, in that they were consultants on the setting up of the SPEs which Enron used to hide its true financial position. It also appears that there was a fear of losing a large and prestigious audit such as Enron, leading to the removal of partners who were disliked by Enron management (similar partner changes occurred on the Arthur Andersen audit of HIH Insurance). There was also a covering up of non-compliance, internal debates about Enron not aired, and a failure to inform investors on Enron's non-disclosures.

In summary, Arthur Andersen's shortcomings included a lack of professional competence, failure of internal quality procedures, failure to follow up where there was a lack of information, and a lack of appreciation of the fiduciary duties of auditors. The company was indicted and convicted in March 2002 for obstruc-tion of justice after personnel in several cities were reported as being involved in the shredding of papers and deletion of electronic data relating to the Enron audit. The consequent conviction resulted in Arthur Andersen's ability to audit companies being withdrawn. Its reputation and ability to function as a firm was rapidly eroded, with Arthur Andersen personnel joining other firms, rival firms taking over its clients and parts of its businesses, and the company eventually imploding. The 'Big Five' became the 'Big Four' in June 2002, and Arthur Andersen's 85 000 employees world-wide were dissipated to other firms or lost their jobs. A firm that had taken 90 years to build an enviable reputation had lost it all in 90 days.

Déjà vu

Poor management, inadequate controls, competition, acquisitions, financing, poor corporate culture and similar issues have continued to be common factors in corporate collapses. However, in looking back at the collapses of the '60s, '70s and '80s in Australia, it is also apparent that the regulation of corporate groups was, and arguably remains, ineffective. On each occasion, regulation has been increased and accounting standards improved, and yet, as noted by Clarke and Dean (2001), there has not been any observable slowing of the manner in which corporate groups feature in corporate crises. In fact, the use of complex corporate structures continues to be a recurrent feature in corporate failures, and the unravelling of the financial impact of the failure of corporate group structures remains bewilderingly complex. For example, in the case of HIH Insurance, the liquidator announced that it would be two years before the first general dividend payment and up to 10 years before the final payment (Sexton 2001).

An additional factor in the recent collapses was sheer greed. Turner (2001) observes that in a system fed by stock options, boardroom perks, and consulting and underwriting fees, enough was never enough. The seeds of the present crisis, particularly in the United States, were sown in the technology stock boom of the early 1990s, with the now bankrupt e-commerce companies then hailed as the way of the future. At the same time, the telecommunications revolution, in a new world of unregulated competition, required billions in investment for fibre optic cables, satellites and microwave towers. For example, the strategic decision by One.Tel to invest in its own telecommunications system was a major reason behind its eventual downfall (Leung & Cooper 2003). These new technologies demanded financial manipulation schemes to ensure that share prices held up, and options, stratospheric salaries and bonuses would continue to be paid. Even a first-year accounting student could work out that this was all financially unsustainable (Leung & Cooper 2003).

Where were the gatekeepers?

Accountants, auditors, investment banks and law firms, whose independence and integrity had been traditionally relied upon, joined the rush – under threat of being left behind – to access the riches from the new dot.com revolution. In the new age of materialism, the belief in the revolution was so pervasive that the gatekeepers became servants to the new players, rather than remain as the independent guardians. The traditional brakes on the system no longer worked

(Scott 2002). As also observed by the American Assembly at Columbia University (American Assembly 2003), all too often those whose mandate it was to act as a gatekeeper were tempted by misguided compensation policies within their firms to forfeit their autonomy and independence. Further to the review above of the famous Enron collapse, which is synonymous with the loss of credibility by the accounting profession, an analysis of three of Australia's biggest corporate collapses, namely HIH Insurance, Harris Scarfe and One.Tel, provides an inside view into how accountants and auditors, together with other professionals such as lawyers, failed in their gatekeeper role.

HIH Insurance

In March 2001, HIH Insurance was placed in provisional liquidation with reported losses of $800 million, although later estimates put the deficiency at between $2.7 and $4 billion, making it Australia's largest corporate collapse (Kehl 2001). HIH was known as a price-cutter and more willing underwriter than its competitors in the insurance industry, and excessive discounting was one of the contributing factors to the failure of the company. However, it was arguably the hostile takeover of FAI Insurance for $300 million, without proper due diligence investigations, that marked the beginning of the end for HIH (Brown 2001). Also, HIH experienced major losses in its operations in the United States and the United Kingdom, which contributed to its eventual demise.

The Royal Commission into the affairs of HIH Insurance by Hon. Justice Owen was announced in June 2001. The terms of reference were wide-ranging and, to enable the Royal Commission to fully investigate the circumstances surrounding HIH's failure, the actions of Commonwealth and state regulatory bodies, and whether changes should be made to the current legal framework, were included in the brief. The report on the failure of HIH Insurance was issued by Hon. Justice Owen in April 2003.

The moral issues that Owen discovered went beyond individuals in HIH's employ to afflict entire professions on the outside. For example, the accountants emerge as the masters of sneaky tricks. Brearley (2003) observes that 'book-cookers' were rife, and some of the instruments they employed, although legitimate tools of their trade, were decidedly shonky. Goodwill was the first offender, an intangible and largely discretionary asset which surged while real assets were squandered. In time, it came to represent fully half of HIH assets. Another major problem with HIH was that it didn't set aside enough reserves to cover future insurance claims and overvalued some assets. Under questioning at the HIH Royal Commission, the finance director denied that carrying out his acknowledged responsibility to be prudent and conservative in assessing policyholders' claims required the use of a safety margin in claims reserves. This was despite the fact that the levels set by the company had proved to be inadequate in the past (AAP 2002).

Hon. Justice Owen was far from satisfied with the accounting systems and procedures adopted by HIH. In one of his observations (HIH Royal Commission 2003, p. *xlvi*), he noted that:

> ... users of HIH accounts may not have understood it at the time, but in 1999 and 2000 – the years to which primary attention was given in the inquiry – the financial statements were distorted by questionable entries, heavy reliance on one-off end-of-year transactions, and aggressive accounting practices ... including, despite significant losses, continuing to record as an asset in its financial statements the full value of the future income tax benefits ...

In relation to the efficacy of the audits, Owen commented that: '... in my view, Andersen's approach in the audit of 1999 and 2000 was insufficiently rigorous to engender in users confidence as to the reliability of HIH's financial statements. This detracted from the users' ability to appreciate fully HIH's true financial position' (HIH Royal Commission 2003, p. *lvii*). Finally, there were also problems with the prima facie independence of the audit committee of the board, whose membership was mainly made up of accountants. The chairman and another member of the committee were both former partners of Arthur Andersen, the auditors of HIH, the finance director was a former Arthur Andersen partner, and another two members of the audit committee had business relationships with the company (Correy 2001).

Harris Scarfe

The retailer Harris Scarfe had operated for 150 years before it was placed into voluntary administration by the directors on 2 April 2001, after discovering irregularities dating back six years. In their report to creditors, the administrators highlighted that the systematic overstatement of profit had been funded by increased debt, both to the bank and the creditors (Peacock 2001). After investigations by ASIC and official examinations by the company's receivers and managers, ASIC alleged the chief financial officer, who has since been jailed, had altered Harris Scarfe's accounts to inflate the company's profits and had created a false picture that Harris Scarfe was in good financial health, permitting it to trade when it was virtually insolvent.

A suit has been filed against Harris Scarfe's auditors by the ANZ Bank, seeking recovery of at least $70 million and alleging the auditors had been negligent because they failed to uncover the accounting discrepancies and irregular entries in the accounts. Also, the former chairman of Harris Scarfe has been charged with a number of offences relating to failure to act honestly, dissemination of false information, and intentional failure to notify the board of falsely inflated profits.

One.Tel

One.Tel was placed in administration and subsequently into liquidation in May 2001 with estimated debts of $600 million. At the same time, ASIC announced it had commenced a formal investigation into One.Tel for potential breaches of the Corporations Act. According to an ASIC spokeswoman, the potential breaches included possible insolvent trading, possible insider trading and market disclosure issues (BBC News 2001). Creative accounting by One.Tel in capitalising expenses had attracted the attention of ASIC, and its insistence that accounting practices be changed led in August 2000 to the company declaring $245 million of costs that would otherwise be hidden (Barry 2002).

The liquidator's inquiry into One.Tel was told how multimillion-dollar bonuses paid to the founders were effectively hidden from public scrutiny by questionable accounting practices. The bonuses totalling $14 million were incurred in 1999, but a change in accounting policy treated the bonuses as deferred expenditure and for set-up costs associated with One.Tel's businesses across Europe and Australia. This treatment, along with other questionable accounting adjustments, had the effect of converting a loss into a profit. It was also claimed that the auditors had supported the questionable accounting (ABC Newsonline 2002).

The fairytale comes true

At the beginning of this paper, the Mad Hatter's tea party included Alice the accountant and auditor, who wanted to join in. Well, the accounting profession *did* join the party of corporate greed and is now paying the price: it is no longer a fairytale. An analysis of the corporate failures in the past provides ample evidence of individual accountants – and, by association, the profession itself – abandoning the traditional gatekeeper role and joining the fray.

Accountants behaving badly

At HIH Insurance, the chief financial officer presided over an accounting system that used complex corporate structures to hide the truth. Inadequate provision was made for future insurance claims, assets were overvalued, and tax losses were turned into assets, even though it must have been known within the company that it was making real losses and that the future income tax benefits were unlikely to ever be realised. Furthermore, the auditors were insufficiently rigorous in their approach to the audit and members of the audit committee were less than independent.

At Harris Scarfe, it was simple manipulation of inventory figures by the chief financial officer, and he got away with it for six years without being detected by the auditors, who are now being sued. At One.Tel, creative accounting in capitalising expenses was practised until the accountants were forced by ASIC to return to the principles they should have learned in Accounting 101 at university. Substantial bonuses that were clearly expense items were capitalised for nebulous reasons, and when later questioned in court, the finance manager admitted that the treatment was 'a bit of a stretch'. And where were the auditors?

While one can argue that it is easy to be critical with hindsight, the fact remains that it has all happened before and we are not 'talking rocket science'. What we *are* now talking about is a loss of public trust. A profession will only survive if it has credibility and can be trusted to serve the public good. For that reason, a profession should be self-regulating, something that is now being lost in Australia. Already the exclusive setting of accounting standards has been taken out of the hands of the profession and the auditing standards are to follow. However, the problem is not confined to Australia, as recognised in the Sarbanes-Oxley Act of 2001 in the United States and the recent IFAC report on rebuilding public confidence in public reporting (IFAC 2003a). It took the dramatic demise of the once great accounting firm of Arthur Andersen to provide the defining moment when public trust was lost. It now has to be rebuilt.

Attempts to restore credibility in financial reporting and auditing

IFAC found that the credibility of reporting is both a national issue in each country and an international issue, with action required at both levels. Some of the specific recommendations of particular relevance to the profession include reduction of incentives to misstate accounts which should require the proper expensing of costs and clear disclosure of the terms of share options; greater attention to auditor independence and corporate governance processes; the raising of auditor effectiveness, primarily through greater attention to audit quality control processes; and the strengthening of auditing and reporting practices and regulation (IFAC 2003a, pp. 2-4). IFAC has also since issued reform proposals that provide for more transparent standard-setting processes, greater public and regulatory input into those processes, regulatory monitoring and public-interest oversight (IFAC 2003b).

The Ramsay Report on auditor independence (Ramsay 2001), the HIH Royal Commission, investigations by ASIC, and the ongoing coverage in the financial press will all impact on the future direction of accounting and audit regulation in Australia. In particular, the latest phase in the Commonwealth Government's Corporate Law Economic Reform Program, resulting in a draft Bill (CLERP 2003), addresses a number of key issues. Of particular importance to the accounting profession are the recommendations in respect of financial reporting and audit reform. Some of the CLERP 9 recommendations have already been implemented.

These include broadening membership of the AASB, increasing Australian involvement in the development of international accounting standards, and developing professional accounting body guidelines for seeking independent advice.

In respect of audit reform, the recommendations include developing higher standards for the independence of auditors, amending the Corporations Act to require an annual audit statement by auditors to disclose all details of their non-audit services, and the imposition of restrictions on retired auditors becoming directors of former client companies.

Conclusion

The above analysis of corporate collapses and the role of accountants and auditors is not a particularly happy one. The profession has lost much of its credibility, public trust has been badly shaken, and the profession has learned the hard way that it should not take its position in society for granted. As the capital market evolved alongside the rapid growth of technology and globalisation, there was an unhealthy shift in attitudes in the corporate world, one that has also existed in earlier times in the development of modern corporations (Leung & Cooper 2003). It is important to understand this phenomenon if any proposed reforms are to be effective in the future. For the sake of the trusting public, let us hope the period of corporate greed so evident in recent years is forever past history. But then, history does have a habit of repeating itself.

References

AAP (Australian Associated Press) 2002, 'Finance Director fronts HIH probe', News.com.au, 21 August, viewed 11 September 2002, http://-www.news.com.au/common/story_page/-0%2C4057%2C4943604%255E22802%2C00.html.

AAP (Australian Associated Press) 2004, 'The head of the National Australia Bank has done the right thing by leaving the bank', *The Age*, 2 February.

ABC Newsonline 2002, 'Accountants hid One.Tel bonuses, inquiry told', viewed 9 September 2002, http://www.abc.net.au/news/business/2002/07/-item200207312161223_1.htm.

American Assembly (103rd) 2003, *The Future of the Accounting Profession*, Columbia University, New York.

Barry, P. 2002, 'One.Tel's cash SOS, then it all fell apart', *Sydney Morning Herald*, 31 July.

BBC News 2001, 'Watchdog 'swoops' on One.Tel HQ', viewed 4 September 2002, http://www.news.bbc.uk/l/hi/business/1365954.stm.

Brearley, D. 2003, 'HIH: Moral Hazard', *The Australian*, 19 April.

Brown, B. 2001, 'Untangling the HIH disaster', *Asiamoney*, London, 7 July.

Carroll, L., *Alice in Wonderland* (any edition).

Chambers, R. J. 1973, 'Observation as a method of inquiry – the background of *Securities and Obscurities*', *Abacus*, vol. 9, no. 1, pp. n/k.

Clarke, F. L. & Dean, G. W. 2001, 'Corporate Collapses Analysed', *Collapse Incorporated*, CCH Australia, Sydney.

Clarke, F. L., Dean, G. W. & Oliver, K. G. 1997, *Corporate Collapse – Regulatory, Accounting and Ethical Failure*, Cambridge University Press, Melbourne.

CLERP (Audit Reform and Corporate Disclosure) Bill 2003, 'Commentary on the Draft Provisions', Commonwealth of Australia, Canberra.

Correy, S. 2001, 'Independence and Auditing: when companies collapse', Radio National, viewed 9 September 2002, http://www.abc.net.au/rn/talks/-bbing/stories/s297499.htm.

Elias, D. 2001, 'Why weren't the HIH bells loud and clear?', *The West Australian*, 1 September.

Gittins, R. 2002a, 'Invasion of the Money Snatchers', *The Age*, 28 August.

Gittins, R. 2002b, 'Getting to the root of modern evil', *Sydney Morning Herald*, 28 August.

Gordon, J., Salmons, R. & FitzGerald, B. 2003, 'Chief's Golden Handshake sparks uproar', *The Age*, 9 January.

Gray, J. 2000, 'The Golden Parachute Club', *Canadian Business*, 12 June, pp. 31-4.

Green, J. 1991, 'Fuzzy Law – a better way to stop the snouts in the trough?', *Company and Securities Law Journal*, vol. 9, no. 3, pp. n/k.

Hewitt, J. 2002, 'The naughty noughties are making greed-is-good '80s refined', *Sydney Morning Herald*, 5 June.

HIH Royal Commission 2003, *The Failure of HIH Insurance*, Commonwealth of Australia, Canberra.

IFAC (International Federation of Accountants) 2003a, *Rebuilding Public Confidence in Financial Reporting*, New York.

IFAC (International Federation of Accountants) 2003b, *Reform Proposals*, New York.

Independence and Ethical Standards 1999, CD-ROM, Arthur Andersen, US.

Kehl, D. 2001, 'Current Issues – HIH Insurance Group', Economics, Commerce and Industrial Relations Group, Department of the Parliamentary Library, viewed 3 September 2002, http://www.aph.gov.au/library/intguide/-econ/hih_insurance.htm.

Kemp, S. 2001, 'Select group should sort claims: ICA', *The Age*, 16 May.

Knott, D. 2002,' Protecting the Investor – the Regulator and Audit', Australian Shareholders Association, viewed 9 September 2002, http://-www.asa.asn.au/%3BArticlesMain/2002-07-01.asp.

Leung, P. & Cooper, B. J. 2003, 'The Mad Hatter's Corporate Tea Party', *Managerial Auditing Journal*, vol. 18, nos. 6 & 7, pp. 505-16.

Mackay, H. 2002, 'Boost the bottom line, pay the CEO less', *The Age*, 5 October.

Myers, D. G. 2000, *The American Paradox – Spiritual hunger in an age of plenty*, Yale University Press, New Haven, CT.

Peacock, S. 2001, 'Probe reveals the extent of Scarfe's debts', *The West Australian*, 11 April.

Powers, W. C., Jr. 2002, 'Report of Investigation,' Special Investigative Committee of the Board of Directors of Enron Corp, viewed 24 March 2004, http:/-/www.news.findlaw.com/hdocs/docs/enron/sicreport/.

Ramsay, I. 2001, *Independence of Australian Company Auditors: review of current Australian requirements and proposals for reform*, University of Melbourne.

Scott, W. 2002, 'Sorry, guys, but greed corrupts absolutely', *Australian Financial Review*, 1 August.

Sexton, E. 2001, 'HIH black hole now 1 bn bigger', *Sydney Morning Herald*, 28 August.

Sykes, T. 1994, *The Bold Riders: Behind Australia's Corporate Collapses*, Allen and Unwin, Sydney.

Toffler, B. L. & Reingold, J. 2003, *Final Accounting: Ambition, Greed and the Fall of Arthur Andersen*, Broadway Books, New York.

Turner, L. 2002, 'Just a few rotten apples? Better audit those books', *Washington Post*, 14 July.

Chapter 9. Management economic bargaining power and auditors' objectivity[1]

Carolyn A Windsor

Abstract

The audit of large organisations relies on a system of professional self-regulation with public-sector oversight. Professional self-regulation of audit is sustained by the fundamental principles of objectivity and independence that are mandatory in the professional code of conduct. The current system of regulation, however, requires auditors to depend directly on the auditee's client management for their economic survival. Using psychometric measures, two studies examine auditors' ability to remain objective when psychologically pressured by client management economic bargaining power in hypothetical audit conflict scenarios. The scenarios tested hypotheses that auditors applied three hierarchical levels of complex decision-making to process independence judgments. The results of two mixed factorial ANOVA-designed studies indicate that auditors' moral reasoning and personal justice beliefs interact with management economic factors when making independence decisions. Auditors' first level of response is immediate and impressionistic to client economic factors: financial condition, size of fees and tendering that result in main effects. Client economic factors interacted with auditors' second-level cognitive moral development and third-level preconscious beliefs in response to management demands, thus showing the difficulty for auditors to be free of personal beliefs and remain objective under intense pressure.

Introduction

The magnitude of recent corporate collapses has provoked public and media ire. Yet again, the spectre of auditor independence and the ability of auditors to remain objective when employed by economically powerful corporate clients is in the news. Unfortunately, auditors have been implicated in fraud after fraud. The Enron scandal brought down Arthur Andersen, which had been one of the

[1]The author gratefully acknowledges the invaluable contribution by the large international audit firms in Australia. Also I am grateful for the opportunity to present this paper at the ANU Audit and Ethics Workshop, December 2003, chaired by Professor Tom Campbell.

profession's 'Big Five' firms. Now a scandal at Italy's Parmalat that was uncovered in late 2003 threatens Deloitte & Touche, another global giant, as well as Grant Thornton, an important second-tier firm. But new scandals are still emerging (*Economist* 2004).

If the public loses confidence in the auditing profession's ability to remain independent, governments will introduce more regulation; consequently the audit profession might have to relinquish their self-regulatory status (see CLERP 9). Moreover, the shock demise of the respectable accounting firm Arthur Andersen emphasised the vulnerability of the profession. The US Congress responded to the wave of corporate scandals with the landmark legislation Sarbanes-Oxley Act of 2002. The broad corporate governance reforms and anti-fraud provisions of the Act were felt in boardrooms across the nation (Labaton 2003) and around the world. The Australian Federal Government also commissioned the Ramsey Report on Auditor Independence (Hayes 2002), following corporate scandals such as the collapse of HIH Insurance.

Every professional auditor is personally mandated to maintain an independent and objective 'state of mind' to provide an unbiased opinion about the veracity of corporate financial reports. Mautz and Sharaf (1961) argue that the auditor's objective judgment should be similar to a judge's decision in a court of law. Hence, independence relies on the personal but unobservable decision-making processes of the engagement auditor to be objective, and free from conflict of interest, bias and prejudice (see IFAC 2001). Objectivity, therefore, is fundamental to auditor independence. The IFAC Code of Ethics for Professional Accountants (IFAC 2001, p. 5) defines objectivity as 'a combination of impartiality, intellectual honesty and a freedom from conflicts of interest'. Yet auditors are human, with the full range of feelings, thoughts, personal strengths and weaknesses, as well as values and beliefs imbued from various life experiences.

The purpose of this research, therefore, is to investigate whether auditors' objectivity is affected by the unconscious stimulation of their cognitive moral development and personal beliefs when resolving a difficult independence decision. In fact, this research examines whether it is possible for all auditors to have the same ethical fortitude to ensure their objectivity. The independence issue in the present study involves the client management, one group which appears to have considerable economic influence on the auditor (Mautz & Sharaf 1961; Goldman & Barlev 1974). Few studies have investigated auditor objectivity, but this research uses psychometric measures to examine some of the auditors' decision-making processes.

Structural power imbalance between management and the auditor

Corporate management is a powerful social and economic institution that directly and indirectly affects the well-being of millions of people worldwide (Kelly 2001). Yet the forces of the capital markets that guide this powerful institution are shrouded in commercial confidentiality rather than democratic principles of openness and public accountability. Instead, government legislators and regulators have created a system of corporate financial disclosure overseen by the self-regulated auditing profession for the benefit of the capital markets, but also ostensibly in the public interest. Through legislation, governments have conferred a special and lucrative franchise on the auditing profession. In return, auditors' conduct and behaviour are governed by professional codes of ethical conduct that emphasise objective judgment independent of all influences, including management (Mautz 1988).

The auditor's role, however, is confusing and conflicting. The profession must implement the regulation of accounting and legislative frameworks on behalf of the public interest, yet at the same time have a business relationship with the auditee company for private economic benefit. Although the owners of the auditee company legally have the power to appoint auditors, more often executive directors (or senior management), as representatives of the owners (shareholders), negotiate the conditions of the auditors' employment and the information to be disclosed on behalf of the auditee firm (Goldman & Barlev 1974). The livelihood of the auditing profession, therefore, relies on fees negotiated with client management. The vulnerability of a large professional service provider working in a business that relies mainly on fees is evidenced by the demise of Arthur Andersen. When the Enron scandal began to fester into huge litigations and US Federal Government investigation, clients fled Arthur Andersen, giving their business and fees to the remaining 'Big Four', and thus leaving Arthur Andersen with an unsustainable cash flow (Morrison 2004). Short-term economic gain of the audit firms (particularly the partners) is at the expense of the long-term good of the profession. Management control of the corporate domain is empowered further by the self-regulation of auditors. Self-regulation perpetuates a lucrative and comfortable professional monopoly that responds pretentiously but ineffectively to audit failures and maintains the status quo.

An example of the failure of self-regulation that pays little heed to the comfortable auditor management relationship was the appointment of KPMG audit partner Chris Lewis to a senior executive position of the National Australia Bank's (NAB) risk management system, shortly after providing an unqualified opinion for the 2000 financial reports (Hoy 2002). Further, 'The problem for KPMG is that the very audit partner, who gave the all clear to National's accounts including

HomeSide, is now the National Bank's general manager of risk management, in clear breach of CLERP 9' (Hoy 2002).

In the 2001/02 financial reports, HomeSide's US business was written off to the amount of A$3.617 million as goodwill, after tax (2001/02 NAB Concise Report, p. 15), although the 2000/01 Annual Report glowingly described the HomeSide business (see the 2000/01 NAB Concise Report, p. 28). Many saw the 2001/02 NAB report into the HomeSide débâcle as sanitised (Hughes 2004). Chris Lewis and other senior executives of the NAB's risk management committee were dismissed from their positions after A$380 million of fictitious foreign exchange trades were revealed that indicated a failure of NAB's risk management system (Hughes 2004).

Rather than break the nexus between the self-serving economic relationship of auditor and management as the example above shows, the American Sarbanes-Oxley Act and the Australian Ramsey Report (Hayes 2002) have focused on mainly behavioural aspects of auditor independence. These reactions to corporate regulatory failure have not addressed the central issue of auditors' working conditions and economic dependence on the auditee as the client. The lofty idealism of professional obligations is at odds with the pragmatism of business to satisfy client needs.

Private interests, public interest and ethical behaviour

The theory of regulatory capture is critical of state intervention. It refers to the capture of state regulation by businesses in a particular industry that the state agency was designed to regulate (Posner 1974). One common way of doing this is to have former or future employees in the industry work for the regulatory agency, to advance private business interests above the public interest. The theory of regulatory capture is somewhat related to the above example, where the former self-regulated auditor is now employed in a lucrative management position in NAB shortly after having provided a clean audit report. In this instance, the auditor's mandated objectivity was compromised by personal self-interest at the expense of the public interest. At this time, the auditor has not been breached or punished in any way by the profession or ASIC.[2] This is a remarkable failure of private and public regulation, where NAB management has not only gotten away with misinforming the public but also reducing NAB owners' wealth through mismanagement and financial irresponsibility.

The power imbalance of the management-auditor relationship in a problematic regulatory system has been known for some time. In fact it was described in the

---

[2]ASIC employs in senior positions retired partners from the large accounting firms whose regulatory experience is mainly a self-regulatory regime.

testimony of an expert witness before the US House of Representatives Commerce Committee, who said (Klott 1985, p. 22):

> If one were starting from point zero today, it would be madness to invent a system where the one to be audited hired the auditor, bargained with the auditor as to the size of fee, was permitted to purchase other management services from the auditor, and where the auditor in turn has the social responsibility for setting the rules and for enforcing them and applying sanctions against themselves.

Nevertheless, auditors are personally required to behave independently of management as mandated by ethical codes of professional conduct. Yet little is known about the decision processes that auditors use to make objective judgments about management-prepared financial statements. This research introduces a complex decision-making model of independence judgments, to examine the auditors' personal objectivity processes under ethical pressure by varying degrees of client management economic power.

The complexity of auditor independence judgments

Auditor independence judgments can be difficult and complex, as they involve personal behavioural and decision-making processes that are difficult to observe. To address some of the complexities of auditor independence judgments, an interactionist model (Trevino 1986) is the basis for this study. Expected findings are that those cognitive processes involving auditors' moral reasoning (Kohlberg 1969) and personal justice beliefs (Lerner 1981) will interact with client management's economic power (Mautz & Sharaf 1961) to affect auditors' objectivity, and so their independence judgments.

The auditors' complex ethical decision-making model posits that auditors use three hierarchical levels of individual decision-making, processing the decision through each sequential level when responding to a thorny situation. The more intense the moral dilemma, the more complex the auditors' decision-making becomes, tapping into embedded beliefs. The last two levels involve high-order interactions, the higher the decision level, the higher the order of interaction. Decisions processed at the higher levels are therefore reflected in interactions between personal beliefs at Level 3, cognitive style at Level 2, and the dilemma to be decided (which triggered the initial response). At Level 2, auditors' responses are the result of thinking processes, which are influenced by cognitive style defined in terms of moral reasoning. Finally, at Level 3, auditors' responses are influenced by processes which involve beliefs defined as 'the belief in a just world'.

The model aims for a more holistic approach to individual decision-making by synthesising its two facets of cognitions and preconscious beliefs imbued from a person's social environment. Kahlbaugh (1993) claims that this approach to individual decision-making gives a better understanding of how these two facets of the person interact. Stage theorists such as Kohlberg assume moral reasoning is stable at each stage, however social learning theorist Bundura (1986) questions this assumption. Bundura suggests that the stages of moral development may be more amenable to social influences than expected by stage theorists (see Optow 1990).

Situation variables – economic bargaining power of client management

Management bargaining power is conceptualized in terms of economic factors that exert pressure on auditors, and therefore influence their objective decision-making processes and independence outcomes. The initial interviews with senior audit partners indicated that the three primary dimensions of management bargaining power were (1) client financial condition (Knapp 1985), (2) size of client fees (Gul 1991), and (3) whether or not the client calls tenders for their audits.

Level 1: Immediate response to situation factors

Level 1 of the complex decision-making model is auditors' immediate response to powerful external stimuli of the situation variables representing client management bargaining (economic) power. We hypothesize that auditors' Level 1 responses to an audit conflict involving client management economic pressure is expected to be spontaneous and immediate, resulting in strong main effects for situation variables, financial condition, size of client fees and tendering.

Level 2: Cognitive processes, moral reasoning and auditor independence

The ethical dilemma must be a powerful enough catalyst to activate auditors' higher levels of individual decision-making processes and responses. When management uses the client firm's economic situation to pressure the auditor's objectivity during an audit conflict, the auditor is faced with an ethical dilemma, hence prompting a different level of reasoning than the impressionistic and immediate responses in Level 1. Trevino (1986) proposed Kohlberg's social-cognitive theory of moral reasoning development (1969) as a key to researching the cognitive component of ethical decision-making in organisations.

The present study utilised Kohlberg's (1969) moral reasoning construct. Although this construct has been subject to some controversy (see Modgil & Modgil 1986), it has been used successfully as a cognitive measure in a number of studies in accounting and organisational settings over recent years (see Louwers, Ponemon & Radtke 1997 for an overview).

Rest (1986) claims the fundamental assumption of Kohlberg's theory is that a person's moral judgments reflect an underlying organisation of thinking. Moral judgments are a part of moral psychology involving how a person judges which course of action is right or just in a social situation. Kohlberg's (1969) theory addresses how the reasoning processes of moral decision-making become more complex and sophisticated with the individual's development. Kohlberg (1969, 1976) identified three broad levels of moral development through which individuals progress: pre-conventional, conventional and post-conventional, with two stages at every level. The pre-conventional level comprises Stages 1 and 2. Here a person responds to notions of right or wrong, particularly when personal consequences are involved (i.e., punishment, reward or an exchange of favours), or when authority figures impose physical power upon the individual. Reasoning at the conventional level consists of Stages 3 and 4, where doing 'right' conforms to the expectations of family, peer groups and society. In post-conventional reasoning (Stages 5 and 6), 'right' is influenced by universal values or principles; the individual defines moral values apart from the authority of groups, and relies upon self-chosen principles to guide reasoning (for a full description of each stage, see Kohlberg 1976, and Colby & Kohlberg 1987).

Rest et al. (1999) acknowledge that there are limits to Kohlberg's approach and that cognitive moral development is one component of the psychological process of morality. They argue that there are four components that lead to moral behaviour; moral judgment, moral motivation, moral sensitivity and moral character. Furthermore, Rest et al. (1999, p. 10) state that 'Some critics have said that Kohlberg's theory (dealing with moral judgement) is too cerebral, that it misses the "heart of morality". But the special function of the construct of moral judgement is to provide conceptual guidance for action choice in situations in which moral claims conflict'. In fact, auditors have to deal with conflicting moral claims of the various interest groups associated with the fair presentation of financial statements (see Goldman & Barlev 1974).

Over the years, criticisms have emerged regarding Kohlberg's theory. Kohlberg and his associates have responded to their major criticisms (see Kohlberg, Levine & Hewer 1983), addressing such issues as stage sequencing, subjectivity in the scoring method, and gender and cultural biases. Snarey's (1985) review of Kohlberg's claim of cross-cultural universality revealed support for much of Kohlberg's theory. Gilligan (1982) voiced criticisms about gender bias. She argued that because Kohlberg focused on justice as the central defining feature of the moral domain, he failed to recognise an important area of morality, namely caring and responsibility. Various researchers, however, such as Lifton (1985), Nunner-

Winkler (1984) and Walker (1984), provide general empirical support for the application of Kohlberg's theory to both sexes.

Level 3: Preconscious socially-learnt belief in a just world

'Personal belief in a just world' (Lerner 1981) is a personality construct from the social justice literature that is suitable for testing auditors' objective decision-making under moral intensity. The auditors' decision-making is characterized by moral reasoning development (Kohlberg 1969) and personal beliefs (Lerner 1981) embedded in the auditors' preconscious, which are stimulated by fractious ethical dilemmas. It is expected that we will find that auditors use their personal beliefs unconsciously, thus affecting their objectivity when making an independence decision. Auditors' decision-making, characterized by decisional levels 2 (cognitive moral development) and 3 (justice beliefs), will be stimulated by an audit conflict when management has the economic advantage, thus affecting auditor objectivity.

Hence, an audit independence dilemma dealing with client economic situational variables is the basis for initiating interactive decisional processes to see if auditor objectivity is maintained. These decisional processes involve an interaction between a 'belief in a just world' personal variable from social learning theory (Rotter 1966) and Kohlberg's (1969) stages of moral cognitions from the cognitive development school. This model aims to show how preconscious personal beliefs from a lifetime of learning influence decision outcomes. Figure 9.1 illustrates the flow of effects in the proposed model of complex decision-making. At Level 1, auditors' responses are a consequence of immediate reactions to situational contingencies (client economic variables), and appear as main effects. At Level 2, auditors' responses are the result of thinking processes, which are influenced by cognitive style defined in terms of Kohlberg's (1969) moral reasoning construct. The decisions resulting from these processes are qualified by cognitions, and are therefore expressed as low-order interactions between cognitions and situational factors. Finally, at Level 3, auditors' responses are influenced by processes which involve beliefs defined as 'the belief in a just world' (Lerner 1981). These are reflected in interactions with cognitive style, personal beliefs and the situational variables:

Figure 9.1. Individual complex decision-making model of auditor independence

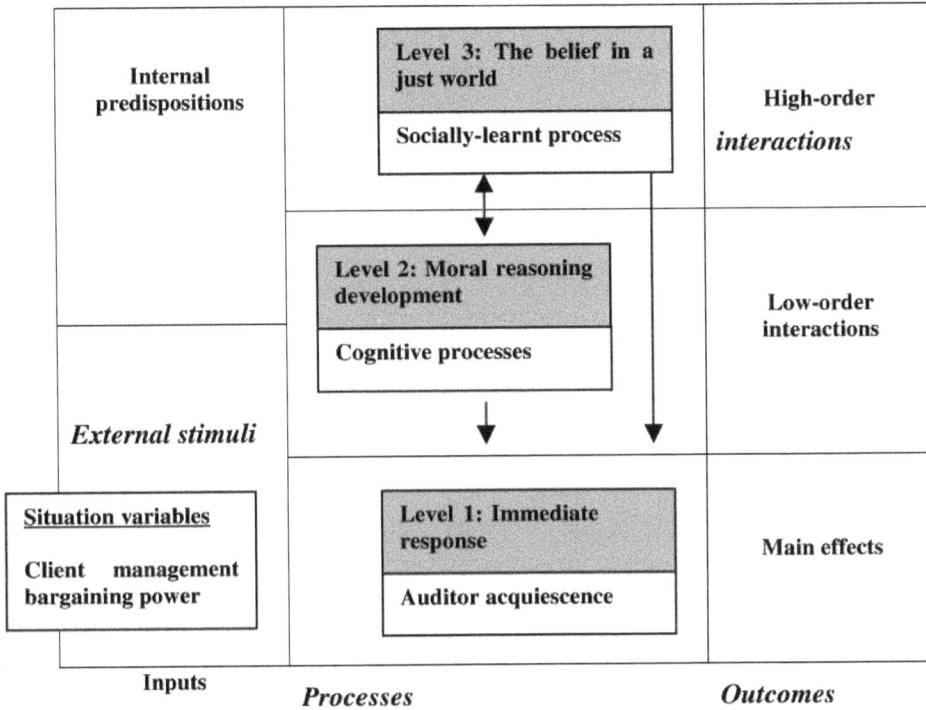

Internal predispositions	**Level 3: The belief in a just world**	High-order
	Socially-learnt process	*interactions*
	Level 2: Moral reasoning development	Low-order interactions
	Cognitive processes	
External stimuli		
<u>Situation variables</u> **Client management bargaining power**	**Level 1: Immediate response**	**Main effects**
	Auditor acquiescence	

Inputs   *Processes*   *Outcomes*

Method and analysis

An ANOVA design used the three repeated measures, (1) client financial condition, (2) size of fees, and (3) tendering. The two between-group independent variables were (1) level of moral reasoning and (2) the belief in a just world. The second hypothesis tests whether auditors' decision-making, characterized by decisional levels 2 (cognitive moral development) and 3 (justice beliefs), will be stimulated by an audit conflict when management has the economic advantage, thus affecting auditor objectivity. This will result in an interaction between management client economic variables, auditors' moral development and justice beliefs.

Two studies comprising ethical dilemmas about management economic power tested auditor independence using the three repeated measures. The dilemmas intended to place auditors in an intense conflict situation with client management, whose economic power was represented by eight scenarios involving company financial condition, size of fees and whether the audit was tendered. The three-story DIT measured auditors' level of moral reasoning. Auditors' justice beliefs were measured using the belief in a just/unjust world dimension. Rest (1979) suggested that the P scores might be categorized into high, mid and low groups corresponding, respectively, to pre-conventional, conventional and post-conventional levels of moral reasoning development. 50 (89%) of the auditors originally contacted responded for the first study. The second study replicated the first, with a 69% response rate.

Results

In the first study, four-way interaction between audit conflict variables of tendering and client financial condition, the belief in a just world variable and moral reasoning development provided support for Hypothesis 1 – that auditors responded immediately and impressionistically to client economic factors, with main effects for financial condition of the client and size of client fees. Hypothesis 2 was also supported, indicating that auditors' moral development and client management economic variables tendering and client financial condition stimulated personal justice beliefs. The results provided general support for the hypotheses that auditors' moral reasoning and personal beliefs are stimulated in a complex decision-making process for thorny audit conflicts. In summary, these results support Lerner's (1981) contention that people's just world beliefs unconsciously affect decision-making, thus affecting auditors' objectivity when faced with an independence dilemma.

Results of the second study supported the first study, with a significant high-order interaction found between client financial condition, the belief in a just world and moral reasoning development. The results of the two studies indicate that intense independence conflicts with management involving the client's economic situation stimulate auditors' personal justice beliefs and moral reasoning, thus reducing the auditors' ability to remain completely objective at a pre-conscious level. As the dilemma intensifies the decision-making process, client economic factors associated with situation affect auditors' cognitive complexity, and stimulate unconscious beliefs that result in higher-order interactions. The results of the two studies indicate that auditors' personal characteristics and beliefs intervene in independence conflicts with management, hence affecting auditors' personal objectivity. Moreover, this points to the structural problem of client management controlling the economic fate of auditors.

General discussion

The two experiments reported here support the notion that a complex decision-making process comprising three hierarchical levels affects auditors' objective decision-making. The professional standards require auditors to make independence judgments objectively, free from conflict of interest, bias, prejudice, feelings and thoughts. The results of the two studies indicate that intense independence conflicts with management involving the client's economic situation stimulate auditors' personal justice beliefs and moral reasoning, thus reducing the auditors' ability to remain completely objective at a preconscious level. At the first level, auditors' immediate response to explicit client economic factors is impressionistic, resulting in main effects. Most everyday decisions are made at this level, however when the decision is not straightforward, particularly for an ethical dilemma, second and third levels of thought-processing are activated.

As the dilemma intensifies the decision-making process, client economic factors associated with situation affect auditors' cognitive complexity and stimulate unconscious beliefs that result in higher-order interactions. Personal beliefs are embedded in the psyche, so that objectivity may be affected when they become part of the decision-making process. As such, the empirical results of this research provide strong support for the interactionist approaches proposed by Trevino (1986).

Results of the two studies reported here, however, are subject to three limitations. The first of these is that the research methodology relies on auditors' responses to hypothetical scenarios, which vary on economic situational variables representing client management bargaining power. Given that the respondents in the three studies were practising auditors expected to meet high professional and ethical standards (in the present instance, IFAC 2001), it would be surprising if they were to indicate high likelihood of acquiescence to management demands. In reality, auditors have been successfully sued for malpractice and are currently facing multibillion-dollar lawsuits. Nonetheless, the audit conflict situation was constructed with the active participation and close consultation of the senior audit partners, so that it constituted a realistic conflict between client management and the auditor.

The second limitation of the present study is that it was based on a repeated-measures design, and therefore subject to problems of demand characteristics (see Knapp 1987). Results obtained using a sample of audit students, however, indicated that the instrument was free of inherent bias. Further, the essential findings of the present study were based on the between-groups design, involving the belief in a just world and moral reasoning development. The third limitation concerns the construct validity of the psychological measures used in this research, and the extent to which they reflect respondents' actual cognitions and beliefs (see Rest 1986; Rest et al. 1999). Using Rest's (1979) DIT P Score and Collins' (1974) belief in a just/unjust world scale, however, is justified in the present research on the basis that the scales are well validated in the literature and provide theoretically interpretable results. Nevertheless, the reported results of the three studies need to be validated in field studies of auditors' behaviour in actual conflict situations.

In conclusion, the implications of these studies suggest that merely prescribing more behavioural and relationship rules to improve auditor objectivity and independence judgments probably will not succeed. The reported experiments indicate that auditors' objective thinking is affected by the corporate economic power controlled by management, the negotiators of audit fees and conditions. Moreover, this points to the regulatory structural problem of client management controlling the economic fate of auditors. In this current situation many auditors find it difficult to dissociate from economic reality and resist management demands when making independence decisions (see Tsui & Gul 1996).

Mautz and Sharaf (1961) maintain that auditor independence relies on the auditors' objectivity, similar to a judge in a court of law. If the judiciary had to support itself through the direct economic patronage of court protagonists by charging fees for services rendered, the judicial system would be compromised. Similarly, auditors whose opinions concern the veracity of corporate financial statements that are relied upon by the public should not be under the direct economic control of the entities that they are examining. Whether regulation should be private, public or a combination is not the issue though. The issue is how the integrity of regulatory systems should be maintained with appropriate checks and balances to encourage the best of human behaviour.

References

Economist 2004, 'The Future of Auditing, Called to Account', Business section, viewed 18 November 2004, http://www.economist.com.

Bundura, A. 1986, *Social Foundations of Thought and Action: A Social Cognitive Theory*, Prentice Hall, Englewood Cliffs, NJ.

Collins, B. E. 1974, 'Four Components of the Rotter Internal-External Scale: Belief in a Difficult World, a Just World, a Predictable World, and a Politically Responsive World', *Journal of Personality and Social Psychology*, vol. 29, no. 3, pp. 381-91.

Goldman, A. & Barlev, B. 1974, 'The Auditor-Firm Conflict of Interests: Its Implications for Independence', *The Accounting Review*, vol. 49, no. 2, pp. 707-18.

Gul, F. A. 1991, 'Size of Audit Fees and Perceptions of Auditors' Ability to Resist Management Pressure in Audit Conflict Situations', *Abacus*, vol. 27, no. 2, pp. 162-70.

Hayes, C. 2002, 'The Ramsey Report and the Regulation of Auditor Independence in Australia', *Australian Accounting Review*, vol. 12, no. 2, pp. 3-11.

Hoy, G. 2002, 'Concerns Around NAB Despite Top Bank Rating', *Inside Report*, ABC TV, 27 October.

Hughes, A. 2004a, 'No Buck-Passing, Sack the Bosses', *Sydney Morning Herald*, Business, 21 January.

Hughes, A. 2004b, 'Give Us a Month, Asks NAB Chair', *Sydney Morning Herald*, Business, 22 January.

IFAC (International Federation of Accountants) 2001, *Code of Ethics for Professional Accountants*, New York.

Kahlbaugh, P. E. 1993, 'James Mark Baldwin: A Bridge Between Social and Cognitive Theories of Development', *The Journal for the Theory of Social Behavior*, vol. 23, vol. 1, pp. 79-103.

Karniol, R. & Miller, D. T. 1981, 'Morality and the Development of Justice', in M. J. Lerner & S. C. Lerner (eds), *The Justice Motive in Social Behavior*, University of Waterloo, Ontario, pp. 73-89.

Kelly, M. 2001, *The Divine Right of Capital: Dethroning the Corporate Aristocracy*, Berrett-Koehler Publishers, Inc., San Francisco.

Knapp, M. C. 1985, 'Audit conflict: An empirical study of the perceived ability of auditors to resist management pressure', *The Accounting Review*, vol. 60, no. 2, pp. 202-11.

Klott, G. 1985, 'Accounting Roles Seen in Jeopardy', *New York Times*, 21 February, pp. 22-3.

Kohlberg, L. 1969, 'Stage and Sequence: The Cognitive-Developmental Approach to Socialization', in D. A. Goslin (ed.), *The Handbook of Socialization Theory and Research*, Rand McNally, Chicago, pp. 347-480.

Kohlberg, L. 1976, 'Moral stages and moralization: the cognitive-developmental approach to socialization', in T. Lickona (ed.), *Moral development and behavior: Theory research and social issues*, Holt, Rinehart & Winston, New York, pp. 31-53.

Kohlberg, L. 1986, 'A current statement on some theoretical issues', in S. Modgil & C. Modgil (eds), *Lawrence Kohlberg: Consensus and controversy*, Falmer Press, Philadelphia, pp. 485-546.

Kohlberg, L., Levine, C. & Hewer, D. 1983, *Moral Stages: A Current Formulation and Response to Critics*, Karger, New York.

Labaton, S. 2003, 'S.E.C.'s Oversight of Mutual Funds Is Said to Be Lax', *New York Times*, viewed 16 November 2003, http://www.nytimes.com/2003/-11/16/business/16FUND.

Lerner, M. J. 1980, *The belief in a just world*, University of Waterloo, Ontario.

Lerner, M. J. 1981, 'The Justice Motive in Human Relations', in M. J. Lerner & S. C. Lerner (eds), *The Justice Motive in Social Behavior*, University of Waterloo, Ontario, pp. 11-35.

Louwers, T. J., Ponemon, L. A. & Radtke, R. R. 1997, 'Examining Accountants' Ethical Behavior: A Review and Implications for Future Research', *Behavioral Accounting Research – Foundations and Frontiers*, American Accounting Association, Sarasota, FA, pp. 188-221.

Mautz. R. K., 1988, 'Public Accounting: Which Kind of Professionalism?', *Accounting Horizons*, vol. 2, no. 3, pp. 112-25.

Mautz, R. K. & Sharaf, H. A. 1961, *The Philosophy of Auditing*, American Accounting Association, Sarasota, FA.

McCrae, R. R. 1985, 'The Defining Issues Test', in J. V. Mitchell (ed.), *The Ninth Mental Measurements Yearbook*, Gryphen Press, Highland Park, NJ, pp. 439-42.

Modgil, S. & Modgil, C. 1986 (eds), *Lawrence Kohlberg: Consensus and controversy*, Falmer Press, Philadelphia.

Morrison, M. A. 2004, 'Rush to Judgment: the Lynching of Arthur Andersen & Co', *Critical Perspectives on Accounting*, vol. 15, no. 3, pp. 335-75.

Opotow, S. 1990, 'Moral Exclusion and Injustice: An Introduction', *Journal of Social Issues*, vol. 46, no. 1, pp. 1-20.

Pearlstein, S. & Behr, P. 2001, 'At Enron, the Fall Came Quickly', *Washington Post*, 2 December, p. A01.

Ponemon, L. A. & Gabhart, D. R. L. 1990, 'Auditor Independence Judgements: A Cognitive Developmental Model and Empirical Evidence', *Contemporary Accounting Research*, vol. 7, no. 1, pp. 227-51.

Ponemon, L. A. & Gabhart, D. R. L. 1994, 'Ethical Reasoning Research in the Accounting and Auditing Professions', in J. R. Rest & D. Narvaez (eds), *Moral Development in the Professions: Psychology and Applied Ethics*, Lawrence Erlbaum Associates, Hillsdale, NJ, pp. 101-20.

Posner, R. A. 1974, 'Theories of Economic Regulation', *Bell Journal of Economics*, Autumn, vol. 5, no. 2, pp. 335-58.

Rest, J. R. 1979, *Revised Manual for the Defining Issues Test: An objective test of moral judgment development*, Minnesota Moral Research Projects, Minneapolis.

Rest, J. R. 1986, 'Issues and Methodology in Moral Judgment', in S. Modgil & C. Modgil (eds), *Lawrence Kohlberg: Consensus and Controversy*, Falmer Press, Philadelphia, pp. 471-80.

Rest, J. R. 1994, 'Background: Theory and Research', in J. R. Rest & D. Narvaez (eds), *Moral Development in the Professions: Psychology and Applied Ethics*, Lawrence Erlbaum Associates, Hillsdale, NJ, pp. 1-26.

Rest, J. R., Narveaz, D., Bebeau, M. J. & Thoma, S. J. 1999, *Post-conventional Moral Thinking, A Neo-Kohlbergian Approach*, Lawrence Erlbaum Associates, Mahwah, NJ.

Rotter, J. B. 1966, 'Internal-External Control of Reinforcement', *Psychological Monographs*, vol. 80, no. 1, whole no. 609.

Rotter, J. B. 1975, 'Some Problems and Misconceptions Related to the Construct of Internal and External Control of Reinforcement', *Journal of Consulting and Clinical Psychology*, vol. 43, no. 2, pp. 56-67.

Shockley, R. A. 1981, 'Perceptions of auditors' independence: an empirical analysis', *The Accounting Review*, vol. 56, no. 4, pp. 785-800.

Trevino, L. K. 1986, 'Ethical Decision-making in Organisations: A Person-Situation Interactionist Model', *Academy of Management Review*, vol. 11, no. 3, pp. 601-17.

Trevino, L. K. & Youngblood, S. A. 1990, 'Bad apples in bad barrels: A causal analysis of ethical decision making behavior', *Journal of Applied Psychology*, vol. 75, no. 4, pp. 378-85.

Tsui, J. S. L. & Gul, F. A. 1996, 'Auditors' Behaviour in an Audit Conflict Situation: A Research Note on the Role of Locus of Control and Ethical Reasoning', *Accounting, Organizations and Society*, vol. 21, no. 1, pp. 41-51.

Chapter 10. Criticisms of auditors and earnings management during the Asian economic crisis

Shireenjit Kaur Johl
Christine A Jubb
Keith A Houghton

Abstract

Auditors were criticised during and after the Asian economic crisis for supplying variable quality across global audit markets. This study examines the level of earnings management as measured by discretionary accruals in the pre-crisis compared to the post-crisis periods as they impacted Malaysia. Both the Jones (1991) and earnings per share frequency distribution methods are used to examine earnings management behaviour. As hypothesised, the pre-crisis period is associated with significantly higher levels of absolute discretionary accruals and increased propensity to meet or beat the prior year earnings per share, whereas the post-crisis period is not. This finding is consistent with auditors responding to the criticisms that were made. However, the propensity to avoid losses is found to be higher in the post-crisis period, indicating that earnings management is not fully constrained.

Introduction

During and after the Asian economic crisis of 1997 and 1998, the large international audit firms were criticised for supplying uneven audit quality across their clients globally (see, for example, *Wall Street Journal* 1998; *Accountancy* 1998a-c, 1999a & b, 2000a & b). This study examines whether in one country affected by the crisis – Malaysia – there appears to be, for the then 'Big Five' audit firms, heightened attention to audit quality in the form of constrained discretionary accruals in the post-crisis compared to the pre-crisis periods. If evidence of differential constraint of discretionary accruals post- compared to pre-crisis *ceteris paribus* is found, then it is possible that the criticism of Big Five audit quality is associated with such a difference.

Malaysia is a country where traditionally there has been little criticism of auditors. To date no litigation against auditors has occurred and even if the professional accounting body, the Malaysian Institute of Accountants, disciplines an audit firm, no publicity surrounding the case is observed (Favere-Marchesi 2000). Malaysia adopts the International Standards on Auditing (ISAs) issued by the International Federation of Accountants (IFAC). Hence, if any heightened constraint of earnings management measured by discretionary accruals is observed, it is unlikely to be the reputation effects associated with litigation or disciplinary action that have motivated it.

Malaysia was affected severely by the crisis during 1997 and 1998, with 1999 seeing the emergence of recovery (Bank Negara Malaysia 1999; Athukorala 2000).

Background

Criticisms of auditors during the crisis

During the Asian economic crisis, the World Bank and the United Nations Conference on Trade and Development (UNCTAD 1998) questioned the quality of audits by Big Five auditors operating in Asia (Petersen 1998; Street & Gray 2001). The following quotations are indicative of the type of criticism levelled at auditors, particularly the Big Five:

> When the financial statements of a corporation or bank receive an unqualified audit opinion [from the Big Five], the external users of these statements tend to feel comfortable about the quality of the audit and the reliability of the information ... therefore, there is an obligation on the part of the international accounting firms to take the necessary steps so the quality of the audit services provided by their national practices all over the world does not fall short of practices in North America and Europe (*Accountancy* 1998b).

> In the precrisis period, the auditors did just what was required by local laws, and the laws were faulty. I think after the crisis they realized that the public sees them as having a responsibility higher than in the past, a responsibility of being a custodian of the interests of the public (Shivakumar, country manager in Thailand for the World Bank, quoted in Crispin 1999, p. 10).

The president of IFAC criticised auditors for asserting that financial statements comply with International Accounting Standards (IASs) when the accounting policies and notes show otherwise (Cairns 1997; Street & Gray 2001). This is evidenced by the formation of the IFAC International Forum on Accountancy Development (IFAD) in response to the 1997 call following the Asian economic crisis from James Wolfensohn, president of the World Bank (*Accountancy* 1999a;

Street & Gray 2001). IFAD, representing an alliance of accountancy groups and firms across the world, is intended to be a platform by which regulators, international financial institutions, investors and representatives of the accountancy and auditing profession act together to promote high-quality financial reporting and reduce the risk of economic downturns such as the Asian economic crisis (Street & Gray 2001).

At the May 2000 conference of IFAC, World Bank advisor Ira M. Millstein criticised the accountancy profession, particularly the Big Five, for failing to offer consistent standards of audit that meet the needs of investors worldwide. The International Auditing Standards Committee stated (IASC 1999) that:

> Identifying and dealing with departures by preparers from International Accounting Standards ... is primarily a matter for auditors, professional accountancy bodies, IFAC, national enforcement agencies and supranational bodies such as IOSCO and the Basel Committee. IASC does not have the resources or the legal authority to do this effectively.

Subsequently, the Forum of Firms (FOF) and the Transnational Auditors Committee (TAC) were formed within IFAC in January 2001. The FOF is a voluntary body made up of international audit firms performing audits across national borders. The founder members were Arthur Andersen, BDO, Deloitte Touche, Ernst & Young, Grant Thornton, KPMG and PricewaterhouseCoopers. These firms agreed to meet certain requirements and undergo a global independent quality review.

Thus, representatives from important institutions made public criticisms of auditors during and after the Asian economic crisis. These criticisms were responded to by auditors with the introduction of various mechanisms to address the issue. This study examines whether evidence consistent with audit firms acting to reduce the level of earnings management exists in Malaysia, one of the countries severely impacted by the crisis.

The pressure on international audit firms to maintain their reputations and supply high-quality audits, it is hypothesised, is likely to lead to constrained earnings management in the post-crisis period compared to the pre-crisis period *ceteris paribus*. It is this hypothesis that is tested in this chapter.

The next part of the chapter examines the research that provides evidence of auditors constraining management of corporate earnings. Then the measurement of earnings management through discretionary accruals is explained. A second method of examining earnings management that uses a frequency distribution of earnings per share (EPS) approach is then explained. Results are analysed before a conclusion is provided which summarises the study, its limitations, and the opportunities it provides for further research.

Prior literature

Auditors and earnings management

Several studies investigate the issue of earnings management and audit quality using archival data and find that higher quality auditors constrain earnings management more than lower quality auditors. Francis and Krishnan (1999) find that 'Big Six' auditors demonstrate greater reporting conservatism – through the modification of audit reports – for firms that record high levels of accruals than auditors from non-Big Six firms. Francis, Maydew and Sparks (1999) find that Big Six auditees record lower levels of discretionary accruals than non-Big Six auditees. Becker et al. (1998) find that Big Six auditees report lower levels of both absolute discretionary accruals, and income-increasing discretionary accruals, compared with non-Big Six auditees. More recently, Kim, Chung and Firth (2003) find that Big Six auditors are more effective in constraining earnings management than non-Big Six only when managers have incentives to engage in income-increasing accruals. Further, Krishnan (2003) finds that Big Five industry specialist auditors are more likely to constrain earnings management than non-specialists.

Amongst the audit judgment studies, Hirst (1994) investigated auditors' sensitivity to management's incentives to manage earnings. The effect of management's incentives to book income-increasing and income-decreasing accruals was examined in association with auditors' judgments of the probability of material misstatement. Management's incentives were manipulated using a management buy-out in one experiment and a bonus in a second experiment. Auditors were found to judge the probability of material misstatement to be higher when management's incentives and the observed unexpected difference were congruent in the first experiment. In the second experiment, auditors appeared not to differentiate between situations in which management had incentives to make either income-increasing or income-decreasing accruals. Hirst speculates that auditor conservatism is the reason for the differential findings, with auditors reacting with scepticism when earnings are expected to be materially overstated, and presupposing management's incentives and the unexpected difference to be congruent.

Nelson, Elliott and Tarpley (2002) found that managers are more likely to attempt earnings management that increases earnings in the current period, while auditors are more likely to recommend adjustments of earnings management attempts where the attempts result in overstated rather than understated earnings. This finding is consistent with differential litigation risk for auditors depending on the direction of the earnings misstatement (Lys & Watts 1994; Heninger 2001). However, as explained earlier, little if any litigation risk is expected in the Malaysian setting.

Earnings management and discretionary accruals

Accruals can be used to modify the timing of earnings recognition. Two key attributes of accruals result in them being the main mechanism by which earnings management is operationalised in the literature. Accruals can be classified as non-discretionary or mandatory accounting adjustments to cash flows required by accounting standards, while discretionary accruals represent voluntary adjustments to cash flows. Accruals can cause earnings to either increase or decrease.

This study utilises the Jones (1991) model as modified by Dechow, Sloan and Sweeney (1995), and Kaznik (1999), in decomposing total accruals into non-discretionary (expected) and discretionary (unexpected or abnormal) accruals. Dechow, Sloan and Sweeney argue that by accounting for the effect of managerial discretion exercised over the timing of receivables in the Jones model, the estimation of discretionary accruals will be better specified. This enhancement is operationalised by subtracting the change in receivables from the change in revenues in the Jones model once the parameters have been estimated. Dechow, Sloan and Sweeney, and Guay, Kothari and Watts (1996), confirm the benefit of this approach. However, this model has been criticised (see McNichols 2000), so a frequency distribution approach is also used.

Time-series data was originally employed to estimate accruals using the Jones model, however Subramanyam (1996), and Bartov, Gul and Tsui (2001), argue that the cross-sectional method of operationalising the model is superior. Since the models are re-estimated each year, an additional advantage of using the cross-sectional approach is that specific year changes in economic conditions affecting expected accruals are filtered out (Teoh, Wong & Rao 1998). Hence, this study employs the cross-sectional modified Jones (1991) model, bootstrap applied within industry categories on a year-by-year basis.

Methodology

The Jones (1991) model

The total accruals model, with organization (i) and year (t) subscripts, is:

$$TA_{it}/A_{i,t-1} = \alpha(1/A_{i,t-1}) + \beta_1(\{\triangle REV_{it} - \triangle REC_{it}\}/A_{i,t-1}) + \beta_2(PPE_{it}/A_{i,t-1}) + \varepsilon_{it}$$

where:

TA_{it} = total accruals at time t is calculated as: $[(\triangle \text{current assets}_{it} - \triangle \text{cash}_{it}) - (\triangle \text{current liabilities}_{it} - \triangle \text{short-term debt}_{it}) - (\text{depreciation and amortisation expense}_{it})$, where $\triangle$ denotes the change between t and t-1 [1]

---

[1] Total accruals are not derived from cash flows because IAS 7, 'Cash Flow Statements', was adopted only in 1996. Given the use of this indirect balance sheet approach, it is possible that the computations for the abnormal accruals are erroneous (Hribar & Collins 2002), and as such may lead bias with respect to the existence of earnings management. Nevertheless, due to data constraints this study acknowledges this limitation.

$A_{i,t-1}$ = lagged (one year) total assets

$\triangle REV_{it}$ = change in operating revenues between t and t-1

$\triangle REC_{it}$ = change in net receivables between t and t-1

PPE_{it} = gross property, plant and equipment

ε_{it} = error term, known as discretionary, unexpected or abnormal accruals (DA).

Non-discretionary accruals are defined as the fitted value from equation (1). Discretionary or abnormal accruals are defined as the residual of (1) – that is, the difference between TA and its fitted value from (1) (Jones 1991). Because each variable is scaled by lagged total assets, the level of abnormal accruals can be tested for significant differences between the pre- and post-crisis periods.

Once the discretionary accruals have been estimated, they are included as the dependent variable in an extended version of an earnings management model developed by Becker et al. (1998). The model takes the following form:

$$ABDA = \alpha + \beta_1 AQ + \beta_2 OCF + \beta_3 LEV + \beta_4 LASSET + \beta_5 ABTA + \beta_6 NEWAUD + \beta_7 OLDAUD + \beta_8 INCSHLD + \beta_9 CON + \beta_{10} IND + \beta_{11} PROP + \beta_{12} PRECRISIS + \beta_{13} POSTCRISIS + \varepsilon_t$$

where, for company i and year t:

ABDA = absolute discretionary accruals estimated as the residual from the Jones (1991) model

BIG5 = dummy variable equal to 1 if the auditor is from a Big Five audit firm and 0 otherwise

OCF = operating cash flow

LEV = leverage (debt/total assets)

LASSET = natural log of total assets

ABTA = absolute value of total accruals/total assets

NEWAUD = first sample year with a new auditor

OLDAUD = last sample year is followed by an auditor change

INCSHLD = increase in total outstanding shares during the year

CON, IND, PROP = industry dummy variables representing consumer trading, industrial products, and construction and property respectively (set equal to 1 if the observation is from these industries, and 0 otherwise)

PRECRIS = dummy variable equal to 1 if the observation is from the period 1994-96 inclusive

POSTCRISIS = dummy variable equal to 1 if the observation is from the period 1999

ε_{it} = unspecified random factors.

$$EM = \alpha + \beta_1 PRECRIS + \beta_2 POSTCRIS + \beta_3 LEV + \beta_4 LASSET + \beta_5 ABTA + \beta_6 NEWAUD + \beta_7 OLDAUD + \beta_8 INCSHLD + \beta_9 CON + \beta_{10} IND + \beta_{11} PROP + \beta_{12} OCF + \varepsilon_t$$

Each of the variables is explained in the following sections, and then, in view of criticism of the modified Jones (1991) model (see McNichols 2000), a second methodology for calculating abnormal accruals under it is explained. This method is used to provide confirmatory evidence and increase the robustness of results.

Hypothesis variables

Indicator variables PRECRIS and POSTCRIS represent the pre-crisis period from 1994 to 1996 inclusive and the post-crisis period in 1999 respectively. It is hypothesised that PRECRIS will be positive and significant and that POSTCRIS will be significant and negative in their respective associations with the absolute value of discretionary accruals.

Control variables

Leverage (LEV)

Although mixed, evidence from the earnings management literature indicates that managers indulge in income-increasing accruals to delay or avoid the costs of debt covenant violations (Press & Weintrop 1990; Defond & Jiambalvo 1994). Consistent with Becker et al. (1998), a measure of leverage (LEV) is included to control for the possible effects of gearing on earnings management. A positive relationship is expected between absolute abnormal accruals (ABDA) and leverage (LEV).

Total accruals (ABTA)

Francis, Maydew and Sparks (1999) argue that firms with greater endogenous accrual-generating potential have greater uncertainty about reported earnings because of the greater difficulty for outside parties to unravel abnormal accruals from total accruals. Thus, as in Becker et al. (1998), the absolute value of total accruals is included in the model to control for the possibility that firms with larger absolute total accruals also have greater inherent earnings management potential. A positive relationship is expected between ABDA and ABTA.

Equity offerings (INSHLD)

Prior studies argue that equity offerings provide increased incentive for managers to increase reported earnings during the offering period due to the potential existence of information asymmetry during this time. These studies (e.g., Teoh, Wong & Rao 1998; Rangan 1998) find that companies undertaking equity offerings show evidence of significant income-increasing abnormal accruals. Thus, consistent with the findings, and as used in Becker et al. (1998), a dummy variable in included in the model to indicate whether outstanding shares have increased by 10% or more from prior year outstanding shares. This INSHLD dummy variable takes a value of 1 if the outstanding shares have increased by 10% or more, or else 0.

Auditor change (OLDAUD and NEWAUD)

Amongst other factors, the occurrence of client-initiated auditor change may be motivated by auditors' preference for conservative accounting choices. DeFond and Subramanyam (1998) argue that firms with a change in auditor are expected to report more negative abnormal accruals in the last year with their predecessor auditor (OLDAUD). However, on the grounds that the successor auditor (NEWAUD) may be willing to adopt a less conservative stance than their predecessor, they argue that abnormal accruals should be less negative in the first year with the successor than those in the last year with the predecessor. Thus, as in Becker et al. (1998), to control for any possible auditor change effect, a dummy variable NEWAUD (OLDAUD) is included and given a value of 1 if the company is experiencing a year (last sample year) with a new auditor (old auditor).

Industry sector

In addition, the Becker et al. (1998) model controls for industry sector, which helps account for expected inter-industry differences in earnings management (Francis, Maydew & Sparks 1999). Kuala Lumpur Stock Exchange (KLSE)-listed firms are generally highly diversified and so the industry categories are collapsed from the KLSE-suggested nine to four – namely, construction and property development (PROP), consumer and trading (CON), industrial products (IND), and natural resources (plantation and mining).

Operating cash flow (OCF)

It is hypothesised that companies with high cash flows (and hence, probable high profits) engage in income-decreasing abnormal accruals to smooth earnings. Becker et al. (1998) find that cash flow has a negative association with discretionary accruals. Because IAS 7, 'Cash Flow Statements' (Malaysian Accounting Standards Board 1996) was operative mid- rather than pre- the period examined in this study (1994-99), to achieve consistency an indirect measurement approach is taken for all years, subtracting net income before extraordinary items from total accruals to derive OCF before deflating it by prior year assets.

Frequency distribution approach (Degeorge, Patel & Zeckhauser 1999)

This study also utilises an additional indirect, simple but powerful test by examining the frequency distribution of reported earnings. This second approach helps address some of the problems in estimating the level of abnormal accruals (e.g., McNichols 2000). This method rests on prior studies suggesting managers manage earnings to meet or beat certain simple earnings benchmarks. Specifically, this study explores the extent to which managers manage earnings to sustain previous years' profits. This involves examining the distribution frequency of firms achieving 0 or 1% or more in change in EPS from the prior year.

Being a relatively new technique in identifying earnings management, the frequency distribution approach has gained popularity because of its simplicity and power in focusing on the density of the earnings distribution after earnings management (McNichols 2000). The approach examines the statistical properties of earnings behaviour around a specified threshold. To date, prior studies (Burgstahler & Dichev 1997; Degeorge, Patel & Zeckhauser 1999) have examined this earnings discontinuities behaviour around three benchmarks; (1) zero earnings, (2) previous year's earnings, and (3) analysts' forecasts.

As pointed out by McNichols (2000), one outstanding feature of this approach is the 'specificity of their predictions regarding which group of firms will manage earnings, rather than a better measure of discretion over earnings' (p. 336). However, McNichols argues that despite this power advantage, there are several disadvantages in that, firstly, 'it seems implausible that the behaviour of the nondiscretionary component of earnings could explain such large differences in the narrow intervals around their hypothesized earnings targets. Stated differently, measurement error in their proxy for discretionary behaviour seems unlikely to be correlated with their partitioning variable' (2000, p. 336), and secondly, the approach is silent on the method applied to manage earnings and the incentives for management to achieve specific benchmarks.

In essence, the methodology used in this approach is to examine the density function of the distribution surrounding the chosen thresholds. If there are signs of earnings management, it is expected that there will be an unusually large number of companies with EPS at or slightly above the threshold, but an unusually low number below the threshold. In order to test the significance of any discontinuities at the chosen thresholds, a univariate statistical test that approximates a t-test is conducted. Specifically, the t-test is computed as follows (Degeorge, Patel & Zeckhauser 1999):

$$\tau_n = \frac{\triangle p(x_n) - \text{mean } \{\triangle p(xi)\}_{i \in R, \, i \neq n}}{\text{s.d } \{\triangle p(x_i)\}_{i \in R, \, i \neq n}}$$

where:

τ_n = t-like test statistic of the desired bin[2]

$\triangle p$ = proportion change of observation that lie in the desired bin with that in the prior bin

x_n = a random sample of x of size n (desired bin)

[2]A 'bin' is defined as histogram interval widths of $0.01 for the range −$0.20 to +$0.20.

x_i = balance of sample excluding observations corresponding to n

s.d = standard deviation.

Consistent with Degeorge, Patel and Zeckhauser, and Plummer and Mest (2000), a discontinuity is evident if the value of τ is greater than 2.0.

Sample

The data is primarily hand-collected from annual reports of companies listed on the KLSE covering financial periods between 1994 and 1999, where 1994-96 is deemed the pre-crisis period, 1997-98 the crisis, and 1999 post-crisis. In addition, incomplete and other required data were supplemented from other sources including (1) KLSE on disk, (2) KLSE handbook, (3) *Corporate Handbook*, (4) KLSE-RIAM online database, (5) Worldscope database and (6) *Investor Digest*.

The initial data-set comprises companies listed on the KLSE for years 1993 to 1999 since lagged variables are required. To be included, companies had to be:

- listed, as well as report in Malaysian Ringgit and be audited by a Malaysian-based auditor
- in an industry other than finance-related and unit trust sectors
- in existence in all or any of the years 1993 through 1999 with all financial report data available
- not newly listed (initial public offering, or IPO) (since differential levels of earnings management are expected within these companies)
- without a change in financial year-end.

In addition, all auditor data had to be available.

The sample size at various stages of data collection is presented in Table 10.1. For the initial regression analysis and the distribution frequency analysis, 1505 observations met the criteria, 599 from the pre-crisis, 643 from the crisis and 263 from the post-crisis periods.

Table 10.1. Sample selection criteria

Selection criteria	No. of valid cases						
	Pre-crisis			Crisis		Post-crisis	
	1994	1995	1996	1997	1998	1999	Total
Approximate number of KLSE-listed companies	478	529	621	708	736	757	3351
Less finance/trust companies	47	47	56	61	63	63	290
Less companies with incomplete financial data and unavailable annual reports	280	285	279	316	334	422	1478
Less IPO companies	2	11	15	14	2	2	46
Less companies with change in financial year end	-	1	2	4	5	7	19
Usable sample (calculation of abnormal accruals)	149	185	270	314	332	270	1520

Selection criteria	No. of valid cases						
	Pre-crisis			Crisis		Post-crisis	
	1994	1995	1996	1997	1998	1999	Total
Less companies with incomplete auditor data	1	2	1	3	-	1	8
Total	148	183	268	311	332	263	1505
Companies with EPS and change in EPS data available for frequency distribution approach	563			611		248	1422
Companies in existence 1996-99 with Big Five auditor for regression approach			150	150	150	150	600

Results

Univariate results

Table 10.2 reports the mean and standard deviation for each variable for periods 1994 to 1999 and for each of the sub-periods 1994-96 (pre-crisis), 1997-98 (crisis) and 1999 (post-crisis). Also reported are t-tests or Chi^2, as appropriate, to test whether the difference between pre- and post-crisis observations for each variable is significant.

Table 10.2. Descriptive statistics and univariate tests

Variable	Overall N = 600		Min	Max	Pre-crisis N = 150		Crisis N = 300		Post-crisis N = 150		Pre-crisis v. post-crisis	
	Mean	Std. dev			Mean	Std. dev	Mean	Std. dev	Mean	Std. dev	t-statistic or Chi²	p-value
ABDA	0.132	0.206	0.000	2.450	0.167	0.281	0.115	0.165	0.133	0.186	−1.911	0.058
LEV	0.326	0.432	0.000	5.143	0.234	0.187	0.321	0.355	0.428	0.665	4.490	0.000
INCSHLD	0.120	0.325	0.000	1.000	0.207	0.406	0.120	0.325	0.033	0.180	14.382	0.000
OLDAUD	0.042	0.200	0.000	1.000	0.033	0.180	0.037	0.188	0.060	0.238	0.337	0.056
NEWAUD	0.028	0.166	0.000	1.000	0.033	0.180	0.040	0.196	0.000	0.000	0.189	0.664
ABTA	0.114	0.216	0.000	2.644	0.083	0.099	0.104	0.188	0.163	0.321	2.942	0.003
LASSET	13.528	1.396	8.884	17.703	13.402	1.361	13.594	1.379	13.522	1.462	1.302	0.194
PRECRIS	0.249	0.433	0.000	1.000								
POSTCRIS	0.251	0.434	0.000	1.000								
CON	0.445	0.497	0.000	1.000								
IND	0.257	0.438	0.000	1.000								
PROP	0.193	0.395	0.000	1.000								
OCF	0.013	0.228	−1.766	0.704	0.038	0.141	−0.006	0.238	0.027	0.272	−2.008	0.045

The variable of interest, absolute discretionary accruals deflated by prior year total assets, is 0.132 overall, reaches a high of 0.167 pre-crisis, drops to 0.115 during the crisis, and settles at 0.133 for the post-crisis. The difference between pre- and post-crisis discretionary accruals is weakly significant at $p = 0.058$. Leverage (total debt/total assets) is increasing across the sub-periods, being 0.234 pre-crisis, 0.321 during the crisis, and 0.428 post-crisis, showing the impact of the crisis on borrowing levels. This difference is significant between pre- and post-crisis at $p < 0.001$.

The impact on share issues of the crisis is shown by approximately 12% of observations reporting an increase of 21% or more pre-crisis, dropping to 12% during the crisis, and 3% post-crisis. The difference in proportions is significantly different at $p < 0.001$ between the pre- and post-crisis periods. Auditor changes, represented by the last year with an auditor, increase across the sub-periods, with 3% of observations in the pre-crisis and crisis and 6% post-crisis. This difference in proportions between pre- and post-crisis is very weakly significant ($p < 0.10$). Distressed companies are known to change auditor more frequently than healthy companies (Schwartz & Menon 1985).

Observations reporting the first year with a new auditor grow across the pre-crisis and crisis periods, but drop in the post-crisis period. In the pre-crisis they represent 3% of observations, in the crisis period they represent 4%, and in the post-crisis period they represent less than 1%. The pre- versus post-crisis proportion is not significant. Deflated absolute total accruals increase across the sub-periods, but do so at a significantly different rate between the pre- and post-crisis periods, at $p < 0.001$. They increase from 0.083 pre-crisis to 0.104 crisis and 0.163 post-crisis. The natural log of company size is similar across the sub-periods. As could be expected, deflated operating cash flows decline from 0.038 pre-crisis to −0.006 during the crisis, and then rise to 0.027 post-crisis. The difference in this variable between pre- and post-crisis is significant at $p < 0.05$.

Table 10.3 reports the Pearson correlations between the variables included in the Becker et al. (1998) model. Although many of the correlations are significant, none are at levels likely to cause problems with the regression. The highest correlations of 0.562 and 0.536 are between deflated absolute total accruals and leverage, and between deflated absolute total accruals and absolute discretionary accruals, which is expected.

Table 10.3. Pearson's correlation N = 600

	ABDA	LEV	INCSHLD	OLDAUD	NEWAUD	ABTA	LASSET	PRECRIS	POSTCRIS	CON	IND	PROP
LEV	0.303***	1.000										
INCSHLD	0.107***	-0.018										
OLDAUD	0.071*	-0.027	0.026									
NEWAUD	0.035	-0.033	0.061	0.015								
ABTA	0.536***	0.562***	-0.054	0.012	-0.013							
LASSET	-0.175***	-0.199***	0.147***	0.014	0.019	-0.212***						
PRECRIS	0.098**	-0.123***	0.155***	-0.024	0.018	-0.082	-0.052					
POSTCRIS	0.000	0.136***	-0.154***	0.052	-0.099**	0.132***	-0.002	-0.333***				
CON	-0.046	0.028	0.010	0.031	0.049	-0.039	0.197***	0.002	-0.002			
IND	0.049	0.057	-0.041	0.011	-0.009	0.048	-0.181***	-0.006	0.010	-0.528***		
PROP	0.041	0.005	0.106**	-0.017	-0.032	0.057	0.047	0.001	-0.011	-0.438**	-0.288**	
OCF	-0.245***	-0.416***	-0.053	-0.031	0.027	-0.420***	0.162***	0.063	0.036	0.082*	-0.011	-0.092**

*** significant at p < 0.01
* significant at p < 0.10
** significant at p < 0.05

Multivariate results

The regression uses data from the same 150 Big Five-audited companies for the years 1996-99, providing 600 observations. Auto-correlation in the panel data is controlled for using the STATA cluster function to identify each observation emanating from the same company. It is important to bear in mind that the estimation of discretionary accruals by year and industry, with bootstrapping, used all available data from 1520 observations, as per Table 10.1.

Table 10.4 shows that the PRECRIS variable is significant and positive at $p < 0.05$, indicating that absolute discretionary accruals are positively associated with the pre-crisis period compared with the crisis and post-crisis periods combined. However, unlike the pre-crisis indicator variable, the post-crisis period indicator is not significant, although it is negative as expected. This result is consistent with absolute discretionary accruals being more constrained in the pre-crisis compared to the post-crisis periods.

Table 10.4. OLS regression

	Big Five auditees in existence across 1996-99			
Dependent variable ABDA	Coef.	Robust std. err	t	P > |t|
LEV	0.005	0.029	0.150	0.878
INCSHLD	0.077	0.032	2.420	0.017
OLDAUD	0.067	0.084	0.810	0.421
NEWAUD	0.040	0.046	0.880	0.378
ABTA	0.505	0.127	3.970	0.000
LASSET	−0.010	0.005	−2.100	0.038
PRECRIS	0.056	0.022	2.510	0.013
POSTCRIS	−0.007	0.014	−0.480	0.634
CON	−0.004	0.019	−0.230	0.820
IND	0.005	0.020	0.260	0.794
PROP	0.001	0.018	0.030	0.975
OCF	−0.004	0.084	−0.050	0.961
BIG5				
Constant	0.187	0.072	2.580	0.011
N	600			
F(13, 379) (13, 184)	11.170			
Prob > F	0.000			
R squared	33.2			
No. of clusters	150			

Significant also are the indicator for a 10% or more increased shareholding ($p < 0.05$) and deflated absolute total accruals ($p < 0.001$). Interestingly, the BIG5 variable is not significant. The regression is significant at $p < 0.001$ with an R squared of 33%. The regression on this panel data controls for observations from the same company and so reduces the risk of auto-correlation arising from the non-independence of observations. Robust regression using the Huber-White sandwich estimator (White 1980) is performed and results reported to cope with potential hetereoscedasticity.

It could be that the need for re-financing from the government agencies of Danaharta or the Corporate Debt Restructuring Committee (CDRC), or from private sources, and the scrutiny entailed in applying for funds, discouraged earnings management (Jaggi & Lee 2002). The regression on the same Big Five auditee sample was re-performed omitting companies that engaged in debt restructuring. This provided 543 observations. The results are not reported but, again, the pre-crisis variable is significant at $p < 0.05$ whilst the post-crisis indicator is not significant.

Results using the frequency distribution approach

This part of the chapter presents results from examining whether sample firms appear to manage earnings to meet or beat prior year earnings or to avoid losses. The aim of this examination is to determine whether the results using the frequency distribution approach support the results of constrained earnings management post-crisis compared to pre-crisis, from the multivariate analysis using the Becker et al. (1998) model in the previous section. Separate analyses for each of the two benchmarks are carried out for each of the distinct periods.

Meet or beat prior year earnings

It is most likely during the post-crisis period that firms will report negative earnings compared to the pre-crisis and, as such, it is unlikely there will be found significant activity around the meet or beat prior year earnings benchmark during the crisis and post-crisis in comparison to the pre-crisis periods. For this reason, the analysis is not performed for the overall period but only for the separately identified macroeconomic periods; that is, 1994-96 for the pre-crisis, 1997-98 for the crisis and 1999 for the post-crisis periods respectively.

Table 10.5 shows the descriptive statistics[3] for the change in earnings per share ($\triangle$EPS) and EPS variables. The mean earnings change between consecutive years is primarily negative when averaged across the whole period, but not exclusively so within each phase of the study period. The change is positive during the post-crisis period, whilst negative in the pre-crisis[4] and crisis periods. In addition, the 1998 (last year of crisis) earnings change appears to confirm the extent of crisis effect, whilst a recovery in the economy is evident in 1999, with companies on average registering positive earnings changes. The mean earnings number is

---

[3]To maximise the number of observations, the histogram analysis on earnings losses and decreases avoidance is carried out for the total sample. However, for descriptive purposes details for both the total and matched-pair samples are provided.
[4]The earnings change in the pre-crisis period for the total sample is negative whilst for the matched-pair it is positive. Analysis by each study year in the pre-crisis period shows that, for the total sample, the driving force for the negative change comes from 1996.

also primarily negative, but not exclusively so throughout the six years from 1994 to 1999.

Table 10.5. Descriptive statistics by period and year for change in earnings per share (△EPS) and earnings (EPS)

	Change in earnings per share (△EPS)					Earnings (EPS)				
	N	Mean	Std. dev.	Min.	Max.	N	Mean	Std. dev.	Min.	Max.
Overall	1422	–0.089	1.489	–39.724	16.236	1453	–0.007	1.373	–32.463	7.261
Pre-crisis	563	–0.037	1.879	–39.724	16.236	588	0.171	1.407	–32.463	7.261
1994	144	0.144	1.354	–0.272	16.236	146	0.196	0.183	-0.180	0.840
1995	168	–0.031	0.854	–10.921	0.855	181	0.265	0.573	–0.365	7.261
1996	251	–0.145	2.524	–39.724	1.204	261	0.092	2.052	–32.463	1.673
Crisis	611	–0.229	1.120	–12.040	10.861	616	–0.144	1.333	–21.602	6.315
1997	297	–0.109	1.027	–4.329	10.861	302	0.004	1.519	–21.602	6.315
1998	314	–0.341	1.193	–12.040	4.634	314	–0.286	1.109	–11.310	1.690
Post-crisis										
1999	248	0.136	1.230	–12.724	5.872	249	–0.089	1.349	–17.158	2.407

As expected, companies registered positive earnings in the pre-crisis period, whilst negative earnings numbers are registered in the crisis and post-crisis periods. Consistent with the earnings change results and other macroeconomic analyses, the extent and depth of the 1997 crisis was certainly also felt in 1998, with companies reporting mean EPS of –0.286 for the total sample and –0.235 for the matched-pair sample.

Figure 10.1. Histogram of change in earnings per share since prior year – prior year earnings performance threshold

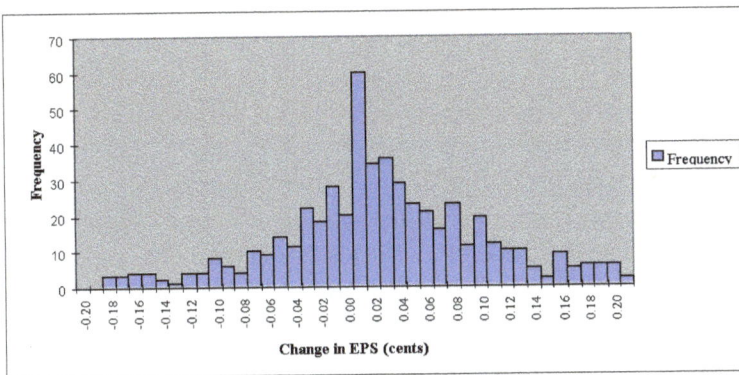

Panel A: Pre-crisis period (1994-96)

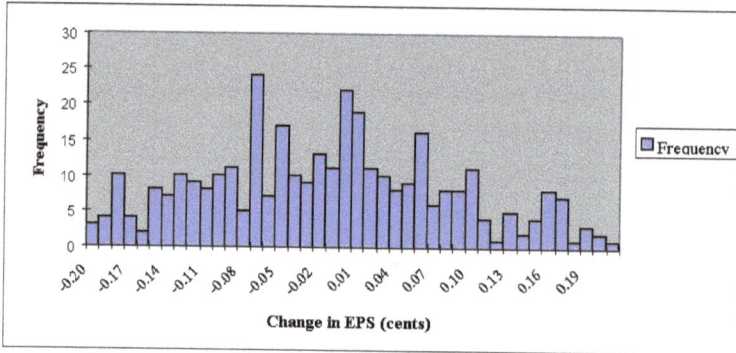

Panel B: Crisis (1997-98)

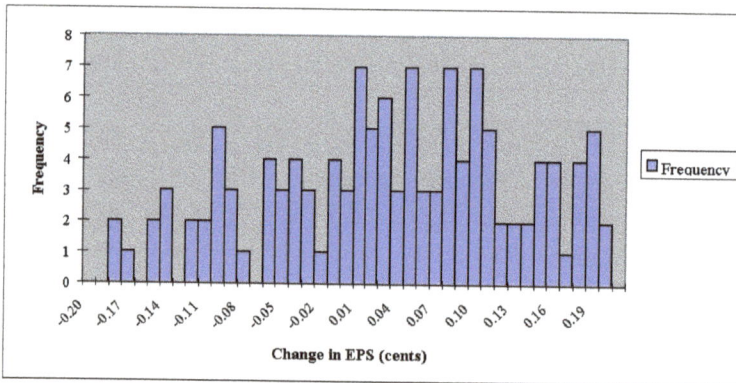

Panel C: Post-crisis (1999)

Figure 10.1, Panels A to C, plot the empirical distribution of change in the EPS variable during the pre-crisis, crisis and post-crisis periods respectively, with histogram interval widths of $0.01 for the range −$0.20 to +$0.20. The figure in Panel A documents a striking single-peaked, almost bell-shaped, distribution with a noticeable discontinuity near 0 (and $0.01) only for the pre-crisis period. The evidence is not surprising because during the crisis companies in general experienced negative earnings, and as such the earnings changes distribution in Panels B and C for both the crisis and post-crisis is not likely to be as normally distributed as that in the pre-crisis. The significance of the discontinuity near 0 and 0.01 is confirmed by statistical tests, in that it provides a T-statistic of 6.310 for the pre-crisis. For the crisis and post-crisis periods, the significance of the discontinuity is less attenuated at T-statistic = 1.884 and T-statistic = 1.744 respectively.[5] These results show evidence of earnings management present in

---

[5] As in Degeorge, Patel and Zeckhauser (1999), and Plummer and Mest (2000), a discontinuity is evident only if the value of T is greater than 2.0.

each period, but particularly so for the pre-crisis. This is as expected, given the strong economy during the pre-crisis period.

Avoidance of earnings loss benchmark

Table 10.5, Panel B, reports the EPS for each distinct macroeconomic period. Figure 10.2, Panels A to C, display the distribution of earnings, again with an interval width of $0.01, for earnings ranging from −$0.20 to +$0.20.

The histogram during the pre-crisis shows a not so smooth bell-shaped distribution (although earnings >+$0.20 are not observable) with the exception of the area near 0 and +0.02 on the x-axis. It is also clear that the earnings distribution seems to fall in the negative and less than +$0.02 earnings region, consistent with the loss avoidance argument. Similarly but with less smoothness, during the crisis period there is some evidence of earnings occurring more frequently in the area beyond the 0, although this is not statistically significant (T-statistic = 1.447). For the post-crisis period, the distribution seems to be erratic, although the frequency of companies reporting +$0.01 EPS is greatest at this point compared to other areas, thus making it significant with a T-statistic = 3.326. Taking these results together and comparing them with the EPS change results in the earlier sub-section, the evidence is consistent with managers strongly desiring to be able to report positive earnings (avoid earnings decreases) as opposed to just breaking even (avoid earnings losses), whilst during the post-crisis period it is evident that companies attempt to avoid earnings losses, although there is still evidence of negative earnings.

Figure 10.2. Histogram of change in earnings per share – loss avoidance threshold

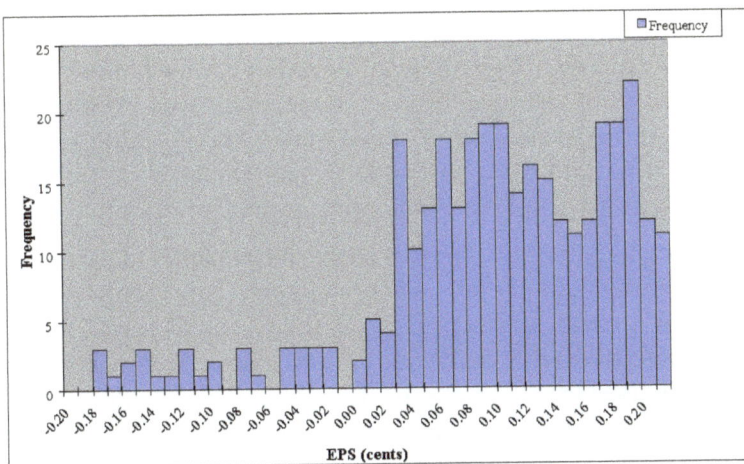

Panel A: Pre-crisis (1994-99)

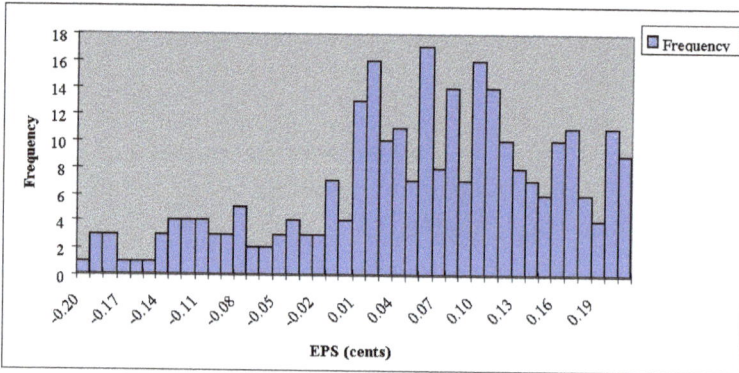

Panel B: Crisis (1997-98)

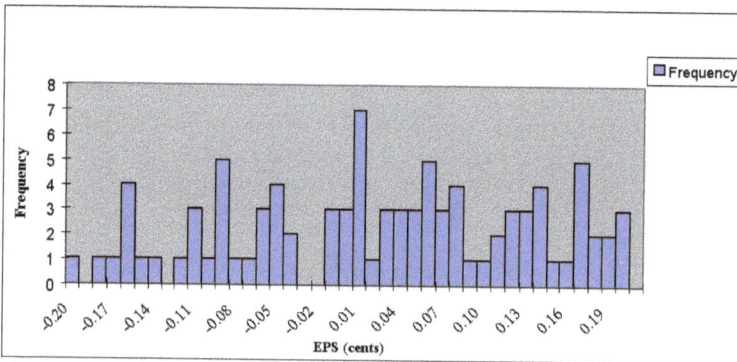

Panel C: Post-crisis (1999)

Conclusion, limitations and further research

This study examines the discrete sub-periods of the Asian economic crisis as it impacted Malaysia in terms of the level of discretionary accruals present. Its purpose is to see whether evidence exists, consistent with the criticisms of auditors by the World Bank and other institutions, that the level of absolute discretionary accruals as a measure of earnings management is reduced.

Regression using panel data consisting of observations of companies in existence from the last year of the pre-crisis (1996), and through the crisis (1997-98) and post-crisis (1999) periods, provides a result showing the pre-crisis period is significantly positively associated with deflated absolute discretionary accruals, whereas the post-crisis period is negatively so, although not significantly. It is acknowledged that care must be taken in interpreting the negative direction in the post-crisis period in the presence of insignificance of the coefficient.

Examining the distribution frequency of change in EPS from the prior year for each crisis sub-period similarly shows evidence of earnings management. A significant discontinuity in the frequency of achievement of earnings to meet or beat the prior year profit is found in the pre-crisis but not in the post-crisis periods. However, in terms of the frequency of avoidance of losses, the post-crisis period demonstrates a significant discontinuity but the pre-crisis period does not.

These results are broadly supportive of constrained earnings management in the post-crisis compared to the pre-crisis periods. However, whether this result is primarily associated with actions by auditors, or primarily an outcome of voluntary actions by the companies themselves, is an issue that cannot be resolved by this study. Alternatively, it may be that the distress in which companies found themselves post-crisis left little opportunity to manage earnings (DeAngelo, DeAngelo & Skinner 1994).

Another limitation is that survivorship bias is a feature of the way the sample is structured. However, because the companies in the sample are likely to be well-established in order to survive the required four turbulent years, it can be argued that these companies are less likely to engage in earnings management than some of their less well-established counterparts. This observation could militate against reporting the result as hypothesised.

Even if it is acknowledged that some of the constrained earnings management is attributable to auditors, the criticisms of auditors by important institutions may not be associated with this. It may be that the heightened distress and need for re-financing from government-established agencies or private sources created a level of scrutiny that encouraged either auditors or clients, or a combination of both, to act to constrain discretionary accruals. However, even with observations removed where debt restructuring was in existence, the finding of pre-crisis association with absolute discretionary accruals remains robust.

Further research to examine the role of Big Five and industry specialist auditors in constraining discretionary accruals across each of the sub-periods of the crisis would be useful. Testing for companies with various motivations to either manage or not manage their earnings would be worthwhile also. Examining the behaviour of discretionary accruals in other countries impacted by the crisis may shed more light on the auditors' role in constraining earnings management.

References

Accountancy 1998a, 'Hard line on standards', international edition, 122 (1263), p. 8.

Accountancy 1998b, 'World Bank takes tough line on standards', 122 (1263), p. 25.

Accountancy 1998c, 'Big Five's key role', 122 (1264), p. 10.

Accountancy 1999a, 'IFAC in uneasy alliance with Big Five on new initiative', 124 (1271), pp. 14-17.

Accountancy 1999b, 'Development forum', international edition, 124 (1271), pp. 12-13.

Accountancy 2000a, 'Firms throw their weight behind ISAs', 126 (1283), p. 9.

Accountancy 2000b, 'Firms told to clean up audit', 126 (1283), p. 9.

Athukorala, P. 2000, 'Capital Account regimes, crisis, and adjustment in Malaysia', *Asian Development Review*, vol. 18, no. 1, pp. 88-120.

Bank Negara Malaysia 1999, *The Central Bank and the Financial System in Malaysia – A Decade of Change*, Kuala Lumpur.

Bartov, E., Gul, F. A. & Tsui, J. S. 2001, 'Discretionary-accruals models and audit qualification', *Journal of Accounting and Economics*, vol. 30, no. 3, pp. 421-52.

Becker, C. L., DeFond, M. L., Jiambalvo, J. & Subramanyam, K. R. 1998, 'The effect of audit quality on earnings management', *Contemporary Accounting Research*, vol. 15, no. 1, pp. 1-24.

Cairns, D. 1997, 'IFAC – 20 years on', *World Accounting Report*, 2 October.

Craswell, A. T., Francis, J. R. & Taylor, S. L. 1995, 'Auditor brand name reputations and industry specializations', *Journal of Accounting and Economics*, vol. 20, no. 3, pp. 297-322.

Crispin, S. W. 1999, 'The power of PwC', *Far-eastern Economic Review*, 23, December.

DeAngelo, H., DeAngelo, L. & Skinner, D. J. 1994, 'Accounting choice in troubled companies', *Journal of Accounting and Economics*, vol. 17, nos. 1 & 2, pp. 113-43.

Dechow, P., Sloan, R. & Sweeney, A. 1995, 'Detecting earnings management', *The Accounting Review*, vol. 70, no. 2, pp. 193-225.

DeFond, M. L. & Jiambalvo, J. 1994, 'Debt covenant violation and manipulation of accruals', *Journal of Accounting and Economics*, vol. 17, nos. 1 & 2, pp. 145-76.

DeFond, M. L. & Subramanyam, K. R. 1998, 'Auditor changes and discretionary accruals', *Journal of Accounting and Economics*, vol. 25, no. 1, pp. 35-67.

Degeorge, F., Patel, J. & Zeckhauser, R. 1999, 'Earnings management to exceed thresholds', *Journal of Business*, vol. 72, no. 1, pp. 1-33.

Favere-Marchesi, M. 2000, 'Audit quality in ASEAN', *International Journal of Accounting*, vol. 35, no. 1, pp. 121-49.

Francis, J. R. & Krishnan, J. 1999, 'Accounting accruals and auditor reporting conservatism', *Contemporary Accounting Research*, vol. 16, no. 1, pp. 135-65.

Francis, J. R., Maydew, E. L. & Sparks, H. C. 1999, 'The role of Big 6 auditors in the credible reporting of accruals', *Auditing: A Journal of Practice and Theory*, vol. 18, no. 2, pp. 17-34.

Grey, S. 1998, 'Barking at the watchdogs', *Accountancy*, 122 (1263), p. 6.

Guay, W., Kothari, S. P. & Watts, R. L. 1996, 'A market-based evaluation of discretionary-accruals models', *Journal of Accounting Research*, vol. 34 (Supplement), pp. 83-116.

Haly, U. C. 2000, 'Corporate governance and restructuring in East Asia: An overview', *Seoul Journal of Economics*, 13, pp. 225-51.

Healy, P. 1985, 'The effect of bonus schemes on accounting decisions', *Journal of Accounting and Economics*, vol. 7, nos. 1-3, pp. 85-107.

Heninger, W. G. 2001, 'The association between auditor litigation and abnormal accruals', *The Accounting Review*, vol. 76, no. 1, pp. 111-26.

Hirst, D. E. 1994, 'Auditor sensitivity to earnings management', *Contemporary Accounting Research*, vol. 11, no. 1, pp. 405-22.

Hribar, P. & Collins, D. W. 2002, 'Errors in estimating accruals: Implications for empirical research', *Journal of Accounting Research*, vol. 40, no. 1, pp. 105-34.

Jaggi, B. & Lee, P. 2002, 'Earnings management response to debt convenant violations and debt restructuring', *Journal of Accounting, Auditing and Finance*, vol. 17, no. 4, p. 295.

Jones, J. 1991, 'Earnings management during import relief investigations', *Journal of Accounting Research*, vol. 29 (Supplement), pp. 193-228.

Krishnan, G. V. 2003, 'Does Big 6 Auditor Industry Expertise Constrain Earnings Management?', *Accounting Horizons*, vol. 17 (Supplement), pp. 1-15.

Krishnan, J(agan) & Krishnan, J(ayanthi) 1996, 'The role of economic trade-offs in the audit opinion decision: An Empirical Analysis', *Journal of Accounting, Auditing and Finance*, vol. 11, no. 4, pp. 565-86.

Lambert, C(hris) & Lambert, C(ecelia) 2001, 'The role of accounting disclosure in the East Asian financial crisis: An evaluation of the lessons learned', Confederation of Asian and Pacific Accountants.

Lane, T. 1999, 'The Asian financial crisis: What have we learned?', *Finance and Development*, September, International Monetary Fund.

Lys, T. & Watts, R. L. 1994, 'Lawsuits against auditors', *Journal of Accounting Research*, vol. 32 (Supplement), pp. 65-93.

MacDonald, E. 1999, 'What happened? A number of problems: Accounting rules are less than rigorous in many countries; It makes all the difference', *Wall Street Journal* (Eastern edition), 26 April, R6.

Malaysian Accounting Standards Board 1996, IAS 7 (revised), 'Cash Flow Statements'.

Nelson, M. W., Elliott, J. A. & Tarpley, R. L. 2002, 'Evidence from auditors about managers' and auditors' earnings management decisions', *The Accounting Review*, vol. 77 (Supplement), pp. 175-202.

McNichols, M. F. 2000, 'Research design issues in earnings management studies', *Journal of Accounting and Public Policy*, vol. 19, nos. 4 & 5, pp. 313-45.

Petersen, M. 1998, 'U.N. report faults big accountants in Asia-crisis', *New York Times*, 24 October.

Phillips, F. 1999, 'Auditor attention to and judgements of aggressive financial reporting', *Journal of Accounting Research*, vol. 37, no. 1, pp. 167-89.

Plummer, E. & Mest, D. P. 2000, 'Evidence on the earnings management of earnings components', *Journal of Accounting, Auditing and Finance*, vol. 16, no. 4, pp. 301-23.

Schwartz, K. B. & Menon, K. 1985, 'Auditor switches by failing firms', *The Accounting Review*, vol. 60, no. 2, pp. 248-61.

Street, D. & Gray, S. 2001, 'Observance of International Accounting Standards: Factors explaining non-compliance', Association of Chartered Certified Accountants (ACCA) Research Report 74, London.

Tay, J. 1995, 'The regulation of financial reporting and quality of information: A comparative analysis of Singapore, Malaysia and Thailand', in H. Y. Pang (ed.), *Contemporary Issues in Accounting*, Addison-Wesley, Singapore.

Teoh, S. H. & Wong, T. J. 1993, 'Perceived auditor quality and the earnings response coefficient', *The Accounting Review*, vol. 68, no. 2, pp. 346-66.

Teoh, S. H., Welch, I. & Wong, T. J. 1998a, 'Earnings management and the underperformance of seasoned equity offerings', *Journal of Financial Economics*, vol. 50, no. 1, pp. 63-99.

Teoh, S. H., Welch, I. & Wong, T. J. 1998b, 'Earnings management and the long-term market performance of initial public offerings', *Journal of Finance*, vol. 53, no. 6, pp. 1935-74.

Teoh, S. H., Wong, T. J. & Rao, G. R. 1998, 'Are accruals during initial public offerings opportunistic?', *Review of Accounting Studies*, 3, pp. 175-208.

Thillainathan, R. 1999, 'Corporate governance and restructuring in Malaysia – A review of markets, mechanisms, agents and the legal infrastructure', working paper, World Bank/OECD Survey of Corporate Governance.

UNCTAD (United Nations Conference on Trade and Development) 1998, 'The role of accounting disclosure in the East Asian financial crisis: Lessons learned', report prepared by M. Z. Rahman.

Wall Street Journal 1998, 'World Bank asks Big 5 to ensure the quality of globe's accounting', Eastern edition, 232 (78), 20 October, B20.

World Bank 2000, *East Asia Brief*, Asia and Pacific Region, September.

Part III. Beyond the auditor: the search for solutions

Chapter 11. Auditor independence: regulation, oversight and inspection

Keith A Houghton
Christine A Jubb

Abstract

Much of what auditors do is unobservable. Indeed, what goes on in an audit has been described as 'secret audit business'. Audits in this context are of financial reports and those financial reports are the representations of the management of those companies, not the auditors. The audits of financial reports are of value in that they provide a competent and independent (of auditee management) attestation of the validity of those management representations. This attestation lowers the 'information risk' for the users of these financial reports.

There has been a marked increase in activity to regulate matters relating to independence. The proposals outlined in CLERP 9 are one example of this. The requirements in the United States under the Sarbanes-Oxley Act are a further example.

Audit firms operate in a highly regulated yet highly competitive market. Evidence exists to suggest that audit firms are active competitors in respect of audit pricing and competency, including specialist industry expertise. Until recently, there has been little or no observable evidence that audit firms compete in respect of independence.

The issues as they relate to audit independence are complex. One issue is that threats to independence are frequently subtle and difficult to observe and measure. Hence, controlling the decisions that relate to them cannot rely solely on regulation which itself inevitably relies on crude definitions and imprecise measures. Additionally, further regulation may not achieve the desired end without other processes being but in place in tandem.

This paper argues that:

1. auditors of certain classes of companies (in particular, those that are publicly traded) should be provided with incentives or requirements to have observable processes on independence

2. the means of observability should be in the form of an inspection and review process focussing on issues critical to the audit, such as independence

3. expert persons not having a current or past financial interest in the firm or in the commercial outcomes of the review should be used in the inspection and review process

4. the review process should have wide-ranging powers of inspection to examine the policies, processes, structures and 'culture' of audit firms

5. the report of the inspection and review should be made public, unedited and in full, and in a timely fashion.

The primary objectives of this proposal are to (1) make more transparent to the market for information the characteristics of the audit firms and their process to ensure audit independence, and (2) provide a rigorous oversight of independence decision-making by persons who have no commercial interest in the outcome of the decision.

Introduction – are audits different?

The regulation of audits has undergone numerous changes since audits first became a part of corporate regulation. It is common for such changes to occur after a major corporate crisis – in particular, a major business failure that gains public interest or notoriety. Where these failures are linked to the belief that there has been audit failure, legislators, corporate regulators, the community at large and the accounting profession all tend to react. Sometimes these reactions result in change to the regulation of audits.

Over time, many of the implemented changes have added to the quality of audit and auditing. However, it continues to be the case that no matter how well an audit is executed and how well the regulation of auditing is implemented, corporate failures continue to occur. This is seen by some as a sign that the audit process is not capable of delivering a product that is of value to the market for financial information. In past years this perception of lack of 'delivery' of the audit product has been described as an 'expectations gap'. It is reasonable to conclude that, at least in part, what is expected by some participants in the market is not achievable. However, there are examples of individuals who might reasonably be expected to be well-informed about the real deliverables of audits having concerns about certain of the qualities of auditing as it is currently practiced. Put another way, there is not just an 'expectations' problem but actual perceived problems with outcomes from audits. This perception is exemplified in the United States by the collapse of Enron in late-2001 and in Australia by the failure of HIH Insurance early in 2001. The outcomes of the HIH Royal Commission detail several of these problems (HIH Royal Commission 2003).

The audit and its characteristics

An audit is a professional service provided by accountants. Much of what goes on is unobservable by anyone except those most intimately involved in the processes. In the 2003 Houghton and Trotman Review, the process has been described as 'secret audit business'. Its key characteristic is that it provides some level of assurance to users of conventional, externally-issued accounting reports that the representations made in those reports are consistent with the underlying economic realities. The demand for this service is, in many instances, involuntary because of legislative or other regulatory requirement. There are, however, occasions where an audit or similar assurance product is voluntary and is the choice of either management or others (including stock or debt holders).

It must be remembered that the financial reports of a company are the representations of the management and directors of that company. It is the board of directors that is ultimately responsible for the content disclosed in those reports. An audit is an attestation of these representations by management by the auditor and assesses the truth and fairness (or in the minds of some, validity or integrity) of those financial reports. This highlights two factors; (1) that the financial reports are indeed simply representations of management and are not primarily the responsibility of the auditor, and (2) that it is the auditor's responsibility to attest to the validity and reliability ('truth and fairness' in the Australian context) of those reports.

For the attestation to be of value in the market for financial information, it must meet two necessary conditions. First, the attestation needs to be competently undertaken and executed. It needs to be undertaken by those with relevant expertise in the practice of auditing. This will include expertise on the planning and execution of the audit itself and may include specific specialist expertise in the industry of the auditee company. To be competent, the audit will need to include relevant and applicable audit processes and methodologies and, where relevant, technologies. Secondly, for an audit to be of value it must be undertaken with judgments made and views held that are independent of the management and board of the auditee company. The auditors' judgments need to test the assertions and representations made by auditee managements.

The information value of audits

The following simple illustration shows why audits have the potential to be highly valuable in the market for financial information. Company A and Company B are two entities that operate in the same industry. They have the same financial structure, they operate in the same industry, they have the same risk profile, cash-flow revenue streams and outlook and the like. In terms of economic substance they are identical. In this hypothetical example, a competent, independent auditor audits Company A. Company B is not audited at all. The question is, if both these companies were traded on a stock exchange, which company would have the higher share price?

Assuming the market is efficient, the answer is Company A. This is because Company A has information conveyed to the market with lower 'information risk'. If there were to be comparison between the two companies in respect of debt costs, Company A would achieve lower costs, again because the information provided to the market is with a lower level of information risk.

Recall that the financial reports produced and used by the stock market, providers of debt and others are the assertions of management. These management assertions are guided by Generally Accepted Accounting Principles (GAAP) and other factors, but they are still simply the representations of management. The processes, including various checks and balances within the auditee that produces these financial reports, do not extend to a critical professional independent review of these representations. Such a review or attestation ideally should be undertaken by persons who are (1) expert in the field, and (2) able to investigate thoroughly the company with a right of access unparalleled by anyone other than those internal to the management of the company. Only where this review and attestation process is both competent and independent of the management of the entity does it add to the market's perception that the financial reports are both valid and reliable. Financial information that is perceived to be more valid and reliable means that the information provided has lower risk. Therefore, financial reports that have attached to them a competent and independent audit have lower information risk in the market; lower risk results in higher stock price and lower cost of debt. Audits do, therefore, add value to a company and have the potential to affect stock price and debt cost.

Consider the slightly more realistic example where two identical companies both have audits, but where one company has an audit provided by an audit firm that has a reputation for high-quality auditing and the other is audited by a firm that has a reputation for providing an adequate audit. The share price difference between these two companies would not be as large as that existing for entities with a competent, independent audit compared with no audit at all, but there would still be a price difference in the stock prices traded by the two companies, other things being equal. Hence, we can conclude that differing audit quality levels have differential value-adding effects. In addition, and perhaps most importantly, the quality difference in the audit converts to a price differential in the shares traded on the stock market.

Similarly, those that trade in the debt of audited companies will attach a different risk premium between companies that are audited and unaudited, and those that are audited by what is seen as a high-quality auditor and those that are not in receipt of that level of quality. Evidence of price premiums for different auditors and their consequential effect on the various markets has been demonstrated in the auditing research literature (e.g., Craswell, Francis & Taylor 1995).

The characteristics of a valuable audit

The value of an audit arises only where the following two necessary conditions are met. That is, where the audit is competent and independent of auditee management. If an audit is not undertaken competently, then it is not of value to users. If an audit is undertaken competently but not independent of management, then the representations made are nothing more than the original views of management. In either case the audit does not lower information risk and would not be valued by the market for information.

The existence of both competency and independence are necessary conditions for the audit to be a value-adding good; one cannot be a substitute for the other.

Audit as an 'experience good'

Unlike many commodities, an audit is not a 'good' that can be observed *ex ante*. An audit is referred to as an 'experience good' (Craswell & Francis 1999). That is to say, it is a 'good' whose qualities cannot be observed prior to purchase. The qualities that are crucial are frequently not observable until the good is actually experienced. This makes audit choice decisions more difficult than in many other markets for goods. Further, even after the audit is purchased and experienced, it is not always possible to observe all the relevant qualities of an audit.

It would be rare for anyone other than those most intimately involved in the audit to be in a position to observe key characteristics of the audit. Even those close to the audit (e.g., those involved in the finance function or with the audit committee of an auditee) are more likely to have some opportunity to observe aspects of competence. Even in these circumstances, it is possible that this elite group will have only a limited ability to observe the characteristics that relate to independence. There are only rare instances where such people are aware of auditor independence threats and can observe how the auditor deals with them. Therefore, relative to competency levels, quality of independence is difficult to observe even in the most intimate of circumstances. It is easy to understand that unless the audit firm initiates means by which the independence processes are made transparent, the market is unlikely to be optimally informed of them.

In Australia, we now have two firms that are, to some degree, seeking to make their processes, or stated processes, observable to the market. The firm first to announce such an oversight and disclosure process was the Australian firm of PricewaterhouseCoopers (PwC). In May 2002, that firm announced the creation of the 'Audit Standards Oversight Board'. The structure and operation followed the principles laid out in submissions made earlier to inquiries emanating from Treasury and the Joint Committee on Public Accounts and Audit (JCPAA) for individual firms to establish an audit independence oversight board (Houghton 2002a & b). The first report of this board was made public and dated August 2003 (PricewaterhouseCoopers 2003). The board was initially made up of three distinguished persons, including a former partner of PwC and a former governor of New South Wales. Using a somewhat different model, the chairperson of the Australian practice of KPMG established an expert review panel to both oversight the independence processes and policies and gather evidence on their operation (see Houghton & Trotman 2002). The two members of the review panel were both persons with audit expertise and neither had a material commercial interest in KPMG. The first report of this review process was issued in October 2002.

Independence

Auditors are exposed often to potential threats to independence during an audit engagement. These threats to independence influence the audit in various ways. Examples of threats to independence include: the joint provision of audit and auditor provided non-audit services (APNAS); the hiring of former audit staff by an auditee (or vice versa); the appointment of former audit firm personnel to the board of directors of an auditee or its audit committee; the employment of close relatives of audit partners or staff by an auditee; and threats issued by an auditee to terminate an audit engagement or put out for tender an audit engagement if an auditor does not withdraw a threatened qualification and/or comply with a particularly assertive or controversial accounting policy choice. Several of these examples do not necessarily prima facie pose a threat to independence, but they have the potential to become a threat in certain circumstances. That is, the existence of a threat to independence may occur only when several factors come together. Put another way, a threat to independence can be a conditional relationship.

A further difficulty is that these potential threats are frequently not easily measurable. A threat to independence can be extremely subtle and it is possible that auditors themselves are not even conscious of it. Threats may be created incrementally and over a lengthy period of time. Indeed, it is possible that both auditors and auditees are not conscious of them. A further threat not well-acknowledged in professional circles relates to the fee dependence issue. Fee dependence by an audit firm may be not just from one auditee, but from a 'family' of auditees all linked by *shared directors*. While the fee earned from each auditee may not represent a threat by itself, when linked together they do potentially pose a significant fee dependence threat in combination via shared directorships.

Testing for auditor independence

It is often said that audits are usually successfully executed, and auditors in general perform their function in a professional and diligent manner. It is our view that the great majority of auditors are intelligent, diligent and professional people who seek to produce a competent independent audit.

In the vast majority of cases it is our belief that competent independent audits are produced, however it is difficult to verify this because it is rare for the independence (and indeed competence) of an audit to be rigorously tested. The only circumstance where a comprehensive examination of the qualities of an audit occurs in a public arena is when an auditee suffers severe financial distress.[1] In the circumstances of corporate failure, there are incentives for persons outside the organisation to rigorously test the competence and independence of the audit. Given the hundreds of business failures each year, it is important to note that only in a small minority of these failures is an auditor even alleged to have not completed a competent independent audit. In some of these circumstances these allegations are not followed through. It is possible that there is no follow-through either because of the significant costs of litigation or other action, or because there is some compromise or settlement on the part of the auditor and/or the auditor's insurance company. In some cases there is significant follow-through. Through this process, a number of these cases end in settlement and/or judgment against the auditors. That is to say, on a non-trivial number of occasions in recent years, audit failure – or at least perceived audit failure – has occurred visibly in a number of jurisdictions.[2]

In respect of allegations of audit failure, there are generally two areas in which allegations are made. These two areas follow the two classic pillars of auditing – competence and independence. With regard to defence strategies relating to competence, it is common for auditors to obtain the services of another auditor to review the working papers and other documentation relating to an audit and reach a judgment as to whether the audit processes have been reasonable and competently executed. With reference to issues of independence, it is not uncommon for the audit review described in the previous sentence to also attempt to cover any issues of independence. It is, however, uncommon in our experience for evidence to be brought forward that can assist in any defence against accusations of a lack of independence. Indeed, while various forms of evidence that demonstrate the competence of an auditor can be pointed to, there is often little

---

[1] In various jurisdictions, peer reviews sponsored by professional accounting associations may be undertaken, but rarely are the results made public.
[2] Note, however, that a settlement does not indicate a clear case of audit failure as it is possible that the cost of settlement is less than the cost of further defending litigation.

that can be identified to assert that judgments and decisions reached were made independent of auditee management.

On the whole, judgments in respect of independence are entirely in-house[3], outside of the observability of those that may be interested in the characteristics of the decision, and more importantly, the decision-making process. In some cases it is reasonable to believe that (1) recognition of threats to independence, (2) determination of alternative courses of action, and (3) final judgment relating to decisions involving independence are all routinely made by those persons within the audit firm who (directly or indirectly) have some commercial interest in the outcome of the decision. In some but not all firms, the policies and procedures that guide the decision process are not subjected to inspection or oversight.

Put simply, auditors have mechanisms and processes to defend accusations of lack of competence. However, they appear to have few, if any, effective defences in respect of accusations of lack of independence. This will be exacerbated by the CLERP 9 definition.

Legislating for auditor independence

There are those who argue that the best way of going forward in relation to audit quality (including both auditor competence and independence) is to enhance the legislation and/or regulation of the market for audit services (e.g., Ramsay 2001). The Corporate Law Economic Reform Program ('CLERP 9') proposals are an example of regulating in an attempt to obtain greater levels of independence. There is some merit in this position.

In respect of auditor competency, it can be argued that ensuring that there is a floor level to competency below which no individual may practise is a desirable thing for those users of the service. The means by which this competency is assessed varies, but often operates to ensure that those who have inadequate expertise and/or inappropriate experience are precluded from entering the market.

There is no regulation or control above this minimum level, and indeed there is evidence of considerable variation in audit quality. It can be argued that this variation in competency comes about because of the existence of competition and the incentives that exist for especially competent audits. The competitive marketplace is the driver of this variation in competency and it is not the outcome of a regulatory or legislative requirement beyond professionally or regulatorily mandated base proficiencies.

In respect of regulating or legislating for independence, the challenges can be seen as (1) efficiency, (2) effectiveness, and (3) completeness.

---

[3]It is acknowledged that while being in-house, there are processes to record these in-house events and decisions; see AUP 32 'Audit Independence' (AARF 1995). This document is to be withdrawn by December 2003, given the introduction of the F1 professional requirements of the two major accounting bodies.

Defining independence

The proposed CLERP 9 Bill offers a definition of independence that has emerged from the report of the HIH Royal Commission. Section 324CA of the Bill gives a general requirement for auditor independence. This means that if an individual auditor or firm has any of the following characteristics they will be seen not to be independent: being an auditor and having a conflict of interest in relation to the auditee. Conflict of interest is defined in Section 324CB and includes:

> ... if the circumstances exist ... That: (a) impair, or might impair, the ability of the auditor, or a professional member of the audit team, to exercise objective and impartial judgment in relation to the conduct of an audit of the audited body; or (b) would give a person, with full knowledge of the facts and circumstances, reasonable grounds for concern that the team, to exercise objective and impartial judgment in relation to the conduct of an audit of the audited body is, or might be, impaired.

This definition is wide and may give rise to a high hurdle, and if a set of circumstances was challenged it seems that the definition would give rise to difficulties for audit firms to defend their actions, even where they might have operated in good faith and with no knowledge of a conflict of interest.

Leaving aside the specifics of the CLERP 9 Bill, there are challenges in the effectiveness of regulating independence by virtue of defining what independence is and more especially what represents a real threat to it. As argued above, many independence threats are hard to identify and observe. Some have argued strongly that the joint supply of audit and non-audit services (NAS) is a threat to audit independence, but this is unlikely to be universally true. It is argued by some that the list of prohibited auditor provided NAS in the Sarbanes-Oxley legislation is a guide, but even then it is not without controversy. Taxation consulting, for example, can be 'benign' in that it can involve relatively 'mechanical' processes, or it can pose a threat to the independence of the auditor if the tax advice gives rise to the company having an aggressive tax position that needs to be provided for in the financial accounts but is not. Thus, even in this simple example we are left with the question, under what conditions does the joint supply become an independence threat? The regulation of independence may result in cases where the law of independence is substituted for the fact of independence. In this circumstance, the economy and the stockholder are, arguably, no better off than in a largely unregulated situation in which no regulated restriction is imposed externally. Rather, it is arguably more efficient for restrictions to exist that are created by market forces, especially those restrictions constructed by the boards or audit committees of auditee companies.

As previously noted, independence is subtle, difficult to observe and often hard to measure. Thus, it can be difficult to regulate efficiently the presence of independence. Even if it can be regulated effectively, deciding on the threat, its measurement, etc. can cause economic inefficiencies. For example, it may be in the clients' (shareholders') best interest to have the auditor undertake certain testing of management controls, as much of that work will have been done as part of the audit. This pre-existing knowledge gives rise to 'knowledge spill-over' effects that represent an economic benefit to shareholders (Beck, Frecka & Solomon 1988). In a high-regulation environment these choices may not be available, thus driving out any such shareholder benefits.

Regulating independence

If there is to be regulation or legislation in respect of matters of independence or threats to independence, we predict that there will be significant costs and problems with inefficiencies.[4] We also believe that such regulation will inevitably lead to issues with the effective management of the independence requirements for the reasons set out below.

Ideally, we would argue independence requires contemporary decision-making that is *ex ante* rather than *ex post*. The avoidance of independence threats is better than dealing with the compromised independence in place (see, for example, IFAC n. d.; CPA Australia & ICAA 2001). It can be argued that any regulatory body or legislative board that is set up to review auditor independence will inevitably examine only independence issues which have been revealed and which are mostly gross, extreme or easily measured. Independence threats typically involve instances of subtle threats, which are not easily measured and therefore not susceptible to an effective legalistic or regulatory intervention and control.

If there is a regulatory process such as a disciplinary board or tribunal, external to the audit firms and removed from the day-to-day operations of the audit, that deals with independence threats, it is our belief that threats to independence would be revealed only after they occur and then only where there has been a damaging outcome and the facts of the case are revealed publicly. This does not aid the efficiency of the market. It also adds no confidence to the market for audit services. Additionally, it also does not enhance the value to shareholders and those that hold the debt of an auditee.

Even if threats to independence can be identified, defined and measured in such a way that they can be subjected to legal or regulatory intervention, threats to independence change and new threats emerge. A decade or more ago the joint supply of audit and non-audit services was not an independence threat because the latter generally did not represent a substantial proportion of the former, but

---

[4]This matter is discussed later on in the chapter in respect of the special case of the joint supply of audit and auditor provided non-audit services noted in the section entitled 'The need for inspection'.

it does often now. If such legislation in respect of auditor independence had been put in place at that time, the joint supply threat would most likely not have been identified as an independence threat. Thus, that legislation would now be seen as incomplete. Additionally, as many threats are so subtle as to not be identified or validly measured, the likelihood of legislation or regulation being comprehensive is low.

Moreover, if auditor independence is enforced via a legal or regulated means, it is possible, even likely, that those in various stakeholder groups might erroneously conclude that the 'problem' is fixed when it is not. The evidence of the absence of a complete 'solution' would not be seen until the inevitable next round of corporate failures.

The need for inspection

Some would have us believe that if accounting firms returned to their position of just being audit providers, and not providers of many other business-related services, the threats to independence would be lowered or even eliminated. Even if this was true and even if it was possible, it can be argued strongly that it is unlikely to derive an optimal outcome. Even if firms were to be only audit suppliers, they will still be supplying a service the characteristics of which remain largely unobservable. The observability of the service provided remains a key issue for the on-going value of the audit service.

Even to those intimately involved in an audit, the characteristics of an audit are not obvious. And those that do have some chance to observe are, by and large, not the clients of the audit – i.e., the shareholders.

As argued above, regulation or legislation that attempts to define and control auditor independence is likely to be both ineffective and economically inefficient. However, with the CLERP 9 proposals implemented, the Financial Reporting Council (FRC) has responsibility to oversight auditor independence. As recently as the Auditing and Assurance Board's Consultative Meeting of 27 November 2003, the current chair of the FRC, Mr Charles Macek, noted that he believed the FRC would choose to oversee not just independence but 'other aspects of audit quality'. The corporate regulator (ASIC, the Australian Securities and Investments Commission) also represented at that meeting and observed that they were building capacity to conduct inspections. These inspections commenced in the first half of 2005. The potential overlap between the two oversight processes is obvious and the need for an understanding between the two bodies seems the only sensible way to proceed. Since then, the chair of the FRC has put the position that the AuASB has a role in auditor independence (comments made at the AuASB board meeting, 13 April 2005). The need to remove overlap is not only to stop the waste of public resources but to guard against the difficulties that might arise if one inspection process concluded that a given firm conducted a competent and independent audit and a second inspection concluded, for the same firm, otherwise.

Perhaps one way to proceed would be for one body, the FRC, to conduct inspections and reviews of policies, procedures and the 'culture' of the audit firm, while the detail of individual audits could be reviewed by the regulator, ASIC. That is to say, the regulator could inspect using as its 'unit of analysis' the individual audit, while the FRC could inspect at the 'policy' level. Reflecting on the collapse of the US firm Arthur Andersen, either of these inspection services would have potentially observed concerns, but it may well have been the policy and 'culture'-level inspection and review that would have seen the warning signals first.

Given the potential inefficiencies and the need to overcome the 'unobservable' processes of an audit, there is a need for the higher-level review (which we propose be undertaken under the authority of the FRC) being highly transparent and the conclusions reached being open to the market for wide consumption. It seems sub-optimal to have the outcomes of an inspection service of an unobservable service itself unobservable. It is arguable that the individual audit inspection undertaken by ASIC might be optimally undertaken privately to ensure some degree of confidentiality of potentially commercially-sensitive client information.

At present the professional bodies have an inspection and quality assurance for those of their members that have public practices, but little is known of the outcomes of these reviews other than they occur at some interval and the outcomes are not readily available to the practices' client bases.

The above arguments would suggest that public-interest control of audit independence may be best affected via a process that permits or encourages both transparency and competition between firms in respect of the quality of independence policies and procedures. Such a process would need to be within an appropriate robust legislative or regulatory environment, but it is the process that affects the oversight of independence, not the legislation itself.

We argue that the preferred process is via inspection and review of an audit firm's independence policies, procedures and structure. It should also be invasive enough to permit understanding and interpretation of the 'culture' of the firm as it relates to independence.

Such an inspection and oversight service has been implemented on a voluntary basis already by some in the market. As indicated above, in Australia we have two examples of voluntary inspection and oversight processes. The first report of the KPMG review came in October 2002 (Houghton & Trotman 2002). The first report for PwC was in August 2003. The second Houghton-Trotman Report of KPMG is due for release in mid 2005. These oversight inspections and reports are important at a time when new challenges are a part of the market for audit services. Market acceptance of them seems substantial.[5]

The voluntary oversight processes of KPMG and PwC have been an important step, but an incomplete one for the market as a whole. One might argue that these processes' quality differentiates KPMG and PwC from other audit firms. They may be a deciding factor in the choice of audit firm by some, but it leaves other parts of the market unprotected. The audit process remains unobservable for those firms that do not subject themselves to this type of oversight and review. An FRC-led transparent inspection process that reviews policies and procedures could ensure a degree of market-wide transparency. If the FRC process is not transparent in the way we suggest, it will fail to meet market expectations in the way those voluntary oversight processes voluntarily undertaken by KPMG and PwC have been able to meet expectations.

An important characteristic of the oversight and inspection process is that those reviewers undertaking this process have no commercial interest in the outcome of their deliberations. That is, the inspection process, while needing audit expertise, should not, in our view, involve persons who are or even have been partners or staff of the firm under review. It is important that this process be lead by a person or persons who are both expert in the area of auditing and independent of the commercial operations of the organisation under review. It is also important that each member of the review or inspection process not benefit commercially, either directly or indirectly, from any determination made in respect of independence. Put bluntly, independence review and oversight should be removed from those who may benefit commercially from those decisions, i.e. the partners of the audit practice.

The reasons why an inspection service with internal access to an audit firm is more effective than high-level regulation alone are as follows:

1. Independence issues, threats and potential threats can be dealt with swiftly and contemporaneously with the audit.
2. The process can deal with commercially sensitive issues without those issues becoming public or accessible by competitors.
3. The quality-control processes of the review process can be observed by the market, which gives rise to the possibility that accounting firms will compete in the market on the basis of having good quality-control procedures for independence, not only for competence or price.
4. Extremely subtle or difficult to access and measure issues can be dealt with sympathetically yet conclusively, and matters where there are conflicting arguments can be dealt with without reference to crude measures.

[5]The first report for KPMG was made available both in print and on the KPMG Australia website. In the first 10 days on the website, the first named author was advised that there were approximately 1500 unique downloads of the report.

5.   Reward structures within audit firms can take account of decisions made by the board in achieving equity across partners responsible for practice growth.

The effect of independence inspection and review

The creation of an inspection and review process is a necessary but not sufficient condition for the effective quality control of independence in an audit process. The inspection process needs to infiltrate and observe all the relevant processes in the audit firm and to affect the culture and ethos of the quality-control processes. The culture needs to be observable, as it is this that is key to the long-term viability of quality-control processes that protect independence. Perhaps more importantly, potential threats need to be recognised *ex ante* and where possible avoided. A dilemma avoided is a more preferred outcome than a threat that is dealt with *ex post*, which might or might not involve a compromise or economic cost.

Development within audit firms: changing the culture of independence

A critical issue in respect of independence is not only the threats to independence but also the ability to recognise a potential ethical dilemma as it relates to independence, rather than just dealing with it when one occurs. Put more bluntly, if a member of the audit firm, be it a partner or employee, recognises a threat to independence before it becomes an actual issue to be dealt with, then many potential threats to independence are unlikely to become actual threats and ethical dilemmas can be minimised. To achieve this, substantial education needs to be put in place both within the firms and across the profession more generally. Such an education process would also probably be useful within the auditee, particularly to audit committee members and possibly more widely to the board of directors.

Some implementation issues

While there are many possible alternative ways to proceed, the above discussion suggests one model that warrants consideration.

The role of regulators and legislatures

While the basis of the model is that auditor independence is essentially an economic problem, it is clear from current evidence that the existing, largely free-market approach in many jurisdictions in the world has resulted in less than optimal outcomes. This free-market approach has had significant negative economic and social effects. While the proposed model relies on competitive processes, it is necessary to have an appropriately strong legislative and regulatory framework. Without this framework it seems possible that the inspection process would potentially fail, as some firms would seek to avoid the level of transparency that would be of benefit to the market for information. The essential framework requires as a minimum the existence of incentives or even requirement for auditors of publicly-traded companies (and possibly others where a significant public interest occurs – such as financial institutions) to be subjected to an inspection and review process. This might also be extended to the audit of other companies as well. This type of requirement may be seen as a parallel to the requirement on the part of audited corporations in many jurisdictions to establish an audit committee of the board of directors of the company.

The second regulatory or legislative requirement is to find the appropriate structure of the review and inspection service. Given the regulatory structure in Australia, it would seem that the process might be under the control and management of the FRC. Clearly some interrelationship between the review and inspection process and the corporate regulator would be desirable.

The professional bodies

The two major professional accounting bodies in Australia have a quality review program. No doubt those involved in these programs will have a view of the quality and integrity of the programs. However, the present writers know of little market evidence that these processes serve to inform the market for information. Additionally, because they themselves are unobservable processes, they do little to provide a competitive transparent environment. They do serve other processes in terms of assisting to keep their memberships on constant alert to enhance the quality of member competence, but an inspection and review process that oversees independence in a way that is observable to the market is a different objective altogether.

The auditees

The proposals do not call for auditees to establish their own quality-control procedures in respect of the independence of their auditor. Market forces will take boards and/or audit committees in this direction in any event. However, it is inevitable that with new disclosures and new information available to auditees arising from internal oversight and the proposed inspection process, some audit-related decisions will need to be considered with greater rigour and frequency than is the case currently. Inevitably, the work of the audit committee will become more burdensome, and auditees need to acknowledge this change in workload. Perhaps the most specific recommendation regarding auditees is that the workload of audit committees must now include assessing these materials on the independence of the auditor. The CLERP 9 draft legislation makes this responsibility even more onerous.

Summary of recommendations

The thrust of the model proposed here includes the following characteristics:

1. The regulatory framework should not attempt to directly and in detail define auditor independence as does the draft CLERP (Audit Reform and Corporate Disclosure) Bill. Nor should it describe or limit certain behavior of audit firms in respect of real or perceived audit independence threats.

2. The regulatory framework should be changed to encourage or require auditors entitled to undertake certain company audits (such as of publicly-traded companies) to demonstrate not only certain levels of competence, but also to develop and maintain review and oversight of their independence processes.

3. The appropriate entity, possibly the FRC, should be empowered to create and approve a review and inspection process for use by company auditors.

4. The review and inspection process should be given the capability of accessing the internal information within auditing firms and oversight the firms' processes to determine threats and perceived threats to independence.

5. The quality-control processes for independence should be observable by a wide section of the market and stakeholders in the market for audit services.

Concluding remarks

Audits require competence and independence. There are a number of mechanisms that can be used to ensure each is present. Competition has driven up the observability – or at least claimed observability – of competence, and yet this mechanism has been slow to drive up observability in respect of independence. The model proposes a solution that will create observability in respect of independence so that the market for information can be better satisfied.

The operation of the market for audit services has both important economic and social implications. Allowing the existing largely free-market approach to auditor independence is now seen as being less than optimal. It can be argued that the efficient and effective operation of this market needs the provision of a carefully constructed regulatory framework. The recommended model proposes a strong review and inspection process to enhance the quality and transparency of independence decision-making in audit firms, and greater disclosure of the auditors' skills and attributes to enhance auditor accountability.

References

AARF (Australian Accounting Research Foundation) 1995, AUP 32 'Audit Independence', CPA Australia and the Institute of Chartered Accountants in Australia Handbook 2001, Sydney.

Beck, P. J., Frecka, T. L. & Solomon, I. 1998, 'A model of the market for MAS and audit services: Knowledge spillovers and auditor-auditee bonding', *Journal of Accounting Literature*, 7, pp. 50-64.

CLERP (Audit Reform and Corporate Disclosure) Bill 2003, 'Commentary on the Draft Provisions', Commonwealth of Australia, Canberra.

CPA Australia & ICAA (Institute of Chartered Accountants in Australia) 2001, *Code of Professional Conduct*, 'Professional Statement F1', Sydney.

Craswell, A. T. & Francis, J. R. 1999, 'Pricing Initial Audit Engagements: A Test of Competing Theories', *The Accounting Review*, vol. 74, no. 2, pp. 201-16.

Craswell, A. T., Francis, J. R. & Taylor, S. L. 1995, 'Auditor brand name reputations and industry specializations', *Journal of Accounting and Economics*, vol. 20, no. 3, pp. 297-322.

HIH Royal Commission 2003, *The Failure of HIH Insurance*, Commonwealth of Australia, Canberra, http://www.hihroyalcom.gov.au.

Houghton, K. 2002a, 'Auditor Independence: A Market Based Model Controlling Independence Decisions', submission to Treasury Inquiry on Independence of Australian Company Auditors Report (March).

Houghton, K. 2002b, 'Auditor Independence: Regulation and Market Competition enhancing Transparency and Objectivity in Independence Decisions', submission to JCPAA Inquiry 'Review of Independent Auditing by Registered Company Auditors' (Report 391), (April).

Houghton, K. & Trotman, K. 2002, 'Review of KPMG Australia's Processes and Policies in respect of Independence, Conflict of Interest and Quality Controls' (October).

Houghton, K. & Trotman, K. 2003, 'Review of KPMG Australia's Processes and Policies in respect of Independence, Conflict of Interest and Quality Controls' (November), http://www.kpmg.com.au.

IFAC (International Federation of Accountants) n.d., *Code of Conduct*, Section 8, 'Independence', New York.

PricewaterhouseCoopers 2003, 'Report to the Board of Partners for Period August 2002 to June 2003', PwC Audit Standards Oversight Board, http://-www.pwcglobal.com.au.

Ramsay, I. 2001, *Independence of Australian Company Auditors: review of current Australian requirements and proposals for reform*, University of Melbourne.

Chapter 12. Improving ethical judgment through deep learning

Kay Plummer

Abstract

Without ethical practice the accounting profession is unable to maintain its part in its contract with society. The accounting profession recognises a need to improve ethical practice through a broad range of strategies. Prior research using Rest's Defining Issues Test has identified education as a way of improving the ethical judgment of individuals, though there has been little Australian research aimed at identifying the educational approaches which can improve ethical judgment. There is, however, evidence that Australian undergraduate accounting students adopt a surface rather than a deep approach to learning. An examination of the description by Biggs of those who are deep learners indicates a similarity to those who perform at higher stages on Rest's Defining Issues Test. This research reports on the findings of a preliminary study that examines the relationship of the ethical judgment skills of accounting students with their approaches to learning.

Evidence is found of a moderate positive relationship between ethical judgment and a deep approach to learning. This suggests that further research examining the impact of teaching approaches that foster deep learning on changes in the ethical judgment of students may be worthwhile.

Introduction

Professionals are characterised by their unique expertise gained through education and training, a commitment to lifelong learning, service to society, a code of ethics, an agreement to abide by their profession's code, and participation in the self-governance and monitoring of the profession. Society grants professions autonomy with the condition that the expertise will be used in the public interest and that members will abide by the profession's code of ethics. Snoeyenbos, Almeder and Humber (1983) have described this as a 'social contract', in which the professional discharges his obligation by operating with high standards of expertise and integrity. When the profession does not maintain these standards the social contract is broken, and society may decide to limit the role or the autonomy of the profession. Society has placed limits on the actions of accounting professionals in the past through legislation, and new restrictions have and are being implemented as a result of corporate failures early in the 2000s.

The directors and the auditors of collapsed Australian corporations such as One.Tel, HIH and Harris Scarfe stated that the accounts of their respective companies had been drawn up so as to give a true and fair view of the then current situation of the company, but subsequent investigation indicated that this was not the case. Directors and auditors are required by Australian corporate law to make a statement about the truth and fairness of the accounts, and the accounts have to be prepared in accordance with the accounting standards. 'Truth and fairness' is not defined in the legislation, but the accepted view is that the adoption of the accounting standards should lead to a true and fair view in all but extraordinary circumstances. In the case of the companies identified above, the accounting standards were not always followed, and the ambiguities and options embedded in the accounting standards were used by management, including accountants, to mislead the shareholders and the public.

As a result, the Australian accounting profession is concerned that the general public could view accountants as being unethical. This is resulting in reduced professional autonomy, with CLERP 9 proposals for increased regulation of the profession, particularly with respect to independence.

Many individual accountants have in the past acknowledged a decline in the ethical standards of the profession, though they did not consider that their own standards had declined. These accountants have suggested a range of remedies to arrest the decline, including stronger professional discipline, the introduction of courses on accounting ethics within university degree programs and continuing professional development (Leung & Cooper 1995).

The professional accounting bodies in Australia have attempted to strengthen the ethics of the profession through updating the Code of Professional Conduct, and ensuring that ethics is included in both undergraduate accounting and professional qualifying programs. As a result of the timing of the introduction of these requirements, there are groups of older members who have only completed a brief study of the Code of Professional Conduct, and have not completed any undergraduate ethics education. This gap has not been addressed within the continuing professional development (CPD) programs offered by the profession, as ethics programs have generally not been available and there does not appear to have been a member demand for such programs (Plummer 2003). In 2002 and 2003 some CPD programs, which included a component on ethics, were offered at the annual conferences of the two Australian professional accounting bodies.

There has been little Australian research on how best to teach ethics in accounting education programs, but there is research that provides some insights into the way that accounting students learn, which may be used to assist in the determination of how ethics could be taught to Australian accounting students. The research reported in this chapter attempts to determine whether or not there is a relationship between ethical judgment and approaches to learning, as this has implications for how professional programs at undergraduate and postgraduate levels could be developed. The second section of the chapter provides the theoretical background for the existence of a relationship between ethical judgment and approaches to learning. The third section describes the empirical tests undertaken and the fourth reports on the results. A summary and conclusions are included in the last section.

Theoretical background and hypothesis

Initial research in accountants' and accounting students' ethics has focused on measuring their abilities to make ethical judgments and, in a few cases, experimenting with interventions that will improve their ability to make those judgments (Armstrong 1987; Ponemon 1993a). The instruments used were initially Kohlberg's Moral Judgment Interview (MJI) and later, and more extensively, Rest's (1986a) Defining Issues Test (DIT). The DIT was developed to extend the work of Kohlberg (1984) in measuring moral judgment development. Kohlberg's work is an extension of Piaget's (1966) work on cognitive development and was initially designed to assist in the development of programs of education for moral development. The MJI was used by Kohlberg to determine the level of an individual's moral development and is based on a structured interview and takes some time to administer. The DIT is a self-administered paper-and-pencil questionnaire, and is based on Kohlberg's six-stage model of moral judgment development.

Kohlberg's model has three levels – pre-conventional, conventional and post-conventional – each of which has two stages. Both Kohlberg and Rest have described these stages differently over the years, and the short descriptions used have led to different interpretations of the developmental process. The stage model depicts a development sequence of problem-solving strategies moving from the simple to the complex; as people age and develop greater understanding, different considerations are recognised as relevant to the solution of moral problems. People operating at lower levels in the model can still make good moral choices, but their lack of understanding of complex issues may inhibit their ability to do so in certain circumstances.

There has been some controversy over Kohlberg's model with respect to the focus on issues of societal justice and the neglect of personal issues, the use of a 'staircase' stage concept, and the rarity of post-conventional thinking, its basis in foundational principalism, and the assumption that this can produce consensus. It is not in the scope of this chapter to discuss all of these issues: the arguments and counter-arguments have been presented by Modgil and Modgil (1986), and summarised, rebutted and updated in Rest et al. (1999).

One issue that may not have been adequately covered is the emphasis on dilemmas as a means of measuring an individual's ethical approach to life. A dilemma-measurement approach does not allow recognition of the ability of individuals to live lives in which there are few dilemmas — where the habit of goodness appears to reduce the occurrence of dilemmas. Colby and Damon (1996) identified a number of these people who they considered to be virtuous moral exemplars. Virtue ethics focuses on the character of individuals and their overall approach to life, and this may not be encapsulated in a response to a small group of dilemmas taken out of context, as is used in the DIT. The moral exemplars studied by Colby and Damon did not score consistently high on Kohlberg's MJI, often only scoring at Stages 3 and 4. While this may be seen as a shortcoming of both the MJI and DIT, their use has identified that people change in the way they conceptualise and judge ethical issues and that, in particular, the DIT measures some of this change.

Rest has attempted to address some of the problems (though not the issue of a dilemma approach) that are recognised in Kohlberg's work, and in doing so has moved from the six-stage model to one of three schemas of an individual's understanding and development of cooperation within society. The three schemas in Rest's updated model are *personal interest, maintaining norms* and *post-conventional*. Rest focuses particularly on the maintaining norms and post-conventional schemas, as the DIT was originally developed as an instrument to measure an adolescent's movement from using conventional to post-conventional thinking (Levels 2 and 3 in Kohlberg's model). Table 12.1 provides a graphic comparison of the two models.

Table 12.1. A comparison of Rest's (1999) schema with Kohlberg's (1976) six-stage model of moral development

Level	Rest	Kohlberg
Level 1	Personal Interest	Pre-conventional
	(not described by Rest et al. 1999)	Stage 1
		To avoid breaking rules backed by punishment, obedience for its own sake, and avoiding physical damage to persons and property.
		Stage 2
		Following rules only when it is in someone's immediate interest; acting to meet one's own interests and needs and letting others do the same. Right is also what is fair, what is an equal exchange, a deal, an agreement.
Level 2	Maintaining norms	Conventional
	An individual recognises that society cannot exist without norms that are publicly set and apply to all, irrespective of whether they benefit all members of society.	Stage 3
		Living up to what is expected by people close to you or what people generally expect of people in your role as son, brother, friend, etc. 'Being good' is important and means having

Level	Rest	Kohlberg
		good motives, showing concern about others. It also means keeping reciprocal relationships, such as trust, loyalty, respect and gratitude.
		Stage 4
		Fulfilling the actual duties to which you have agreed. Laws are to be upheld except in extreme cases where they conflict with other fixed social duties. Right is also contributing to society, the group or the institution.
Level 3	**Post-conventional**	Post-conventional
	An individual recognises the moral criteria that underpin the norms and uses these for guidance as they strive to achieve an ideal of cooperation within society which is shared and in which all benefit equally.	**Stage 5**
		Being aware that people hold a variety of values and opinions; that most values and rules are relative to your group. These relative rules should however usually be upheld, in the interest of impartiality and because they are the social contract. But some non-relative values and rights, like life and liberty, must be upheld in any society and regardless of majority opinion.
		Stage 6
		Following self-chosen ethical principles. Particular laws or social agreements are usually valid because they rest on such principles. When laws violate these principles, one acts in accordance with the principle. They include the universal principles of justice: the equality of human rights and respect for the dignity of human beings as individual persons.

Rest's maintaining norms schema is similar to the conventional level in Kohlberg's model and integrates such issues as:

- the need for norms, i.e. in a society-wide system of cooperation a set of norms limits the need to debate every issue
- duty orientation, i.e. a person obeys authority out of respect for the social system
- society-wide scope, i.e. individuals recognise the importance of and need for a society-wide system of cooperation
- uniform, categorical application, i.e. that the norms, laws and rules are publicly set and known and apply to all
- partial reciprocity, i.e. that individuals will obey the norms and laws and expect others to do the same even though not all may benefit equally.

An accountant who is at this level of moral development would be one who recognised the importance of various corporate and tax laws, and accounting and auditing standards, and complied with them; understanding that sometimes this compliance would benefit them and that sometimes it would not, but recognising that obeying these laws and standards is important for general harmony within society. Operating at this level may seem the ideal for an accountant, but it does not ensure that the accountant can make good decisions when there are options and ambiguities within accounting and auditing standards, nor does it ensure that they have the ability to make good decisions when business circumstances arise that are outside of the current laws, norms and standards.

The accountant's role is to tell a story – to make an account – of a series of business activities. This story can be told from many perspectives and can therefore result in many different accounts. It is the role of the accountant to use the laws and accounting standards to determine the perspective to be taken, but these laws and accounting standards contain options and ambiguities. A higher level of understanding is required to deal with these differing perspectives, the options and ambiguities that exist within the standards, and the unexpected occurrences of business life. This higher level of understanding is encapsulated in the post-conventional schema.

The post-conventional schema integrates such issues as:

*   recognition of the primacy of moral criteria, i.e. the individual recognises that they do not have to follow the norms but seeks the moral criteria behind the norms for guidance in action
*   an appeal to an ideal way in which humans can cooperate
*   a cooperative development of ideals that can and have been justified to a wider audience and are open to rational critique
*   full reciprocity, i.e. the idea that everyone should benefit equally.

In deciding whether or not a set of accounts is true and fair, the accountant operating at this level is applying an ideal which has been developed and shared within the profession, the application of which they should be able to justify to a wider audience while being open to coherent and balanced criticism. Operating at this level would therefore appear to be the ideal at which accountants should aim.

The use of Rest's schema, with its societal basis, is also considered appropriate within the accounting domain, as many of the dilemmas that accountants face have a society-wide scope; e.g. lack of independence on an audit is a societal justice issue, as is submitting to client pressure for tax evasion. Accounting is an activity that facilitates the operation of – and cooperation within – society, and as such the ethical dilemmas that fall within it need to be considered within a society-wide scope.

Rest's schema is embedded in the DIT, the evaluation of which results in a P score. This is the relative importance a subject gives to responses appropriate for individuals who make judgments using the post-conventional schema (or Level 3 incorporating Stages 5 and 6 of Kohlberg's six-stage model), i.e. the higher the P score, the greater a subject's ability to make moral judgments based on the moral purpose behind society's conventions. Although the P score ranges from 0 to 95, it is unusual to have someone scoring over 60. Ideally, accountants should score highly on this range.

Rest also developed a four-component model of moral action, each component of which must be present before the moral action will be undertaken. The components are:

1. *moral sensitivity*: interpreting the situation as one in which there is a moral dilemma
2. *moral judgment*: judging which action is morally right/wrong
3. *moral motivation*: prioritising moral values relative to other values
4. *moral character*: having courage and persistence, overcoming distractions, and implementing skills.

The DIT attempts to measure the moral judgment component of moral action, i.e. Component 2. Much of the research to date has focused on Component 2, with some research on Component 1 (Rest 1986a; Rest et al. 1999). There is no formal sequence for the components in the model, but some level of moral sensitivity must exist before a moral judgment can be made. It is possible to measure a level of moral sensitivity, but an instrument has not been developed that separates the moral sensitivity component from the moral judgment component when moral judgment is being measured using the DIT. In the research presented in this chapter the focus is on Component 2, as there is evidence that growth in moral judgment occurs within education (Rest 1986a; McNeel 1994; Rest et al. 1999). How much of this growth reflects a growth in moral sensitivity and how much reflects a growth in moral judgment has not yet been examined.

McNeel (1994) identified strong longitudinal growth in moral judgment development across his student subjects' four years of college, with a P score moving from an average of 35.7 to 46.4 (n = 216). In his study, McNeel examined the growth among the various major subject areas and identified this growth as being greater, and with significantly higher P scores, for seniors in psychology, nursing and English than among business and education majors. McNeel related this growth to majors in which the focus was on understanding the contradictions within each person and the variation between people, i.e. being able to take different viewpoints. This requires empathy and sensitivity to the impact of actions on others, as well as reflection and the ability to integrate the viewpoint of others with one's own world-view. McNeel also recognised that the growth could be due to the way the majors were taught, differences in the students who chose these majors, and other unidentified factors.

As an outcome of his and others' extensive research on moral development, Rest (1986a, p. 57) described people who achieve greater development in moral judgment as:

> ... those who love to learn, who seek new challenges, who enjoy intellectually stimulating environments, who are reflective, who make plans and set goals, who take risks, who see themselves in the larger social contexts of history and institutions and broad cultural trends, who take responsibility for themselves and their environs. On the environmental side of the equation, those who develop in moral judgment have an advantage in receiving encouragement to continue their education and their development. They profit from stimulating and challenging environments, and from social milieus that support their work, interest them, and reward their accomplishments. As young adults, the people who develop in moral judgment are more fulfilled in their career aspirations, have set a life direction of continued intellectual stimulation and challenge, are more involved in their communities, and take more interest in the larger societal issues. This pattern is one of general social/cognitive development.

This description comes from the early research using the DIT and provides a strong connection between moral developers and learning – as does the more recent research of McNeel – and highlights the need to more effectively explore connections between learning and moral development.

Specific ethics education programs in the general population have concentrated on the discussion of moral dilemmas and conflict, and this focus has encouraged the growth of abstract moral judgment, though this is not necessarily translated into moral action (Rest 1986a). The interventions used in accounting ethics education programs initially included ethical dilemma discussion, consideration of professionalism, codes of conduct and dilemma resolution models (Ponemon 1993b). The aim of these courses appears to be that of sensitising students to the range of moral issues that they will face as accountants and giving them some tools to resolve those issues.

Some of the teaching techniques adopted by accounting and business ethics lecturers are provided in the accounting ethics education literature and listed in Table 12.2, but the literature provides little description and analysis of the teaching/learning and assessment strategies adopted in these programs, nor does it generally provide an analysis of the student responses to the interventions. This is unfortunate as it provides the accounting lecturer with little information about how to teach or not teach ethics to accountants, but it does provide accounting lecturers with a selection of techniques that can be used as a basis of research in their own classes. Providing diverse ways in which an area of study can be experienced gives the students greater opportunities to more effectively personalise the knowledge and attitudes embedded in the area of study and to relate it to their own lives (Gardner 1999; Marton & Trigwell 2000; Marton, Watkins & Tang 1997) – that is, it can promote deep learning.

Table 12.2 provides a list of ways of teaching that have been suggested for ethics education. No one way has been identified as superior but as suggested above, ways of teaching which incorporate diversity, personalisation, integration and reflection may well provide a deep learning environment, which may foster ethical development.

Table 12.2. Ways of teaching ethics

Ways of teaching ethics	Author
Andragogy	Brookfield (1998), Leicester & Pearce (1997), Segon (1996)
Case	Buchholz & Rosenthal (2001), Loo, Kennedy & Sauers (1999), Alam (1998), Mintz (1996), Segon (1996), Leung & Cooper (1994), Welton, Lagrone & Davis (1994), Langenderfer & Rockness (1989), Gandz & Hayes (1988)
Collaborative learning	Hill & Stewart (1999), Mintz (1996), Damon & Colby (1996)
Cooperative learning	Mintz (1996)
Critical reflection and critical education	Hill & Stewart (1999), Levitt (1999), Carroll (1998), Brookfield (1998), Leicester & Pearce (1997), McDonald (1997), Segon (1996), Damon & Colby (1996)
Debate	Levitt (1999), Carroll (1998), Leung & Cooper (1994)
Decision models	Leung & Cooper (1994), Langenderfer & Rockness (1989), Gandz & Hayes (1988)
Dialogue	Brookfield (1998), Milton-Smith (1996)
Drama	Winston (1999), Basourokas (1999)
Emotion and feeling	Segon (1996)
Exhortation	Armstrong, Ketz & Owsen (2003)
Experiential learning – this includes activities like participating in community enrichment programs and service learning	Sims (2002), Buchholz & Rosenthal (2001), LeClair & Ferrell (2000), Glass & Bonnici (1999), Hill & Stewart (1999), Armon (1998), Kitwood (1998), Damon & Colby (1996), Morton & Troppe (1996)
Habit	Levitt (1999), Damon & Colby (1996)
Instruction (lectures)	Milton-Smith (1996), Leung & Cooper (1994)
Logic	Penn (1990), Colby & Kohlberg (1987), Rest (1986)
Meditation	La Forge (2000), Levitt (1999)
Mentor relationships, role models, moral exemplars	Armstrong, Ketz & Owsen (2003), Watson (2003), Hill & Stewart (1999), Levitt (1999), Damon & Colby (1996), MacIntyre (1984)
Movies and videos	Giacalone & Jurkiewicz (2001), Mintz (1996)
Presentations	Leung & Cooper (1994)
Reading stories/storytelling	King & Down (2002), Hill & Stewart (1999), Mintz (1996)
Reflection	Levitt (1999), Hill & Stewart (1999), McDonald (1997), Segon (1996)
Resolution of dissonant experiences	Brookfield (1998), Leicester & Pearce (1997)
Role plays, role taking	Kitwood (1998), Bebeau (1994), Mintz (1996), Segon (1996) Penn (1990), Colby & Kohlberg (1987), Rest (1986)

Identifying ways of successfully teaching ethics is important to the accounting profession as this will help ensure the continuance of a largely ethical profession and may address what appears to be a shortfall in ethical decision-making capabilities within the profession. In the United States, accounting students and accountants who completed the DIT were found in general to have lower P scores than those of comparable groups (Armstrong 1987; Lampe & Finn 1992; Ponemon 1990, 1992a, 1992b; Shaub 1994), though there were some exceptions (Jeffrey 1993; Shaub 1994), and accounting students who participated in an ethics education program did not significantly improve their scores on the DIT (Ponemon 1993), apart from those who undertook an elective subject in professional ethics (Armstrong 1993). In his Australian study, Dellaportas (2002) also found a lack of growth in the DIT scores of accounting students who participated in an ethics education program. Armstrong and Ponemon (1993) concluded that traditional accounting education inhibits moral judgment development.

In the education discipline, greater moral growth has been found in interventions that provide experiences of moral challenge and accompanying moral emotions or commitments (Armon 1998), i.e. where students have been fully engaged in the subject matter and with the people with whom they were working, while in dentistry greater moral growth has been achieved through a combination of cooperative learning and role taking (Bebeau 1994).

Traditional accounting education has been identified as emphasising shallow, reiterative learning (Gray, Bebbington & McPhail 1994), where students do not fully engage with the subject and do not develop a deep approach to learning. The type of education accountants receive could therefore be inhibiting the development of moral judgment skills by not creating a need for a deep reflective approach to learning (Gray, Bebbington & McPhail 1994). Accounting lecturers could be using educational processes which encourage a surface approach to learning, and which may not be consistent with improved moral judgment in accounting students.

Recognition of a range of approaches to learning has existed for some time. For example, Ramsden and Entwistle (1981) identified a number, one of which was an 'understanding' approach, which involves the search for meaning and is related to intrinsic motivation, and corresponds to the deep approach called for by Gray, Bebbington and McPhail. Biggs (1987a) developed an instrument, the Study Process Questionnaire (SPQ), which has been widely used to identify common student approaches to learning in particular courses or classes. Biggs identified four approaches; *surface*, *achieving*, *deep* and a composite, *deep achieving*. Each of these approaches has two sub-scales, *motive* and *strategy*. These approaches are not mutually exclusive, so it is possible to score highly on more than one scale, though Biggs (1987a) indicates that students tend to favour one approach over another.

Students will adopt an approach depending upon a number of factors, some of which are personal – such as prior learning experiences, personality, intelligence and the issues that are affecting their lives at the time – and some situational.

Situational factors include such issues as subject content, methods of teaching and evaluation, and course structure (Biggs 1987b). This makes it difficult to validly compare students' scores on an SPQ across courses – and even perhaps across institutions – without taking into account the differences in the situational factors.

Students can score between 7 and 35 on each approach sub-scale, resulting in possible scores for each approach ranging from 14 to 70. Biggs (1987a) found that undergraduate students in general become increasingly surface and decreasingly deep in their orientation to learning over the course of their undergraduate studies, though his studies did not include accounting students. Booth, Luckett and Mladenovic (1999) had accounting students at two universities in Sydney complete the SPQ and a brief summary of the results is outlined in Table 12.3.

Table 12.3. Mean SPQ scores of Australian accounting students

Accounting students	Surface approach	Deep approach	Achieving approach
Males (n = 187)	51.5	43.0	44.3
Females (n = 158)	51.3	41.7	43.2
Combined (n = 345)	51.2	42.2	43.6

(Adapted from Booth, Luckett & Mladenovic 1999)

These accounting students were found to have a higher surface approach than deep approach to learning, and this is consistent with the findings of Gow, Kember and Cooper (1994). They identified a number of situational factors that encouraged a surface approach and these included 'excessive workload, surface assessment demands, lack of intrinsic motivation, a didactic teaching style, [and] high staff/student ratios' (p.118), while Jackling (2003) identified students' perceptions of good teaching, an appropriate workload in which there weren't too many topics and there was enough time for understanding, and clear goals associated with greater use by students of deep learning strategies. Some common themes in these situational factors appear to be time for reflection and integration (understanding), and good teaching.

Biggs (1987a, p. 15) described a student who adopts a deep approach as one who:

- is interested in the academic task and derives enjoyment from carrying it out
- searches for the meaning inherent in the task (if a prose passage, the intention of the author)
- personalises the task, making it meaningful to their own experience and to the real world
- integrates aspects or parts of tasks into a whole (for instance, relates evidence to a conclusion) and sees relationships between this whole and previous knowledge

- tries to theorize about the tasks – forms a hypothesis.

Similarities can be found between the different descriptions of those who achieve high moral judgment growth and the descriptions of deep learners. One example of this is that people who achieve higher levels of moral development love to learn and enjoy intellectually stimulating environments, as – naturally enough – do deep learners. Moral developers are also described as 'reflective', and deep learners, while not described in this way, are characterised as searching for inherent meaning, personalising the learning and attempting to theorise about the tasks, all of which use reflective abilities. Both groups further use reflection and integration in seeing themselves within a broad social context, relating their experiences to the wider world and recognising relationships between concepts. Therefore, deep learners and higher moral developers have a number of similar characteristics largely centred on their reflective and integrative abilities. It could therefore be expected that a deep approach to learning correlates with a higher P score. From this can be developed a hypothesis:

H_1 *Students who are deep learners will have a higher P score.*

Students who have a surface approach to learning are only motivated to meet the minimal requirements of the course: they balance failure with working more than necessary and operationalise this through only studying the bare essentials, focusing on facts that can be reproduced by rote learning (Biggs 1987b). As a result they do not reflect upon the subject matter of the course, nor do they attempt to integrate any knowledge gained with previous knowledge. These students are likely to reproduce the facts they have learnt but are unlikely to place those facts within a structure that can be later used to deal with other facts. They may not even have the skills of reflection and integration. These people are therefore more likely to be operating at a pre-conventional level or at the lower end of the conventional level, where there is a focus on the self and the need to do things such as obeying laws and norms because it means looking after oneself. It could therefore be expected that a higher surface approach to learning is correlated with a lower P score. The following hypothesis is therefore also suggested:

H_2 *Students who are surface learners will have a lower P score.*

Biggs (1987b) describes an achieving approach to learning as characterised by ego-driven motives. Students are driven to get the highest grades because of their competitive nature, wanting to do well irrespective of their interest in the material. This results in good organisation of their learning environment, time and activities. Where this ego-driven motive is strong it could be expected that these students would operate at the pre-conventional level, where ego is a major determinant of moral decisions, but these students may have also developed some reflective and integrative skills which are necessary in some courses to achieve high grades, and these skills may have given them a deeper understanding of moral issues. It is therefore not expected that there will be any correlation between an achieving approach to learning and P score.

There has also been extensive work correlating P score with a number of demographic variables. Higher P scores are associated with age (Rest 1986a) and being a female accounting student (Ponemon 1993a; Shaub 1994). From these two, further hypotheses have been developed and will be examined:

H_3 *Students who are older will have higher P scores.*

H_4 *Female students will have higher P scores than male students.*

Findings of a positive relationship between deep learning and P score may mean that accounting educators at all levels should be looking at ways to reverse the trend to a surface approach to learning, and to provide learning activities that encourage the development of integrative, reflective practice, as this may also assist in developing moral judgment skills. While students may be using a deep approach in non-accounting courses in which they are enrolled, they are not seeing its application as relevant to accounting. They therefore do not see reflection and integration as necessary components of accounting practice and this may limit their abilities to make good accounting decisions, and good ethical decisions within the accounting sphere.

Reviewing assessment and other teaching practices, and providing examples where lecturers demonstrate reflection and integration and have students practise these with respect to accounting, are some ways in which a deep approach to learning may be fostered. Activities such as the development of 'concept maps' help students understand the basic structure of the knowledge being presented, as well as providing them with a demonstration and practice in integration and reflection. In auditing classes, for example, concept maps can be used to identify the range of knowledge areas that underpin auditing and highlight the importance of a true and fair view.

In the teaching of accounting ethics other types of activities that provide deep learning experiences could be used. One of these is the use of a movie to trigger a range of discussions and role plays. One movie that has been successfully used is *The Dish*, a gentle comedy giving a fictionalised account of the role of the Parkes radio telescope in the successful 1969 moon landing and walk by Neil Armstrong. Part of this movie tells the story of a lie told by scientists in order to protect their professional reputation. Leung and Cooper (1995) identified the issue of integrity in admitting mistakes made by oneself as being one of the key ethical issues faced by accountants in Australia, and this movie can be used to help bring this issue to life with undergraduate accounting students.

After watching the movie, some students seem to consider that it was right to tell the lie – in the movie it did seem to save the scientists' reputation – but as the students more thoroughly analyse the scenario, they see that the reputation wouldn't necessarily have been lost if the scientists had told the truth: that by lying the scientists shifted the blame elsewhere, which would have been hard on those to whom it was shifted, and that the risk to their reputations and to their continuing role in the moon mission that arose from lying was extremely high. At this point, students can then be asked to identify similar situations in which they may have been involved, such as where lies have been told to them about products and services they have purchased. Some of these situations can then be role played, highlighting the damage that such lies cause.

Undergraduate students in Australia often do not have the knowledge of accounting practice that would enable them to identify the accounting situations in which such lies might be told, but these can be described by the lecturer and the students asked to identify who might be harmed in these circumstances. In doing this they are being sensitised to the issues that arise in practice and are reflecting on the impact of these on others.

For this type of lesson to be effective, the teacher needs to be prepared with a range of questions that direct students' reflection on the issues of importance. Such lessons allow the students to experience the ethical issue in a number of ways and help them to relate it to their own lives – and to reflect on the impact of such lying on society – and in so doing they offer students a deep learning experience.

Empirical tests

The data to test the relationship between deep learning and ethical judgment was collected in 2002 and 2003, and drawn from students studying an elective second-year subject in business ethics and from students studying a compulsory third (final)-year subject in accounting theory. The students were asked to complete the SPQ, a short demographic survey and a three-scenario DIT.

The SPQ has 42 questions with responses given on a five-point Likert scale, ranging from 'Never' scored as 1 to 'Always' scored as 5. As mentioned earlier, three approaches are measured, deep, surface and achieving (the composite deep achieving is not relevant here), and each of these has two sub-scales, motive and strategy, resulting in a questionnaire with six factors. There are seven questions for each factor, resulting in possible factor scores ranging from 7 to 35 (Biggs 1987b).

The DIT contains three scenarios in which an ethical dilemma is posed. Students were asked to read each scenario and determine the action that they would take. Under each scenario there is a list of 12 statements reflecting issues relevant to the ethical question raised in the scenario. Each of the statements represents one of the *schemas* in the model or is included as a measure of reliability. Students then had to indicate on the Likert scale the importance each issues statement had in determining their decision on the action to be taken. The four issues statements which were the most relevant to the student's decision had to be selected and ranked, 4 through to 1, with 4 being the most important and 1 being the fourth most important. Of these four, those that related to post-conventional thinking were rank-summed and the proportion of these was calculated as the P score (Rest 1986b).

The business ethics students completed all questionnaires during their class; there were 19 usable responses, after two were eliminated for choosing issues that sounded important but were meaningless. The accounting theory students completed the DIT in class and were asked to complete the SPQ after class and return it to the lecturer. Of the 13 DITs completed, two were eliminated for choosing issues that were meaningless, leaving 11 usable responses. Seven SPQs were returned and all were usable. As these were not all the same students there were only six responses that could be used to test H_1 and H_2, resulting in a combined class sample size of 25.

The variables extracted from the instruments are:

- *P score*, calculated from the results of the student responses to the three-scenario DIT
- *age*, recorded as the age within a range at the time of completing the questionnaire; the ranges were 18-20 years old (recorded as 1), 21-25 (2), 26-30 (3), 31-40 (4), and 41+ (5)
- *gender*, recorded as male = 1 and female = 0
- *deep*, the combined deep motive and strategy score on the SPQ
- *surface*, the combined surface motive and strategy score on the SPQ.

Results and discussion

Means of all P scores, and the deep and surface learning approach scores in total and for each class, were calculated and are shown in Table 12.4. The mean P score of each class differs by 4.55, with students doing the elective business ethics class having the higher P score. These students also exhibited a 4.7-higher deep approach to learning and a 7.5-lower surface approach to learning than the accounting theory class. An independent samples t-test was used to examine the significance of these differences. The differences in means between classes on the P score and deep approach were not significant, but the difference in means on the surface approach was significant at $p < 0.05$. The surface approach mean of the accounting theory class was also consistent with the surface approach means identified by Booth, Luckett and Mladenovic (1999), while the deep approach means of the business ethics students were 5.6 higher than those of the combined accounting students surveyed by Booth, Luckett and Mladen-ovic.

Table 12.4. Mean scores of each class

Class	P score	Deep approach	Surface approach
Accounting theory	31.51 (n = 11) sd = 12.24	43.14 (n = 7) sd = 3.33	51.86 (n = 7) sd = 5.43
Business ethics	36.06 (n = 19) sd = 20.89	47.84 (n = 19) sd = 8.03	44.36 (n = 19) sd = 7.01
All	34.39 (n = 30) sd = 18.09	46.57 (n = 26) sd = 7.32	46.38 (n = 26) sd = 7.3

The range of situational factors impacting on the business ethics and accounting theory classes may explain the higher surface learning approach scores achieved by the accounting theory class and the higher deep approach scores achieved by the business ethics class. Business ethics is an elective, with assessment by essays and a range of in-class activities that the students generally didn't consider to be an excessive workload, and which provided a number of diverse ways of reflecting upon the subject. Accounting theory, by comparison, is a compulsory subject in the accounting core of the degree program assessed through essays, debates and a final exam. Students considered the reading workload necessary to pass the assessment events in this subject excessive. Where the workload is considered excessive, students generally do not spend additional time exploring the subject as they do not consider that they have the time to do so – that is, they take a more surface approach to the subject.

Table 12.5 provides a summary of the key correlations using the combined results of both the accounting theory and business ethics classes. The correlation of DIT P scores with approaches to learning shows a moderate, positive and significant relationship with a deep approach to learning ($r = +0.493, n = 25, p = 0.006$). The results for the sub-scale deep motive are significant ($r = +0.518, n = 25, p = 0.004$). There was also a mild significant correlation with a deep strategy ($r = +0.392, n = 25, p = 0.026$). Thus, there is some positive support for H_1, i.e. that students who are deep learners have a higher P score. Evidence of this positive relationship between deep learning and P scores suggests that it would be useful to examine the impact of teaching interventions that support a deep approach to learning within accounting and ethics courses, and the effect of these on the moral judgment ability of students. The milder correlation with a deep strategy may be the result of a lack of student understanding as to how to turn their motives into effective action, or it may be that the amount of work students do both within and outside of degree programs means that they do not have the time – or perhaps the inclination – to turn their motives into effective strategies.

There is no support for H_2 as there was no significant relationship between P score and a surface approach to learning $(r = -0.193, n = 25, p = 0.177)$.

Table 12.5. Correlations of variables using the combined classes

		Deep approach	Deep motive	Deep strategy	Surface approach	Surface motive	Surface strategy
P score	R	0.493**	0.518**	0.392*	−0.193	−0.090	−0.227
	Sig. (1-tailed)	0.006	0.004	0.026	0.177	0.335	0.138
	N	25	25	25	25	25	25

**correlation significant at the 0.01 level

* correlation significant at the 0.05 level

There was no support for H_3 either, i.e. that older students would have a higher P score $(r = 0.089, n = 30, p = 0.344)$. This is not surprising as there was very little difference in the age of the students. Further studies using a wider age-range group will be needed to examine this hypothesis.

Table 12.6. Mean scores of males and females

	Gender	Number	Mean
P score	Male	13	30.25
	Female	17	37.57
Deep approach	Male	11	46.64
	Female	15	46.53
Surface approach	Male	11	47.09
	Female	15	45.87

The data used to examine H_4 is given in Table 12.6. Female students' mean P score was 37.57, 7.32 higher than the male students' score of 30.25. These means were compared using an independent samples t-test that indicated that there was a significant difference between the means $(p < 0.10)$. Therefore, there was support for H_4, i.e. that female business students have a higher P score than male business students. There were no significant differences between the means of males and females on the approaches to learning.

Table 12.7. DIT P Score means of college/university students from a range of disciplines and countries

Author	Sample	Mean P score
McNeel (1994)	US senior college students (n = 216)	46.4
Shaub (1994)	US accounting students with ethics intervention (n = 30)	44.7
Rest (1986a)	US average college students	42.3
Shaub (1994)	Senior auditing students (n = 91)	41.3
Shaub (1994)	Accounting students without ethics intervention (n = 61)	39.7
Ponemon (1993)	US graduate accounting students with ethics intervention (n = 53)	39.2
Thorne (2001)	Cooperative education students (n = 56)	38.9
Jeffrey (1993)	Senior liberal arts students (n = 41)	38.8

Author	Sample	Mean P score
Jeffrey (1993)	Lower division accounting students (n = 57)	37.6
Jeffrey (1993)	Senior business students (n = 195)	37.4
Thorne (1999)	Canadian graduate accounting students (n = 144)	37.2
Dellaportas (2002)	Aust. senior accounting students with ethics intervention (n = 47)	36.1
This study	**Aust. business ethics students (n = 19)**	**36.06**
Thorne (2001)	Cooperative education students (n = 54)	35.9
Thorne (1999)	Canadian accounting students (n = 70)	35.5
McNeel (1994)	US freshman college students (n = 216)	35.7
This study	Aust. business and accounting students (n = 30)	34.39
Rest (1986a)	**US average senior high school students**	**31.8**
This study	**Aust. accounting theory students (n = 11)**	**31.51**

The overall mean DIT P score in this study was 34.39, and this is lower than that found in Dellaportas' Australian study (2002). The differences could be because the students in the Dellaportas study had completed their ethics subject and as a result improved their ethical judgment skills, while students in this study had not completed their ethics studies. The results from this study are similar to those found by McNeel (1994) at a freshman level and are lower than a range of studies from the United States. These Australian results provide further evidence for the proposition that accounting and business students do not perform as well at ethical judgment as students from other disciplines or other countries. A comparison of DIT P score means from a number of studies that provide evidence for this proposition is seen in Table 12.7.

Conclusion

While there is support for the hypothesis that students who are deep learners will have a higher P score, it should be remembered that this is only a preliminary study and that the sample size is small; however, the results offer a promising line of enquiry into ways of teaching accounting and ethics. At this stage further research needs to be undertaken, increasing the sample size and examining the relationship between deep and surface learning and P score before and after ethics education interventions that emphasise a deep approach to learning. McNeel recognised that the growth in P score may be a result of differences in teaching, as well as a result of the types of students who select accounting as a profession and other factors such as the different extracurricular activities that business students undertake. A study examining the teaching interventions and their effect on students will enable further clarification of these relationships, and provide information to the profession and to accounting academics about ways in which the ethical judgment of members of the profession may be improved.

The lack of support for the hypothesis that students who are surface learners will have a lower P score may be a result of problems with the SPQ, as recent research indicates that some of the strategies included within the surface learning approach underpin deep learning as well and that there may be confusion between the factors.

As Rest (1986a) suggests, moral judgment is only one factor in determining moral action: educational interventions at all levels need to also incorporate activities designed to sensitise people to ethical issues and to build moral character. Further research also needs to be undertaken to determine how this can be done within the accounting educational context.

References

Armon, C. 1998, 'Adult moral development, experience and education', *Journal of Moral Education*, vol. 27, no. 3, pp. 345-70.

Armstrong, M. B. 1987, 'Moral development and accounting education', *Journal of Accounting Education*, vol. 5, Spring, pp. 27-43.

Armstrong, M. B. 1993, 'Ethics and professionalism in accounting education: a sample course', *Journal of Accounting Education*, vol. 11, no. 1, pp. 77-92.

Armstrong, M. B., Ketz, J. E. & Owsen, D. 2003, 'Ethics education in accounting: moving toward ethical motivation and ethical behavior', *Journal of Accounting Education*, vol. 21, no. 1, pp. 1-16.

Basourakos, J. 1999, 'Moral Voices and Moral Choices: Canadian drama and moral pedagogy', *Journal of Moral Education*, vol. 28, no. 4, pp. 473-89.

Bebeau, M. J. 1994, 'Influencing the Moral Dimensions of Dental Practice', in J. R. Rest & D. Narvaez (eds), *Moral Development in the Professions: Psychology and Applied Ethics*, Lawrence Erlbaum Associates, Hillsdale, NJ.

Biggs, J. 1987a, *Student approaches to learning and studying*, Australian Council for Education Research, Melbourne.

Biggs, J. 1987b, *Study process questionnaire manual*, Australian Council for Educational Research, Melbourne.

Booth, P., Luckett, P. & Mladenovic, R. 1999, 'The quality of learning in accounting education: the impact of approaches to learning on academic performance', *Accounting Education*, vol. 8, no. 4, pp. 277-300.

Brookfield, S. 1998, 'Understanding and facilitating moral learning in adults', *Journal of Moral Education*, vol. 27, no. 3, pp. 283-300.

Buchholz, R. A. & Rosenthal, S. B. 2001, 'A philosophical framework for case studies', *Journal of Business Ethics*, vol. 29, nos. 1 & 2, pp. 25-31.

Burton, S., Johnston, M. W. & Wilson, E. J. 1991, 'An experimental assessment of alternative teaching approaches for introducing business ethics to undergraduate business students', *Journal of Business Ethics*, vol. 10, no. 7, pp. 507-17.

Carroll, R. 1998, 'A model for ethical education in accounting', in C. Gowthorpe & J. Blake (eds), *Ethical Issues in Accounting*, Routledge, London.

Colby, A. & Kohlberg, L. 1987, *The Measurement of Moral Judgment*, Cambridge University Press.

Damon, W. & Colby, A. 1996, 'Education and Moral Commitment', *Journal of Moral Education*, vol. 25, no. 1, pp. 31-7.

Dellaportas, S. 2002, 'Moral Developments in Accounting Education', AAANZ 2002 Annual Conference, Accounting Association of Australia and New Zealand.

Gandz, J. & Hayes, N. 1988, 'Teaching business ethics', *Journal of Business Ethics*, vol. 7, no. 9, pp. 657-69.

Gardner, H. 1999, *Intelligence Reframed*, Basic Books, New York.

George, R. 1987, 'Teaching business ethics: Is there a gap between rhetoric and reality', *Journal of Business Ethics*, vol. 6, no. 7, pp. 513-18.

Giacalone, R. A. 2001, 'Lights, camera, action: Teaching ethical decision making through the cinematic experience', *Teaching Business Ethics*, vol. 5, no. 1, pp. 79-87.

Giacalone, R. A. & Jurkiewicz, C. L. 2003, 'Right from Wrong: The Influence of Spirituality on Perceptions of Unethical Business Activities', *Journal of Business Ethics*, vol. 46, no. 1, pp. 85-97.

Glass, R. S. & Bonnici, J. 1997, 'An Experiential Approach for Teaching Business Ethics', *Teaching Business Ethics*, vol. 1, no. 2, pp. 183-95.

Gow, L., Kember, D. & Cooper, B. 1994, 'The teaching context and approaches to study of accountancy students', *Issues in Accounting Education*, vol. 9, no. 1, pp. 118-30.

Gray, R. H., Bebbington, J. & McPhail, K. 1994, 'Teaching ethics and the ethics of accounting teaching: educating for immorality and a possible case for social and environmental accounting education', *Accounting Education*, vol. 3, no. 1, pp. 51-75.

Griseri, P. 2002, 'Emotion and cognition in business ethics teaching', *Teaching Business Ethics*, vol. 6, no. 3, pp. 371-91.

Hill, A. & Stewart, I. 1999, 'Character education in business schools: pedagogical strategies', *Teaching Business Ethics*, vol. 3, no. 2, pp. 179-93.

Jackling, B. 2003, 'Learning approaches of accounting students: A cross-sectional and longitudinal study', AFAANZ Annual Conference 2003, Accounting Association of Australia and New Zealand.

Jeffrey, C. 1993, 'Ethical development of accounting students, non-accounting students, and liberal arts students', *Issues in Accounting Education*, vol. 8, no. 1, pp. 86-96.

King, J. & Down, J. 2001, 'On taking stories seriously: Emotional and moral intelligences', *Teaching Business Ethics*, vol. 5, no. 4, pp. 419-37.

Kitwood, T. 1998, 'Professional and Moral Development for Care Work: some observations on the process', *Journal of Moral Education*, vol. 27, no. 3, pp. 401-11.

Kohlberg, L. 1976, 'Moral stages and moralization: The cognitive developmental approach in Moral development and behavior', in T. Lickona (ed.), *Moral development and behavior*, Holt, Rinehart & Winston, New York.

Kohlberg, L. 1984, *Essay on moral development, volume two: the psychology of moral development*, Harper and Row, San Francisco.

Kuit, J. A., Reay, G. & Freeman, R. 2001, 'Experiences of reflective teaching', *Active Learning in Higher Education*, vol. 2, no. 2, pp. 128-42.

La Forge, P. 2000, 'Business ethics through philosophy: Meditation, Readings, Case Work', *Teaching Business Ethics*, vol. 4, no. 1, pp. 69-83.

Lampe, C. J. & Finn, D. W. 1992, 'A model of auditors' ethical decision processes', *Auditing: A Journal of Practice and Theory*, vol. 11 (Supplement), pp. 33-59.

Langenderfer, H. Q. & Rockness, J. W. 1989, 'Integrating Ethics into the Accounting Curriculum: Issues, Problems, and Solutions', *Issues in Accounting Education*, vol. 4, no. 1, pp. 58-69.

LeClair, D. T. & Ferrell, L. 2000, 'Innovations in experiential business ethics training', *Journal of Business Ethics*, vol. 23, no. 3, pp. 313-22.

Leicester, M. & Pearce, R. 1997, 'Cognitive Development, Self Knowledge and Moral Education', *Journal of Moral Education*, vol. 26, no. 4, pp. 455-72.

Leung, P. & Cooper, B. J. 1994, 'Ethics in accountancy: a classroom experience', *Accounting Education*, vol. 3, no. 1, pp. 19-33.

Leung, P. & Cooper, B. J. 1995, *Professional Ethics – A Survey of Australian Accountants*, Ethics Centre of Excellence, Australian Society of Certified Practising Accountants, Melbourne.

Levitt, H. M. 1999, 'The development of wisdom; An analysis of Tibetan Buddhist experience', *The Journal of Humanistic Psychology*, vol. 39, no. 2, pp. 86-105.

Lickona, T. 1996, 'Eleven principles of effective character education', *Journal of Moral Education*, vol. 25, no. 1, pp. 93-100.

Loo, K. H., Kennedy, J. & Sauers, D. A. 1998-99, 'Are Students Really Less Ethical Than Business Practitioners?', *Teaching Business Ethics*, vol. 2, no. 4, pp. 347-69.

MacIntyre, A. 1981, *After Virtue*, Notre Dame University Press, New York.

Marton, F. & Trigwell, K. 2000, 'Variato Est Mater Studorium', *Higher Education Research and Development*, vol. 9, no. 3, pp. 381-95.

Marton, F., Watkins, D. & Tang, C. 1997, 'Discontinuities and continuities in the experience of learning: an interview study of high-school students in Hong Kong', *Learning and Instruction*, vol. 7, no. 1, pp. 21-48.

McAlpine, L., Weston, C. B. & Beauchamp, J. 1999, 'Building a metacognitive model of reflection', *Higher Education*, vol. 37, no. 2, pp. 105-31.

McDonald, R. 1997, 'Information and Transformation in Teaching Business Ethics', *Teaching Business Ethics*, vol. 1, no. 2, pp. 151-62.

McDonald, R. 1999, 'Seven exercises to get students thinking', *Teaching Business Ethics*, vol. 2, no. 4, pp. 411-32.

McNeel, S. P. 1994, 'College teaching and student moral development', in J. R. Rest & D. Narvaez (eds), *Moral Development in the Professions: Psychology and Applied Ethics*, Lawrence Erlbaum Associates, Hillsdale, NJ.

Milton-Smith, J. 1996, 'Forces for cultural change: The findings of the Australian business ethics project', in K. E. Woldring (ed.), *Business Ethics in Australia and New Zealand: Essays and Cases*, Nelson, Melbourne.

Mintz, S. 1996, 'Aristotelian virtue and business ethics education', *Journal of Business Ethics*, vol. 15, no. 8, pp. 827-38.

Modgil, S. & Modgil, C. (eds) 1986, *Lawrence Kohlberg: Consensus and controversy*, Falmer Press, Philadelphia.

Morton, K. & Troppe, M. 1996, 'From the margin to the mainstream: campus compact's project on integrating service with academic study', *Journal of Business Ethics*, vol. 15, no. 1, pp. 21-32.

Narvaez, D. 2002, 'Does reading moral stories build character?', *Educational Psychology Review*, vol. 14, no. 2, pp. 155-71.

Nouri, H. & Shiarappa, B. 1996, 'An empirical examination of senior accounting students' ethical reaction to grade inflation', *Accounting Education*, vol. 5, no. 1, pp. 17-24.

Penn, W. Y. 1990, 'Teaching Ethics – A direct approach', *Journal of Moral Education*, vol. 19, no. 2, pp. 124-38.

Piaget, J. 1966, *The moral development of the child*, Free Press, New York.

Plummer, K. 2003, 'Ethics in ICAA CPE', in P. Rushbrook (ed.), *Innovations in professional practice: Influences and perspectives*, Charles Sturt University, Bathurst.

Ponemon, L. A. 1990, 'Ethical judgments in accounting: a cognitive-development perspective', *Critical Perspectives on Accounting*, vol. 1, no. 2, pp. 191-215.

Ponemon, L. A. 1992a, 'Ethical reasoning and selection-socialisation in accounting', *Accounting, Organisations and Society*, vol 17, nos. 3 & 4, pp. 239-58.

Ponemon, L. A. 1992b, 'Auditor underreporting of time and moral reasoning: An experimental lab study', *Contemporary Accounting Research*, vol. 9, no. 2, pp. 171-89.

Ponemon, L. A. 1993a, 'Can ethics be taught in accounting?', *Journal of Accounting Education*, vol. 11, no. 2, pp. 185-210.

Ponemon, L. A. 1993b, 'Ethical reasoning in auditing education', *The Auditor's Report*, vol. 16, no. 3, p. 6 (one-page article).

Ramsden, P. & Entwistle, N. 1981, 'Effects of Academic departments on students' approaches to studying', *British Journal of Educational Psychology*, vol. 51, no. 3, pp. 368-83.

Rest, J. R. 1986a, *Moral development: Advances in research and theory*, Praeger, New York

Rest, J. R. 1986b, *Manual for the defining issues test*, Centre for the study of ethical development, Minneapolis.

Rest, J. R. & Narvaez, D. (eds) 1994, *Moral Development in the Professions: Psychology and Applied Ethics*, Lawrence Erlbaum Associates, Hillsdale, NJ.

Rest, J. R., Narvaez, D., Bebeau, M. J. & Thoma, S. J. 1999, *Post-conventional Moral Thinking: A Neo-Kohlbergian Approach*, Lawrence Erlbaum Associates, Mahwah, NJ.

Rogers, V. & Smith, A. 2001, 'Ethics, moral development, and accountants-in-training', *Teaching Business Ethics*, vol. 5, no. 1, pp. 1-20.

Segon, M. 1996, 'Ethics training: the professions and academia', in K. E. Woldring (ed.), *Business Ethics in Australia and New Zealand: Essays and Cases*, Nelson, Melbourne.

Shaub, M. K. 1994, 'An analysis of the association of traditional demographic variables with the moral reasoning of auditing students and auditors', *Journal of Accounting Education*, vol. 12, no. 1, pp. 1-26.

Sims, R. R. 2002, 'Debriefing experiential learning exercises in ethics education', *Teaching Business Ethics*, vol. 6, no. 2, pp. 179-97.

Snoeyenbos, M., Almeder, R. & Humber, J. 1983, *Business Ethics, Corporate Values and Society*, Prometheus Books, Buffalo.

Thorne, L. 1999, 'An analysis of the association of demographic variables with the cognitive moral development of Canadian accounting students: An examination of the applicability of American based findings to the Canadian context', *Journal of Accounting Education*, vol. 17, nos. 2 & 3, pp. 157-74.

Thorne, L. 2001, 'Refocusing ethics education in accounting: an examination of accounting students' tendency to use their cognitive moral capacity', *Journal of Accounting Education*, vol. 19, no. 2, pp. 103-17.

Watson, C. E. 2003, 'Using Stories to Teach Business Ethics – Developing Character through Examples of Admirable Actions', *Teaching Business Ethics*, vol. 7, no. 2, pp. 93-105.

Welton, R. E., Lagrone, R. M. & Davis, J. R. 1994, 'Promoting the moral development of accounting graduate students: an instructional design and assessment', *Accounting Education*, vol. 3, no. 1, pp. 35-50.

Wilson, J. 1996, 'First steps in moral education', *Journal of Moral Education*, vol. 25, no. 1, pp. 85-91.

Winston, J. 1999, 'Theorising Drama as Moral Education', *Journal of Moral Education*, vol. 28, no. 4, pp. 459-71.

Chapter 13. Can we teach auditors and accountants to be more ethically competent and publicly accountable?[1]

Bryan Howieson

Abstract

Education and training in ethics has been given increased importance and urgency by recent corporate collapses of high-profile companies. These events have encouraged the media and public to question the ethical standards and behaviours of auditors and accountants. There is a high level of cynicism and scepticism in the profession that ethics can be 'taught' to auditing and accounting students and practitioners. This chapter seeks to counter these perceptions by arguing that the ethical awareness of auditors can be raised by attacking certain widely-held 'myths' about the nature and teaching of ethics. These myths include cynicism that the teaching of ethics can make any difference, or that ethics is simply a matter of personal opinion, or that the study of ethics must start with the study of ethical theory rather than practical experience. This chapter emphasises that ethics is about power relationships and responsibility, and that developing the practical skills of students and practitioners in values clarification, ethical decision-making and ethical policy-setting can not only raise ethical awareness in the professions of auditing and accounting, but also improve standards of practice. It is argued that improving ethical competence in the profession and striving for excellence in practice are not just starry-eyed ideals, but achievable with relevant curriculum planning and the use of effective teaching methods.

[1]This chapter draws heavily on experiences gained in collaboration with Ian Thompson (University of Edinburgh) in our experiments in teaching ethics to students of accounting and business, and in joint ethics consultancy to a variety of public- and private-sector organizations. I wish to acknowledge Ian's influence and inspiration behind some of the ideas I have developed in this chapter. I also thank Ian for his comments on an earlier draft of this chapter.

Introduction

Can ethics be taught? This is an ancient question that continues to exercise the minds of those in many different professions.[2] There are also many papers that have sought to explore the relationship between ethics and accounting and auditing practice. As a generalisation, many of these have tended to emphasise lamentations about the 'poor' ethical behaviours of accountants and auditors as exhibited in high-profile corporate crises.[3] Alternatively, they adopt an overwhelmingly empirical perspective and test whether various types of ethical courses or interventions can change the ethical character and behaviour of accounting and auditing students and practitioners.[4] There is very little written in the accounting and auditing literature that explores the underlying conceptual issues associated with whether ethics can be taught to accountants and auditors. This chapter seeks to explore some of these conceptual issues.

Whether ethics can be taught to accountants and auditors is viewed by many as something of an oxymoron. There is widespread cynicism about the ability to 'teach' ethics in business generally and in accounting in particular.[5] Some of this cynicism comes about, for instance, from a belief that people's ethical character is determined early in life and cannot later be changed.[6] The role of some accountants and auditors in corporate fraud and failure also tends to confirm stereotypical perceptions by the press and public that members of these professions are driven by greed rather than public interest and high moral standards. For example, Hill (1995, p. 585) has observed that 'the fruits of a profound cynicism are now with us, as prominent figures find themselves in court to defend their actions, and seem amazed that they are accused of doing anything wrong at all'. This chapter seeks to counter this cynicism by reflecting upon what ethics training might realistically and productively achieve, and by attacking misperceptions about the nature of ethics.[7]

A resolution of the question as to whether ethics can be taught depends very much on the underlying and interrelated questions of 'what' and 'how' ethics is to be taught and, as previously mentioned, what objectives can realistically

---

[2]Some examples of papers that have sought to explore the issue of teaching ethics within different professions and fields of employment include Gutmann (1993) on lawyers, Smith (1998) on members of the insurance industry, Thompson (1998) on politicians, and Toner (1998) on members of the US military.
[3]See, for example, Smith (2003). In a similar vein, there are a number of empirical papers that purport to demonstrate the poor moral character of accounting and auditing students; for instance, Haswell and Jubb (1995).
[4]See, as just one example, Ponemon (1993). Despite the enticing title 'Can Ethics Be Taught in Accounting?', the paper is really a report on a study of whether certain teaching interventions impacted upon the moral development and ethical behaviour of accounting students. The accounting and business ethics literature is replete with such studies. A review of the mixed results of some of this research can be found in Wright (1995).
[5]See, for instance, Henderson (1988), Luoma (1989), Piper (1993) and Hill (1995), who describe the general perceptions of cynicism about the extent to which ethics can be effectively 'taught'.
[6]Luoma (1989, p. 14), and Harris and Brown (1990, p. 855), for instance, acknowledge this as a common perception.
[7]Cynicism is not a coherent moral position. Rather, it is the adoption of an attitude of intellectual superiority that makes one invulnerable to criticism, and exempt from the responsibility to do anything about the corruption of the world. Like the ancient cynics (who earned their nick-name 'dogs' from their habit of urinating on objects of public veneration), modern cynics undermine confidence in public institutions.

be met by the teaching of ethics. Much of the emphasis of this chapter is devoted to the issues of what is to be taught and what can be achieved by the study of ethics in the context of the *applied* practice of accounting and auditing. Space does not permit an extended discussion of how ethics can be taught, although this issue will be touched upon as appropriate.

What can ethics teaching achieve?

There can be little argument with the general observation that ethics is an important component of accounting and auditing practice. Like any professional group, accountants and auditors are expected to put the public interest before their own private interests. This is reflected in the profession's Code of Professional Conduct by the principles of 'the public interest' and 'ethical behaviour' (CPA Australia & ICAA 2004). However, at regular intervals the ethical character of accountants and auditors is called into question by high-profile cases of corporate fraud and failure. In the United States, the spectacular frauds committed by executives at Enron and other companies have resulted in the Sarbanes-Oxley Act, that has sped up the process by which accounting firms split their auditing and managerial consulting activities into separate non-related entities. The Act has also seen the creation of the Public Company Accounting Oversight Board to impose a new level of regulation on auditors. In Australia, these events, along with our own corporate scandals such as the HIH collapse, have resulted in the Commonwealth Government proposing a series of major reforms to, *inter alia*, auditing practice aimed at increasing perceived and actual audit independence (see CLERP 2003). As part of these reforms, it is proposed that the Financial Reporting Council (FRC) will play a greater supervisory role of the auditing profession, including having the function of 'promoting the teaching of professional and business ethics by the professional accounting bodies, universities and other tertiary institutions' (CLERP 2003, p. 13).

To date the FRC has been silent on how it proposes to undertake this function, but should this responsibility ultimately find its way into legislation, then the teaching of ethics may be viewed as an even more important activity than at present. This of course raises important questions about what should be taught and how it should be taught.

A key point in any discussion on the teaching of ethics is an understanding about what the study of ethics can realistically achieve. Henderson (1988, p. 52) observes that:

> Those who claim ethics can't be taught are really saying it can't be taught in such a way that everyone who has had a course in business ethics will from that day forth cease and desist from all unethical activity. ... That's a tougher assignment than that given to other required courses in business schools. For example, is there any certainty that students will

practice random-walk market theory when they become stockbrokers? Will all students be supply-side economists if they graduate from the University of Chicago? Of course not. Why, then, does business ethics evoke different expectations?

When people call for greater teaching of ethics to accountants and auditors in the hope that misbehaviour can be swept away, or, at the other extreme, express disbelief or contempt for the efficacy of ethics courses, too much or too little is claimed about the power of education. In the real world, human behaviour is complex and subject to a diverse mix of powerful risks, rewards and constraints.[8] It is naïve to expect that the usual style of training via a short-term course in ethics will reap quick changes in people's individual and corporate values and behaviours, or isolate them from the common limitations of the human condition such as fatigue or errors of judgment. With this in mind it is important to rethink both the content and methods for teaching ethics to accountants and auditors. In particular, there needs to be an acknowledgment that:

- because moral behaviour is complex and the causes of corruption in practice are multi-factorial, multi-modal strategies are needed to change individuals and the culture of business corporations and audit firms. Simple educational interventions will never be enough on their own. However, if part of a coherent package of other measures (including professional standards, corporate governance and both individual training and team-building), education and training can become very effective
- the development of relevant ethics education and training requires a lot more careful thought and planning, as well as rigorous evaluation of courses, both with respect to their content and the efficacy of pedagogical methods employed.

If the teaching of ethics will not remove all 'bad' behaviour, what then can it achieve? The answer, perhaps, lies in the exhortation of Socrates that 'the life which is unexamined is not worth living' (Plato 1999 (1871), p. 541). Although there are clearly examples of unethical behaviour that are conscious and premeditated, the majority of unethical behaviour arises because the person or people concerned do not make the effort to reflect upon their behaviour or possess the skills necessary to do so. Kidder (1995, p. 43) has referred to this as 'drowsy morality', particularly in the context of people who lack clarity about their own values, or those of their organisation or profession. He notes that the problem of drowsy morality is particularly important today because technology 'leverages'

---

[8]For example, see Wyatt (2004), who describes how a change in the mind-set of large accounting firms occurred, subtly over time, in which the value of 'independence' was replaced with a management consulting paradigm that emphasized the maximisation of the accounting firms' profits. The end result of this change in mind-set was the Enron, WorldCom, etc. corporate collapses and the tarnishing of the audit profession's reputation.

the consequences of moral errors (Kidder 1995, p. 34).[9] For example, one person, Nick Leeson, was able to bring down a major bank on the basis of his access to, and use of, sophisticated trading technology. Kidder (1995, p. 38) notes that three factors are important in such cases; intelligence, size and moral awareness. If Leeson lacked intelligence, then he may not have even reached the position he held in Barings Bank. If the foreign currency trading had been small, then its collapse may not have irreparably damaged the bank. If Leeson had had the necessary moral awareness to reflect on the propriety of what he was doing, then he might never have undertaken the actions he did.[10] Kidder's point is summarised when he states (1995, p. 35):

> But these days the danger lies not only in the hands of madmen, tyrants, or obvious exponents of evil. Nowadays, it also lies in the hands of more-or-less well-meaning experts – whose only failings, perhaps, are a fuzziness at the moral core and a consequent limiting of the vision. The danger increasingly lies in the hands of otherwise ordinary people – people you and I know and like. They are not willfully [sic] setting out to create the next [Barings or Enron]. Yet they may be operating in a systemic and personal ethical vacuum that, in the end, leaves them unable to tell right from wrong. The great danger, it seems, is that at the critical moment of decision they may simply not understand the one most crucial fact – that they are walking straight into a world-class moral temptation.

Ethics training can help combat this 'drowsy morality' by assisting accountants and auditors to become more aware of the personal, organisational and professional values they bring to their work, and which serve as the basis for their public accountability. It can also attempt to sensitise them to the need to employ these values in the work environment and to reflect upon the consequences of the potential courses of action they face in any particular circumstances. In the 'real world', time or other pressures can create incentives for professionals to approach their work with a drowsy morality, but the colourful words of Henderson (1988, p. 53) should warn them otherwise: 'There is tremendous pressure upon corporate executives to manage only to the quarterly bottom line. That's like jumping off a tall building and boasting half way down that "everything's all right so far".'

Kidder (1995, Chapter 1) points to a second and related benefit of the teaching of ethics which is providing people with the skills and tools needed to deal with the more difficult ethical decision problems. He distinguishes between 'right-versus-right' choices and 'right-versus-wrong' choices. He argues that the latter category is the less problematic type of ethical problem for most people because

---

[9]Kidder (1995) uses the example of the Chernobyl nuclear disaster to illustrate the leveraging effects of technology.
[10]Of course, Leeson's behaviour was not discouraged by an organisational culture that emphasized and rewarded 'profit' above other objectives and values.

a moment of simple reflection is usually enough to recognise that the 'wrong' option is indeed 'wrong'. Kimm (2003, p. 65) has sought to demonstrate this by noting:

> ... typical ethics subjects like whistleblowers or lying in negotiations are challenging but not at the heart of business ethics. Enron, while deliciously salacious, is mundane from a business-ethics point of view. It's pretty straightforward – they did wrong. A more interesting ethical dilemma may be: Is sub-prime lending ethical? Many low-income borrowers could not get access to capital without these loans, but at what point do the loans become emblematic of predatory lending?

Right-versus-right choices, on the other hand, are far more difficult because they involve the decision-maker being forced to make trade-offs between core values.[11] When faced with such difficult choices, many people may lapse into a sort of moral paralysis, unable to make the choice one way or the other. Although training in ethics may not necessarily reduce the emotional pain of such choices, it can offer systematic problem-solving-based models that offer some hope and direction for decision-making. This issue will be pursued further later in this chapter when the issue of ethical 'dilemmas' is addressed.

The teaching of ethics can also encourage the development of moral courage. Moral courage is, of course, important to auditors when they are expected to 'take a stand' against unscrupulous or domineering CEOs who are proposing to 'cook the books' or indulge in other clearly unethical behaviour. However, moral courage is also important in less dramatic and mundane circumstances where conflict between parties is less apparent or not readily observable. Consider, for example, the so-called 'Abilene Paradox' that is described by Harvey (1974, p. 66) as follows: 'Organizations frequently take actions in contradiction to what they really want to do and therefore defeat the very purposes they are trying to achieve'. The Abilene Paradox argues that there are circumstances in which individual organisational members privately believe that an action or activity is inappropriate (and even, perhaps, unethical) but they collectively (e.g., during meetings) support the action in public. In the words of Harvey (1974, p. 73, emphasis in original), 'each person in a self-defeating, Abilene-bound organization *colludes* with others, including peers, superiors, and subordinates, sometimes consciously and sometimes subconsciously, to create the dilemma in which the organization finds itself'.

---

[11]Kidder (1995, p. 18) suggests that such trade-offs are typically between truth versus loyalty, or individual versus community, or short-term versus long-term, or justice versus mercy. In addition, one might also consider the difficulties of 'wrong-versus-wrong' decisions in which one might be forced to choose between the 'lesser of two evils'.

The Abilene Paradox is thus self-destructive and has the potential to lead people who are otherwise ethical into unethical actions.[12] Harvey (1974, pp. 70-2) suggests that the Abilene Paradox arises because of four factors:

1. *action anxiety*: the individuals become anxious about taking the 'right' action in contradiction to what is presently happening in the organisation
2. *negative fantasies*: the individuals anticipate and emphasise only negative outcomes if they act the 'right' way
3. *real risk*: taking the 'right' action might risk the individual being in a worse position (e.g., sacked) than if the current set of circumstances were left to run their course
4. *fear of separation*: individuals don't wish to risk being ostracised by their work colleagues and others (a very real problem faced by whistleblowers, for instance).

Managing the Abilene Paradox clearly requires someone in an organisation to have the moral courage and sound ethical arguments to confront the collective 'wisdom', as well as the skills to manage this process. Ethics teaching that emphasises the development of 'virtues' or characteristics that promote agreed standards of excellence offers the possibility that auditors, who must promote and maintain independence, can be equipped to handle situations exhibiting the Abilene Paradox. Again, this issue is addressed later in the chapter.

Given that the teaching of ethics offers value to students and practitioners of accounting and auditing, what needs to be taught to convey these benefits?

The next section of the chapter reviews a variety of common attitudes to ethics and approaches to teaching ethics to accountants and auditors and highlights the more significant limitations of these approaches. This is followed by an alternative view about what aspects of ethics might be taught to maximise the benefits to students and practitioners alike in the applied disciplines of accounting and auditing.

Some typical ways in which ethics is taught to accountants and auditors

In practice, a variety of educational styles and methods are used in the teaching of ethics in accounting and auditing to university students and practitioners. However, there are some common themes found in the great majority of accounting ethics courses around Australia that are identified below. These are teaching ethics as synonymous with *ethical theory*, *rules*, *individual judgment* (inter-personal relativism), or as *dealing with 'dilemmas'*.

---

[12]Harvey (1974), for example, uses testimony from the Watergate hearings to demonstrate that although the majority of conspirators claimed that they each privately objected to their collective actions, they were not prepared to voice these objections because of their fears concerning the expected reactions of the other conspirators and President Nixon.

It will be argued that none of these approaches is either effective or efficient in the education or training of people for a practical profession like accounting. A focus on any of these approaches will do little to enhance either the competence of practitioners in ethical decision-making or give them confidence that they have a better understanding of applied ethics. Instead, they each tend to create a disjunction between ethics and the practice of accounting and auditing, as shall be seen.

Ethics as ethical theory

Almost invariably, undergraduate courses in accounting or business ethics begin with an analysis of ethical theories such as utilitarianism and deontology, among others. As a teacher, one of the things one discovers early is the need to match one's material to the appropriate level of the audience. If we are honest, the great majority of accounting and auditing students have not undertaken studies in these disciplines to become philosophers and may have little, if any, background in ethics traditions (Sommers 1993, p. 7). As such, unfortunately they quickly lose interest in any 'theoretical' material that does not seem to be immediately related to the practice of accounting and auditing. By starting with ethical theories that many students find less than accessible, teachers lose the attention and interest of their students, and this makes it more difficult to reach out to them later when they are asked to apply these theories to case studies and other activities. The problem is exacerbated because the specialised language of philosophy is seen as irrelevant and alien to accounting students and this prevents them from taking applied ethics seriously. In the words of Hill (1995, p. 585): 'As Socrates pointed out long ago, ethics is not a theoretical science, which can be taught and learnt as dispassionately as mathematics. It is practical, and so engages teacher and pupil in an entirely different way'. By beginning with the theoretical we immediately disengage students from what is practical in ethics, and strengthen the illusion that knowledge of ethical theory is a key to competence in ethical decision-making.

In addition, a more powerful reason why teaching ethical theory is inappropriate, and 'puts the cart before the horse', is that many people learn, without being exposed to moral theory, to exercise what Aristotle calls 'prudence' or practical wisdom. This he defines as the ability to integrate both theoretical knowledge and skilled practice, and to combine the intellectual and moral virtues in such a way that we are able to make sensible decisions. This means being able to apply universal principles to particular situations in such a way that we choose the best available means to achieve a good outcome (if that is at all possible). To be able to exercise the virtue of prudence certainly does not require a prior knowledge of Kant, Mill or even Aristotle. Ethical theory only becomes relevant when we seek meta-ethical means to justify the ethical policies we adopt either as individuals, or as societies.

The above remarks should not in any way be viewed as an attack on the role of ethical theory, but rather as a plea to remember that the audience of accounting and auditing students or practitioners are focussed upon more immediate concerns in their proposed or current workplaces, and good teaching would dictate that the relevance of one's material should be readily recognisable and accessible. For instance, it is not necessary to use the formal language of ethical theory to communicate the essential elements of different theoretical models. Utilitarianism can be dressed in the language of 'consequences' and 'costs and benefits', or 'inputs', 'outputs' and 'outcomes'. Similarly, deontology can be expressed in terms of 'duties' or 'responsibility' and 'accountability'. In this way these terms can be made more accessible and relevant to students and practitioners, and they would be more readily able to identify with them in discussions of organisational policy. If it is felt to be necessary or helpful to introduce students to the philosophical underpinnings of applied ethics, and to introduce them to moral philosophy, then ethical theory can be taught in a course on accounting and auditing ethics. However, experience suggests that this is best done towards the *end* of the course, when students have become familiar with the language of 'consequences' and 'duties' in using practical decision models. The relevance of meta-ethical debate about moral theory can then be more apparent and helpful to students.

As discussed later in this chapter, rather than begin a course with ethical theories, it is better to begin with a discussion of the nature of ethics, highlighting the role of ethics in personal and business 'communities' as well as the importance of developing practical skills in the application of ethics.

Ethics as rules

The importance of rules in ethics is another theme that is typically overemphasised in the teaching of ethics to accountants and auditors. Usually this means focusing upon the rules contained in the accounting profession's Code of Professional Conduct and sometimes includes references to legislation and corporate codes of conduct. Indeed, some textbooks on ethics and accounting/auditing discuss virtually nothing but the application of professional rules and codes of conduct.[13] Rules are, of course, a very important element of ethics. They are an efficient means by which any community (such as the accounting profession) can communicate its expectations as to what behaviour promotes the community's interests and what to avoid. However, a course in ethics that explicitly or impli-

---

[13]See, for example, Windal (1991), Mintz (1992) and Maurice (1996). Of course, not all accounting ethics books discuss only compliance with professional rules, but even ethics training for entrance to the professional accounting associations is dominated by a focus on candidates' compliance with codes of professional conduct and other professional pronouncements.

citly equates ethical behaviour with compliance with professional rules could leave students with the following narrow perceptions:

- that compliance with rules is the same as ethical behaviour. Ethics and rules, however, are different. We use our ethical principles and values to judge the appropriateness of any rule. If, in our minds, we conflate rules with ethics, then we lose our ability to object to any particular rule as inappropriate, unfair, or unethical

- that rules are the starting (and ending) point for any ethical question and that rules are objective measures of ethical standards. In fact, rules are the result of prior value judgments (either by ourselves or those that came before us) as to what is good and right for our community. In this sense, rules are no more objective than any other value judgment, although they do reflect the community's consensus view about good behaviour

- rules-based decision-making creates a black and white ('right' or 'wrong') mentality that does not admit that solutions to ethical problems might lie somewhere along a good/bad continuum. Accountants and auditors who are trained to view ethical issues within this concrete framework are likely to suffer a moral paralysis when encountering problems for which there is no readily apparent rule. In such cases they may be unable to reach a decision, or may focus on an ill-considered 'quick fix'

- an overemphasis on 'codes' of behaviour tends to reinforce a perception of ethics as being punitive and does not promote the positive aspects of ethics that are designed to promote the well-being of an accounting firm and its clients, as well as standards of excellence in the profession. As Thompson (1998, p. 50) notes, 'The negative connotations of codes, associated with the codes of civil and criminal law, tend to focus attention on crime and conflict, rather than on the skills that are necessary to build and change the culture of moral communities'

- the possibility that professional ethics is confused with professional etiquette. Professional etiquette is an accepted set of behaviours about polite conduct between members of the profession. Etiquette is one important manifestation of ethics because important ethical principles such as respect for persons underlie polite (and thus respectful) behaviour (Chismar 2001). However, the great majority of the contents of the accounting profession's Code of Professional Conduct reflects etiquette between members of the profession (or other professions such as lawyers) rather than more explicit guidance on the relationship between professionals and their clients. For example, the Australian profession's Code of Professional Conduct consists of six major sections of which only Section B, *Fundamental Principles of Professional Conduct applicable to all members*, and Statement F1, *Professional Independence*, can be said to explicitly concern themselves with the professional account-ant's duties to his/her clients.

Teaching ethics by the rulebook only raises awareness of one aspect of profes-sional ethics. Compliance with the rules does not guarantee that accountants and auditors will behave ethically. In the words of Russell (1992 (1954), p. 40):

> Nine of the Ten Commandments are negative. If throughout your life you abstain from murder, theft, fornication, perjury, blasphemy, and disrespect towards your parents, your Church, and your King, you are conventionally held to deserve moral admiration even if you have never done a single kind or generous or useful action. This very inadequate notion of virtue is an outcome of taboo mentality and has done untold harm.

Ethics and individualism/relativism

One of the more serious objections to the current approaches to teaching account-ing and auditing ethics relates to the very common remark in ethics classes that 'there is no "right" answer' to an ethical problem. The general basis for such a statement lies in the belief that everyone is entitled to his or her opinion about what is right and wrong. Although respect for others' opinions is a laudable principle, it does leave students of ethics with the very unproductive and incor-rect impression that 'anything goes' in ethics.[14] Such a perspective on ethics is based on two presumptions. First, that ethics is a matter personal to the individual and is akin to issues of personal taste and preference, a perspective that Thompson, Melia and Boyd (2000, pp. 63-4) describe as the 'privatisation of ethics'. They note that such a conception of ethics runs counter to the majority of our Western tradition, where ethics has in fact been seen as a community issue. Henderson (1988, p. 53) also rejects the individualistic notion of ethics and states 'ethics, like politics, is a public matter for open discussion by all'. Allowing students to view ethics only within the private rather than public domain risks the chance that they are unable to properly appreciate the full extent of the role of the accountant and auditor in business. Further, saying any opinion is okay and that there is no one right answer rapidly generates frustration among students of ethics because the question of what is appropriate behaviour in any particular case remains unresolved – and unresolvable! Such frustration only assists in perpetuating the perception that ethics cannot be taught.

---

[14]Sommers (1993, pp. 7-8) takes issue with the 'everyone's view is valid' approach. She states:

> ... it seems to me that the hands-off posture is not really as neutral as it professes to be. ... One could also make a case that the new attitude of disowning responsibility probably contributes to the student's belief in the false and debilitating doctrine that there are no "plain moral facts" after all. In tacitly or explicitly promoting that doctrine, the teacher contributes to the student's lack of confidence in a moral life that could be grounded in something more than personal disposition or political fashion.

The second, and related, presumption underlying the 'anything goes' approach to ethics is an appeal to ethical relativism. Relativism, the view that all moral points of view are equally valid, extends beyond the individual/interpersonal perspective just noted to include cultural and philosophical relativism (Thompson, Melia & Boyd 2000, pp. 20-1). Relativism allows, for instance, the position that a specific behaviour (e.g., bribery) is 'unethical' in one culture but 'ethical' in another where it is the accepted norm. Consequently, the acceptance of a relativistic perspective tends to mean that students' thinking is dominated by concentrating on what makes people different and fails to recognise that there may also be common ethical ground. Harris and Brown (1990, p. 857) note that relativism can be an attractive 'cop-out' to those people who find reflection on ethical issues just too hard. Luoma (1989, p. 14, emphasis in original) rejects relativism: '... an ethicist responds that it *is* possible to make judgments about cultural norms and to establish moral standards that are universal. An ethicist believes that ethics "is not culturally relative," and most ethicists reject any assertion that morality is relative to individual standards of conduct'.

This chapter endorses that sentiment on the grounds that relativism is an unproductive basis on which to create incentives for accountants and auditors to reflect upon the ethical dimensions of their behaviour and decisions. The benefits of highlighting the role of universal ethical principles are explored later in this chapter.

Ethics as 'dilemmas'

One final methodological problem in the contemporary teaching of accounting and auditing ethics is the overwhelming tendency to portray all ethical issues as 'dilemmas', whether they are true dilemmas or not. Academic literature, the media and teaching materials nearly always use this term to describe an ethical issue. The problem for teaching ethics is that the term 'dilemma' immediately conveys connotations that *all* ethical issues are difficult and, strictly speaking, irresolvable.[15] This perception is exacerbated in a teaching environment that explicitly or implicitly promotes individual and relativist views of ethics. One teacher of ethics has concluded (Sommers 1993, p. 7): 'I have come to see that dilemma ethics is especially lacking in edificatory force, and indeed that it may even be a significant factor in encouraging a superficial moral relativism or agnosticism'.

She goes on to note that case studies which portray ethics as dilemmas do not provide incentives for students to fully explore the ethical implications of decision-making (Sommers 1993, p. 12): 'In a dilemma there is no obvious right

---

[15] 'In a course specifically devoted to dilemmas and hard cases, it is almost impossible *not* to give the student the impression that ethics itself has no solid foundation' (Sommers 1993, p. 6, emphasis in original).

and wrong, no clear vice and virtue. The dilemma may engage the students' minds; it only marginally engages their emotions, their moral sensibilities'.

To combat the negative and perhaps even defeatist mind-set created by calling all ethical issues 'dilemmas', it would be more helpful for the ethical development of members of the profession to assist them to see that most ethical quandaries can be recast as 'problems' to which we can apply appropriate problem-solving methods. Kidder (1995, p. 23) recognises that even the majority of the more difficult 'right-versus-right' ethical issues can be transformed into 'an ultimately manageable problem, bearing strong resemblance to lots of other problems and quite amendable to analysis' using well-established problem-solving methods.[16] Adopting problem-solving methods encourages the positive view of ethical decision-making that it is a practical and everyday type of activity and largely avoids the possibility of moral paralysis. Problem-solving methods are also very familiar to accountants and auditors from their technical training and can be easily modified to incorporate ethical considerations, thus combating the laziness associated with drowsy morality. Practical skills in ethics are explored further in a later section of this chapter.

Revising our approach to teaching ethics to accountants and auditors

The discussion so far has sought to demonstrate that many of the common approaches and methodologies for teaching ethics to prospective and practicing accountants and auditors are not productive of the desired behaviour change or skills acquisition because they:

- 'mystify' ethics by abstracting the theoretical aspects of ethics from people's real world experiences
- equate ethics with compliance with professional rules, so encouraging rigid and mechanistic thinking about ethics
- encourage cynicism, confusion and frustration about ethical decision-making by promoting ethical relativism and representation of every case as a 'dilemma' rather than as a problem which requires a practical solution.

The remainder of this chapter sets out to counter these limitations by presenting an alternative methodology for teaching ethics within the applied context of accounting and auditing that draws upon Aristotelian traditions and virtue ethics.

The nature of ethics

It has previously been argued that far too much emphasis is placed upon the privatised view of ethics where the centre of attention is the individual and an

---

[16]Also see Thompson, Melia and Boyd (2000, pp. 10 & 63).

introspective consideration of ethical issues. This in turn promotes an unproductive relativism in the discussion of ethics. Aristotle's approach to ethics is a powerful methodology for awakening accountants and auditors to their responsibilities in the business and wider community.

Ethics is fundamentally about what is good and right for human beings. As such, it demands a consideration of what factors will encourage the flourishing of society and what factors inhibit society's development and well-being. Reminding accountants and auditors that ethics is a community enterprise, not a matter of individual opinion, highlights the service role of these professionals in the efficient and effective operation of our market-based system.

Accountants and auditors operate in teams. Of necessity, ethics cannot be treated as a matter only for the individual – as the Abilene Paradox demonstrated, a failure to take the 'right' action/decision is often a collective responsibility. Adopting an approach that emphasises the communal context of ethics (whether that be work teams, departments, accounting firms or business corporations) means that accountants and auditors must take responsibility for building a culture within that community that fosters and develops personal and community integrity, competence and excellence.

Aristotle saw ethics as a question related to how power was shared among the members of society and how power was employed to benefit or harm society's well-being.[17] The notion of how power is exercised dovetails very well with the everyday activities and responsibilities of accountants and auditors, who are frequently in positions of power relative to clients, investors and others because of their technical expertise, legal duties and access to privileged information. Without the ability to consciously reflect on how their actions or inactions might harm others, accountants and auditors can (and have) misused their power to harm investors and other parties.

Finding common ground

If ethics is concerned with the flourishing of communities and the exercise of power within and across communities, this is also true for the business community and its customers. It is important for students to identify what common ground exists for rational deliberation about ethical issues within the community in question. This is particularly important as an antidote to the prevalence of the entrenched ethical relativism within the profession and among students and the general public.

For good practical reasons, we are taught to be 'tolerant' or 'accepting' of the opinions and practices of people of other countries (e.g., to minimise conflict and promote understanding). However, in liberal societies we advocate tolerance

[17]See Aristotle (2003 (1976)).

as a moral principle that should be applied universally. This viewpoint shows respect for others – which is commonly viewed as an important ethical behaviour, and relates to a universally recognised moral principle; that is, respect for persons and their rights.[18] The downside, however, of tolerant acceptance of diversity is that it tends to treat moral and cultural differences between communities as fundamental rather than focussing attention on the basic commonalities between peoples that make it possible for people around the world to, for example, sign up to the UN Universal Declaration of Human Rights. Uncritical relativism encourages the misconception that anything goes in ethics and any viewpoint is acceptable (or at least must be 'tolerated'). As mentioned before, taken to its extreme, this relativism paralyses moral discourse and in fact is ultimately a nonsense. If it were true that *everyone's* ethics were different, then it would be impossible to reach agreement on any matter (except, perhaps, by chance) – we would not be able to make international treaties, conduct business overseas, have institutions like the United Nations, and so on. Fortunately, many philosophers and commentators have been able to demonstrate that there are a number of principles and values that are shared across all societies[19] around the world as a result of the fundamental commonalities of human life.[20]

In our teaching and consultancy, Ian Thompson and I have found it beneficial to distinguish between 'fundamental ethical principles' and 'cultural values'. Fundamental ethical principles are the underlying universally shared common ground of ethics across all cultures. Values are a community's expression as to the specific qualities and conditions they perceive to be necessary for that community to flourish. Principles are the starting point from which social duties and responsibilities are derived on the basis of each community's experience as to what values will promote its particular well-being. When we observe differences in values across communities, it is not because each community has fundamentally different ethics, but rather the differences are the result of each community giving different priority to different fundamental ethical principles, and/or finding different ways to translate these principles into the idiom of their own language and culture. In the light of the universal demands of *beneficence*, *justice*, and *respect for persons*, the communities make their own choices about how their well-being is best promoted, given each community's history, environment, resources and values.[21]

---

[18] See, for example, Chismar (2001).
[19] For a more detailed discussion see, for example, Luoma (1989, p. 14), Sommers (1993, pp. 6-7), Kidder (1995, pp. 88-92), ICAA (1997, pp. 15-16), and Thompson, Melia and Boyd (2000, pp. 17-18).
[20] We share many common life experiences, trials and tribulations from birth to death.
[21] For instance, the emphasis on individual rights in the United States reflects an emphasis on the principle of respect for persons, while the dominance of the State in Soviet Russia reflected that community's emphasis on a principle of beneficence (care).

These three fundamental ethical principles represent the moral common ground and are described in Table 13.1, 13.2 and 13.3 below:[22]

Table 13.1. The principle of beneficence

PRINCIPLE OF BENEFICENCE (or principle of responsible care)
Duty of the strong to do good to others (beneficence) and avoid doing them harm (non-maleficence), e.g. to dependants, clients and customers.
Duty of care, on the part of the strong to protect the weak and the vulnerable.
Duty of advocacy, defending the rights of those unable to defend their own rights.

Table 13.2. The principle of justice

PRINCIPLE OF JUSTICE (or principle of universal fairness)
Duty of universal fairness or equity, viz. both justice in terms of equality of opportunity for individuals and equitable outcomes for groups.
Duty to treat people with dignity, treating them as ends in themselves, never simply as means to some other end, i.e. the duty not to exploit other people.
Duty to avoid discrimination, abuse or prejudice against people on grounds of race, age, sex, class, gender, religion, etc.

Table 13.3. The principle of respect for persons

PRINCIPLE OF RESPECT FOR PERSONS (or principle of respect for the rights of others)
Duty to respect the dignity, freedom and rights of other people as persons, e.g. the right to know, the right to privacy, etc.
Duty to promote the happiness, well-being and autonomy of other people – to assist them to develop their potential.
Duty to be truthful, honest and sincere with other people – honesty is a demand of respect for other people, just as lying or deceit shows contempt toward other people.

One important attribute of these principles is that they are an effective means of demonstrating the relationship between ethics and power. The principle of beneficence reflects our reciprocal duty to use power responsibly for the good of one another, rather than to do harm, for we are all weak at times and must rely on the protective care of others when we are vulnerable and need help. The principle of justice requires power-sharing as expressed here by the test of universalisability. Justice demands that any rule we apply to our own actions should also be capable of being applied equally to everybody else. Finally, respect for persons is about empowerment of other persons to enable them to achieve their own fulfilment. When placed within the context of everyday working scenarios, these power-related principles can be a very effective means of encouraging accountants and auditors to reflect upon the ethics of their relationships with clients and others. For example, an accountant who is acting as liquidator for a company has a duty under the principle of beneficence to ensure that he or she uses their power as liquidator to maximise the value of the liquidation process (rather than realising assets at minimal prices for the benefit of him or herself

---

[22]These principles have been successfully employed in teaching and consultancy. For example, the three fundamental ethical principles were adopted by the WA Government as the major component of its Code of Ethics for the state's public sector and the principles have been used by Western Australia's public-sector agencies in the development of their agency-specific Codes of Conduct; see Public Sector Standards Commission (1995a, 1995b). In an accounting context, we have also used these principles in the development of training materials for the ICAA's Professional Year Ethics Module; see ICAA (1997).

or friends and acquaintances) so that employees and creditors (who have little or no power in such a situation) can receive their entitlements or have their debts repaid. Similarly, when an accountant is asked to prepare a tax return on behalf of a client, justice demands that that return is prepared with the same competence and quality as for any other client and in compliance with the taxation laws. In a situation where a client approaches an accountant for assistance in establishing a new business, the principle of respect for persons would demand that the accountant take all reasonable steps to transfer whatever skills and knowledge are appropriate on running the business to the client. This empowers the client to take charge of his or her own affairs, rather than being left dependent upon (and at the mercy of) the accountant. Gutmann (1993, p. 1769), for instance, writing in the context of the legal profession, has recognised the ethical importance of empowering one's clients by joining with them to understand their needs rather than the professional imposing his or her perceptions of what is in the client's best interests: 'If [professionals] do not deliberate with their clients, if they pursue their own independently-arrived-at conception of their clients' interests ... then they act paternalistically, treating their clients as children ... using them as mere means rather than ends in themselves'.

Although knowledge of the fundamental ethical principles is advantageous to accountants and auditors, these principles on their own are not sufficient for promoting ethical behaviour and quality accounting and auditing practice. At least two further components are needed. First is the development of an understanding as to how these principles are to manifest themselves in the practical context as one's personal, organisational and professional values. Second is the need to develop and practise the application of these values using systematic methods for decision- and rule-making within organisations and the profession so as to promote the well-being of these communities.

Ethics as excellence

One of the great advantages of teaching ethics from an Aristotelian perspective is the ability to highlight the role of ethics as a practical vehicle for promoting excellence of performance in one's profession for the good of the community. Aristotle's discussion of 'virtues' is of particular relevance in applied disciplines such as accounting and auditing because it requires us to give consideration to what 'virtues' or competencies, or knowledge and skills, promote excellence in accounting and auditing practice. Aristotle distinguished between intellectual and moral virtues – the former relate to competence in the application of technical knowledge (e.g., accounting and auditing standards) in a systematic way, while the latter include courage and temperance for self-discipline and justice. As mentioned previously, prudence or practical wisdom is the key virtue of being able to combine both the intellectual and moral virtues to achieve a good outcome in any specific case. Competency in the intellectual and moral virtues and skill in practical wisdom allow people to achieve self-fulfilment and the well-being of their firm and the wider community.

Virtue ethics relates well to the notion of 'professionalism' and 'professional behaviour' by combining technical competencies with moral competencies. As Gutmann (1993, p. 1760) observes in the context of the legal profession and as paraphrased below:

> Far worse than being a zealous [accountant] is being a lazy or incompetent one, unwilling or unable to take on someone else's [affairs] as your own. [Accountants] who [work for] their clients simply for the sake of making a living, and therefore do not [serve] them well as long as they can get away with it, use their clients merely as means to their own self-interested ends.

Ethics training based on what 'virtues' are necessary to become an 'excellent' accountant or auditor is also able to immediately engage students and practitioners alike because it emphasises the relevance of ethics to the workplace. Sommers (1993, p. 8) has noted that:

> Once the student becomes engaged with the problem of what kind of person to be, and how to *become* that kind of person, the problems of ethics become concrete and practical and, for many a student, moral development is thereafter looked on as a natural and even inescapable undertaking.

By focusing on both intellectual and moral virtues, virtue ethics is also an effective means of broadening accountants and auditors' understanding of ethics beyond mere compliance with standards and rules that predominately reflect the intellectual and technical expertise of accounting and auditing practice. Only a little reflection is needed to recognise that the combination of the intellectual and moral virtues is absolutely fundamental in the context of auditing – an audit only has value if the auditor is both technically competent (an intellectual virtue) *and* independent in attitude (a moral virtue).

Emphasis on practical and applied skills

The discussion of Aristotle's virtues indicated the importance of the virtue of prudence or practical wisdom in the development of excellence in accounting and auditing practice. An auditor who possesses outstanding technical skills but lacks moral virtues could cause untold damage, while an auditor who lacks technical competence but has strong moral virtues may be unable to implement his or her laudable objectives. Prudence can develop over time in the light of our experiences, but this can be a serendipitous and *ad hoc* process. One major benefit of ethics training can be the education of accountants and auditors in practical skills designed to develop these professional skills in practical wisdom. As the virtue of prudence is designed to assist in the marriage of both intellectual and moral virtues, these practical ethical skills can also reinforce the message that ethics is a part of all everyday activities, not a subject divorced from day-to-day life. Kimm (2003, p. 66) has reinforced this point when he states: 'A framework for evaluating ethical issues should be a part of our tool kit right next to Porter's Five Forces. By making ethics a consistent part of our analysis of any situation, we incorporate it into our operating principles'.

There are three important and interrelated skills:

1. skills in clarifying and applying personal, organisational and professional values in everyday practice
2. skills in making responsible and accountable decisions ethically
3. skills in developing sound, ethical organisational and professional rules.

Space considerations do not allow a detailed overview here of each of these skills but some general comments might be helpful. When the accounting profession, for instance, promotes in its Code of Professional Conduct the fundamental values of 'the public interest', 'integrity', 'objectivity', 'independence', 'confidentiality', 'technical and professional standards', 'competence and due care' and 'ethical behaviour' (CPA Australia & ICAA 2004), it does so because of the belief that these values represent key virtues that promote excellence in the practice of accounting and the well-being of the accounting profession. When a new member joins the profession it is important for him or her to understand what these values represent and how they manifest themselves in day-to-day accounting and auditing practice. It is important, therefore, that induction into the values of the profession should help build the consensus and commitment of all partners in the business to the same values, and to prevent these being dismissed as simply 'motherhood statements', serious work needs to be done by work teams to operationalise these values.

If an accountant or auditor does not truly adopt these values as his or her own, then that person may be unable to act in ways that promote the well-being of the community. Similarly, the accountant or auditor will have his or her own values and must also understand, and operate within, the values of his or her organisation. An inability to clearly understand and own these various sets of values can create confusion or result in conflict if the values are not congruent. Various techniques of values clarification can be used to assist accountants and auditors to understand these different sets of values and to reflect upon how they might be used to promote the well-being of their organisation and profession.

If values are well understood, they can be used to assist accountants and auditors in their day-to-day decision-making. The 'drowsy morality' mentioned previously in this chapter occurs, in part, when people and communities do not adopt systematic methods for approaching ethical issues. Lack of a clear decision model perpetuates the myth that ethical issues are unresolvable dilemmas and means that decision-makers are not always able to discern relevant and practical courses of action or identify competing duties. Once ethical issues are viewed as 'problems' rather than 'dilemmas', they can be analysed using standard decision-making methods and models. One well-known model for incorporating ethics into decision-making is the so-called 'AAA model' (May 1990, pp. 1-2), which suggests seven stages to the decision-making process:

1. determine the facts
2. define the ethical issue
3. identify major principles, rules, values
4. specify the alternatives
5. compare values and alternatives, see if a clear decision emerges
6. assess the consequences
7. make your decision.

One might argue about the relative merits of alternate decision models[23], but the key issue remains that training accountants and auditors to use systematic methods to make decisions ethically allows for more reflective, consistent and justifiable decisions that will tend to maximise well-being, or at least minimise harm.

Finally, a few comments should be made about rule- and policy-setting within organisations and communities. Much has been made here about ethics as the promotion of a community's well-being. To help achieve this, communities (whether accounting firms, the accounting profession or society in general) put in place rules. Just as decisions should be informed by the values to which the community aspires, rule-setting also needs to build upon accepted and well-understood values. This process, too, should be systematic and reflective to ensure that the rules are inclusive and do indeed promote the community's flourishing. As accountants and auditors work in a world of considerable regulation (such as legislation, accounting and auditing standards, and professional by-laws and regulations), ethics training should also develop skills in setting rules and policies on an ethical basis. This will assist accountants and auditors to develop policies that promote the well-being of their work teams, organisations and the profession, and also provide them with the tools to make informed judgments and to present justifiable evidence in advice to governments and to others on matters of public policy.[24]

---

[23]For example, the DECIDE model reported in Thompson, Melia and Boyd (2000, pp. 280-1) has the advantage that it includes a feedback loop with which decision-makers can learn from their prior decisions.
[24]A more detailed discussion on the ethical development of policy and rules can be found in Thompson (1998) and Thompson, Melia and Boyd (2000).

Conclusion

This chapter has argued that ethics can be taught to students and practitioners of accounting and auditing. However, to do so it has been argued that realistic expectations need to be placed upon what outcomes courses on ethics can practically achieve and the need for accountants and auditors to develop their own practical wisdom in the context of their work experiences. Contemporary approaches to teaching accounting and auditing ethics tend to be unproductive by abstracting ethics from its practical applications. They typically present all ethical decisions as 'dilemmas', the resolution of which depends more on an individual's tastes and preferences than as problems to be resolved by applying commonly shared ethical principles with appropriate skill and judgment. To counter this perspective, it has been suggested here that the teaching of ethics needs to be firmly grounded and integrated into the practical and applied experience of accounting and auditing students and practitioners. The emphasis must be upon the development and practice of the applied skills of values clarification, ethical decision-making and ethical policy-setting. This approach is founded upon traditional views that ethics is a community enterprise about how power is to be used responsibly and distributed among members of the community. Ethics as a community enterprise challenges ethical individualism and relativism and allows the opportunity for students to explore the common ground between people, rather than to simply concentrate on what makes them different. The approach promoted here also reflects the perspective that, as members of an applied discipline, accountants and auditors are rightly concerned about developing those practical virtues or characteristics that lead to excellence in their profession. These arguments are summarised in the following table that Ian Thompson and I have published elsewhere (ICAA 1997, pp. 13-14).

Table 13.4. Nature of ethics

WHAT ETHICS IS NOT	WHAT ETHICS IS
ETHICS IS NOT simply about matters of a private nature or about personal feelings, attitudes and values.	ETHICS IS a community enterprise, based on universal principles and reasoned public debate.
ETHICS IS NOT about mysterious occult processes, feelings in the gut, or privileged access to moral truth.	ETHICS IS about real power relations between people and the basis of power-sharing between them.
ETHICS IS NOT exclusively a business for experts, for religious authorities, lawyers, philosophers or gurus.	ETHICS IS about participation in a moral community and ownership of the policies it develops.
ETHICS IS NOT about endless disputes, disagreements and dilemmas, nor about grandstanding our opinions.	ETHICS IS a problem-solving activity based on knowledge of principles and skills in their application.
ETHICS IS NOT a matter of innate knowledge, special powers of intuition or supernatural revelation.	ETHICS IS an educational process in which we can discover what it means to be responsible moral agents.

The teaching of ethics is a challenging activity − it requires creativity on the part of the teacher as well as the sensitivity and composure needed to assist those students who would prefer not to be shifted from their 'comfort zone'. Although the teaching of ethics to accountants and auditors cannot eliminate all cases of professional misconduct, it can assist in minimising such occurrences by waking professionals out of their state of drowsy morality and inspiring them to develop their professional competence (or virtues) and promote excellence in accounting and auditing practice.

References

Aristotle 2003 (1976), *Ethics*, J. A. K. Thomson & H. Tredennick (trans.), J. Barnes & A. C. Grayling (eds), The Folio Society, London.

Chismar, D. 2001, 'Vice and Virtue in Everyday (Business) Life', *Journal of Business Ethics*, vol. 29, nos. 1 & 2, pp. 169-76.

CLERP (Audit Reform and Corporate Disclosure) Bill 2003, 'Commentary on the Draft Provisions', Commonwealth of Australia, Canberra.

CPA Australia & ICAA (Institute of Chartered Accountants in Australia) 2004, Joint Code of Professional Conduct, Section B, *Fundamental Principles of Professional Conduct Applicable to All Members*, Sydney.

Gutmann, A. 1993, 'Can Virtue Be Taught to Lawyers?', *Stanford Law Review*, vol. 45, no. 6, pp. 1759-71.

Harris, C. & Brown, W. 1990, 'Developmental Constraints on Ethical Behavior in Business', *Journal of Business Ethics*, vol. 9, no. 11, pp. 855-62.

Harvey, J. B. 1974, 'The Abilene Paradox: The Management of Agreement', *Organizational Dynamics*, vol. 3, no. 1, pp. 63-80.

Haswell, S. & Jubb, P. 1995, 'Unethical Tendencies', *Charter*, vol. 66, no. 3, pp. 102-3.

Henderson, V. E. 1988, 'Can Ethics Be Taught?', *Management Review*, vol. 77, no. 8, pp. 52-4.

Hill, J. 1995, 'Can We Talk About Ethics Anymore?', *Journal of Business Ethics*, vol. 14, no. 8, pp. 585-92.

ICAA (Institute of Chartered Accountants in Australia) 1997, *Ethics: Professional Year Programme 1997*, Sydney.

Kidder, R. M. 1995, *How Good People Make Tough Choices: Resolving the Dilemmas of Ethical Living*, William Morrow and Company, Inc., New York.

Kimm, S. J. 2003, 'How Ethics Should Be Taught', *Across the Board*, vol. 40, no. 1, pp. 65-6.

Luoma, G. A. 1989, 'Can 'Ethics' Be Taught?', *Management Accounting*, vol. 71, no. 5, pp. 14-16.

Maurice, J. 1996, *Accounting Ethics*, Pitman Publishing, London.

May, W. M. (ed.) 1990, *Ethics in the Accounting Curriculum: Cases and Readings*, American Accounting Association, Sarasota, FA.

Mintz, S. M. 1992, *Cases in Accounting Ethics and Professionalism*, 2nd edn, McGraw-Hill, Inc., New York.

Piper, T. R. 1993, 'Rediscovery of Purpose: The Genesis of the Leadership, Ethics, and Corporate Responsibility Initiative', in T. R. Piper, M. C. Gentile & S. D. Parks (eds), *Can Ethics Be Taught?*, Harvard Business School, Boston, pp. 1-12.

Plato 1999 (1871), 'The Apology', in B. Jowett (trans.), *The Essential Plato*, The Softback Preview, http://www.etsp.co.uk. Introduction by A. De Botton.

Ponemon, L. A. 1993, 'Can ethics be taught in accounting?', *Journal of Accounting Education*, vol. 11, no. 2, pp. 185-210.

Public Sector Standards Commission 1995a, *Guidelines for Developing Codes of Conduct*, Perth, WA.

Public Sector Standards Commission 1995b, *Western Australian Public Sector Code of Ethics*, Perth, WA.

Russell, B. 1992 (1954), *Human Society in Ethics and Politics*, Routledge, London.

Smith, G. M. 1998, 'Can Insurance People Be Taught Ethics?', *National Underwriter*, vol. 102, no. 43, pp. 7 & 24.

Smith, L. M. 2003, 'A Fresh Look at Accounting Ethics (or Dr. Smith goes to Washington)', *Accounting Horizons*, vol. 17, no. 1, pp. 47-50.

Sommers, C. H. 1993, 'Teaching the Virtues', *The Public Interest*, 111, pp. 3-13.

Thompson, I. E. 1998, 'Inducing Change. Can Ethics Be Taught?', *Legislative Studies*, vol. 13, no. 1, pp. 40-63.

Thompson, I. E., Melia, K. M. & Boyd, K. M. 2000, *Nursing Ethics*, 4th edn, Churchill Livingstone, Edinburgh.

Toner, J. H. 1998, 'Mistakes in Teaching Ethics', *Airpower Journal*, vol. 12, no. 2, pp. 45-51.

Windal, F. W. 1991, *Ethics and the Accountant: Text and Cases*, Prentice Hall, Englewood Cliffs, NJ.

Wright, M. 1995, 'Can Moral Judgement and Ethical Behaviour Be Learned?', *Management Decision*, vol. 33, no. 10, pp. 17-28.

Wyatt, A. R. 2004, 'Accounting Professionalism – They Just Don't Get It!', *Accounting Horizons*, vol. 18, no. 1, pp. 45-53.

Chapter 14. Do auditor provided non-audit services (APNAS) fees impair auditor independence?

Christopher Ikin

Abstract

For over 40 years there has been active debate about whether joint provision of audit and non-audit services by a company's incumbent auditor compromises auditor independence in fact and/or appearance. This chapter analyses the existing literature in the English speaking world and concludes that while there is some evidence supporting a *perceived* threat to auditor independence, no substantial evidence exists that there is any threat to independence *in fact* as a consequence of the auditor's fee dependence.

Introduction

For more than 40 years, regulators, the accounting profession and academics have been debating and researching whether the joint provision of audit services and non-audit services by a company's incumbent auditor compromises auditor independence in fact or in appearance. Regulators have reacted promptly to recent corporate scandals, despite the lack of convincing corroborative evidence from the auditing research literature. In this chapter I analyse that body of literature which investigates whether auditor independence is impaired as a consequence of the auditor's fee dependence on auditor provided non-audit services (APNAS). I conclude that while there is some evidence supporting a *perceived* threat to auditor independence, no substantial evidence exists that supports the notion that there is any threat to independence *in fact* as a consequence of the auditor's fee dependence on APNAS.

This review of the APNAS fee research literature is not exhaustive – it excludes, for example, the experimental markets literature and the analytical literature. My intention is to provide an overview and to draw insights from its major findings and propose avenues for future profitable research. The subject matter is both topical and important, as regulatory agencies and professional bodies rush to shore up public confidence in the auditing profession after some notable and highly visible company (and audit) failures. Such reactive responses need to be tempered with insights and evidence from academic auditing research. Research into auditor independence is currently blossoming and it is timely that results to date be brought together and evaluated. Two review articles have appeared recently (Simnett & Trotman 2002; Nelson 2004), but neither deals specifically with APNAS fee dependence nor covers the same breadth of research paradigms.

The rest of the chapter is set out as follows. I begin with a brief overview of the historical setting, and an indication of the current economic climate and theoretical underpinnings that have given rise to the present debate. The next sections describe the literature according to their different perspectives on the way the problem might best be investigated. Archival studies about financial statement users' perceptions of auditor independence in the presence of APNAS, archival studies into independence *in fact*, and a small body of literature that investigates the relation between APNAS and independence from a purely audit firm/audit partner point of view are all discussed in turn. Finally, I draw some conclusions and offer some suggestions for future research.

APNAS and conflicts of interest

Background

The first requirements for compulsory audits conducted by independent auditors arose as a result of the share speculation and corporate fraud in the 1920s. Requirements appeared in legislation to regulate the formation, conduct and dissolution of companies and to regulate the capital markets.[1] About this time, too, the professional bodies became active in setting standards of conduct for members in public practice.[2]

Fundamental to the notion of auditor independence is the recognition that the added credibility that an external audit brings to a company's financial statements, and the investing public's perceptions of that credibility, are beneficial to an efficient capital market. In a sense, the accounting profession has been trusted by the public to be a 'gatekeeper', protecting investors' confidence that company financial statements are true and fair. The accounting profession, and since 1984 the US courts[3], have upheld the dual elements of auditor independence – independence in fact and independence in appearance.

---

[1] In Australia, prior to the enactment of the *Uniform Companies Act 1961*, the various State Companies Acts, from as early as 1920, contained basic requirements for auditor independence. In the United States, the first independence rules were promulgated by the Federal Trade Commission (the forerunner of the Securities and Exchange Commission (SEC), which was established in 1934), soon after the enactment of the Securities Act (1933).
[2] The American Institute of Certified Public Accountants (AICPA) was established in 1921 (although it had various predecessors in several states). In Australia, the ICAA was founded by Royal Charter as a national professional accounting body in 1928.
[3] *United States v. Arthur Young and Co.*, 465 U.S. 805 (1984)

For the past 50 years it has been recognised that the notion of independence demands that the auditor should not be a material investor or borrower in, or a director or employee of, the audit client. However, as public accounting firms increased their revenues from performing APNAS for their clients, and as the number of large audit firms gradually fell (from eight in 1960s to five by 2000 and four by 2002), questions were repeatedly asked about the extent of real competition in the market for audit services and the extent to which fees paid to auditors might be compromising auditor independence.

Greater APNAS (both in terms of variety and dollar-value) meant that investors became sceptical about how auditors, who were increasingly promoting themselves as 'one-stop shops' for all professional services, and providing client management with a wide portfolio of services that helped ensure the auditee operated effectively and that its financial statements were trustworthy, could remain truly objective when it came to audit matters. This scepticism was derived from a number of concerns including the possibility of (1) fee dependence, (2) auditors having to attest to their own recommendations, (3) auditors usurping some managerial functions, and (4) auditors acting as advocates for the company.

This chapter addresses only the first of these concerns.

Current environment

An economic analysis of auditor independence in the United States was commissioned by the AICPA in 1997 (Antle et al. 1997). The Executive Summary reported, *inter alia*, that (1) non-audit service fees are material (accounting firms earn substantial and growing revenues from supplying non-audit services) and that all the real growth in 'Big Six' audit firms' revenues since 1990 was attributable to non-audit service fees, (2) there is a strong intuitive case for economies of scope between audit and non-audit services, and (3) there was no evidence that the supply of non-audit services threatened auditor independence – references to APNAS are absent in all auditors' professional indemnity insurance policies and virtually all negligence suits against auditors.

At least in the United States, nearly all audit firms have now segregated their core audit, accounting and tax divisions from their other consulting activities by selling or spinning off their consultancy divisions into legally separate entities.[4] However, consultancy fees have continued to rise through the mid-1990s to the early 2000s.

Banker, Chang and Cunningham (2003) provide descriptive statistics showing that, between 1995 and 1999, US public accounting firms had grown management

---

[4]Arthur Andersen was the first. It formed Andersen Consulting (now Accenture) in 1989. KPMG sold off a fifth of KPMG Consulting to Cisco Systems in 1999, Ernst & Young spun off their consulting arm to form Cap Gemini Ernst & Young in the mid-1990s, but sold out completely to Cap Gemini in 2000, PricewaterhouseCoopers sold PwC Consulting to IBM in June 2002, and Deloitte Touche Tohmatsu spun off Deloitte Consulting in February 2002.

advisory services at the expense of audit and accounting services (and tax services) over that period. Data collected on 64 auditing firms showed that, on average, while total firm revenue had almost doubled (from US$269.7 million in 1995 to US$485.3 million in 1999), audit and accounting services fees had in fact fallen (from US$49.5 million in 1995 to US$42.2 million in 1999). On a per company basis, since fees disclosures were made mandatory in the United States in 2000, levels of APNAS fees seem to be about equivalent in dollar terms to audit fees. Francis and Ke (2003) report a mean fee ratio (APNAS/total fees) of 51.9% (based on 1588 observations in 2000), Reynolds, Deis and Francis (2004) report a fee ratio of 49.1% (based on 2507 observations in 2001), and Larcher and Richardson (2003) report a fee ratio of 48.3% (based on 5103 observations in 2000 and 2001).

In Australia, where the level of audit APNAS fees has long been a disclosure requirement for listed companies, Carson et al. (2003) report that over the 16 years to 1999, APNAS has become a material component of total fees paid to auditors and continues to grow. By 1999, the mean APNAS fee per listed company client was $117 800, with a mean APNAS fee ratio of 49.4% (compared to averages for the whole period of $93 600 and 38.8% respectively). Carson et al. note that there is a robust positive association between APNAS and audit fees, suggesting that audits are not being used as loss leaders in order to obtain access to more lucrative consulting fees. They also observe some differences in the pricing of audit and APNAS between the big accounting firms – some earn premia on audit fees while those that don't appear to have higher APNAS fee revenues. More recent statistics show an interesting reversal of the trend occurring in 2003. The *Business Review Weekly* (Walker & Andrews 2004) reports that for Australia's top 100 companies (by market capitalisation) there was a huge, 32.7% reduction in APNAS fees between 2003 and 2002. At the same time audit fees increased nearly 10%.

A number of very public accounting scandals[5] in the last five years have caused regulators to turn their eyes again towards the auditing profession. In the United States, the Independence Standards Board (ISB), which was set up in 1997 by the SEC and the AICPA, was effectively disbanded in 2003 when the SEC issued its own Auditor Independence Rule (SEC 2003). In 2002 the Sarbanes-Oxley Act was passed by Congress, imposing onerous rules governing the way companies and auditors interact.

Increased public awareness in Australia has seen two government enquiries into the role of auditing in financial reporting (Ramsay 2001; JSCPAA 2002), the reissuance of the joint professional accounting bodies' ethical rules relating to

---

[5]For example, in the United States, Enron, WorldCom, Tyco, Adelphia, HealthSouth, Xerox and Arthur Andersen, and in Australia, HIH Insurance, One.Tel and Harris Scarfe.

auditor independence in May 2002, and introduction of the Corporate Law Economic Reform Program (Audit Reform and Corporate Disclosure) Bill – 'CLERP 9' – into Parliament in 2004.

These developments have affected the provision of APNAS to audit clients by (1) the proscription of some types of APNAS, (2) requiring Audit Committees to pre-approve all APNAS, and (3) improving the disclosure of APNAS and audit fees, but in neither country has 'fee dependence' been defined in terms of quantitative parameters.

Agency/costly contracting problems explained

The two major professional accounting bodies in Australia, the Institute of Chartered Accountants in Australia (ICAA) and CPA Australia (CPAA), require their auditor members to ensure that in the conduct of their audits they maintain independence from their client both in appearance and in fact.[6] Why is auditor independence so important?

In brief, auditor independence helps ensure an efficient and effective capital market. According to 'agency theory' and 'costly contracting theory' (see Watts & Zimmerman 1986), principals (who are assumed to be rational, self-serving but not risk averse) and agents (who are also assumed to rational and self-serving but not risk-takers) are bound to have differing goals and objectives. This is because they have different time horizons, different attitudes to risk and different work ethics. And if we consider company owners as principals and their appointed managers as agents, then these differing goals and objectives imply that company managers may attempt to operate companies in ways that suit themselves rather than the owners. For various reasons, owners are concerned that managers may have incentives to misreport the financial performance and the financial position of the companies they manage. These reasons may include, for example, to boost their bonuses by inflating profits, or to obscure the effects of excessive perks enjoyed by managers, or to influence the market price of company shares so that their options are more likely to be 'in the money'.

Owners are not economically able to fully monitor the behaviour of managers, and hence owners will deduct from managers' negotiated remuneration the estimated costs to them of managers' incongruent behaviour. Rational managers realise this and therefore have incentives to prove to owners that they have nothing to hide and, *inter alia*, agree to engage the services of an independent person to attest to the fairness of the reported financial performance and position. These independent attestors are auditors. Their report to the shareholders, stating that management's representations in the financial statement are true and fair,

---

[6]Kemp and Knapp (2004), Statement B4, *Independence*, p. 1106.

adds credibility and reliability – and in doing so eliminates information asymmetry between company and investors, which helps maintain an efficient market.

The agency arguments outlined above apply to an investor or equity ownership setting. Agency arguments can similarly be applied to the debt-provider setting. Here the financiers or debt-providers can be considered the principals and the managers (on behalf of the companies) can be considered agents, in the sense that the financier makes funds available to a company which are expected to be managed responsibly until the funds are repaid at some future time. Again, because agents have differing goals and objectives from principals, there is a fear that agents might mismanage the funds, allowing a transfer of resources away from debt-providers to the company. *Ceteris paribus*, the cost of finance will be higher because of these likely losses to the debt-providers. Hence companies have incentives to keep interest rates down by, *inter alia*, agreeing to have their financial statements audited by a reputable independent auditor. There is some evidence that this is in fact the case (see, for example, Pittman & Fortin 2004). The audit report in this case will add credibility to management's representations that the company is exercising good stewardship over the financier's funds.

Similar costly contracting theory arguments have been put forward to explain why auditors' reports may help a company minimise the political costs to which it is exposed by virtue of its operations in the wider business and social community.

However, the degree of credibility and reliability that attaches to an audit report depends largely on two factors; the auditor's competence and the auditor's independence (DeAngelo 1981). For the audit function to have value, there needs to be a belief in the minds of all parties that misstatements in the financial statements prepared by management will, in the first place, be discovered by the auditors (an issue of competence), and in the second place, be unbiasedly reported to users of those financial statements in the auditor's report (an issue of independence).

There is a large body of research that explores the competence with which auditors undertake audit engagements and make judgments about the truth and fairness of financial statements based on the evidence they collect. However, the academic auditing literature reviewed here is not concerned with the quality aspects of auditors; it focuses more specifically on aspects of auditor independence.

A well-informed and transparent market for audit services requires that auditors should not only be independent in fact, but that they should also appear to be independent. There are many threats to auditor independence in fact and in appearance. The ICAA/CPAA Joint Code of Professional Conduct identifies five such threats:[7]

1. *self-interest threats*: where the auditor could obtain a benefit, either financial or otherwise, from the audit client

2. *self-review threats*: where (a) the auditor in undertaking the audit engagement is required to form a judgment on other work (assurance or non-assurance) previously performed for the audit client, and/or (b) the auditor was previously associated with the audit client and is in a position to influence the outcome of the audit engagement

3. *advocacy threats*: where the auditor promotes an audit client's position or opinion to the point that objectivity may be – or may appear to be – compromised

4. *familiarity threats*: where the auditor becomes too familiar and sympathetic with the audit client

5. *intimidation threats*: where the auditor is deterred from acting objectively because of threats from the audit client.

Narrowing the focus again, this chapter considers the research about only the first of these, namely self-interest threats. These arise most commonly through fee dependence when an auditor, who receives materially large fees from a client, may be inclined not to unbiasedly report misstatements in the client's financial statements for fear of displeasing the client, and consequently being removed from the audit and thereby losing the future income stream attaching to the engagement.[8] This argument is only valid, of course, if management have the authority to hire and fire auditors or if auditors negotiate with management to receive fees that are contingent upon a certain type of audit report being issued. In Australia, contingent fees for audit services are banned[9], and auditors are appointed and removed on the vote of shareholders not at the discretion of management.[10] This being so, one might argue the opposite case – that auditors will be unlikely to side with managers against shareholder interests by not faithfully reporting financial misrepresentation to owners for fear of being found out by shareholders and consequently dismissed by them. However, there is anecdotal evidence that managers are highly influential in the appointment and removal of auditors. And because of information asymmetry between auditors and shareholders, there remains some doubt about the efficacy with which shareholders could, in the absence of company failure and/or subsequent litiga-

---

[7]Kemp and Knapp (2004), Statement F1, Appendix 1, para. 1.22 et seq.
[8]The ICAA/CPAA Joint Code of Professional Conduct, Statement F1, Appendix 2, discussed the threat of fee dependence (at para. 2.102 et seq.). The Code suggests that when audit fees from any one client reach 15% of the audit firm's total fees, auditors should have external parties conduct reviews and such reviews should be documented. Should the client's fees form 'an unduly large proportion' (not further defined) of total firm fees, then the auditor is required to refuse to perform, or withdraw from, the audit engagement.
[9]See Kemp and Knapp (2004), Statement F6.
[10]See the Australian *Corporations Act 2001* (at Part 2M.4).

tion, discover mendacious reporting by the auditor. Thus fee dependence continues to be perceived as a threat to auditor independence.

To the extent that shareholders have the power to appoint, instruct, remunerate and remove auditors, then auditors are agents of the shareholders. To the extent that management has the power to appoint, instruct, remunerate and remove auditors, then auditors are agents of management. It must be said that in Australia, listed company boards generally appoint an audit committee to oversee the company's arrangements with the auditor. Management may or may not be represented on the audit committee. Such a committee adds another layer in the principal-agent structure. It is a matter of some speculation whether auditors are agents of the shareholders, the audit committee or management.

Some have argued that auditors can never be truly independent simply because they are always subject to unconscious self-serving biases that arise in any number of ways, but including the effects of simply receiving a fee for service from their client companies (Bazerman, Morgan & Lowenstein 1997). Others have argued the impossibility of auditor independence because of the inevitable conflict that arises when auditors perform work for one party (shareholders) but are paid by another party (managers) (O'Connor 2002). Various alternate structural arrangements have been suggested for the market for audit services (for example, Coffee 2001; O'Connor 2002; Ronen 2002; Sunder 2003), but none has been considered seriously by company management and the accounting profession. Perhaps this is because the status quo suits both those parties too well.

While investigating the pricing of audit services, Simunic (1984) noted that the provision of APNAS would exacerbate the self-interest (fee dependence) faced by auditors. He reasoned that not only would the APNAS fee add to the level of fees derived from the audit client, but further, that the joint provision of audit and non-audit services might cause knowledge spillovers between the audit and the consultancy, enabling the auditor to perform either or both of these services more cheaply than a competitor supplier. These knowledge spillovers are sometimes referred to as 'economies of scope'.[11] To the extent that these 'efficiencies' are not passed on to the client by way of lower fees, they represent an economic rent (or a quasi-rent) to the auditor. If the APNAS services are recurring, the future stream of economic rents could be substantial.

The other worrisome aspect of APNAS is that it provides management with the opportunity to offer consultancy to the incumbent auditor (often referred to as

---

[11]There appears to be little published evidence as to the exact nature and incidence of these economies on audit costs. Antle and Demski (1991, p. 2) speculate:

> Some types of internal control deficiencies may generate high audit costs, but low costs for consulting to correct them. A client that generates high audit costs from a bad control environment due to improper attention from top management may be easier or harder to conduct an executive search for than an average client. The costs of conducting market surveys may be unrelated to audit costs.

'side payments') which, in contrast to audit fees, could be awarded on a contingency basis. In other words, management have the discretion to reward auditors with a stream of APNAS fees conditional upon the auditor concurring with management's representations in the financial statements. Such discretion is not subject to specific review and approbation by shareholders.

So herein lies the problem at the foundation of all APNAS fee research: does APNAS impair auditor independence through fee dependence? The question of whether APNAS causes the audit (and/or the consultancy) to be performed more efficiently and effectively is not as important as the independence issue because, notwithstanding an efficient and effective audit, shareholders are no better off – and likely worse off – if fee dependence is able to sufficiently influence auditors to bias their reports in favour of management.

In the remainder of this chapter, I review the extant empirical research literature that attempts to answer the specific question, does fee dependence occasioned by APNAS impair auditor independence?

Evidence from the archival literature – perception studies

APNAS and knowledge spillovers

It has been argued that the provision of APNAS by a company's incumbent auditor strengthens the economic bonding between auditor and client company and hence impairs the auditor's perceived independence. This is because the added economic benefits of the APNAS fees (being the quasi-rents associated with synergies/knowledge spillovers from or to the existing audit) strengthen the reluctance of the auditor to risk losing the audit through some disagreement with management (Simunic 1984).

Many studies have investigated this 'perceived lack of independence' by trying to determine if there is a measurable effect on audit fees in the presence of APNAS fees paid to incumbent auditors. Simunic (1984), Simon and Francis (1988), Abdel-khalik (1990), Turpen (1990), Butterworth and Houghton (1993), Ezzamel, Gwilliam and Holland (1996) and Houghton and Jubb (1998) collected public auditee data, while Palmrose (1986) and Ezzamel, Gwilliam and Holland (2002) surveyed public companies, and Davis, Ricchiute and Trompeter (1993) collected private audit firm production data to examine this relationship. Some used initial audit settings to incorporate 'low balling' effects into the picture.

It was generally thought that in a competitive market the benefit of knowledge spillovers (if they existed) would, in part at least, be passed on to the auditee and thus would operate in such a way as to hold audit fees *down* in the presence of APNAS fees purchased from incumbent auditors.

The results of the tests of this proposition were far from expected. The research generally supports the finding that there is a significant *and positive* relationship between APNAS fees paid to incumbent auditors and audit fees.[12] Simunic's (1984) conclusion was that auditors' cost functions for audit services and APNAS *were* significantly interdependent – the results consistent with knowledge spillovers flowing from audit to APNAS as well as the other way around, provided the demand for audit services is elastic.

The theoretical arguments supporting a positive relationship have not been well developed. Other explanations have been proposed to explain the positive relationship: for example, auditee financial difficulty causing higher levels of both APNAS and audit fees (Simunic 1984); APNAS fees related to major changes in auditee organisational structure (including changes in the accounting and internal control systems), which might require greater auditor effort (Palmrose 1986); and lack of competition in the market for APNAS (Solomon 1990).

Davis, Ricchiute and Trompeter (1993) in fact set out to test such alternative explanations for the incidence and level of APNAS fees and found APNAS and audit fees were related to increased audit effort – a result that was inconsistent with the view that performing both might provide the auditor with incentives to compromise 'objectivity' (p. 149). Ezzamel, Gwilliam and Holland (2002) surveyed UK companies in 1995, soliciting information not only about APNAS paid to incumbent auditors but also non-audit services purchased from other consultants, as well as information about the size of the companies' internal audit functions. They then used a number of models to evaluate the relationship between audit fees and various components of APNAS and non-audit services supplied by others.[13] They found audit fees were significantly positively associated with corporate finance advice and tax advice supplied by the auditor, but that audit fees were not associated with any of the non-incumbent supplied management consulting advice. They conclude (p. 13):

> We interpret these results as supporting explanations of the positive association between fees paid for non-audit services and audit fees in terms either of client specific differences, for example organisational complexity, or of events giving rise to the purchase of more audit and non-audit services rather than in terms of direct economic linkages between cost productions for audit and non-audit services. More tentatively, we speculate that the presence of another auditing firm at the client in a consulting capacity may exert competitive pressure on the fee for external audit.

[12]However, at least one of the US studies, Abdel-khalik (1990), failed to find any relationship.
[13]It seems to me a great opportunity missed that Ezzamel, Gwilliam and Holland (2002) didn't use their survey data to attempt to answer the question, what explains the level of APNAS fees out of a total level of non-audit services fees paid by a company to both incumbent auditor and other consultants?

However, few clear implications for auditor independence can be drawn from the above line of research.

Another, and potentially more fruitful, line of research has been proposed that attempts to model directly the level of APNAS fees paid to incumbent auditors with perceived notions of auditor independence. This research strives to determine the relationship between the demand and/or supply drivers of APNAS fees and the perceived lack of auditor objectivity (rather than investigating the level of APNAS fees as one of a number of components of audit fees). A summary of that research is set out below.

APNAS and surveys of market users' perceptions

There is a large body of research that has investigated whether the mere existence of APNAS causes different classes of external users of financial statements to infer a lack of independence between auditor and client, and whether – and if so, how – such a perceived lack of independence might cause those users to alter their attitudes towards, and contractual relationships with, the audited company. Some of this research looks at the appearance of independence threats arising from the *level* of APNAS (self-interest threats), while some addresses the appearance of independence threats from the *nature* of APNAS (self-review threats):[14] in this chapter, I review only the former.

Pany and Reckers (1988) allude to more than 20 years of surveys that indicated that users of financial statements were concerned about possible loss of auditor independence in cases where the incumbent provided audit and significant non-audit services concurrently. McKinley, Pany and Reckers (1985) argued that biased phrasing of some questions in some of these early survey instruments might have caused the severity of this so-called 'perception problem' to have been overstated. As an alternative to employing a survey instrument, McKinley, Pany and Reckers asked subjects whether they would approve or reject a loan application from a small company for which the level of APNAS was manipulated. Their results showed that users' perceptions of auditor independence and of financial statement reliability were unaffected by the level of APNAS. The McKinley, Pany and Reckers study was conducted on a relatively small scale and manipulated APNAS in just a binary fashion (0 or 30% of audit fees). Pany and Reckers (1988) sought to overcome these limitations by conducting a larger survey of bank loan officers and financial analysts, who were asked a series of questions about whether a loan to, or an investment in, a company was sound, given levels of APNAS that ranged between 0 and 90% of audit fees. Various other questions were asked about the perceived levels of auditor independence

---

[14] An early example of this sort of research is Shockley (1981). More recently, Lowe, Geiger and Pany (1999) elicit loan offer perceptions about auditor independence when the client company outsources internal audit work to the incumbent auditor.

and financial statement reliability. Bank loan officers were significantly more willing to provide loans when APNAS stood at the 25%-level, while at other levels there was no significant difference in perceptions (i.e., bank loan officers perceived independence risk no differently when APNAS was 90% to when it was set at 0%). Financial analysts were influenced (negatively) in their perceptions about the company's short-term riskiness only in the case where APNAS was 90%. The authors concluded that they were unable to find any real support that APNAS results in changed perceptions of auditor independence.

Some years later, Arthur Andersen won a battle with the SEC enabling its newly formed but legally separate consulting 'arm', Andersen Consulting, to undertake all manner of non-audit services for Andersen audit clients. Other Big Six accounting firms were not given the same opportunity and there was a renewed debate at the time into auditor independence. Lowe and Pany (1995) obtained the views of 401 loan officers as to whether, *inter alia*, the dollar amount of the consulting relationship (manipulated between subjects as either material or immaterial) affects perceptions of auditor independence. Interestingly, Lowe and Pany defined 'material' fees as being 12% of the audit firm's *office* total revenue. In addition, two levels relating to the recurrence of the APNAS were tested — in one case, the APNAS was treated as a one-off project, in the other as a 'continuous association' between client and auditor. Their survey results indicated strong support for the assertion that user perceptions of auditor independence are affected by the materiality of the APNAS, and weaker support for the proposition that user perceptions are affected by the continuity of the APNAS.

In 1996 a survey of company finance directors and audit partners was conducted in the United Kingdom to gauge perceptions about auditor independence and the effectiveness of recent UK regulatory changes to mitigate threats to auditor independence (Beattie, Brandt & Fearnley 1999). Questions about APNAS fee dependence (measured as the percentage of APNAS to audit fees) were included in the survey instrument and this threat to independence was ranked sixth in importance by finance directors and equal twelfth in importance by audit partners. Interestingly, Beattie, Brandt and Fearnley report that perceived economic dependence by audit partners on their audit clients was ranked very highly by both groups of respondents.

In a pre- and post-Enron study, Thornton, Reinstein and Miller (2004) surveyed bank executives and loan officers (representing well-informed financial statement users) and audit and non-audit CPA practitioners (representing financial statement preparers) to determine their attitudes about a number of issues associated with auditor independence and the provision of APNAS. By replicating some of the questions previously used by Reinstein and Lander (2001), they were able to test for changes in perceptions before and after the Enron scandal became headline news in the United States. The results of the survey are interesting but not surprising:

- An equal amount of subjects (41%) thought APNAS would be likely to compromise auditor independence as those who thought it wouldn't, but auditors (and other CPAs, including those in industry) are significantly less concerned about a potential compromise than bankers.
- Public audit CPAs are significantly more likely than others surveyed to perceive that APNAS increases the client's power over the auditor and that APNAS improves the quality of the audit.
- However, public audit CPAs are less likely than other respondents to perceive that high APNAS implies a breach of independence in fact.
- Bankers and audit CPAs agreed more often than non-audit CPAs that litigation threats affected auditor credibility more than auditor independence.
- Significant differences pre- and post-Enron were observed. Generally, perceptions about the importance of auditor independence and client power afforded by APNAS over the auditor strengthened for all groups of respondents.

As an aside, the survey showed that respondents displayed little homogeneity about what types of APNAS were most serious in compromising independence, which indicates 'that regulators may not be able to satisfy all users' and preparers' desired level of auditor independence through a series of non-audit service proscriptions' (Thornton, Reinstein & Miller 2004, p. 19).

APNAS and market responses

Concern about APNAS fee dependence was confirmed in an Australian study by Gul and Tsui (1999), who investigated shareholder responses to varying levels of APNAS disclosed by 500 Australian publicly-listed companies in 1993 and 1994. Gul and Tsui obtained market evidence as to whether the returns accruing to a holder of a share were affected by the level of reported APNAS. They hypothesised an inverse relationship due to the expected reduced investor reliance on the integrity and objectivity occasioned by higher levels of APNAS. Using an OLS regression model, which included an interaction term (APNAS multiplied by earnings yield) as the variable of interest, they find a significant and negative relationship between returns and APNAS as hypothesised. However, after controlling for audit firm quality (using a Big Six dummy variable), they find that Big Six 'quality' auditors significantly moderate investors' negative association with APNAS. Gul and Tsui (p. 12) conclude: 'The results suggest that concerns regarding the adverse effects of [APNAS] on investor confidence are warranted only when [APNAS] is provided by non-Big 6 auditors'.

Another study (Brandon, Crabtree & Maher 2004) investigates the debt market's perceptions of independence impairment caused by APNAS. Using corporate disclosures about audit and non-audit service fees required in the United States under SEC Rule S7 (SEC 2000), the authors regress company bond ratings against APNAS fees and a number of control variables. The regression shows a significant and inverse relationship between the dependent variable and APNAS. The APNAS variable is operationalised three ways (APNAS as a percentage of audit fees, the total of APNAS plus audit fees, and APNAS and audit fees separately) and in all cases the regression coefficient is significantly negative. However, Brandon, Crabtree and Maher are unable to improve the prediction accuracy of a benchmark bond-ranking prediction model by including an APNAS variable.

APNAS and auditor reappointment

Raghunandan (2003) uses a novel setting in which to examine shareholder perceptions of auditor independence. He analyses shareholder voting in 172 *Fortune 1000* companies in the United States which elected to adopt shareholder ratification of management-nominated auditor re-appointments between February and April 2001. Raghunandan finds evidence to support the argument that one would be expected to observe less shareholder support for auditors who supplied large APNAS to their clients. However, the implications of these results need to be cautiously drawn because even in cases where APNAS was high, shareholder ratification of the re-appointment was, on average, still 97%.

APNAS and management's perceptions

Another body of empirical research has investigated management's perceptions about the relationship between the level of APNAS and agency costs. This research posits that companies with high agency costs (usually measured by ownership dispersion and managerial share ownership and leverage) will have incentives to signal to shareholders and financiers that their financial statements are credible and reliable. Given that managers have the discretion to issue APNAS consultancies, if managers perceive that APNAS will impair auditor independence (either in their own eyes or those of owners and debt-providers) then, *ceteris paribus*, high agency cost companies will be expected to report lower APNAS than low agency cost companies.

Parkash and Venable (1993) set out to test the above agency theory-inspired proposition. They argue further that recurrent APNAS represents an annuity and therefore is likely to be perceived as more of an impairment to auditor independence than non-recurrent APNAS. Using US information about APNAS made available under the old ASR 250 disclosure rules, Parkash and Venable combine data sets of approximately 250 listed companies for 1978, 1979 and 1980, and regress APNAS against agency cost variables. Both univariate and multivariate analysis support the hypotheses that lower levels of recurrent APNAS are associated with lower levels of managerial/director ownership, lower levels of owner dispersion, and higher levels of leverage (as a surrogate for closeness to debt covenant limits). The results, however, revealed some temporal anomalies. The regression for 1978 reflects in substance the overall pooled results. However, the 1979 indicator variable is only significant for larger auditees, while the 1980 indicator variable is only significant for smaller auditees. Similarly, when recurrent APNAS fees are broken down into the categories of tax, pensions and personnel, and systems, the explanatory power of the agency variables is mixed. A major limitation of the study not specifically addressed by Parkash and Venable is the underlying assumption that the demand for APNAS is cross-sectionally and temporally homogeneous. This is unlikely to be the case in practice. The reason why an auditee purchased less APNAS from its auditor in a particular period may be because it had less of a *need* of non-audit services in that period – and *not* because of agency theory-related incentives for an independent auditor.

In a much more recent study, but using the same ASR 250 data as Parkash and Venable (1993), albeit with a much larger selection of companies, Hackenbrack (2003, p. 23) reports that the disclosure of APNAS during those years altered management's appetite for APNAS:

> The evidence reported in this study is consistent with the SEC's policy substantively changing behaviour. The percentage of companies jointly sourcing audit and [APNAS] dropped from 54% to 42% during the effective period of ASR 250, a time when consulting industry revenues were expanding at 20% annually. Investors' reactions to the mandated disclosure are positively related to managements' subsequent purchases at two levels: the likelihood a company chose to jointly source audit and [APNAS] and the overall (relative) purchase levels for the 14% of the sample that purchased high levels of [APNAS].

Firth (1997) was the first to attempt to overcome the assumption of cross-sectional homogeneity of non-audit services. The incidence of APNAS must be predicated on the *ex ante* economic need for such consulting/management services. He hypothesised that such a demand is likely to be a function of:

- corporate restructuring
- the installation of a new information system
- the recruitment of a new CEO, within the current or previous two years, from outside the company
- high asset growth
- the financial performance of the company.

Firth regressed APNAS fees paid to incumbent auditors (deflated by the audit fee) against agency cost variables after controlling for the above economic need variables. He used data collected from the 500 largest UK *industrial* listed companies, which were required to disclose APNAS fees paid to incumbent auditors for the first time in 1993. His results indicated that, except for company performance, growth and new information system installation, all 'economic need' variables were significant. All of the agency theory independence variables were also significant and displayed the expected directional sign. This led Firth to conclude that his study 'finds evidence in support of agency variables influencing the relative use of auditor-provided consultancy services' (Firth 1997, p. 19).

In an Australian setting, Houghton and Ikin (2001) posit a three-factor model to explain the level of APNAS paid by Australian companies to their incumbent auditor. The first factor is an '*ex ante* need for consulting services' (operationalised similarly to Firth (1997), but including the error term from a parsimonious audit fee model to capture the jointness of audit and APNAS fees), the second factor is a requirement for the incumbent to be an APNAS industry specialist, and the third is a willingness by the auditee to appoint the auditor. This 'willingness to appoint' construct is argued to be determined by agency and political cost pressures, together with management's perceptions of the strength of the auditee's portfolio of corporate governance practices, of which the appointment of an independent auditor is one such. In other words, the authors argue that if a company employs a number of strong corporate governance practices, these might mitigate against any pejorative perceptions arising from a high level of APNAS and thus help restrain any increase in agency or political costs. Using OLS regression on data collected from a sample of 432 companies selected from among the largest 500 companies listed on the Australian Stock Exchange (ASX) in 1997, Houghton and Ikin find general support for their model. In particular, equity (but not debt) agency costs and political costs were significantly and negatively related to levels of APNAS, which is consistent with the notion that management perceives the loss of independence associated with high APNAS as impacting the cost of doing business with stakeholders, and manipulates the levels of APNAS downwards accordingly. Further, they find some evidence that other good corporate governance practices offset this effect – the number of non-executive directors on the audit committee and the activity of the board were both significantly and positively associated with levels of APNAS.

Summary

It seems clear that perceptions of impaired auditor independence are aroused in the minds of financial statement stakeholders (if not auditors) by the incidence of high levels of APNAS.

Evidence from the archival literature – more direct tests

This section reviews the extant academic literature that specifically examines the relationship between auditor independence and the provision of APNAS. The concerns expressed by the public and regulators – that the joint provision of audit services and APNAS appear to compromise auditor independence – have motivated all the research described below.

Dopuch and King (1991) conducted an experiment using two abstract markets that modelled the contracting offers and acceptances between auditors and clients. In one market auditors could offer to provide APNAS as well as audit services, in the other market they could not. Since the interactions between market participants were complex, the results are difficult to interpret and extrapolate into the real world.

Unlike the research studies noted in the previous section (and unlike Dopuch & King 1991), each of the following studies directly explores the relationship between the level of APNAS fees paid to incumbent auditors and various proxies of auditor independence *in fact*. The different measures of independence used include the length of auditor tenure, the frequency of qualified audit opinions, auditor changes ('switches') and various agency theory-related incentives for auditor independence.

APNAS and auditor tenure

Beck, Frecka and Solomon published their research into the relationship between APNAS and auditor independence in two papers. The first (1988a) proposed an analytical, supply-side model of the bonding that develops between auditor and auditee in the presence of APNAS fees.[15] Assuming a competitive market for non-audit services, they argued that incremental bonding will be greatest in the case of recurrent APNAS when there are effective barriers to entry into the market (i.e., when the APNAS start-up costs and APNAS switching costs are greater than audit cost savings through knowledge spillovers). In the case of non-recurrent APNAS, they predicted that incremental bonding will only occur when there are real knowledge spillovers between the audit and APNAS engagements because the incumbents will then have lower costs than their competitors. The researchers were faced with a major limitation – audit and APNAS start-up costs, and audit and APNAS switching costs and spillover benefits are not directly observable to external parties. So Beck, Frecka and Solomon needed to make one further assumption in order to test their model – that as bonding increases so too will audit tenure (i.e., the length of time the incumbent auditor remains incumbent). In fact, of course, without this data on costs and benefits, their

---

[15] In fact, they extended the DeAngelo model (1981) by including the market for APNAS fees.

model cannot really be tested. Nevertheless, despite the inability to test the precepts of the model, their research does permit the empirical testing of the effect APNAS fees has on audit tenure (as a proxy for bonding and, inversely, for independence) and hence is instructive for this study. In their second paper (1988b), Beck, Frecka and Solomon empirically tested the relationship between various levels of APNAS fees (by categories) and audit tenure on US listed companies in 1978 and 1979. They selected 50 companies in both years with high levels of different categories of APNAS and compared them with 50 companies with low levels of APNAS. Overall the results are mixed. Limited support was found for increased tenure (increased bonding – decreased independence) in the case of some of the recurrent APNAS categories (systems, and pension and personnel – but oddly not tax) in the 1978 sub-sample. This was not replicated in the 1979 sub-sample. The difference in the means of audit tenure in the high APNAS groups varied only slightly in absolute terms with the low APNAS groups (the differences were significant, however). No significant results were found in respect of the non-recurrent APNAS. Dopuch (1988) finds the results unconvincing, especially since their sub-samples were so highly skewed.

Dopuch noted the low level of auditor switches that were evident in the Beck, Frecka and Solomon (1988b) sample compared to other research. He suggests (at p. 90) that it might be 'useful to look at client auditor switches for each of the accounting firms in their samples to see whether the frequency of switches of an accounting firm's high [APNAS] clients differs from that of switches of its low [NAS] clients'. DeBerg, Kaplan and Pany (1991) report how they took up Dopuch's challenge. They tested the assertion that companies with higher levels of APNAS would switch their auditors less often than companies with lower levels of APNAS. Using a matched pair research design, they compared levels of APNAS for all listed US companies that changed auditors between September 1978 and February 1982 with levels of APNAS fees reported by similar companies that did not change auditors in that time period. Like Beck, Frecka and Solomon (1988b), they used the disclosure requirements of ASR 250 to obtain data about APNAS fees and used the same categories of recurrent and non-recurrent APNAS. Despite the good motivation of the research, they failed to find any significant differences in the levels of total APNAS, recurrent APNAS and non-recurrent APNAS between the two groups of 'treatment' and 'control' companies. The claim that higher levels of APNAS increased bonding between auditor and auditee was thus rejected, as also, by inference, was the claim that APNAS fees might impair auditor independence. In an extension to their prime research question, DeBerg, Kaplan and Pany (1991) investigated whether the decision to change auditors was related to changes in the purchase of APNAS. Levels of APNAS before and after the auditor switches were analysed. The results indicated that lower levels of total APNAS and recurring APNAS were purchased from the successor auditor compared to the predecessor auditor and also to the non-change company group.[16]

APNAS and qualified opinions

The notion that a less independent auditor is less likely to issue qualified or modified audit opinions is appealing, and many studies have now been undertaken to examine the effect APNAS fees might have on the incidence of qualified audit opinions. Initially, most of these were Australian studies because for many years APNAS fees were required by legislation to be disclosed in company annual financial statements.

Barkess and Simnett (1994) were concerned with two issues relating to APNAS – the pricing of APNAS as well as the association, if any, between APNAS and auditor independence as measured by audit report qualifications (and by auditor switches; see notes). They drew their sample from the top 500 listed companies in Australia for each of the five years 1986 to 1990. Data was not pooled.

A parsimonious OLS model was proposed that would identify any relationship between APNAS and predicted drivers of the level of APNAS – namely, audit fees, auditee size and auditor. To this was added an independent variable to identify qualified audit reports.

The results relating to auditor independence observed by Barkess and Simnett indicated that there was no support for the contention that auditors would be less likely to issue qualified audit reports when they are selling higher levels of APNAS to their clients. Univariate analysis failed to reveal any significant differences between the level of APNAS in companies receiving qualified and unqualified audit reports in each of the five years. This was confirmed in the regression analysis – the audit qualification indicator variable was insignificant in all years except 1989 (where it was significant and *positive*).

Wines (1994) stated that while many researches have investigated financial statement users' *perceptions* of auditor independence in the presence of APNAS fees, none had examined the connection between the output of the audit process – the audit report – and APNAS fees. He claimed that observations of variations in the nature of audit reports issued is likely to tell us more about real independence effects than users' perceptions of independence effects. Wines selected the 76 largest Australian listed companies that survived during the 10-year period 1980 to 1989, and analysed the pooled data by regressing APNAS fees as an independent variable against audit report qualifications as the dependent dummy

[16]In an Australian study, Barkess and Simnett (1994) also investigated the relationship between APNAS fees and auditor switches (although they claim to be testing auditor tenure). A summary of their research appears in the section 'APNAS and qualified opinions', but briefly their results indicated that there was no significant relationship between the two variables. In contrast to DeBerg, Kaplan and Pany (1991), they noted that the average level of APNAS fees increased sharply in the year after the auditor switch and concluded that companies 'may change auditors in order to gain access to higher levels of other services' (Barkess & Simnett 1994, p. 106).

variable. The probit model is very parsimonious, controlling only for auditee size and dummy variables for industry and auditor. Wines found a significant – and negative – relationship between audit qualifications and APNAS fees, as predicted.

Craswell (1999) was motivated by the desire to reconcile the conflicting results of Wines (1994) and Barkess and Simnett (1994). He regressed APNAS fees as an independent variable against audit report qualifications as the dependent dummy variable. Craswell included 'emphasis of the matter'-type comments in auditors' reports as qualifications, while Wines did not. (Craswell's dependent variable could more accurately be described as 'modified audit report' rather than 'qualified audit report'.) Craswell's logit model controlled more carefully for the (audit risk and complexity) factors that prior research had identified as being responsible for producing cross-sectional differences in qualified audit reports. These included size, profitability, leverage and asset composition. The model also included a dummy variable as a control for cases in which auditors had issued a qualified audit report in the prior year and another to indicate whether the auditor was a member of the Big Eight or not. The data sets of the three studies overlap in time – Craswell selected all listed Australian companies in 1984, 1987 and 1994, but analysed each year's data separately. Craswell (1999) failed to find any significant relationship between the incidence of modified audit reports in the presence of APNAS fees paid to incumbent auditors.

Craswell appears to be the more complete and robust research, however various limitations in all studies are evident. These include:

- the failure to adequately control for audit quality (a co-requisite with audit independence for an audit qualification)
- the inability to determine, from publicly available data, precisely those companies that experienced circumstances that would normally have given rise to a qualified audit opinion but did not receive one from the incumbent auditor
- the existence of alternative explanations for the results (the consequence of the APNAS consultancy might be to so improve accounting systems, for example, that an audit qualification becomes no longer appropriate).

In another Australian study, Houghton and Jubb (1999), while not investigating auditor independence *per se*, found that audit qualifications were costly both in terms of audit fees (particularly in the year following the qualification) and also APNAS fees (in the year of the qualification).

Craswell, Stokes and Laughton (2002) conduct an investigation of the effects of audit fee dependence on an auditor's propensity to issue qualified audit opinions. Again set in Australia, the authors use qualified opinions only as their dependent regression variable, on the basis that modified opinions do not constitute the exercise of 'serious' independent judgments by auditors. As an extension of prior research, Craswell, Stokes and Laughton consider an auditor's audit fee dependence at a local office level as well as at a national level. Variables are included in the regression to control for other company characteristics generally associated with the issuance of a qualified opinion and for the impact of the level of APNAS fees. Listed Australian company data for two years (1994 & 1996) are collected and analysed separately (i.e., the data are not pooled). The results of the study indicate that 'the fee dependence variables do not have a statistically detectable impact on the exercise of independent judgement in the formulation of the audit opinion' (Craswell, Stokes & Laughton 2002, p. 271). The authors note that any observed incidence of a qualified audit report must have arisen as a coincidence of two factors – viz, an *ex ante* error in the financial statements and an auditor sufficiently unbiased as to qualify the audit report – and that the first factor should be controlled for in studies such as these. Unfortunately, *ex ante* errors in financial statements are not observable, but some have argued (for example, Whittred 1980) that delays in issuing audit reports are evidence of client-auditor negotiations over financial statement misstatement and might serve as a useful proxy. Craswell, Stokes and Laughton analyse whether late reporters are systematically different from the rest of their companies and conclude in the negative.[17]

Since 1992, UK companies have been required to disclose levels of APNAS in addition to levels of audit fees. Firth (2002) extends his prior research into the effect of agency costs on levels of reported APNAS (Firth 1997, see above) by investigating (1) whether levels of audit fees and APNAS fees are driven by common events and characteristics that create a demand for APNAS as well as an increase in the amount of audit effort, and (2) whether, after controlling for cross-sectional differences in an auditee's need for consulting services, higher levels of APNAS lead to a higher incidence of unqualified audit opinions. It is the second question that is of interest here. Audit report qualifications are modelled as a function of the size of client, its financial performance, leverage, asset composition, risk characteristics, Big Six status of the auditor and various fee dependence measures including the ratio of APNAS to total assets, the ratio of audit fees to total assets, and the ratio of audit and APNAS fees to the total fee income of the audit firm. 1112 listed UK companies are selected using 1996 data. The probit regression results show that the coefficient of the variable of interest, APNAS/total assets, is significantly negative, indicating that the higher the APNAS, the more likely it is that the audit report will be 'clean'. The fee

---

[17]Knechel and Payne (2001) use proprietary information obtained from an international public accounting firm to examine the causes of lags in audit reports. They find that, in addition to incremental work effort, the existence of contentious tax issues and the level of staff experience, one factor that helps explain audit report lag is APNAS – which works to *decrease* the lag. They conclude that this indicates the synergistic relationship between APNAS and audit effort. However, such a finding is also consistent with the notion that APNAS increases independence threats.

dependence argument is reinforced by the moderately significant and negatively signed variable APNAS/total APNAS + audit fee.[18] This result confirms Wines (1994), but is at odds with other similar research. Note that there is, of course, an alternative explanation for any observed negative relationship between APNAS and qualified opinions – namely, that high APNAS might have so improved the auditee's accounting systems and internal controls and/or operations that the reasons for qualified opinions are substantially reduced.

A couple of US studies fail to replicate Firth's (2002) results. DeFond, Raghunandan and Subramanyam (2002) test the proposition that going concern qualifications are negatively associated with levels of fee dependence. Fee dependence is measured both in terms of APNAS and total fees (i.e., APNAS + audit fees). They choose going concern qualifications specifically because of the serious consequences for both client and auditor of misreporting when financial failure might be imminent. Their sample of 4105 companies lodging proxy statements with the SEC between February and October 2001 included 160 with going concern qualifications. Their analysis is rigorous, and after controlling for cross-sectional variation in the demand for audit and consulting services to derive unexpected fees[19], they report (p. 1250):

> Our results provide no support for either hypothesis. That is, we find no evidence of a significant association between the auditor's propensity to issue a going concern opinion and any of our fee measures. This finding is robust to replacing all fee variables with their respective unexpected components, and after controlling for the simultaneity bias induced by endogeneity among non-audit fees, audit fees and going concern opinions.

DeFond, Raghunandan and Subramanyam's results are supported by Geiger and Rama (2003), who investigated the effect that different levels of fees paid to auditors had on the incidence of going concern qualifications for stressed manufacturing companies. The selection of a smaller sample than DeFond, Raghunandan and Subramanyam – they examined only 66 companies – enabled them to test a richer model. In particular, Geiger and Rama collected data relating to a company's default status, management plans and audit committee composition, all of which have been shown to be associated with US audit opinions. Their regression showed a significant and positive association between the auditor's propensity to issue going concern opinions and audit fees, but no such association with APNAS. Similar to DeFond, Raghunandan and Subramanyam, their results are unchanged after controlling for the endogeneity of audit opinions, audit fees

---

[18]Interestingly, Firth (2002) found no observed association between audit fees and audit qualifications. The reason might be as explained by Houghton and Jubb (1999), who observed a lagged effect between the two.
[19]The authors here draw on prior research by Craswell, Francis and Taylor (1995) and Whisenart, Sankaraguruswami and Raghunandan (2003) for variables explaining audit fees, and Parkash and Venable (1993), Firth (1997), Whisenart, Sankaraguruswami and Raghunandan (2002; see References), and Frankel, Johnson and Nelson (2002) for variables explaining APNAS.

and APNAS. In other words, they found no evidence of APNAS having any significant adverse effect on auditor reporting judgments in their sample of stressed companies.

The results of both DeFond, Raghunandan and Subramanyam (2002) and Geiger and Rama (2003) are compatible with the findings of Reynolds and Francis (2001). They also use the incidence of going concern audit reports to determine whether large audit clients (i.e., large in terms of audit fees at an audit firm office level) affect the propensity for auditors to issue biased audit reports. They cannot find any evidence that economic dependence causes auditors to report more favourably for larger clients. On the contrary, they conclude that auditors generally report more conservatively (i.e., with less concern for self-serving bias) for larger clients, attributing this to greater litigation and reputation risk associated with misreporting for those larger clients where fee dependence is high.

In another interesting Australian study, Barkess, Simnett and Urquhart (2002) take a different perspective on the debate. They set out to determine if audit firms which receive material fees from clients are less likely to issue qualified opinions by examining audit fee data on a firm-by-firm basis. They collected client fee data on Australia's largest 25 audit firms over the years 1988 to 1992. A number of tests were performed:

- comparing the rate of audit qualifications of those clients that contributed more than 0.5% of total firm revenues with the rate of qualifications across all companies
- using an audit opinion prediction model first propounded by Monroe and Teh (1993), comparing actual opinions with predicted opinions for those 77 companies that contributed more than 0.5% of audit firm revenues in 1991 and 1992
- including a fee dependence ratio in the audit opinion prediction model to determine if that improved the specification (i.e., the accuracy of prediction) of the model.

Barkess, Simnett and Urquhart (2002) found no support in any of their tests for the proposition that audit firms allowed their reporting judgments to be biased in favour of high fee paying clients.

APNAS and earnings management

Much attention was given to the work of Frankel, Johnson and Nelson (2002) when it was published. It was the first to publish results using the audit and APNAS fee data that was required to be disclosed in all US company proxy statements lodged after April 2000. It seems a number of researchers had thought of using earnings management as a measure of earnings quality, and then testing the notion that economic bonding between auditor and client through fee dependence might be associated with lower earnings quality and therefore higher earnings management. Frankel, Johnson and Nelson used three measures of earnings management (meeting or just beating earnings forecasts, absolute discretionary accruals, and the share price reaction to disclosed audit and APNAS fees) and two measures of fee dependence (ratio of APNAS fees to the total of audit and APNAS fees, and the rank of the magnitude of APNAS for the auditor across clients in the sample). Their sample comprised 3074 US companies disclosing APNAS and audit fee data in proxy statements filed with the SEC between February and June 2001. After controlling for various auditor and company characteristics affecting earnings management, they find a significant and positive relationship between APNAS and small earnings surprises and the size of discretionary accruals. This finding supported the UK results of Gore, Pope and Singh (2001).

Kinney and Libby (2002) raised some conceptual and model specification concerns in the Frankel, Johnson and Nelson (2002) study which have been addressed to some extent by other researchers. For example, Ashbaugh, LaFond and Mayhew (2003) used a modified discretionary accruals model that controlled for company performance (and could not find any association between their APNAS ratio and earnings management for those companies reporting positive discretionary accruals).[20] Ashbaugh, LaFond and Mayhew also respecified the regression modelling 'benchmark beating' (and could not replicate the Frankel, Johnson & Nelson finding). In summary, they state: 'Overall, our study indicates that [Frankel, Johnson & Nelson 2002]'s results are sensitive to research design choices, and we find no systematic evidence supporting their claim that auditors violate their independence as a result of clients purchasing relatively more nonaudit services' (p. 611).

Similarly, Antle et al. (2002) address the endogeneity issue concerning the joint determination of audit fees, APNAS fees and to some extent earnings management. Contrary to the findings of Frankel, Johnson and Nelson (2002), the evidence provided by their 1994-2000 UK company data indicates that increased discretionary accruals are associated with a *decrease* in APNAS. Antle et al. claim that their results are robust to preliminary tests on US data.

Francis and Ke (2003), who focus only on beating earnings forecasts as a proxy for earnings management and hence poor quality reporting, make three improvements to the Frankel, Johnson and Nelson study. First, they respecify the model to exclude companies with large negative earnings surprises, second they consider quarterly earnings benchmarks rather than annual benchmarks, and third they measure 'fee dependence' by using three additional metrics. They find no sys-

---

[20]This is a significant finding because there is evidence that companies engage in earnings management in a hierarchical order; the first objective is to report positive earnings, next to report a positive change in earnings, and then, given the first two objectives are achieved, to meet or just beat analysts' forecasts (Degeorge, Patel & Zeckhauser 1999).

tematic evidence that companies paying high fees (APNAS or audit or both) are more likely to manage earnings to meet analysts' forecasts.

Another study to investigate this question was Larcher and Richardson (2003). Initially replicating the research design used by Frankel, Johnson and Nelson (2002), they find a positive association between the absolute value of discretionary accruals and APNAS paid to auditors. However, after applying 'latent class mixture models', using additional measures of fee dependence (including *unexpected* fees), and including some corporate governance control variables, they report that this positive association is driven by a small cluster of companies (only 8.5% of companies in their large sample) that have a relatively small market capitalisation, lower book-to-market ratio, lower institutional shareholding and higher managerial ownership. Further, these companies concurrently show symptoms of weakness in corporate governance mechanisms. The overall results show a *negative* association between auditor independence (as proxied by four alternate fee measures) and earnings quality (as proxied by discretionary accruals).

Chung and Kallapur (2003) strengthened the case for no independence impairment. They failed to find an association between earnings management and APNAS fees (measured in terms of relative importance to the audit firm at both a national and office level) after controlling for industry and geographical segments, auditor industry expertise, audit tenure and some additional company corporate governance characteristics.

The latest US study follows the trend. Reynolds, Deis and Francis (2004) expand the Frankel, Johnson and Nelson model to include control variables for auditor litigation risk and reputation protection, company industry membership and IPOs. Their highly explanatory model (R^2 of approximately 75%) shows that neither of their fee dependence measures (ratio of APNAS to total fees paid to the auditor and the natural log of total fees) is significantly related to discretionary accruals and hence not to earnings management.

However, the latest UK study (Fergusson, Seow & Young 2004) does find a positive association between earnings management and APNAS purchases between 1996 and 1998. Three measures of earnings management were used, including a measure of the likelihood that the auditee's accounting policies were publicly criticised or subject to investigation by regulators. Three measures of APNAS fee dependence were also employed; (1) the ratio of APNAS fee to total auditor fees, (2) the log of APNAS fees, and (3) the decile rank of the auditee's APNAS fees in the auditor practice office. The authors note that the UK environment during the period of the study was one of stable economic growth, few corporate collapses and low auditor litigation.

One Australian study adopts a different measure of earnings management. Ruddock, Taylor and Taylor (2003) posit that auditors who are fee dependent may have incentives to monitor client reporting less thoroughly and that this may lead to a noticeable reduction in reporting conservatism (the notion of anticipating losses but not profits). They use three measures of reporting conservatism (one as reflected in share returns, another as reflected in the time series of earnings, and the last in the time series of the relation between cash flows and accruals) proposed by previous researchers (Basu 1997; Ball & Shivakumar 2002) and various measures of APNAS and client importance to audit firms. Ruddock, Taylor and Taylor summarise their results in the following way (p. 5):

> With only one exception, we are unable to identify any statistically significant incremental decrease in earnings conservatism associated with relatively larger amounts of [APNAS]. ... However, further analysis indicates that this [exception] is driven by client year observations drawn solely from one of the Big Six audit firms. Additional tests indicate our results are robust to alternative measures of [APNAS] (and client) significance, as well as attempts to control for the potentially endogenous relation between the demand for [APNAS] and earnings conservatism. We therefore interpret our results as being inconsistent with the claim that relatively larger amounts of [APNAS] results in reduced auditor independence in fact, but consistent with the view that market forces such as litigation risk, the more general loss of reputation and alternative governance mechanisms serve to discipline auditors from reducing their independence in order to gain increasing [APNAS] fees.

The overriding impression from the above body of research is that as models become better specified, the prospects of finding positive associations between APNAS and the quality of reporting become more remote. However, few would disagree that our current ability to accurately model 'earnings management' or indeed 'earnings conservatism' is not able to be improved upon. At present they remain at best noisy proxies for aggressive reporting. Perhaps a stronger measure of earnings quality (or the lack of it) is the degree to which companies restate the numbers in their financial statements to correct past errors.

APNAS and profit restatements

The *Economist* magazine recently reported a study by two Cornell University professors (Eisenberg & Macey 2004) investigating whether the failed Arthur Andersen was very different from its peers, in terms of clients who restated earnings as a result of errors subsequently discovered in prior year financial statement which had received clean audit opinions. The study indicates that Arthur Andersen's record of having large clients which subsequently restated earnings was no worse than the other Big Five auditing firms. Over a five-year period ending 2002, there was no significant difference between the restatement rates for all audit firms (Deloitte & Touche had the highest rate at 5.6%, while Arthur Andersen had the second lowest rate at 2.8%). And, interestingly, restatement rates increased over the period and as client size increased.

Like qualified auditor reports, restatements of profits provide an *ex post* indication of auditor quality and auditor independence. This has prompted a number of studies into the association between the coincidence of APNAS and subsequent earnings restatements by their audit clients.

Raghunandan, Read and Whisenant (2003) test the relationship between the incidence of restatements and three measures of fees paid to auditors; APNAS fees themselves, the ratio of APNAS to the sum of audit and APNAS fees, as well as total fees as a single amount. They calculated what they called the 'unexpected' levels of all three measures. The motivation for this was to control for economic factors and firm characteristics that might have caused APNAS to vary between companies (after Firth 1997, Houghton & Ikin 2001, and DeFond, Raghunandan & Subramanyam 2002, as previously discussed).[21] Comparisons were made between 110 US companies that restated earnings in 2000 and 2001, with some 3500 'control' companies. They report (p. 232):

> The results, based on a comparison of the distribution of unexpected values, indicate no statistically significant differences across the two groups for any of the three measures. Thus, these findings are not consistent with concerns that non-audit fees or total fees paid to the auditor inappropriately influence the audit such that the financial statements are subsequently adjusted.

Earnings restatements and corporate governance mechanisms were the focus of a study by Agrawal and Chadha (2003). However, they used the ratio of APNAS to total fees paid to incumbent auditors as a proxy for potential auditor conflicts. A total of 159 US companies that reported restatements in 2000 and 2001 were matched on size and industry with the same number of control companies that did not restate. Agrawal and Chadha find that several key corporate governance mechanisms (such as the independence of the board and the independence of the audit committee) are unrelated to the probability of earnings restatements. However, interesting for our purposes is the finding that APNAS is found to have no association with low-quality reporting inferred by the restatement of earnings.

Another study, by Kinney, Palmrose and Scholz (2004), sought to determine if certain types of APNAS were related to the restatement of earnings for previous financial statement misstatements (caused by serious 'core' errors rather than

---

[21]Noting Whisenant, Sankaraguruswami and Raghunandan (2003), they also control for the jointness of APNAS and audit fees.

'technical' errors). Kinney, Palmrose and Scholz surveyed the seven largest US public accounting firms to collect a breakdown of audit and APNAS fees paid by their audit clients between the years of 1995 and 2000. Their sample consisted of 374 'fee-years' (187 that restated earnings and 187 matching observations that didn't). If restatements represent poor quality reporting then they would expect to find higher levels of APNAS among the restatement group than the control group. However, for only one category of APNAS fees, 'other consulting and all other services', which represented about 23% of all APNAS fees paid, was there evidence of such an association. Other categories were either negatively correlated with restatements ('tax' 33%) or not significantly correlated at all ('financial information systems design and implementation' 8%, 'internal audit' 1%, and 'audit related' 35%).

APNAS and *ex post* litigation

In addition to earnings restatements, subsequent litigation against auditors of listed companies for biased reporting represents another potential setting to ascertain whether auditors have been independent *in fact*. In Australia, most claims against auditors for breach of contract or for negligence seem to be settled out of court – the number of such cases going to full trial are very small. One would expect greater scope to be open to researchers in other countries with larger capital markets. However, I can find little evidence of active research in this area. Antle et al. (1997, p. 23) report:

> In Minet's risk management database of 610 claims against auditors, there are only 24 claims in which the claim mentions that the auditor also supplied consulting services. In 19 of those cases it does not appear that independence was an issue. In two of the remaining five cases, there were allegations of lack of independence, but the allegations were not directed at the supply of consulting services. This leaves us with only three out of 610 cases in which there were allegations that independence was somehow impaired by the supply of consulting services.

They further report that they supplemented the Minet data with their own evidence gathered from informal questions to lawyers who could be expected to be well-informed about such claims against the Big Six and they failed to uncover any additional cases.

Similarly, Palmrose (1999) reported that her auditor litigation database, compiled since 1969, contained less than 1% of instances of lawsuits against auditors that alleged non-audit services impaired independence (cited in Kinney 1999).

Summary

The overall conclusion that is apparent from this line of research is that there is no persistent evidence that the level of APNAS fees impacts auditor independence *in fact*. This conclusion is robust across various measures of auditor independence – namely, audit tenure, propensity to issue qualified audit opinions, the level of client earnings management, the degree of earnings conservatism, client *ex post* profit restatements and *ex post* litigation against auditors.

Evidence from the archival literature – auditor focus

Because audit firms are not regulated to disclose business information in annual reports as listed companies are required to do, much important data about audit firms – e.g., their internal financial results and arrangements at an office, state, national and global level, their activity in different business sectors, their financial arrangements with consulting divisions and associated entities, and partner remuneration and review, etc. – are not publicly observable. This has meant that survey and experiment have been the main avenues by which researchers have endeavoured to explain audit judgments in different settings.

The issue here is whether – and if so, to what extent – auditors take into consideration the level of APNAS fees (current and/or proposed) when making client acceptance and continuance decisions. How do firms, and partners within firms, weigh the benefits, such as the firm's enhanced profitability and reputation, and individual partners' enhanced remuneration and career prospects, against the potential costs, such as the potential compromise of reputation and independence in appearance, the potential loss of independence in fact, and the associated increase in business risk including litigation risk? Similar questions arise when auditors make judgments about the truth and fairness of contents and disclosures in clients' financial statements.

Early work in this area (Pany & Reckers 1980; Shockley 1981; Knapp 1985) suggested that total fees and/or APNAS fees are an important factor in auditors' judgment processes and decision behaviours. Lord (1992) introduced various 'contextural' variables into his investigation into how pressure affects auditors' decisions about reporting judgments. Two of these manipulated variables related to fee dependence; one was client revenue contribution (significant/moderate), the other APNAS fees (consistent/seldom). Significant interaction action effects were noted between pressure, client revenue contribution, APNAS and client financial condition, and the auditor's likelihood of issuing an unqualified opinion when faced with a reporting dilemma. Results are somewhat difficult to interpret, but one conclusion seems to be that 'pressured' auditors of smaller, financially healthier clients are more likely to accept management's suggested accounting treatment if APNAS is increased.

Chang and Hwang (2003) provide further experimental evidence supporting the proposition that audit judgments about clients' aggressive reporting would be influenced by the levels of professional fees paid to the auditor by the client. Chang and Hwang surveyed practitioners about how they would react to a reporting dilemma, while at the same time manipulating the degree of client business risk and client retention incentives. They operationalised retention incentives three ways; audit and APNAS fees, auditor competition (as a measure of dismissal threats), and individual partner career prospects being tied to client outcomes. Chang and Hwang found that when client risk is high, auditor judgments do not appear to be compromised by high retention incentives, but when client risk is low, it appears they might be. Unfortunately, individual components of retention risk were not themselves manipulated, so the results could just as well have been driven by either or both of the other components as by fee dependence.

Another 'angle' was investigated by O'Keefe, Simunic and Stein (1994). The positive association between audit fees and APNAS fees is only a threat to auditor independence if the extra fees charged for the audit work are not accompanied by extra audit effort. In other words, the impairment of independence might be observed if auditors exploited their existing fee relationship with the client by charging an audit fee premium over and above the level of audit work performed. Obtaining actual audit cost production data (audit hours by staff classification), O'Keefe, Simunic and Stein find no increase in audit effort (in any of the four staff categories) when APNAS is increased. They also find no premium for APNAS. In contrast, Hackenbrack and Knechel (1997) find some evidence of increased audit effort across audit activities (especially planning) and in labour mix (especially among partners and managers).

Johnstone and Bedard (2001) re-examine this issue in an initial engagement setting. They obtained proprietary data from one audit firm's initial engagement tender documents and analysed how planned audit effort and tender pricing varied with various levels of client business risk and the provision of APNAS. They report (p. 201):

> Our results also show that the firm plans more for clients purchasing additional services, and proposes a small but significant fee premium after controlling for the incremental effort. Supplementary analysis reveals no evidence that additional services clients have problems that might lead the firm to plan more effort or seek a higher fee. However, we do find more frequent use of industry experts, which may imply assignment of engagement personnel who can better integrate the multiple services provided. When we analyse the accepted bid group separately, no fee premium remains. This suggests that while the firm may try to charge a premium, the implied promise of cross-service

synergy does not induce clients to pay a higher fee. In sum, the results of our analysis of accepted vs. rejected bids imply that fee premia charged for additional services are bid away in the market, while risk premia remain.

There is some experimental evidence that threats of formal sanctions (e.g., litigation risk and peer review risk) have a deterring influence on an auditor's propensity to suborn unbiased judgments about aggressive client reporting. In one study (Shafer, Morris & Ketchand 1999), while fees were not explicitly stated as the basis of the audit judgment dilemma, the case materials described the auditee as 'a valued client', and the potential to lose the client should the auditor not accept management's representations in the financial statements was clearly implied. Formal sanctions (with the exception of disciplinary action by professional bodies) were found to reduce the likelihood of auditors concurring with clients on the treatment in the financial statement of an aggressive asset valuation adjustment.[22]

Most research treats the engagement partner and audit firm as one. Promising research could be conducted into the intra-firm dynamics of partner and firm. For example, if engagement audit partners' remuneration and career prospects are tied in some way to the fees derived from their clients, and if audit partners have private information about the client that is not available to other partners in the audit firm (which seems likely to be the case), then engagement partners may have incentives to issue mendacious audit reports even in the absence of any contingent APNAS fees being offered by management.

Summary

This is an underdeveloped research area. We do not know very much at all from auditors themselves about whether they take into consideration the level of APNAS fees (current and/or proposed) when making judgments on (1) client acceptance and continuance, or (2) management's aggressive reporting practices. The little evidence that we do have is contradictory and inconclusive.

Conclusions

After reviewing the above literature, I summarise the conclusions as follows:

- There is evidence that financial statement users *perceive* that APNAS fees impair auditor independence. However, auditors do not necessarily hold the same view.
- There is mounting, robust evidence that the level of APNAS fees does not impair independence *in fact*, whether this is measured by audit tenure,

---

[22]The survey respondents were fairly mature AICPAs with auditing experience. Interestingly, they estimated that a majority of auditors would issue a clean audit opinion even if the amount of the misstatement was 40% of profits after tax. I doubt if auditors would now hold similar views in this post-Enron world.

propensity to issues-qualified audit opinions, the level of client earnings management, the degree of earnings conservatism, client *ex post* profit re-statements, or *ex post* litigation against auditors.

- Evidence from auditors themselves about the impact that present and pro-spective levels of APNAS have on their day-to-day professional judgments is sparse and inconclusive.

While the accounting profession and regulators can take some comfort from the evidence about auditor independence *in fact*, the evidence about auditor inde-pendence *in appearance* is worrisome. It is of concern, too, because, for an efficient capital market to exist, it is just as important for the investing public to price the reliability of financial information into their transactions by a belief in aud-itor independence as it is for there to be independence in fact. It should be noted that this finding relates only to the level of APNAS fees – the nature of those APNAS services (that might compromise independence through the threat of self-review) are another matter altogether.

It appears that there is an 'expectation gap' between auditors and financial statement users as to the costs and benefits of APNAS. Recent company account-ing scandals have probably exacerbated this gap. In addition to an education program such as the one mounted to address the audit expectation gap in Aus-tralia 15 years ago, one solution to this perception problem might be for the profession and/or regulators to establish some dollar-value limit to the level of APNAS fees above which auditor independence might be assumed to be com-promised.

Any investigations that improve our knowledge about the following matters would be useful avenues for future research:

1. the effectiveness of different monitoring mechanisms (e.g., audit committees, audit firm reputation, auditor integrity and legal sanctions) in moderating the pejorative effect APNAS has on auditor independence
2. the internal mechanics of audit firms. In particular, the structure of audit partner remuneration packages and how these might influence incentives to breach independence, and whether this is exacerbated in the presence of APNAS
3. refining tests on stakeholder perceptions to determine limits to acceptable levels of APNAS
4. improving proxies for auditor independence in fact (e.g., actual data on the waiving of auditor-proposed year end adjustments, in the vein of Nelson, Elliott & Tarpley 2002)
5. increasing the period over which observations about auditor independence are collected. Australia and the United Kingdom have an immediate advant-age here

6. identifying and investigating companies that have powerful characteristics and settings (as in Larcher & Richardson 2003).

The first three lend themselves well to an experimental and/or survey design, while the last three are best tested in an archival setting. Access to 'market-disciplined' data will remain a challenge.

References

Abdel-khalik, A. R. 1990, 'The jointness of audit fees and demand for MAS: A self selection analysis', *Contemporary Accounting Research*, vol. 6, no. 2, pp. 295-322.

Agrawal, A. & Chadha, S. 2003, 'Corporate governance and accounting scandals', working paper, University of Alabama.

Antle, R. & Demski, J. S. 1991, 'Contracting frictions, regulation, and the structure of CPA firms', *Journal of Accounting Research*, vol. 29 (Supplement), pp. 1-24.

Antle, R., Gordon, E. A., Narayanamoorthy, G. & Zhou, L. 2002, 'The joint determination of audit fees, non-audit fees, and abnormal accruals', working paper, School of Management, Yale University.

Antle, R., Griffin, P. A., Teece, D. J. & Williamson, O. E. 1997, 'An economic analysis of auditor independence for a multi-client, multi-service public accounting firm', prepared by The Law & Economics Consulting Group, Inc. on behalf of the American Institute of Certified Public Accountants (AICPA), pp. 1-31.

Ashbaugh, H., LaFond, R. & Mayhew, B. W. 2003, 'Do nonaudit services compromise auditor independence? Further evidence', *The Accounting Review*, vol. 78, no. 3, pp. 611-39.

Ball, R. & Shivakumar, L. 2002, 'Earnings quality in UK private firms', working paper, London Business School.

Banker, R. D., Chang, H. & Cunningham, R. 2003, 'The public accounting industry production function', *Journal of Accounting and Economics*, vol. 35, no. 2, pp. 255-81.

Barkess, L. & Simnett, R. 1994, 'The provision of other services by auditors: Independence and pricing issues', *Accounting and Business Research*, vol. 24, no. 94, pp. 91-108.

Barkess, L., Simnett, R. & Urquhart, P. 2002, 'The effect of client fee dependence on audit independence', *Australian Accounting Review*, vol. 12, no. 3, pp. 14-22.

Basu, S. 1997, 'The conservatism principle and the asymmetric timeliness of earnings', *Journal of Accounting and Economics*, vol. 24, no. 1, pp. 99-108.

Bazerman, M. H., Morgan, K. P. & Lowenstein, G. F. 1997, 'The impossibility of auditor independence', *MIT Sloan Management Review*, vol. 38, no. 4, pp. 89-94.

Beattie, V., Brandt, R. & Fearnley, S. 1999, 'Perceptions of auditor independence: U.K. evidence', *Journal of International Accounting, Auditing and Taxation*, vol. 8, no. 1, pp. 67-107.

Beck, P. J., Frecka, T. L. & Solomon, I. 1988a, 'An empirical analysis of the relationship between MAS involvement and audit tenure: Implications for auditor independence', *Journal of Accounting Literature*, 7, pp. 65-84.

Beck, P. J., Frecka, T. L. & Solomon, I. 1988b, 'A model of the market for MAS and audit services: Knowledge spillovers and auditor-auditee bonding', *Journal of Accounting Literature*, 7, pp. 50-64.

Brandon, D. M., Crabtree, A. D. & Maher, J. J. 2004, 'Nonaudit fees, auditor independence and bond ratings', *Auditing: A Journal of Practice and Theory*, vol. 23, no. 2, pp. 89-103.

Butterworth, S. & Houghton, K. A. 1993, 'Auditor switching and the pricing of audit services', *Journal of Business Finance and Accounting*, vol. 22, no. 3, pp. 323-34.

Carson, E., Simnett, R., Soo, B. & Wright, A. M. 2003, 'A longitudinal investigation of the audit and non-audit services fee markets (1984 to 1999)', working paper, University of New South Wales, Sydney.

Chang, C. J. & Hwang, N.-C. R. 2003, 'The impact of retention incentives and client business risks on auditors' decisions involving aggressive reporting practices', *Auditing: A Journal of Practice and Theory*, vol. 22, no. 2, pp. 207-18.

Chung, H. & Kallapur, S. 2003, 'Client importance, nonaudit services, and abnormal accruals', *The Accounting Review*, vol. 78, no. 4, pp. 931-55.

Coffee, J. C. 2001, 'The acquiescent gatekeeper: Reputational intermediaries, auditor independence and the governance of accounting', working paper, Columbia University Law School, New York.

Craswell, A. 1999, 'Does the provision of non-audit services impair auditor independence?', *International Journal of Auditing*, vol 3, no. 1, pp. 29-40.

Craswell, A., Francis, J. R. & Taylor, S. 1995, 'Auditor brand name reputation and industry specializations', *Journal of Accounting and Economics*, vol. 20, no. 3, pp. 297-312.

Craswell, A., Stokes, D. J. & Laughton, J. 2002, 'Auditor independence and fee dependence', *Journal of Accounting and Economics*, vol. 33, no. 2, pp. 253-75.

Davis, L. R., Ricchiute, D. N. & Trompeter, G. 1993, 'Audit effort, audit fees and the provision of non-audit services', *The Accounting Review*, vol. 68, no. 1, pp. 135-50.

DeAngelo, L. E. 1981, 'Auditor size and audit quality', *Journal of Accounting and Economics*, vol. 3, no. 3, pp. 183-99.

DeBerg, C. L., Kaplan, S. E. & Pany, K. 1991, 'An examination of some relationships between non-audit services and auditor change', *Accounting Horizons*, vol. 5, no. 1, pp. 17-28.

DeFond, M. L., Raghunandan, K. & Subramanyam, K. R. 2002, 'Do non-audit service fees impair auditor independence? Evidence from going concern audit opinions', *Journal of Accounting Research*, vol. 40, no. 4, pp. 1247-74.

Degeorge, F., Patel, J. and & Zeckhauser, R. 1999, 'Earnings management to exceed thresholds', *Journal of Business*, vol. 72, no. 1, pp. 1-33.

Dopuch, N. 1988, 'Discussion of 'A model of the market for MAS and audit services: Knowledge spillovers and auditor-auditee bonding' and 'An empirical analysis of the relationship between MAS involvement and audit tenure: Implications for auditor independence'', *Journal of Accounting Literature*, 7, pp. 85-91.

Dopuch, N. & King, R. R. 1991, 'The impact of MAS on auditors' independence: An experimental markets study', *Journal of Accounting Research*, vol. 29 (Supplement), pp. 60-98.

Eisenberg, T. & Macey, J. 2004, 'Was Arthur Andersen different?: An empirical examination of major accounting firms' audits of large clients', *Journal of Empirical Legal Studies* (forthcoming), pp. 1-34, cited in the *Economist*, 4 December, 2003.

Ezzamel, M., Gwilliam, D. R. & Holland, K. M. 1996, 'Some empirical evidence from publicly quoted UK companies on the relationship between the pricing of audit and non-audit services', *Accounting and Business Research*, vol. 27, no. 1, pp. 3-16.

Ezzamel, M., Gwilliam, D. R. & Holland, K. M. 2002, 'The relationship between categories of non-audit services and audit fees: Evidence from UK companies', *International Journal of Auditing*, vol. 6, no. 1, pp. 13-35.

Fergusson, M. J., Seow, G. & Young, D. 2004, 'Nonaudit services and earnings management: U.K. evidence', *Contemporary Accounting Research*, vol. 21, no. 4, pp. 813-42.

Firth, M. 1997, 'The provision of nonaudit services by accounting firms to their audit clients', *Contemporary Accounting Research*, vol. 14, no. 2, pp. 4-21.

Firth, M. 2002, 'Auditor-provided consultancy services and their association with audit fees and audit opinions', *Journal of Business Finance and Accounting*, vol. 29, no. 5, pp. 661-93.

Francis, J. R. & Ke, B. 2003, 'Do fees paid to auditors increase a company's likelihood of meeting analysts' forecasts?', working paper, University of Missouri-Columbia.

Frankel, R. M., Johnson, M. F. & Nelson, K. K. 2002, 'The relation between auditors' fees for nonaudit services and earnings management', *The Accounting Review*, vol. 77 (Supplement), pp. 71-105.

Geiger, M. A. & Rama, D. 2003, 'Audit fees, non-audit fees and auditor reporting on stressed companies', *Auditing: A Journal of Practice and Theory*, vol. 22, no. 2, pp. 53-69.

Gore, P., Pope, P. F. & Singh, A. K. 2001, 'Non-audit services, auditor independence and earnings management', working paper, Lancaster University, UK.

Gul, F. A. & Tsui, J. 1999, 'Management advisory services, perceived auditor quality and informativeness of earnings', working paper, City University of Hong Kong.

Hackenbrack, K. 2003, 'Mandatory disclosure and the joint sourcing of audit and management advisory services', working paper, University of Florida, Gainesville.

Hackenbrack, K. & Knechel, W. R. 1997, 'Resource allocation decisions in audit engagements', *Contemporary Accounting Research*, vol. 14, no. 3, pp. 481-99.

Houghton, K. A. & Ikin, C. C. 2001, 'Auditor provided non-audit services: Modelling fees and willingness to buy', working paper, University of Tasmania, Hobart.

Houghton, K. A. & Jubb, C. A. 1998, 'Auditor low balling: Fee recoupment and non-audit services', working paper, University of Melbourne.

Houghton, K. A. & Jubb, C. A. 1999, 'The cost of audit qualifications: The role of non-audit services', *Journal of International Accounting Auditing and Taxation*, vol. 8, no. 2, p. 215.

Johnstone, K. M. & Bedard, J. C. 2001, 'Engagement planning, bid pricing, and client response in the market for initial attest engagements', *The Accounting Review*, vol. 76, no. 2, pp. 199-220.

JSCPAA (Joint Standing Committee on Public Accounts and Audit) 2002, Review of Independent Auditing by Registered Company Auditors, Report 391, Commonwealth of Australia, Canberra. (The Charles Committee Report)

Kemp, S. & Knapp, J. (eds) 2004, ICAA/CPAA Joint Code of Professional Conduct *Auditing and Assurance Handbook 2004*, Pearson Education, Sydney.

Kinney, W. R. 1999, 'Auditor independence: A burdensome constraint or core value?', *Accounting Horizons*, vol. 13, no. 1, pp. 69-75.

Kinney, W. R. & Libby, R. 2002, 'Discussion of 'The relation between auditors' fees for nonaudit services and earnings management'', *The Accounting Review*, vol. 77 (Supplement), pp. 101-14.

Kinney, W. R., Palmrose, Z.-V. & Scholz, S. 2004, 'Auditor independence, non-audit services, and restatements: Was the US Government right?', *Journal of Accounting Research*, vol. 42, no. 3, pp. 561-88.

Knapp, M. C. 1985, 'Audit conflict: An empirical study of the perceived ability of auditors to resist management pressure', *The Accounting Review*, vol. 60, no. 2, pp. 202-11.

Knechel, W. R. & Payne, J. L. 2001, 'Additional evidence on audit report lag', *Auditing: A Journal of Practice and Theory*, vol. 20, no. 1, pp. 137-46.

Larcher, D. F. & Richardson, S. A. 2003, 'Fees paid to audit firms, accrual choices and corporate governance', working paper, The Wharton School, University of Pennsylvania.

Lord, A. T. 1992, 'Pressure: A methodological consideration for behavioural research in auditing', *Auditing: A Journal of Practice and Theory*, vol. 11, no. 2, pp. 89-108.

Lowe, D. J., Geiger, M. A. & Pany, K. 1999, 'The effects of internal audit outsourcing on perceived external auditor independence', *Auditing: A Journal of Practice and Theory*, vol. 18 (Supplement), pp. 7-26.

Lowe, D. J. & Pany, K. 1995, 'CPA performance of consulting engagements with audit clients: Effects on financial statement users' perceptions and decisions', *Auditing: A Journal of Practice and Theory*, vol. 14, no. 2, pp. 35-53.

McKinley, S., Pany, K. & Reckers, P. M. J. 1985, 'An examination of the influence of CPA firm type, size and MAS provision on loan officers decisions and perceptions', *Journal of Accounting Research*, vol. 23, no. 2, pp. 889-96.

Monroe, G. & Teh, S. 1993, 'Predicting uncertainty audit qualifications using publicly available information', *Journal of Accounting and Finance*, vol. 33, no. 2, pp. 79-106.

Nelson, M. W. 2004, 'A review of experimental and archival conflicts-of-interest research in auditing', working paper, Cornell University.

Nelson, M. W., Elliott, J. A. & Tarpley, R. L. 2002, 'Evidence from auditors about managers' and auditors' earnings management decisions', *The Accounting Review*, vol. 77 (Supplement), pp. 175-202.

O'Connor, S. M. 2002, 'The inevitability of Enron and the impossibility of "auditor independence" under the current audit system', working paper, School of Law, University of Pittsburgh.

O'Keefe, T. B., Simunic, D. A. & Stein, M. T. 1994, 'The production of audit services: Evidence from a major public accounting firm', *Journal of Accounting Research*, vol. 32, no. 2, pp. 241-61.

Palmrose, Z.-V. 1986, 'The effect of non-audit services on the pricing of audit services: Further evidence', *Journal of Accounting Research*, vol. 24, no. 2, pp. 405-11.

Palmrose, Z.-V. 1999, *Empirical Research on Auditor Litigation: Considerations and Data*, American Accounting Association, Sarasota, FL.

Pany, K. & Reckers, P. M. J. 1980, 'The effects of gifts, discounts and client size on perceived auditor independence', *The Accounting Review*, vol. 55, no. 1, pp. 50-61.

Pany, K. & Reckers, P. M. J. 1988, 'Auditor performance of MAS: A study of its effects on decisions and perceptions', *Accounting Horizons*, vol. 2, no. 2, pp. 31-8.

Parkash, M. & Venable, C. 1993, 'Audit incentives for auditor independence: The case for non-audit services', *The Accounting Review*, vol. 68, no. 1, pp. 113-33.

Pittman, J. & Fortin, S. 2004, 'Auditor choice and the cost of debt capital for newly public companies', *Journal of Accounting and Economics*, vol. 37, no. 1, pp. 113-36.

Raghunandan, K. 2003, 'Nonaudit services and shareholder ratification of auditors', *Auditing: A Journal of Practice and Theory*, vol. 22, no. 1, pp. 155-63.

Raghunandan, K., Read, W. J. & Whisenant, S. 2003, 'Initial evidence on the association between nonaudit fees and restated financial statements', *Accounting Horizons*, vol. 17, no. 3, pp. 223-34.

Ramsay, I. 2001, *Independence of Australian Company Auditors: review of current Australian requirements and proposals for reform*, Report to the Minister for Financial Services and Regulation, Department of Treasury, Canberra (The Ramsay Report).

Reinstein, A. & Lander, G. 2001, 'Examining auditor's independence in relation to management consulting engagements', proceedings, AAA Annual Meeting, Atlanta.

Reynolds, J. K., Deis, D. R. & Francis, J. R. 2004, 'Professional service fees and auditor objectivity', *Auditing: A Journal of Practice and Theory*, vol. 23, no. 1, pp. 29-52.

Reynolds, J. K. & Francis, J. R. 2000, 'Does size matter? The influence of large clients on office level auditor reporting decisions', *Journal of Accounting and Economics*, vol. 30, no. 3, pp. 375-400.

Ronen, J. 2002, 'Post-Enron reform: Financial statement insurance, and GAAP revisited', *Stanford Journal of Law, Business and Finance*, vol. 8, no. 1, pp. 39-68.

Ruddock, C., Taylor, S(arah) & Taylor, S(tephen) 2003, 'Non-audit services and earnings conservatism: Is auditor independence impaired?', working paper, University of New South Wales.

SEC (Securities and Exchange Commission) 2000, *Final Rule: Revision of the Commission's Auditor Independence Requirements*, New York.

SEC (Securities and Exchange Commission) 2003, *Final Rule: Strengthening the Commission's Requirements Regarding Auditor Independence*, 17 CFR Parts 210, 249 and & 274, RIN 3235-AI73, New York.

Shafer, W. E., Morris, R. E. & Ketchand, A. A. 1999, 'The effects of formal sanctions on auditor independence', *Auditing: A Journal of Practice and Theory*, vol. 18 (Supplement), pp. 85-101.

Shockley, R. A. 1981, 'Perceptions of auditors' independence: An empirical analysis', *The Accounting Review*, vol. 56, no. 4, pp. 785-800.

Simnett, R. & Trotman, K. T. 2002, 'Research methods for examining independence issues: Experimental and economics-of-auditing approaches', *Australian Accounting Review*, vol. 12, no. 3, pp. 23-31.

Simon, D. T. & Francis, J. R. 1988, 'The effects of auditor change on audit fees: Tests of price cutting and recovery', *The Accounting Review*, vol. 63, no. 2, pp. 255-69.

Simunic, D. A. 1984, 'Auditing, consulting, and auditor independence', *Journal of Accounting Research*, vol. 22, no. 2, pp. 679-702.

Solomon, I. 1990, 'Discussion of 'The jointness of audit fees and demand for MAS: A self selection analysis'', *Contemporary Accounting Research*, vol. 6, no. 2, pp. 323-8.

Sunder, S. 2003, 'Rethinking the structure of accounting and auditing', working paper, Yale International Centre for Finance.

Thornton, J., Reinstein, A. & Miller, C. L. 2004, 'Non-audit services and perceived auditor independence post-Enron', working paper, Washington State University (Tri-Cities).

Turpen, R. A. 1990, 'Differential pricing on auditors' initial engagements: Further evidence', *Auditing: A Journal of Practice and Theory*, vol. 9, no. 2, pp. 60-76.

Walker, K. & Andrews, B. 2004, 'The checkers checked', *Business Review Weekly*, 4-10 March, pp. 68-71

Watts, R. L. & Zimmerman, J. L. 1986, *Positive accounting theory*, Prentice Hall, Englewood Cliffs, NJ.

Whisenant, S., Sankaraguruswami, S. & Raghunandan, K. 2003, 'Evidence on the joint determination of audit and non-audit fees', *Journal of Accounting Research*, vol. 41, no. 4, pp. 721-44. (Initially a working paper produced at the University of Houston in 2002.)

Whittred, G. 1980, 'Audit qualifications and the timeliness of corporate annual reports', *The Accounting Review*, vol. 55, no. 4, pp. 563-77.

Wines, G. 1994, 'Auditor independence, audit qualifications and the provision of non-audit services: A note', *Journal of Accounting and Finance*, vol. 34, no. 1, pp. 75-86.

Chapter 15. Conclusion: Restorative strategies

Keith A Houghton
Colin Dolley

The focus for the discussion of ethics and auditing has been the recurring financial failures of large public companies not only in Australia but also in the Anglo-American accounting world. To the extent that these failures are evidence of systemic problems in the auditing and accounting profession, it is unlikely that regulatory responses that do not take account of the systemic issues will lead to an improvement in financial reporting and auditing. This summary is based around three themes developed in the book: frameworks for understanding the role and duties of the auditor, the analytical and empirical review of the underlying issues in financial reporting and auditing, and finally some proposals to support improvement in financial reporting and auditing.

On one level, the role and duties of auditors can be explained in a relatively straightforward manner. Hamilton and Stokes (Chapter 4) outline the role of the auditor using an economics of auditing approach. Within this framework, a firm has an incentive to enter into contracts with external auditors in order to reduce the contracting costs between the firm and external parties such as creditors. Ethics has a role in this contracting process in that it bears on the fairness of decisions made by contracting parties in the completion of the contract.

In the legal context, Bottomley (Chapter 1) sets out the statutory functions and powers of the auditor, as well as the duties of the auditor imposed by common law. Bottomley identifies the more recent reforms to the statutory independence requirement of auditors and concludes that auditor independence has become 'a much more complex regulatory goal'. Underlying the economic and legal framework understanding the nature of auditing are some fundamental issues about the audit firm-client relationship and the way in which it impacts on auditor independence, as well as the financial reporting climate in which the auditor is required to engage.

One approach to the examination of financial crises is an understanding of the financial reporting climate in which auditors engage. Campbell (Chapter 5) identifies two issues: the role of the auditor and the audience for audit reports. Campbell returns to the concept of a 'true and fair view' as the basis for an ethical scheme to assist in understanding the audit process. He finds this concept attractive because it associates the auditor's role with developing (or destroying) the trust which is critical to business relationships. A true and fair view concept also raises issues about the potential conflict in the representation of financial information for different stakeholders.

In contrast to the notion of a true and fair view that reflects economic reality, McBarnet (Chapter 2) draws attention to behaviours where financial reporting may be 'technically proper and perfectly legal', and yet exploits gaps and loopholes in regulatory statements. This view highlights the situation that whilst there may be a few spectacular corporate failures, there is an underlying approach to financial reporting that seeks to exploit gaps in accounting rules and principles. Despite commitments in corporate ethical codes to compliance with the law, these commitments do not require company managers to abide by the spirit of the law. A similar theme is pursued by Cooper (Chapter 8), who detects that 'materialism' represents a fundamental change in corporate and professional culture. Cooper further asserts that the declining ethical standards of auditors and accountants can be viewed against the inclusion of materialism in professional culture.

An example of the flexibility in accounting standards and auditing is provided by Johl, Jubb and Houghton (Chapter 10). Their study was motivated by the criticism of auditors, including international auditors, of the variability of audit quality following the Asian financial crises. Johl, Jubb and Houghton examine earnings management by Malaysian companies prior to and following the Asian financial crisis. They found evidence of higher levels of earnings management prior to the crisis, but there was no association with earnings management and the post-crisis period.

As noted by Bottomley, auditor independence is a complex matter. Two aspects of auditor independence explored in the book are the provision of services to the client other than audit services, and the relationship between companies with interlocking directorates and auditors.

Spence (Chapter 6) identifies the situation in which auditors provide both audit and other financial services to the same client as a conflict of interest. Spence proposes that the best way to deal with conflicts of interest such as these is to avoid the arrangement where possible. The next best solution is to disclose the conflict so that the relationship between the parties is transparent. However, Spence argues that apparent conflicts of interest can generate ethical problems because of the uncertainty created in the minds of users of financial statements about the credibility of the financial reporting process.

It is significant that in his review of the literature on auditor independence and the provision of non-audit services, Ikin (Chapter 14) concludes that there is evidence that financial statement users perceive that the provision of non-audit services does impair auditor independence. There is little evidence from auditors on the impact of non-audit services on their professional judgments, and what evidence there is is inconclusive. However, the evidence on other aspects of auditor independence and non-audit services suggests that auditor independence is not impaired. Ikin concludes that the provision of non-audit services is not associated with issues such as audit firm tenure, the propensity to issue an audit qualification and earnings management.

Auditor independence can also be weakened by the fundamental relationship between the audit firm and the corporate client where the audit firm is economically dependent on the client. Professional accounting societies state that auditor independence is associated with objectivity in decision-making. The question arises as to what extent the auditor's decision-making is influenced by client management bargaining power. Windsor (Chapter 9) reports that the results of two experiments indicate that auditors' objective thinking is influenced by client economic variables.

There may be situations in which the engagement of an audit firm by a client company is not an independent decision. That is, there may be directors that are members of the board of a number of companies that are able to influence the decision through their 'personal attachment' to appoint an auditor. In their review of prior research, Courtney and Jubb (Chapter 7) report findings of a positive association between companies with interlocking directorates and the choice of audit firm. Courtney and Jubb investigate whether companies with interlocking directorates will be associated with audit firm tenure, and find that auditor-director links are positively associated with audit firm tenure. Such a finding lends support to the view that longer audit firm tenure may be associated with attenuated auditor independence.

As noted above, professional accounting bodies state that auditor independence is associated with objectivity in decision-making. Professional bodies develop codes of professional conduct to support objectivity in decision-making, as well as including sessions on ethics and accounting in professional training. As part of the reforms to auditing practice, it is proposed that the Financial Reporting Council (FRC) promotes the teaching of business and professional ethics.

Plummer (Chapter 12) examines improving the ethical judgment of individuals in the context of undergraduate accounting education. In particular, Plummer explores the relationship between ethical judgment and approaches to learning. One approach – deep learning – occurs where a student has an intrinsic interest in the academic task and relates the task to their experience. Plummer finds a moderate positive relation between ethical judgment and a deep approach to learning, and suggests that further research on this relationship may be worthwhile.

Howieson (Chapter 13) argues that the development of ethics education requires multimodal strategies and careful thought and planning. According to him, the outcomes of such well-planned ethical training can result in increased sensitivity to ethical issues, develop people with the tools and skills required to deal with more difficult ethical problems, promote the development of moral courage, and broaden auditors' understanding of ethics to embrace it as excellence in professional performance.

A number of authors are wary of increases in regulation as a response to the current crisis in financial reporting and auditing. Cooper notes that the response to previous financial crises' increased regulation has been ineffective. Hamilton and Stokes review the positive accounting theory approach to the political process and note that regulatory reform may not always be in the public interest. They suggest that such a view of the regulatory process is consistent with the selective use of research evidence. From their review of the auditing literature, Hamilton and Stokes argue that the regulatory reforms are unlikely to result in more efficient solutions in that they provide lower contracting costs for participants in the audit contract.

Proposals to increase the independence of the audit profession (Simnett and Smith, Chapter 3) and to signal the independence of audit firms (Houghton and Jubb, Chapter 11) are cognizant of the requirement to develop regulation of auditing that is in harmony with the efficient operation of the audit market.

Simnett and Smith examine a proposal to improve the independence of the audit profession. In a number of countries, a public oversight board has been proposed to achieve the outcome of increased transparency and independence for the audit profession. Members of a public oversight body are selected on the basis that they are independent of the audit profession. Simnett and Smith compare and contrast public oversight board proposals across the dimensions of selection of board members, whether there should be separation of oversight and standard-setting, the extent of disciplinary and investigative powers, and the scope of the board's activities. They conclude that the proposed Australian public oversight board will achieve the objective of increasing investor confidence without reducing market efficiency. Tensions that may arise with an Australian public oversight board are with it being a local oversight board while auditing standards are developed by an international body, and concern also the scope of the board's activities across a range of organisations and across a range of assurance standards.

Houghton and Jubb develop a proposal that is designed to provide information to the market about the independence of audit firms. Such information would have value in the marketplace because auditor independence, in the absence of such information, is typically *ex ante* unobservable. The information about the independence of audit firms would be based on a report by external inspectors on an audit firm's processes to determine threats and perceived threats to audit independence. Houghton and Jubb propose that the requirement for a review and inspection service be under the control of the FRC.

The way in which the future of audit may be crafted will depend in large part upon regulatory imposition, and entrance or exits from the audit for market services from both the supply and demand side. In respect of the matter of auditor independence – the key component to auditor quality – the present state of play in Australia has a mixed and somewhat confusing set of overlapping responsibilities and authorities. For example, at one level the FRC has a high-level responsibility and substantial authority in respect of the area, given the relevant legislation. However, in respect of audits of corporations, the Australian Securities and Investments Commission (ASIC) also has legal authority, and in recent times has used that authority to perform inspections on the larger audit firms with regard to their audits of organisations formed under the Corporations Act. It is understood that these inspections will be complete and that a report, which will be available to the public, will be in place by the middle of 2005. Additionally, the two major professional bodies, the Institute of Chartered Accountants in Australia (ICCA) and CPA Australia, have professional guidance and quality assurance reviews that also in part touch on the area of independence. These quality assurance programs also cover areas of auditor competence, and indeed management of accounting firm practices. In the recently revised structure and operation of the Auditing and Assurance Standards Board (AuASB), it too has responsibility for providing guidance and even setting standards in respect of independence. This was recently confirmed by the chairman of the FRC, who at the April 2005 board meeting of the AuASB made it clear that both auditor competence and independence were components for the work program of the board. It is also understood that the FRC has a memorandum of agreement with the two professional bodies, the AuASB and direct oversight of the AuASB. It should take command of the issue of independence and harness the energy of all these organisations to ensure that the market for audit services has good quality controls and processes in respect of auditor independence. In the eyes of some, this will cut across the long-standing tradition of the professional bodies being responsible for ethics. It is understood that tension between the professional bodies and the corporate regulator, ASIC, has meant that a shared understanding of the guidance on ethical behaviour has not been established, and indeed if this disagreement exists between these powerful and important organisations, the present regime dominated by the Professional Standard F1 is unlikely to be sustained or sustainable.

What is the future of audit?

Many of the contributions to this book state that there is clearly a degree of instability, even turmoil, within the market for audit services, including behaviours within that market. The regulatory framework for going forward is unlikely to be perceived as being clear-cut by many and the challenges are no less than they were a decade or even two decades ago. Indeed, we now know more about behaviours, and possessing that greater knowledge provides more questions than solutions in respect of the ethics of auditors and their behaviour, particularly relating to independence. All of this leads to the conclusion that the country requires a more comprehensive investigation into what is the future of audit. To this end, the two professional bodies and other stakeholders are challenged to create, fund and implement research programs that will provide both a clear pathway and structure so that auditing will have, and be seen to have, a future contribution to the Australian economy and society.

The contributions of the authors to this book have been both important and thought-provoking. These debates lead to further questions – important questions that need to be addressed by those in the market for audit services and those who seek to regulate this market.

Index

www.ingramcontent.com/pod-product-compliance
Lightning Source LLC
Chambersburg PA
CBHW050100220326
41599CB00049B/7203